THE NEW PSYCHOLOGY OF MONEY

The New Psychology of Money is an accessible and engrossing analysis of our psychological relationship to money in all its forms.

Comprehensive and insightful, Adrian Furnham explores the role that money plays in a range of contexts, from the family to the high street, and asks whether the relationship is always a healthy one. Discussing how money influences what we think, what we say and how we behave in a range of situations, the book places the dynamics of high finance and credit card culture in context with traditional attitudes towards wealth across a range of cultures, as well as how the concept of money has developed historically.

The book has various themes:

- **Understanding money:** What are our attitudes to money, and how does nationality, history and religion mediate those attitudes?
- **Money in the home:** How do we grow up with money, and what role does it play within the family? What role does gender play, and can we lose control in dealing with money?
- **Money at work:** Are we really motivated by money at work? And what methods do retailers use to persuade us to part with our money?
- **Money in everyday life:** How do we balance the need to create more money for ourselves through investments with the desire to make charitable contributions, or give money to friends and family? How has the e-revolution changed our relationship to money?

Radically updated from its original publication in 1998, *The New Psychology of Money* is a timely and fascinating book on the psychological impact of an aspect of daily life we generally take for granted. It will be of interest to all students of psychology, economics and business and management, but also anyone who takes an interest in the world around them.

Adrian Furnham is Professor of Psychology at University College London. He has lectured widely abroad and held scholarships and visiting professorships at, amongst others, the University of New South Wales, the University of the West Indies, the University of Hong Kong and the University of KwaZulu-Natal. He has also been a visiting professor of Management at Henley Management College. He has recently been made Adjunct Professor of Management at the Norwegian School of Management.

THE NEW PSYCHOLOGY OF MONEY

Adrian Furnham

Routledge
Taylor & Francis Group

LONDON AND NEW YORK

First published 2014
by Routledge
27 Church Road, Hove, East Sussex BN3 2FA

and by Routledge
711 Third Avenue, New York, NY 10017

Routledge is an imprint of the Taylor & Francis Group, an informa business

British Library Cataloguing in Publication Data
A catalogue record for this book is available from the British Library

Library of Congress Cataloging in Publication Data
Furnham, Adrian.
The new psychology of money / Adrian Furnham.
pages cm
ISBN 978-1-84872-178-4 (hbk) -- ISBN 978-1-84872-179-1 (pbk) 1.
Money--Psychological aspects. I. Title.
HG222.3.F867 2013
332.401'9--dc23
2013038605

ISBN: 978-1-84872-178-4 (hbk)
ISBN: 978-1-84872-179-1 (pbk)
ISBN: 978-0-20350-601-1 (ebk)

Typeset in Bembo
by Saxon Graphics Ltd, Derby.

MIX
Paper from
responsible sources
FSC   FSC® C013056
www.fsc.org

Printed and bound in Great Britain by
TJ International Ltd, Padstow, Cornwall

For Michael Argyle
My co-author, DPhil (Oxon) supervisor, and guide
Godspeed

CONTENTS

List of illustrations   ix
List of tables   xi
Preface   xiii

1   The psychology of money   1

2   Money today   15

3   Different approaches to the topic of money   33

4   Money and happiness   55

5   Money attitudes, beliefs and behaviours   81

6   Understanding the economic world   115

7   Economic socialisation and good parenting   139

8   Sex differences, money and the family   165

9   Money madness: money and mental health   183

10 Money and motivation in the workplace   211

11 Behavioural economics   237

12 Persuasion, pricing and money   259

Appendix 1   *281*
Appendix 2   *285*
References   *289*
Index   *308*

LIST OF ILLUSTRATIONS

4.1 The evidence for the Easterlin hypothesis   65
5.1 Materialism and work–family conflict   107
9.1 A strategy to understand typologies   198
9.2 Questions to determine type   199
10.1 Money and performance   215
10.2 Key variables in performance-related pay   225
11.1 The pain and pleasure of loss and gain   239

LIST OF TABLES

1.1	Unusual items which have been used as money	7
2.1	Today's equivalent to £1m in the past	19
2.2	Reasons for millionaires' wealth accumulation	20
4.1	Income as a predictor of happiness and well-being	71
4.2	Impacts on the money/happiness relationship	75
5.1	Factor loadings for the Money Ethic Scale	83
5.2	The money contented and the money troubled	87
5.3	Money associations and gender	88
5.4	Four-factor measure of attitudes to money	93
5.5	Four dimensions of money	96
5.6	Empirical studies: methodological characteristics and demographic and personality factors that do and do not influence money attitudes	99
5.7	The items for the Money Attitudes scale	102
5.8	The Economic Beliefs Scale: instructions, items, format and scoring	104
6.1	Dates, samples and stages found in studies of the development of economic understanding	117
6.2	Percentage of participants nominating the 11 'issues' on which government spends taxation money	129
6.3	Percentage of participants specifying taxes (other than income tax) that (British) people have to pay	129
7.1	Children have a large disposable income: consider the British data from the Walls' annual survey, in the last century	144
7.2	The proportion of respondents who believe schools should teach 11 finance-related topics at secondary school, and levels of significance for the logistic regression analyses with the seven background variables	146
7.3	British parents' beliefs	150

8.1	Money grams	176
9.1	Money pathology of the British people	185
9.2	A test of the anal character	188
10.1	Reactions to inequity	218
10.2	Effectiveness of merit-pay and bonus incentive systems in achieving various desired effects	228
10.3	Advice for managers	230
12.1	Increasing donations	266
12.2	Common pricing techniques	276

PREFACE

The Psychology of Money was published in 1998. It has been reprinted half a dozen times and translated into various languages including Chinese and Portuguese. It has been quoted over 350 times in the academic literature and was well reviewed. It has been bought in bulk by banks as well as conference organisers, and I once recall signing 300 copies in one session for those attending a conference.

It was written by myself and Michael Argyle, my PhD (DPhil) supervisor at Oxford. The reason we collaborated on the book was really a chance remark made 15 years after I graduated. Michael used to tell people that he kept a "secret list" of topics that, for some reason, psychology had neglected and about which he intended to write books. One was happiness and he was among the first to write a book on that topic, foreshadowing Positive Psychology. Another was *money*. We had both noticed that even work/organisational psychology seemed to really neglect the issue, and it was rare to find any psychology textbook that had money in the index. It was as if psychology had left the topic completely to the economists, who, as we shall see, treated the topic very differently. They believed it was the measure of all things but that it cannot itself be measured. They believed we were all rational beings bent on money accumulation.

I had been working on the topic for some time and had published various papers on it. In 1984 I developed a measure to assess attitudes to money which is now one of my most quoted papers. I had been particularly interested in children and money; more particularly how they think about, and use, money. I had in fact started writing the book, called *The Psychology of Money*, when Michael mentioned the topic and his plan. I told him my story and we jointly agreed to write the book together. It was not our first and we knew each other well. We had somewhat different interests and rather different styles but that was relatively easily sorted out. I wrote many of my chapters while working in New Zealand.

Michael wrote four of the chapters: those on possessions, money and the family, giving money away and the very rich. All have been radically changed. In this book I have completely revised all the chapters on donating/giving money away and enormously expand the chapter on the very rich to include biographies of those with odd money habits. I have added new sections and the references have almost doubled. There is a whole new chapter on perhaps the most important new development in the area, namely *behavioural economics*. There is also a whole chapter on pricing and persuasion, and the way commercial organisations exploit our thinking about money. The chapter on children and money has been radically revised. The chapter on attitudes towards, and beliefs about, money has been greatly expanded. This is as much a new book as a second edition.

It is, of course, quite right that the book is dedicated to Michael. He was the kindest and most generous of men and I miss him still. He gave me confidence in my abilities at an early age and encouraged me to write and research topics I found of interest. I was one of his 50 doctoral students and his legacy is immense. I am not sure that he would have approved of all the contents of the second edition but know he would be forgiving of my misjudgements and peculiar enthusiasms.

I have tried to make this book both academically sound and well referenced but also approachable for those simply interested in the topic. I have found when giving both academic and popular talks about money that almost everyone is interested in some aspect of the topic. They recognise their (and others') foibles and fantasies, hopes and fears, rational and arational beliefs.

The topic of this book has attracted a lot of attention because money remains of great interest to many people. The BBC and other networks, I am sure, must have a file and next to the word *money* is my name. I am asked to appear on radio or television at least half a dozen times a year very specifically to talk about money-related issues. I did a dozen programmes on lottery winners as well as famous misers, tax dodgers and spendthrifts. I am also asked to talk about children's pocket money and how to make them more economically responsible and literate.

The media are particularly beguiled by the *Easterlin hypothesis* and how little money you need to achieve maximal/optimal happiness. The issue is the very contentious relationship between money and happiness and how much of the former you need to maximise the latter. The media, and I think people in general, have an insatiable desire to know more about money and why people seem so obsessed and irrational about it. All the recent work on "obscene banker bonuses" and the feeding frenzy of people in the money world still attracts attention. There are endless articles on the problems, particularly the unintended consequences, of performance-related pay.

But I certainly know that writing this book will not make me rich! Indeed, it is not intended to do so. My own money beliefs, behaviours and indeed pathology are to be found in the appendices, should anyone be interested. Further, I should confess that most of our family money affairs and issues are dealt with by my wife. We academics are strangely incompetent at practical issues.

I have been helped and assisted by many people in the writing of this book. I need to thank particularly various groups of individuals. First, there are my colleagues at *Mountainview Learning*, especially Gorkan Ahmetoglu and Evengiya Petrova. They have helped me enormously in some areas, such as the psychology of pricing and behavioural economics as well as policies of donating: two chapters that are as much their work as mine. Indeed much of Chapters 10 and 11 are reliant on our joint work and reports that we presented to different organisations, such as the Office of Fair Trading.

Next there have been my research assistants from Bath university over the years, particularly Rebecca Milner, Kate Telford, Sharon Boo and Will Ritchie, who have located and summarised articles and set me straight on various topics. Will, in particular, has spent hours checking references as well as doing proofreading, which I am famously bad at, as well as helping me to get the last revision into shape.

Third, there have been my academic colleagues, particularly Sophie von Stumm and Tomas Chamorro-Premuzic, who have helped on numerous papers and projects. To be surrounded by talented, positive, attractive people while working on something that interests one is surely a very great privilege. Others, like Richard Wolman, Thomas Bayne and John Taylor have always been a good sounding board and source of new ideas for me to work on.

Of course, I have to take full responsibility for all errors and misjudgements in the text.

Adrian Furnham
Bloomsbury 2013

1

THE PSYCHOLOGY OF MONEY

Money is like promises – easier made than kept.

Josh Billings

If you wonder why something is the way it is, find out who's making money from it being that way.

Anon

I do everything for a reason, most of the time the reason is money.

Suzy Parker

Always remember, money isn't everything – but also remember to make a lot of it before talking such fool nonsense.

Earl Wilson

Introduction

The *New Oxford (Colour) Thesaurus* defines money thus:

> **Money n:** affluence, arrears, assets, bank-notes, inf bread, capital, cash, change, cheque, coin, copper, credit card, credit transfer, currency, damages, debt, dividend, inf dough, dowry, earnings, endowment, estate, expenditure, finance, fortune, fund, grant, income, interest, investment, legal tender, loan, inf lolly, old use lucre, mortgage, inf nest-egg, notes, outgoings, patrimony, pay, penny, pension, pocket-money, proceeds, profit, inf the ready, remittance, resources, revenue, riches, salary, savings, silver, sterling, takings, tax, traveller's cheque, wage, wealth, inf the wherewithal, winnings.

The above definition gives some idea of all the money-related issues that will be discussed later in the book. Money not only has many different definitions – it has multiple meanings and many uses. The sheer number of terms attests to the importance of money in society.

Money is, in and of itself, **inert**. But everywhere it becomes empowered with special meanings, imbued with unusual powers. Psychologists are interested in attitudes toward money, why and how people behave as they do toward and with money, as well as what effect money has on human relations.

The dream to become rich is widespread. Many cultures have fairy tales, folklore and well-known stories about wealth. This dream of money has several themes. One theme is that money brings *security*, another is that it brings *freedom*. Money can be used to show off one's success as well as repay those who in the past slighted, rejected or humiliated one. One of the many themes in literature is that *wealth renders the powerless powerful and the unloved lovable*. Wealth is a great transforming agent that has the power to cure all. Hence the common desire for wealth and the extreme behaviours sometimes seen in pursuit of extreme wealth.

However, it is true to say that there are probably *two* rather different fairy tales associated with money. The one is that *money and riches are just desserts for a good life*. Further, this money should be enjoyed and spent wisely for the betterment of all. The other story is of the *ruthless destroyer of others* who sacrifices love and happiness for money, and eventually gets it but finds it is of no use to him/her. Hence all they can do is give it away with the same fanaticism that they first amassed it. Note the moralism in the story, which is often associated with money.

The supposedly fantastic power of money means that the quest for it is a very powerful driving force. Gold-diggers, fortune hunters, financial wizards, robber barons, pools winners, and movie stars are often held up as examples of what money can do. Like the alchemists of old, or the forgers of today, money can actually be **made** (printed, struck, or indeed electronically moved). Money through natural resources (oil, gold) can be **discovered** and exploited. Money through patents and products can be **multiplied**. It can also **grow** in successful investments.

The acceptability of openly and proudly seeking money and ruthlessly pursuing it at all costs seems to vary at particular historical times. From the 1980s to around 2005 it seemed quite socially acceptable, even desirable, in some circles to talk about wanting money. It was acceptable to talk about greed, power and the "money game". But this bullish talk appears only to occur and be socially sanctioned when the stock market is doing well and the economy is thriving. After the various crashes this century, brash pro-money talk is considered vulgar, inappropriate and the manifestation of a lack of social conscience. The particular state of the national economy, however, does not stop individuals seeking out their personal formula for economic success, though it inevitably influences it. Things have changed since the great crash of 2008.

Money effectiveness in society now depends on people's expectations of it rather than upon its intrinsic or material characteristics. Money is a social convention and hence people's attitudes to it are partly determined by what they collectively think everyone else's response will be. Thus, when money becomes "problematic" because of changing or highly uncertain value, exchange becomes more difficult and people may even revert to barter. In these "revolutionary" times long-established, taken-for-granted beliefs are challenged and many people find themselves articulating and making explicit ideas and assumptions previously only implicitly held.

One of the most neglected topics in the whole discipline of psychology, which prides itself in the definition of the science of human behaviour, is the psychology of money. Open any psychology textbook and it is very unlikely that the word money will appear in the index.

An overlooked topic

It is true that not all psychologists have ignored the topic of money. Freud (1908) directed our attention to the many unconscious symbols money has that may explain unusually irrational monetary behaviours. Behaviourists have attempted to show how monetary behaviours arise and are maintained. Cognitive psychologists showed how attention, memory and information processing leads to systematic errors in dealing with money. Some clinical psychologists have been interested in some of the more pathological behaviours associated with money, such as compulsive saving, spending and gambling. Developmental psychologists have been interested in when and how children become integrated into the economic world and how they acquire an understanding of money. More recently economic psychologists have taken a serious interest in various aspects of the way people use money, from the reason why they save, to their strategies of tax evasion and avoidance.

Yet it still remains true that the psychology of money has been neglected. There may be various reasons for this. Money remains a *taboo topic*. Whereas sex and death have been removed from both the social and research taboo lists in many Western countries, money is still a topic that appears to be impolite to discuss and debate. To some extent psychologists have seen monetary behaviour as either relatively rational (as do economists) or beyond their "province of concern".

Lindgren (1991) has pointed out that psychologists have not studied money-related behaviours as such because they assume that anything involving money lies within the domain of economics. Yet economists have also avoided the subject, and are in fact not interested in money as such, but rather in the way it affects prices, the demand for credit, interest rates, and the like. Economists, like sociologists, also study large aggregates of data at the macro level in their attempts to determine how nations, communities, and designated categories of people use, spend, and save their money.

It may even be that the topic was thought of as trivial compared to other more pressing concerns, like understanding brain anatomy, or the causes of schizophrenia. Economics has had a great deal to say about money but very little about the behaviour of individuals. Both economists and psychologists have noticed but shied away from the obvious irrationality of everyday monetary behaviour.

Lea and Webley (1981) wrote:

> We do not need to look far to understand this negligence. Psychologists do not think about money because it is the property of another social science, namely economics. Economists can tell us all there is to know about money; they tell us so themselves. It is possible, they admit, that there are certain small irregularities of behaviour, certain deficiencies in rationality perhaps. Thus, psychologists can try to understand, if this amuses them. But they are of no importance. As economic psychologists, we disapprove of both the confidence of economist and the pusillanimity of psychologist. (p. 1)

It is, of course, impossible to do justice to the range and complexity of economic theories of money in this book. Economists differ from psychologists on two major grounds, though they share the similar goal of trying to understand and predict the ways in which money is used.

First, economists are interested in **aggregated** data at the **macro** level – how classes, groups and countries use, spend and save their money under certain conditions. They are interested in modelling the behaviour of prices, wages, etc. – not often people, though they may be interested in certain groups like "old people" or migrants. Thus, whereas economists might have the goal of modelling or understanding the money supply, demand and movement for a country or continent, psychologists would be more interested in understanding how and why different groups of individuals with different beliefs or different backgrounds use money differently. Whereas individual differences are "error variance" for the economists, they are the "stuff of differential psychology".

Second, whereas economists attempt to understand monetary usage in terms of rational decisions of people with considerable economic knowledge and understanding, psychologists have not taken for granted the fact that people are logical or rational in any formal or objective sense, though they may be self-consistent. Indeed it has been the *psychological,* rather than the *logical,* factors that induce people to use money the way they do that has, not unnaturally, fascinated psychologists.

A number of books have appeared entitled *The Psychology of Money* (Hartley, 1995; Lindgren, 1991; Ware, 2001). Most reveal "the secrets" of making money, though what was left unsaid was the motive for the writing of that particular kind of book itself! Often those readers most obsessed with finding the secret formulae, the magic bullet, or the "seven steps" that lead to a fortune are the ones least likely to acquire it.

Many famous writers have thought and written about monetary-related matters. **Marx** (1977) talked about the fetishism of commodities in capitalistic societies because people produced things that they did not need and endowed them with particular meanings. **Veblen** (1899) believed that certain goods are sought after as status symbols because they are expensive. Yet this demand for the exclusive leads to increase in supply, lowered prices and lessened demand by conspicuous consumers who turn their attention elsewhere. **Galbraith** (1984), the celebrated economist, agreed that powerful forces in society have the power to shape the creation of wants, and thus how people spend their money.

This book is an attempt to draw together and make sense of a very diverse, scattered, and patchy literature covering many disciplines. A theme running through the book is not how cool, logical and rational people are about acquiring, storing and spending money, but the precise opposite.

The history of money

Historians have long been interested in the financial history of the world. Ferguson (2009), like others, was fascinated by manic stock market rises and falls. He noted that all seemed to go through a highly predictable cycle: displacement where economic circumstances offer new and very profitable opportunities for some; euphoria or overtrading; mania or bubble where first-time investors and swindlers get involved; distress when insiders see that expected profits cannot justify the trades and start to sell; and finally revulsion or discredit – when the bubble bursts due to a stampede for the exit.

In many ways the history of money is the story of boom and bust, and how all aspects of the financial system are the result of human behaviour with all its fruitless foibles. In his book *The Ascent of Money: A Financial History of the World*, Ferguson (2009) notes that he had three particular insights.

First, that poverty is *not* the result of wicked, rapacious financiers exploiting poor people but rather an area or country not having effective financial institutions like well-regulated banks.

Second, money amplifies our tendency to over-read, causing swings from boom to bust. The way we use our skill and money causes dramatic inequality between people.

Third, few things are harder to predict accurately than the timing and the magnitude of financial crises. History shows that big crises often happen, but few economists can say when.

The history of money is about the establishment of great financial institutions as well as great and dramatic events like the South Sea Bubble, the Great Depression, etc. Every generation seems to experience national and global crises that affect the whole monetary system. Further, technological changes, such as the invention of automated telling machines or credit cards and electronic money, alter the behaviour of individuals and whole societies. Individuals are products of their time and circumstance, but are not governed by it.

There is a fascinating literature on the history of money as opposed to financial institutions. Most countries have coins and notes. Each has a *history* of when they were introduced; who designed them and the name of the issuing authority. Each has a *function*, which is in effect its nominal value as well as the name of the guaranteeing institution. It also has *identity*, including a serial number and information about the conditions under which the value is payable and to whom.

As Gilbert (2005) notes, there is an iconography of national currencies that may self-consciously reflect or attempt to strengthen a sense of national identity. In some countries it is banks that issue notes while in others it is the government. Money, like stamps, can be used to underlie political agendas. Just as countries that move out of one political system to another – colony to dominion to republic – change their flag and state symbols, so they change their money. Note the problem for the design of the Euro!

Earliest human records show evidence of what Adam Smith called "truck, barter and exchange". Bartering, which still goes on today for those who have no cash or wish to avoid taxation, has obvious drawbacks. These include: the necessity of the **double coincidence of wants**: both parties in the exchange must want exactly what the other has. Barter does not help in establishing the **measurement** of worth; the **relative value** of the changed products: whilst it may be possible to exchange multiple items of less worth for a single item of greater worth, it may be that only one item of less worth is required, i.e. it does not work well if things cannot be divided; barter cannot easily be **deferred**: some items perish and need to be consumed relatively rapidly.

Hence as barter transactions grew more sophisticated, people formed the habit of assessing "prices" in terms of a standard article, which in turn came to enjoy preferential treatment as a medium of exchange (Morgan, 1969). Thus cattle, slaves, wives, cloth, cereals, shells, oil and wine, as well as gold, silver, lead and bronze have served as a medium of exchange (see Table 1.1).

Often religious objects, ornaments or model/miniature tools served as the medium of exchange. During the post-war period in Germany, coffee and cigarettes became the medium of exchange, and in the 1980s bottled beer served that function in war-torn Angola. The cowrie shell (as well as pigs) until the middle of this century (in New Guinea) was a very popular Asian medium of exchange.

Using cattle or oxen in exchange for other goods was a cumbrous system. Traders took time to make a settlement (if they reached an agreement at all). The quality of the animals varied, as did the quality of the goods for which they were exchanged. Cattle and oxen, when used as money, were portable and recognisable, but not durable, divisible, or homogeneous.

The next step in the development of money came about when the trading countries around the Mediterranean began to use metal for exchange purposes. The metals were gold, silver, and copper: precious enough to be wanted, useful and decorative enough to be generally acceptable, and their quality did not vary with time. Some believe the earliest people to use metal money were the Assyrians of Cappadocia, whose embossed silver ingots date back to 2100 BC. The Assyrians may even have had a primitive banking system including what we now call "interest": payment for loans and debts.

TABLE 1.1 Unusual items which have been used as money

Items	Country/region
Beads	Parts of Africa and Canada
Boars	New Hebrides
Butter	Norway
Cigarettes	Prisoner-of-war camps and in post-war Europe
Cocoa beans	Mexico
Cowries (shells)	World-wide (South Sea Islands, Africa, America and Ancient Britain)
Fish hooks	Gilbert Islands
Fur of flying fox	New Caledonia
Fur of black marmot	Russia
Grain	India
Hoes and throwing knives	Congo
Iron bars	France
Knives	China
Rats (edible)	Easter Island
Salt	Nigeria
Shells	Solomon Islands, Thailand, New Britain, Paraguay
Skins	Alaska, Canada, Mongolia, Russia, Scandinavia
Stones	South Sea Islands
Tobacco	USA
Whale teeth	Fiji

Source: Furnham and Argyle (1998)

Precious metal

By the eleventh century BC, bars of gold and electrum were traded between merchants. Electrum is a naturally occurring mixture of gold and silver. The bars or lumps of electrum were not coins, for they were of differing weights, but they had great advantages over the exchange of goods by barter and the use of animals as a form of money. Metals do not rot or perish, so deferred payments could be arranged. Yet these metal bars were bulky. They did not easily pass from hand to hand. They were difficult to divide. The quality and quantity of the metal in different bars was not the same. The ratio of gold and silver in electrum varied. Traders in different parts of the world often used different weights, so all metal bars had to be weighed before goods could be exchanged.

Because of the need to weigh metals to ensure that they were of the correct value, traders tried to identify their own metal bars by marking them. Smaller pieces of metal, easily handled, were later produced, and marked in the same way as the larger pieces had been, so that they, too, would be recognisable by traders.

At first it was not clear how much metal should be exchanged for cattle. Eventually the amount of gold, silver, or copper was made equal to the local value of an ox. The Greeks called this measure a *talanton* or "talent": a copper talent weighed 60 lb. The Babylonians used shekels for their weights: 60 shekels equalled one manah, and 60 manahs equalled one biltu, which was the average weight of a Greek copper talent.

The process of marking small pieces of metal was probably how the first coins were produced in 700 BC, when the Lydians of Asia Minor gave their electrum pieces the head of a lion on one side and nail marks on the other. From Lydia the use of coins like these spread to other areas such as Aegina, and the states of Athens and Corinth; to Cyrenaica, Persia, and Macedon. China, Japan, and India were also using coinage by about this time.

Some media of exchange were weighed; others counted. Coins eventually compromised between two principles because their characteristics (face, stamp) supposedly guaranteed their weight and fineness and hence they did not have to be weighed.

Metal discs have been found in both the Middle East and China that date back more than ten centuries BC. In the seventh century BC it became possible to stamp coins on both obverse and reverse sides so as to distinguish between different denominations and guarantee quality. As today the coinage of one country could be, indeed had to be, used by others.

Because money could serve as a payment for wages it could bring benefits to a wide section of the community. Even slaves could be paid a ration allowance, rather than being fed by their masters. Precious metal coins have been dated to the Peloponnesian Wars of 407 BC: gold for large transactions, bronze for very small ones. Alexander the Great, who spread the use of money in his empire, was the first to have his face on coins. The Romans varied the appearance of their coinage for political ends but also manipulated its value to suit the financial needs of the state. Nero, amongst others, reduced the weight in coins and caused a crisis of confidence in the currency.

Until this century the means of payment in commercial societies were, with rare exceptions, either coins made from precious metals or notes or bank deposits convertible into coin. The inconvertible paper note and the deposit repayable in such notes is a very recent development, which has now displaced the precious metals for internal transactions in all the highly developed economies of the world. So long as they retain public confidence, they have great advantages in convenience, but they are liable to abuse and, on many occasions in their short history, they have broken down.

Banks have gone bankrupt in many Western countries through bad debt, incompetence or financial crises they could not foresee. Sometimes investors are partly recompensed by government; often they are not! The government that adopts an inconvertible currency, therefore, takes on a heavy responsibility for maintaining its value. Indeed paper money – that is documents rather than actual notes – is now being transferred electronically such that a person might fly 1,000 miles, go into a bank in a foreign country never before visited, and emerge with the notes and coinage of that country.

There are various ways to approach the history of money. Usually one starts with primitive money, followed by the first use of coinage, then onto banking, credit, and gold/silver standards, and, finally, on to inconvertible paper and plastic money. Chown (1994) has explained some of the concepts associated with money. It costs money to manufacture coins from silver or gold, and the mint authority charges a turn (usually including a profit) known as "**seignorage**". Issuers can cheat, and make an extra profit by **debasing** the coinage. If this is detected, as it usually is, the public may value coins "**in specie**" (i.e. by their bullion content) rather than "**in tale**" (their official legal value). The purchasing value of coins may change without any debasement; the value in trade of coinage metal itself may change. The monetary system may be threatened by **clipping** and **counterfeiting** and, even if rulers and citizens are scrupulously honest, the coinage has to contend with fair wear and tear.

In medieval and early modern time coins were expected (although in some places and times only by the naïve and credulous) to contain the appropriate weight of metal. The use of more than one metal raised problems. This is sometimes referred to collectively as "tri-metallism", but is more conveniently divided into the two separate problems of "bi-metallism" (the relationship between silver and gold) and "small change" (the role of the "black coins"). The new and more complicated coinages also caused problems by definition – "ghost money" and "money of account". For much of the late medieval period, there would be more than one coinage type in circulation in a country. This creates a serious problem for the modern historian, as it presumably did for the contemporary accountant. "Ghost money" units consist of accounts which have names based on actual coins that have disappeared from circulation. They arose, of course, from depreciation and the phenomena of bi-metallism and petty coins.

Money is used as a "unit of account" as well as a medium of exchange and store of value. Some system was needed by which debts could be recorded and settled, and in which merchants could keep their accounts. It was convenient to have a money of account for this purpose. This could be based on a silver and gold standard or, very occasionally, on black money. Two systems often existed side by side. The value of actual real coins could fluctuate in terms of the appropriate money of accounts and this was often based on a ghost from the past. Money could be used as cash or stored in a bank.

Cash

Derived from the French word *caisse*, meaning money-box or chest, cash is often known as "ready or liquid" money. Traditionally it comes in two forms: coins and bank-notes.

(A) Coins: Standard coins, where the value of the metal is equal to the face stamped on the coin, are comparatively rare but used in the collecting world. **Token** coins are more common: here the metal (or indeed plastic) content is worth (far) less than the face value. The Jewish shekel was first a weight of metal,

then a specific coin. Monasteries were the first mints because it was thought they would be free of theft.

Wars or political crises often lead to the debasing of a country's coinage. Precious metal coins are filed down (shaved), made more impure, or give way to token (non-metallic) coins. But even coins that began as standard could come to a bad end. Unscrupulous kings rubbed off metal from the edge of gold coins, or put quantities of lead into silver coins to gain money to finance wars. In Henry VIII's time the coins issued in 1544 contained one-seventh less silver than those issued in 1543; Henry continued in this way until, by the time coins were issued in 1551, they contained only one-seventh of the original amount of silver.

The idea of a standard coin was that it should be a coin of guaranteed weight and purity of metal. That remained true until coins became tokens in the sense that their intrinsic metal value was not the same as their face value.

(B) Paper: Paper money was primarily introduced because it made it much easier to handle large sums. Second, coins could not be produced in sufficient amounts for the vastly increased world trade that developed from the seventeenth century onwards. Third, trade inevitably demonstrated that there were more profitable uses for metal than as exchange pieces. Finally, it was argued that paper money (cheques, credit cards) reduced the amount of cash in transit and therefore reduced the possibility of theft.

Cash money probably developed from the practice of giving a receipt by a gold or silversmith who held one's precious metal for "safe-keeping". In time this receipt, although it had no real value of its own, became acceptable in payment of debt among the literate. Banknotes, printed by banks, first appeared in the twentieth century. Up till the beginning of the First World War in Britain notes were called **convertible** paper because they could be exchanged for gold. Alas now all notes are **inconvertible** paper. Clearly one of the disadvantages of convertible paper money is that the supply and issue of notes is related to the amount of gold held by the issuing authorities (government, banks) and not to the supply of goods. Another disadvantage of the old convertible money is that prices depend on the world market not simply gold supply. A government cannot control its country's prices without taking account of what is going on in other parts of the world. Equally, imprudent governments can literally print (issue) as much money as they wish, with too much money chasing too few goods leading to a concomitant fall in the value of the money.

China printed money in the Ming Dynasty (1368–1644), while the Swedes were the first Europeans to issue paper money, in 1656. Notes can have any face value and the variation within and between countries is very wide. They have also varied considerably in shape, size, colour and ornamentation. Provided paper money is immediately acceptable in payment of debt, it fulfils the criteria of being money. Cheques, postal orders, credit cards, electronic transfers, etc., are "claims to money", sometimes referred to as **near** money.

(C) Plastic, virtual and local money: For a discussion of this topic see Chapter 2.

Banks

Goldsmiths were the first bankers. They soon learnt to become fractional reserve banks in that they kept only a proportion of the gold deposits with them and invested the rest. Many failed, as did banks this century, because they could not immediately pay back deposits on demand because they did not have enough reserves or "liquid money". The cash ratios or the amount of actual cash kept by banks is about 6–10% of all the money deposited with them. Another 20–25% of deposits are kept as "near money", which are investments that can be turned back into cash almost immediately.

The Christian church objected to usury and moneylenders, which opened up the profession particularly to Jews (see Shylock in Shakespeare's *Merchant of Venice*). Islam, too, disapproves of interest and has been more zealous than Christianity in trying to discourage it. Some Christians later lent money free for a short period, but if the debt was not paid back at the time promised Church laws appeared to allow the delay to be charged for. The Crusades and the industrial revolution were a great impetus to banking because people needed capital. Goldsmiths, rich landowners, and prosperous merchants pioneered modern banking by lending to investors and industrialists.

By manipulating the liquidity rate and their preferred patterns of lending, banks are inevitably very powerful institutions. However, they are not the only institutions that lend money. Building societies make loans to house buyers; finance houses lend money for hire-purchase transactions; and insurance companies have various funds available for borrowers. The relationship of money to income and capital may be summarised as follows. First money circulates, or passes from hand to hand in payment for:

a.   goods and services which form part of the national income;
b.   transfers and intermediate payments, which are income from the point of view of the recipients but which are not part of the national income;
c.   transactions in existing real assets, which are part of the national capital; and
d.   transactions in financial claims, which are capital from the point of view of their owners but which are not part of the national capital.

Money is also held in stock. Stocks are, however, very different in the time for which they are held, and the intention behind the holding. Money in stock is part of the capital of its owners, but it is not part of the national capital unless it is in a form that is acceptable to foreigners. New money can be created by a net addition to bank lending, and money can be destroyed by a net payment of bank loans. For a closed community, income and expenditure are identical, but for an individual they are not. An individual can spend less than his income and so add to his stock of money or some other asset, and he can spend more than his income by reducing his stock of money or other assets or by borrowing.

For most people the "high street bank" is the primary source of money. They borrow from, and lend to, banks, which are also seen as major sources of advice. Estimates are that over three-quarters of all UK adults have a current bank account or chequing account and in the past five years there has been a considerable increase in such accounts as well as building society accounts.

The cheque (or "check" in the USA) arose about 300 years ago directly out of the use of exchanged receipts or promissory notes and was illegal to begin with and certainly regarded as highly immoral, but the convenience quickly outweighed any moral considerations and the legalities soon followed. Until 1931 there was a national responsibility not to issue more hard currency than could be backed up by gold deposits. So, in effect, until that date if everyone handed in their notes for value, there would have been enough gold to go around. Today, if we *all* demanded our face-value gold, the banks and the nation would go bankrupt overnight. There is currently enough gold on deposit in the Bank of England's vaults to cover around one-third of the issued currency. It is no longer possible, in fact, to receive face value gold.

The biggest difference between a bank in the UK and a bank in the USA is that in the UK, in order to open a bank account, it used to be necessary not only to have money but also to have friends. A reference provided by a bank-account holder had to be furnished before a new account could be opened. The process took about two weeks. In the USA, and now in most developed countries, anyone can walk into almost any bank and open an account on the spot, receive a cheque book and use it, provided they deposit enough money in the account to cover the cheques. One of the reasons why this is so is that in New York State it is a crime to write a cheque without having funds to back it. In the UK, however, a bouncing cheque will not send you to prison.

In addition, in the USA, with some of the competing banks, opening an account and depositing a fixed amount of cash will bring you free gifts. British banks have copied this trend, especially in attempting to lure young people (i.e. students) to open accounts with them.

Banks all over the world lend money to each other. This is called the Interbank lending system and it occurs because the larger banks have more money on deposit than the smaller ones, and all banks must balance their accounts each day – so they borrow and lend among themselves. Thus, if you leave a lot of money in your current account each day, even though the banks are not paying you any interest on that money they are making interest on it through the overnight Interbank lending market – about 11% per annum in the UK. In the USA almost all money in all accounts earns interest, if only at a low rate, and this system is slowly happening in the UK too, with various different names. No bank is giving anything away with these accounts; they are simply reducing their profits slightly to attract more custom.

Themes in this book

There are six themes in this book.

First, people are far from rational in the way they think about, accumulate, spend and save money. They are essentially psychological rather than irrational. Money is imbued with such power and meaning that people have difficulty thinking rationally about it.

Second, we all apply a range of (sometimes unhelpful) heuristics when thinking about money. These short cuts or rules of thumb explain why we make so many "mistakes".

Third, many of these money beliefs come from childhood and early education. We learn about money and its power and allure early on in life and carry these ideas and associations into adulthood.

Fourth, money and happiness/well-being are only tangentially related. Many factors contribute to our unhappiness and money is only one factor.

Fifth, money is a more powerful demotivator than a motivator at work. If people are paid equitably, given their comparative inputs, money has surprisingly little motivational power.

Sixth, a knowledge of how people think about and use their money in typical (and arational) ways has meant businesses often try to "exploit" them. These processes and procedures can be understood in order to help people guard against any form of attempted manipulation.

2

MONEY TODAY

Human capital has replaced dollar capital.

Michael Milken

Business ethics is to ethics as Monopoly money is to money.

Harold Hendersen

Beauty is potent, but money is omnipotent.

Anon

Nothing is more admirable than the fortitude with which millionaires tolerate the disadvantages of their wealth.

Rex Stout

Introduction

It is true, as well as a truism, that the world is changing fast. This is as true of money as of everything else. Technological changes have deeply affected how people use, store and spend their money. The world of cash is fast disappearing. People now pay for their car parking from their mobile phone; and transfer high sums of money (legally and illegally) around the world electronically. Currencies change and both appear and disappear. There are now local currencies and virtual currencies.

The distribution of wealth has also changed dramatically. Many countries have many thousands of millionaires and it seems the gap between the rich and the poor is changing dramatically. However, some things are constant, like the bizarre behaviour of (often very rich) people with respect to their money.

This chapter will look at some of the changes in the world of money today.

The story of the credit card

The use of credit cards originated in the United States during the 1920s, when individual firms, such as oil companies and hotel chains, began issuing them to customers. Early credit cards involved sales directly between the merchant offering the credit and credit card, and that merchant's customer.

Around 1938, companies started to accept each other's cards. Today, credit cards allow you to make purchases with countless third parties. The inventor of the first bank-issued credit card was John Biggins of the Flatbush National Bank of Brooklyn in New York. In 1946, Biggins invented the "Charge-It" program between bank customers and local merchants. Merchants could deposit sales slips into the bank and the bank billed the customer who used the card.

By the early 1960s, more companies offered credit cards, advertising them as a time-saving device rather than a form of credit. American Express and MasterCard became huge successes overnight, allowing the consumers a continuing balance of debt, subject to interest being charged.

These are a few handy facts about credit cards:

- There are 609.8 million credit cards held by US consumers (Source: "The Survey of Consumer Payment Choice", Federal Reserve Bank of Boston, January 2010).
- Average number of credit cards held by cardholders: 3.5, as of year-end 2008 (Source: "The Survey of Consumer Payment Choice", Federal Reserve Bank of Boston, January 2010).
- Average APR on new credit card offer: 14.91% (Source: CreditCards.com Weekly Rate Report, 6 July 2011).
- Average APR on credit card with a balance on it: 13.10%, as of May 2011 (Source: Federal Reserve's G.19 report on consumer credit, released July 2011).
- US credit card 30-day delinquency rate: 3.3% (Source: Moody's, May 2011).
- Forty-one per cent of college students have a credit card. Of the students with cards, about 65% pay their bills in full every month, which is higher than the general adult population (Source: Student Monitor annual financial services study, 2008).
- Eighty per cent of Americans who are 65 or older indicated they used a credit card in the month preceding the September 2008 survey. That's 13 points higher than any other age group. They also used debit cards far less than other age groups. Only 47% of those over 65 said they had used a debit card in the month before the survey, 19 points lower than any other age group (Source: Javelin, "Credit Card Spending Declines" study, March 2009).
- Just 51% of Americans aged 18 to 24 indicated they had used a credit card in the month preceding the September 2008 survey. Seventy-one per cent of that age group said that they had used a debit card in the same period (Source: Javelin, "Credit Card Spending Declines" study, March 2009).

- One in 12 households in London (or 8%) has used credit cards to pay their mortgage or rent in the last 12 months. Across Great Britain, 6% of households did the same, equivalent to more than one million people (Source: Shelter Media Centre, January 2010).
- There were 60.7 million credit cards in circulation in the UK at the end of November 2009, 69% of which had a balance outstanding (Source: British Bankers Association, January 2010).
- Outstanding credit card balances stood at £63.5 billion in November 2009, nearly £3 billion lower than a year earlier (Source: British Bankers Association, January 2010).

Children as young as 14 carry credit and debit cards. Most adults have many cards and they are often a source of considerable problems.

The story of online banking and shopping

The concept of online banking as we know it today dates back to the early 1980s, when it was first envisioned and experimented with. However, it was only in 1995 that Presidential Savings Bank first announced the facility for regular client use. Inventors had predicted that it would be only a matter of time before online banking completely replaced the conventional kind. Facts now prove that this was an over-optimistic assessment – many customers still harbour an inherent distrust of the process. Despite this, the number of online banking customers has been increasing at an exponential rate. The speed with which this process happens online, as well as the other services possible by these means, has translated into a boom in the banking industry over the last five years.

Seventy-one per cent of survey respondents said they had logged into their credit card account via the Internet (ComScore, 2009).

One of the first known Web purchases took place in 1994. It was a pepperoni pizza with mushrooms and extra cheese from Pizza Hut. When Amazon came on the scene not long after, selling books online was a curious idea, but eventually a revolutionary change in culture and groupthink took place. Buying things online was all about price and selection.

Now 83% of consumers say they are more confident in making a purchase when they have conducted research online as opposed to speaking to a salesperson in a store. And, despite the economic recession, online retail in the USA grew 11% in 2009, according to a March 2010 report from Forrester Research. More than 150 million people – about two-thirds of all Internet users in the USA – bought something online last year. It's a staggering leap for an industry used by only 27% of the nation's online population a decade ago.

Local currencies

One of the more interesting features of "the new money" is the rise of what are called "local currencies". In London the Brixton Pound (B£) exists in paper and electronic format (also known as Pay by Text). The paper version was launched in September 2009 and the electronic currency was launched in September 2011. Around 200 businesses accept the B£ paper notes and about 100 are signed up to Pay by Text.

The notes are printed on watermarked paper by specialist secure printers. Each B£ is worth £1 sterling, so B£1 = £1, B£5 = £5, B£10 = £10, and B£20 = £20. The sterling backing for all B£ in circulation is held at a local bank. B£ notes are not exchangeable back to sterling, however businesses may redeem them at face value.

Some traders offer B£ customers special offers for using the money (like a loyalty card for Brixton). The 1st Edition of the notes expired on 30 September 2011, with the 2nd Edition being in use since. Pay by Text customers receive a 10% bonus automatically added onto their account every time they credit it. The notes have already become highly collectable items and, together with the Pay by Text service, they are attracting a lot of media attention and encouraging new visitors to go to Brixton.

This currency has the potential ability to raise awareness of prosocial issues (e.g. the importance of shopping locally) rather than its claimed economic effect of keeping more value local by facilitating local spending. The idea is to "keep money in Brixton". By swapping real money for Brixton currency, you are obliged to spend it with local retailers (since no one else will accept it). Arguably it raises awareness of the importance of buying locally as it inevitably gets people talking about the issue (because they have the currency in their pocket and it's newsworthy).

Bristol in England recently introduced the "*Bristol Pound*" in a bid to increase local commerce. By making the currency only available to spend within the city, each spend using the money will in turn force an equivalent spend on local goods and services, unless the money is converted back to British sterling at the 3% fee rate.

Unlike previous attempts at a local currency the Bristol Pound is available to be spent online. More than 350 local companies have signed up, making the Bristol Pound the UK's largest alternative to sterling. In fact, Bristol's mayor is taking his entire salary in Bristol Pounds.

Not far from Bristol, in Stroud, Gloucestershire, a "Stroud Pound" experiment that started in 2009 has failed to take the town by storm, with only half the amount of Stroud Pounds issued last year as in the first year. Local businesses do say, however, that customers have committed to buying locally because of it.

Local currency systems encourage not only local business growth, but local responsibility. The creation of new jobs and new projects in any region will stimulate not only economic but also social growth.

Millionaires

Traditionally, to be a "millionaire" meant having over £1million in the bank. Yet it seems this definition may be changing. Goldstein (2011) describes how in recent years the term "millionaire" has come to relate instead to someone who earns over £1million a year. There is a considerable difference between the two definitions. Someone earning over £1million a year is much more elite. Barclays Wealth (2011) said there were 619,000 millionaires – including property assets – currently living in the UK at the end of 2010, up from 528,000 in 2008. However, only 11,000 people in the UK earn over £1million each year (Office for National Statistics, 2009). Therefore, changing the definition from assets toward annual income redefines "millionaires", pushing them up the economic ladder. This is highly rational, as having a million pounds does not make you as rich as it used to, with the cost of living having increased dramatically. Today, you would need £17.5million to enjoy the equivalent lifestyle of a person with £1million in 1958 (Table 2.1; Bank of Scotland, 2008).

So who becomes a millionaire? Spectrem Group (2011) found that those with over $1million in assets were more likely to have a degree than those in the lower $100,000–$1million segment. Interestingly, those in the middle affluent segment ($1m–$5m) either currently or have previously worked for more than 60 hours each week, while 47% of those in the well-off segment ($5m–$25m+) worked less than 40 hours per week.

How do millionaires become so wealthy? (Table 2.2).

Spectrem Group (2011) investigated the method through which affluent households believed they had obtained their wealth, with the predominant reason offered being through hard work. Those in households with $1–5million and $5–25million of net worth believed that education and smart investing were the most significant contributing factors. Yet those in households with $100,000–$1million net worth placed more emphasis on frugality than education. Though many mayspeculate that the majority of such wealthy people inherit their money, the four main sources those in wealthy homes believe they gain their riches through are hard work, education, smart investing and frugality. Inheritance was specified as a source of wealth by just a quarter of individuals in each wealth segment.

TABLE 2.1 Today's equivalent to £1m in the past

1958	£17.500m
1968	£12.991m
1978	£4.297m
1988	£2.009m
1998	£1.318m
2008	£1.000m

Note: According to estimates by the economic consultancy, cebr (The cebr Forecasting Eye, 14 August 2006). Figure relates to 2006.

Source: The Cebr Forecasting Eye (2006)

TABLE 2.2 Reasons for millionaires' wealth accumulation

Reason	$100,000–$1,000,000*	$1,000,000–$5,000,000*	$5,000,000–$25,000,000*
Hard work	93%	95%	95%
Education	71%	89%	92%
Smart investing	67%	83%	85%
Frugality	66%	81%	77%
Taking risks	42%	67%	72%
Being in the right place at the right time	33%	45%	62%
Inheritance	23%	28%	26%

Note: *Not including principle residence.

Source: Spectrem Group, 2011, Affluent Market Insights.

These findings are supported by Skandia (2012) "millionaire monitor" research. Seventy-four per cent of UK millionaires were found to have made their wealth through employment, with 57% acknowledging that investments contributed to their fortune. Fifteen per cent of the surveyed millionaires made their money from their own business. This all indicates that hard work and smart investing are key. However, 41% had inherited money, contributing to their fortunes. The research showed that the top jobs through which wealth was earned were manufacturing (21%), IT/Telecoms (21%), finance (18%) and the service industry (17%). The project found that 29% of UK millionaires made their wealth through setting up their own business.

Interestingly, research shows that the majority of UK millionaires (79%) are wealthier than their parents (Skandia, 2012). The research also found that the majority of millionaires make their fortune when they are young, with 31% of entrepreneurs in the survey making their fortune before they were 30, and over half (53%) of those making their money before they were 25. Hong Kong was the country in which millionaires earned their fortune most rapidly, with two-thirds of entrepreneurs making their money within five years. Whereas in the UK, 60% made their earnings from their business in a decade or less.

What do they do with their money? Data from Skandia (2012) research shows that Britain's millionaires tend to invest their wealth in residential property, with just under a third of money being held here. The next most popular areas that wealth is invested in are cash (18%), shares (16%) and managed investment funds (13%).

Some spend money on moving to a different country. Skandia (2012) research found that almost one in ten millionaires in Italy, France and Dubai say they intend to leave their country (they are considered a millionaire if conversion of their net disposable assets relates to GB£+1million). In the UK almost 45% would consider relocating. A widely stated reason for moving was the weather (22%), with improved living standards also being hoped for (20%).

There are a few famous examples of eccentric millionaire behaviours:

1. **Salvatore Cerreto:** the 71-year-old property magnate was found to have been defecating in front of shops and restaurants in the dead of night in his local town of North Ryde.
2. **Robert Clark Graham:** the late millionaire optometrist opened a sperm bank in 1980 to be mostly stocked with donations from Nobel laureates, in a bid to create a master generation. When the bank closed in 1999 after his death, none of the children fathered from the stocks had a Nobel laureate father.
3. **Ailin Graef:** this Chinese woman became the first person to make a million from the online avatar community *Second Life* by developing property online and selling it on, converting the online currency to real money as per the game's rates.
4. **Karl Rabeder:** grew up poor, and upon realising his £3 million fortune was making him unhappy, gave it all away, with all proceeds going to charitable foundations he set up in Central and Latin America, from which he will not take a salary.
5. **Gunther IV:** received his inheritance from his father Gunther III, who received it in turn from the German countess Karlotta Liebenstein. Gunther is worth around $372 million now thanks to his growing trust fund. None of which is remarkable, until you find out that Gunther and his father are German shepherd dogs.
6. **Graham Pendrill:** the Bristol millionaire visited Kenya for a month last year, and was awarded the title of elder after helping resolve a conflict. He has since decided to sell his house and move to Kenya to live in a mud hut with the Masai tribe.
7. **Scott Alexander:** the 31-year-old lifestyle millionaire decided to buy his own town in Bulgaria for £3 million and is turning it into a holiday hotspot. He has named the town after himself – Alexander.
8. **Karen Shand:** became the first person to win £1 million live on TV when she won ITV's "The Vault". Despite this, she has not quit her £25,000 job as a nurse in Kirkcaldy, Fife.
9. **Nicholas Berggruen:** known as the "homeless billionaire", Berggruen lost all interest in acquiring material goods, so decided to sell his properties and live in hotels. He plans to leave his fortune to charity and his art collection to a museum in Berlin.
10. **Thaksin Shinawatra:** the Thai Premier's youngest daughter works in McDonald's in Thailand. He got her the job through the president of McThai, but insisted that she be treated like any other employee in order to teach her the value of money.

Famous (modern) people with odd money habits

One way to understand people's difficult, often bizarre, relationships with their money is to examine case studies of famous people. Their story is readily available on Wikipedia and other public sources.

Misers

1. Benny Hill

Benny Hill was a famous British TV comedian, starring in the popular *Benny Hill Show*.

Hill lived in a small apartment, keeping the many awards he had won throughout his career in a large box, with none being openly displayed. Despite Hill having earned millions of pounds over the course of his career, he did his own grocery shopping, and never used the second floor of his modest rented flat. Friends described Hill's home as being characterised by an unmade bed, dirty dishes, and heaps of paper everywhere.

The *Daily Star*, a popular British newspaper, referred to him as "Mr Mean", after regular sightings in his local area of a distinctly un-showbizzy-looking Benny poring over tins of food in a supermarket, and trudging home with plastic bags.

Benny Hill died in 1992, aged 68, leaving an estate worth over £7 million. Despite his fortune, Benny Hill died alone watching TV and his death was not discovered for several days. In many ways his is a classic story of someone for whom money represented security more than anything else.

2. Lester Piggott

Piggott remains the most famous jockey in British racing history. Known affect-ionately as "the Long Fellow", he won the world famous Epsom Derby nine times, including his first victory in the famous race in 1954 aged only 18. He also rode more than 5,300 winners worldwide during 47 years in the saddle. He was also famously mean.

Piggott tarnished his good name, and sacrificed his OBE, when he was jailed in 1987 for tax fraud for failing to declare income of £3.25m to the Inland Revenue in the biggest tax-evasion case of its time. The jockey, whose fortune was estimated at £20 million, spent a year in prison.

3. Howard Hughes

Howard Hughes was the son of the founder of the Hughes Tool Company, which revolutionised oil well drilling. Hughes inherited 75% of the company in 1924, following the death of his father. He then proceeded to buy out his relatives' shares in the business, becoming the owner of the Hughes Tool Company.

Hughes moved to Hollywood aged 23 and began producing films, winning Academy awards, as well as being successful at the Box Office. He became famous and even richer.

Hughes went onto develop a passion for aviation, forming the Hughes Aircraft Company in 1932. In 1934, Hughes built and test-piloted the H1, the world's most advanced plane, as well as setting a new speed record in 1935.

Hughes then went on to move to Las Vegas, where he purchased four hotels and six casinos. Hughes is also remembered for his eccentric behaviour and reclusive lifestyle in later life, caused in part by an obsessive-compulsive disorder. He spent the last 20 years out of the public eye living in hotel penthouses around the world.

Hughes was described as never being the same after suffering a fiery plane crash in 1946. He avoided socialising, stopped playing his beloved golf, and his germ obsession began to spiral out of control. This included a fear of flies. Hughes hired three guards to work in eight-hour shifts at the bungalow where he lived to intercept the insects.

Also in 1946, he threw out his golf clubs and clothes, convinced they were contaminated with syphilis. Over the next 20 years, Hughes became an increasingly reclusive shell of a man. He wore tissue boxes for shoes, began storing his bodily waste in glass jars and drafted lengthy memos on the proper way to open tin cans without touching them.

X-rays taken at autopsy revealed broken hypodermic needles lodged in his arms, and his six-foot-four frame weighed less than 90 lb (41 kg). He had been seen by so few people for so long that the Treasury Department had to use fingerprints to identify his body. On his death in 1976, Hughes left an estate estimated at $2 billion.

This was a classic and very sad psychiatric case where high sums of money seemed to make him worse rather than better off.

Spendthrifts

1. Michael Jackson

Michael Jackson went from being the richest musician in the world, having sold 61 million albums in the USA alone, to having mounting debts as a result of a lavish and bizarre lifestyle.

Jackson's highly successful music career included his 1982 hit "Thriller", which still holds the record for the second best-selling US album of all time. During his success, Jackson purchased the famous *Neverland* ranch for $14.6 million, a fantasy-like 2500-acre property. His life changed in 1993 when child molesting allegations were revealed, and financial troubles became apparent.

In 2003 Michael Jackson was said to be more than $230 million in debt. At the time, he was stated to be spending $20 to $30 million more than he was earning per year by accountancy experts, with *Neverland* costing as much as $120,000 a month to look after. Upon Jackson's death in 2009, his debts were estimated at $500 million.

2. Viv Nicholson

Nicholson became famous in 1961 when she won £152,319 (equivalent to more than £3 million today), and announced that she was going to "spend, spend, spend". This she did. Born into a modest working-class home, she set about spending this massive windfall immediately.

Viv went on to purchase a large bungalow priced at £11,000 for herself and her family, as well as a pink Chevrolet, which she changed for a different luxury car every six months. Her husband bought a racehorse, the children were sent to boarding school, and the family enjoyed luxurious holidays around America and Europe.

Around half of her winnings had been spent by the time her husband was killed in a car accident in 1965. She then ran into financial trouble, with banks and tax creditors deeming her bankrupt, declaring that all her money, and everything she had acquired with it, belonged not to her but to her partners' estate.

Following a three-year legal battle, Viv gained £34,000 from her husband's estate, yet went on to lose the money she had been awarded on the stock market and through unsuccessful investments. She ended up penniless, and by 1976 was unable to afford to bury her fourth husband, having failed to regain her position in the public eye through promoting a singing career. In 2007 Nicholson described how she was now living on £87 a week, and finding it difficult to find a job, yet talked about her financial situation with ease – "It may have served me right – maybe I was wild and crazy. But it is *my* life and I won't be told how to live it."

Investors

1. Warren Buffett

Buffet, perhaps the most famous investor of all time, began investing his money in his early life. At 14 years old, he invested $1,200 of his savings from delivering newspapers in 40 acres of farmland, and in high school he then purchased a used pinball machine for $25, which he placed in a nearby Barber Shop. Within months, he owned three machines in three different locations, and went on to sell his pinball business for $1,200. Buffett continued to invest his savings in a series of similar entrepreneurial ventures. By the time he went to study at the University of Nebraska in 1946, he had saved $6,000, which was a considerable amount of money at the time.

Having graduated and spent a period of time working in New York, he started his own investment company when he was 25 years old with $100. Seven limited partners contributed a total of $105,000 towards the stock market trading partnership. The partners were rewarded with 6% on their investment and 75% of the profits above this target amount annually. Buffett received the remaining 25% of profits. Over 13 years, he compounded money at an annual rate of 29.5% through stock market trading activities, whilst the Dow Jones Industrial Average *declined* in value during five of these years.

By 1969, Buffett believed that the stock market had become speculative and ended the stock market trading investment partnership, with his share of the investment partnership having grown to be worth over $25 million.

He also invested in a number of companies, including a leading textile manufacturer called Berkshire Hathaway. In 1969, he was having difficulty finding reasonable investments in the stock market, so he liquidated his partnership. His initial investors received $30 for every dollar they invested in 1956 – a compounded annual return of almost 30%. Buffett invested his share of the partnership profits into Berkshire Hathaway.

In 1967, Buffett began diversifying Berkshire's business interests by purchasing two insurance companies. Over the next decade, he added several more insurance companies to his arsenal. He became, in effect, the investment manager for the insurance companies' premium-based capital (or "float"). But instead of returning the profits from his investments to his partners, he reinvested them in his company.

His company, Berkshire Hathaway, owns many companies. In 2007, Buffett was named *The World's Second Richest Man*, after Bill Gates. Despite this, he still lives in the same small three-bedroom house that he bought after he got married 50 years ago. Buffett drives his own car everywhere and does not have a driver or security people around him. He never travels by private jet, although he owns the world's largest private jet company. He is now mainly concerned with giving away his great wealth.

2. The "Google Guys"

Sergey Brin and Larry Page are the co-founders of Google, having studied computer science together at Stanford University. Google began in 1996 as a project by the pair. In their research project they came up with a plan to make a search engine that ranked websites according to the number of other websites that linked to that site, and ultimately came up with the Google we have today.

The domain google.com was registered on 14 September 1997 and Google Corporation was formed a year later in September 1998. Google started selling advertisements with its keyword searches in 2000. These advertisements used a system based on the idea that you only paid for your advertising if someone clicked on your ad link – hence the term Pay Per Click (PPC) was born.

In 2004, Google launched its own free web-based email service, known as Gmail. This service was made to rival the free online mail services supplied by Yahoo! and Microsoft (hotmail). This new free email service shook up the very foundation of free email with its enormous 1 GB of storage, which dwarfed its rivals tenfold.

In 2004 Google also launched Google Earth. Google Earth is an amazing creation: a map of the earth based on satellite imagery. This interactive map of the world allows you to type in a search for any place in the world and you will automatically be taken there.

Google has a dominant controlling share of the search market. It is the most widely used search engine on the Internet, with an 85.72% market share in August 2011, with Google receiving about a billion search requests per day – and with estimates that Google makes 12 cents for every search you perform.

As of 2011, Larry Page and Sergey Brin are estimated to each be worth $19.8 billion.

Tycoons

1. Mohamed Al-Fayed

Mohamed was born in Egypt, with his first real business opportunity coming when he and his brothers set up the shipping company Genavco, which turned out to be highly successful. However, the President of Egypt decided to "nationalise" all substantial private companies, removing control of Genavco from the Fayeds. The family then decided to relocate to London. Despite this setback, in 1966 the Fayeds re-established Genavco's headquarters in Genoa, Italy, and opened additional offices in London. Mohamed's fleet of Genavco ships frequently traded between Alexandria and Dubai, and in the mid-1960s he travelled there to meet with its ruler, Sheikh Rashid al Makhtoum.

Mohamed discussed with the Sheikh why, with so many boats trading in the Gulf and sailing right past Dubai, he did not build a harbour which would allow Dubai to offer bunkering and other such services to the ships and their crews. Sheikh Rashid invited Mohamed to gather the resources needed to build Dubai's first significant piece of modern infrastructure.

When the harbour was complete, the Sheikh asked Mohamed to help him find a company to search for oil, something most large companies did not want to do. Mohammed flew experts from a leading technology firm out to Dubai to set to work. Some 300,000 barrels of oil were found. The Sheikh was delighted, and charged Mohamed with revolutionising Dubai. Mohamed was committed to fulfilling the Sheikh's vision for Dubai and chose to purchase a 30% stake in Richard Costain (the British construction company he had entrusted with the majority of the work) to ensure it fulfilled its promises to the Emirate. The architectural overhaul of Dubai was vast; construction took almost a decade to complete and laid the foundations for the phenomenal growth Dubai enjoys today.

Mohamed insisted on using British companies and workers for the projects, and consequently introduced British financiers and construction companies to Dubai. As a direct result of Mohamed's industry and enterprise, Britain earned £8 billion at a time when the UK economy was struggling.

The year 1968 was when Mohamed established International Marine Services (IMS), which carried out salvage, towing and servicing work for the fleets of oil tankers trading in Dubai's waters. IMS became one of the world's leading companies in this specialised field.

In 1979, Mohamed learnt that L'Hotel Ritz in Paris was for sale, and made an offer on it, which was accepted. He went on to renovate the hotel, spending the equivalent of US$1 million per suite in the process.

In November 1984, Mohamed and his brothers acquired a 30% stake in House of Fraser (which included Harrods). In March 1985, the Fayeds made an offer for the remaining 70%, which was subsequently accepted. House of Fraser employed 30,000 people and was badly in need of capital investment, which Mohamed provided. He also hired leading retailers to take charge and ensured that everyone kept their jobs. Without Mohamed's efforts, House of Fraser would not enjoy the success it does today. Mohamed had also begun to restore Harrods, investing more than £400 million in the renovation.

Mohamed and his brothers decided to float House of Fraser Group on the London Stock Exchange in 1994, retaining Harrods and its subsidiary companies (including Harrods Aviation, Harrods Bank, and Harrods Estates) as an independent, family-run business. In 1996, Mohamed spotted a gap in the aviation industry, and launched Air Harrods, a luxury helicopter chartering service.

In 1997, Mohamed learned that the Second Division team, Fulham Football Club (FFC) was for sale, saw its potential, and bought it. He promised the fans that within five years FFC would be playing in the Premiership. Mohamed poured money into the club's grounds, players and management, instructing Kevin Keegan to take over as club manager. As a result, Fulham was transformed. Within three years, the club had enjoyed two league championship wins and promotion to the Premiership.

Al-Fayed has enjoyed widespread success, and his wealth is currently estimated at $1.2 billion.

Experimental studies of coins and notes

On a much more concrete level, attitudes to money have been studied by looking at the public's reaction to their actual currency. One reason for this is the public misunderstanding or misuse of currency, along with hostility to changes in it. Notes and coins, though being overtaken by "plastic" and "electronic" money, are still the physical manifestation of money to most people. Looking at attitudes to national currency certainly gives insight into money attitudes.

One experiment undertaken in 1947 has led to considerable research being done on the psychology of coins from various countries. Bruner and Goodman (1947) argued that values and needs play a very important part in psychophysical perception. They entertained various general hypotheses: the greater the social value of an object, the more it will be susceptible to accentuation: and the greater the individual need for a socially valued object, the more marked will be the operation of behavioural determinants. Researchers asked rich and poor ten-year-olds to estimate which of an ascending and descending range of circles of light corresponded to a range of coins. Another control group compared the circle of light to cardboard discs of identical size to the coins. They found, as predicted, that coins (socially valued objects) were judged larger in size than grey discs, and that the greater the value of the coin the greater was the deviation of apparent size from actual size. Second, they found that poor children overestimated the size of coins considerably more than did rich children. Furthermore, this was true both with coins present and with coins from memory.

Because this experiment demonstrated that subjective value and objective needs actually affected perception of physical objects, it provoked considerable interest and many replications have been done. Studies have been done in different countries (Dawson, 1975; McCurdy, 1956) with different coins (Smith, Fuller & Forrest, 1975) and with poker chips as well as coins (Lambert, Soloman & Watson, 1949) and it was found that although there have been some differences in the findings, the effects have been generalisable. Tajfel (1977) noted that about 20 experiments have been done on the "overestimation effect" and only two have yielded unambiguously negative results. Nearly all the researchers have found that motivational or valuable stimuli had effects on subjects' perceptual judgements of magnitude as well as size, weight, and brightness.

Two other methodologically different studies have looked at the value–size hypothesis. Hitchcock, Munroe and Munroe (1976) compared 84 countries' per capita incomes and the average size of the currency to determine whether "persons in poor countries have greater subjective need than persons in wealthy countries, and whether a country's coinage allows institutional expression of the level of need" (p. 307). They found a correlation of − .19 ($p < .05$) between GNP per capita and the mean size of all coins minted for a country, and a correlation of − .25 ($p < .025$) between GNP per capita and the size of the least-valued coin.

They concluded that these data indicate the potential usefulness of viewing institutional-level data from a psychological perspective. The difference was especially marked when the countries' lowest-level coins were compared. The governments of the poorer countries seemed to be using the principle that although the low-value coins (used more by the poor than the affluent) would buy very little, if they could be given substantial size and weight they would at least be psychologically reassuring.

Furnham (1985a) did an unobtrusive study on the perceived value of small coins. The four smallest coins of the country (England) were dropped in the street and observers recorded how people who saw the coins reacted. In the study of over 200 people, 56 people who saw the smallest (½p) coin ignored it, 44 ignored the 1p coin, 16 the 2p coin and 10 the 5p coin. It was concluded that because of the fact that money is both a taboo and an emotionally charged topic, unobtrusive measures such as these are particularly useful, particularly in times of high inflation or unemployment, or where there were changes in the coinage.

Bruce, Gilmore, Mason, and Mayhew (1983) were interested in the introduction of two new coins into British currency that were small relative to their value compared with other coins present in the system. They were made because small coins are cheaper to produce and easier to handle, and it brought British coinage into line with the coins of other nations. In a preliminary series of studies the authors found that it was not the colour of a coin (gold vs. copper vs. silver) that made it appear more valuable, but rather its thickness and elaborate edge. Further, in Britain "seven-sidedness", rather than a purely circular coin, is seen as more valuable. In the main study they found that their adult subjects appeared to follow specific "rules" about the value-conferring features of coins. These rules refer to the shape, colour, edge and sidedness of the coins.

In a second series of studies, Bruce, Howarth, Clark–Carter, Dodds and Heyes (1983) looked at the extent to which the new British £1.00 coin might be confused with existing coins. They found that the new coin could easily be confused with a coin one twentieth of its value and a different colour, but of similar circumference. Where coins have the same shape and circumference it is most important that the thickness of the more valuable is sufficiently great to make the weight difference between the two coins very easily detectable. They concluded that more ergonomic work is needed before coins are introduced into circulation in order to study problems of confusion to the public.

Furnham and Weissman (1985) showed all the British coins to over 60 Americans (in America) who had never been to Britain, or previously seen British currency. Only one subject was able to rank order the coins correctly according to worth. Whereas over half of the sample could identify the relative worthlessness of the two smallest coins (1p, ½p), less than a third correctly identified the rank of the top five coins.

In a second study the authors asked 4- and 9- to 10-year-old children various questions about British coins when showing them all the coins of the realm, e.g. "Which coin can you buy most with?" and "Point at the 10p piece". They found that whereas the 9- to 10-year-olds were accurate in their answers (90% or more), in each case 4-year-olds were often wrong. The 4-year-olds seemed to be operating on much the same principles as the American adults had done. That is, given the choice the children (and foreign adults) assumed that size was positively correlated with worth (circumference, not volume) and that silver coins were more valuable than copper or gold-coloured coins.

Some studies have looked at the effects of inflation on the perception of money, one using coins, the other notes. Subjects are shown paper cuts of circular coins or oblong notes and required to estimate the correct size. Lea (1981) showed that subjects tended to overestimate the sizes of identical coins as a function of inflation. That is, subjects made bigger estimates of coins given their old pre-decimalisation names (2 shillings) than their new name (10 pence). Although there are some alternate hypotheses that may be entertained, the most satisfactory explanation appears to be that because inflation has reduced the actual worth of the same sized coin, they are perceived as smaller.

Furnham (1983) found evidence of the same phenomenon when considering notes. Subjects were asked to identify rectangles corresponding in shape to a £1.00 note withdrawn from circulation in 1979 and a £1.00 note currently being used. The notes differed slightly in colour, shape and design but were broadly similar. As predicted, subjects tended to overemphasise the size of the old note (10.71 cm vs. 9.69 cm) and underemphasise the new note (8.24 cm vs. 9.05 cm).

Together these studies provide evidence for the value/need money perception hypothesis and the effects of inflation on the perceived size of actual money. These results could be extrapolated to the abstract, nebulous concept of money rather than just actual coins and notes. Indeed these results confirm non-experimental observations in the area such as that poorer people overestimate the power of money.

Leiser and Izak (1987) argued that a culture with high inflation – such as Israel in the 1980s – leads to people having changing attitudes to their coinage. They found that it was the attitude of the public to a given coin that best predicted what they called the money size illusion. Further, the biases in estimated sizes remained even after the coin was withdrawn.

The introduction of a new coin offers interesting and important opportunities for research. One example was the introduction of the euro in 2002. Numerous studies were done such as those by Jonas, Greitemeyer, Frey, and Schulz-Hardt (2002), who showed how the size and denomination of the currency changed (i.e. German Deutschmark, Italian lira) had a powerful anchoring effect on what people thought about their new currency.

One recent study proved what many of us know: we react differently to money notes/bills as a function of their use. Di Muro and Noseworthy (2012) found that people spend small notes/bills quickly because they are often worn, dirty and seen as contaminated. Their conclusion was that money is not as fungible as previously thought – its physical appearance influences the way it is spent:

> People actively seek to acquire and retain crisp currency because it affords a source of pride to be expressed around others; however, people actively seek to divest worn currency because they are disgusted by the contamination from others. This suggests that the physical appearance of money matters more than traditionally thought, and like most things in life, it too is inextricably linked to the social context (p. 12).

In another scatological study Kardos and Castano (2012) showed that some money stinks, in the sense that it is acquired immorally. They showed that the greater the guilt felt by acquiring money (lottery ticket on procurement) the less likely it is to be spent because of the desire not to handle "dirty" money.

Money today

Certainly changes in technology have changed our money. Most of us use plastic rather than metal or paper money. We transfer money electronically from our personal computers. Yet, our follies and foibles with regard to money remain.

There persists a great interest in very rich people as well as famous people whose money habits remain very unusual.

3

DIFFERENT APPROACHES TO THE TOPIC OF MONEY

I sell, therefore I am. You buy, therefore I eat.

Craig Dormanen

What better way to prove that you understand a subject than to make money out of it?

Harold Rosenberg

Money changes people just as often as it changes hands.

Al Batt

The entire economic system depends on the fact that people are willing to do unpleasant things in return for money.

Scott Adams

Introduction

There are no grand psychological "theories" of money, although various psychological paradigms or traditions have been applied to the psychology of money. These include psychoanalytic theories, Piagetian development theories, behaviourist learning theory and, more recently, interesting ideas emerging out of economic psychology and behavioural economics.

Lea, Tarpy and Webley (1987) have noted that there is an experimental and social psychology of money, as well as numerous important psychometric studies on the topic. They argue that we need to move toward a new psychological theory of money that takes cognisance of the symbolic value of money. They believe psychologists need to move on from arguing and demonstrating that people are clearly irrational or arational with regard to money and look at the many institutions and rituals that accept, sanction, even encourage less than rational economic behaviour.

They argue that money represents not only the goods that it can purchase but also the source of the goods and how they were obtained. Its meaning is also derived from its form. They believe that money's function of expressing value can be carried out at various levels of measurement.

---

1. **Nominal:** Here money operates only at the level of equivalence. That is with a particular kind of money you can buy a particular item of goods or service.
2. **Ordinal:** Here money has different forms that can be ranked greater or less than each other.
3. **Interval/Ratio:** This means we have a true zero and a ratio scale such that we know and accept the difference between £20 and £30 is the same as between £70 and £80. This is the system we have today.

Lea, Tarpy and Webley's theory is that money is deeply symbolic. Behaviour toward and with money can only be understood through an historical and developmental perspective. Principally money represents an exchange evaluation, but there are many subsidiary meanings, which affect how it is used and can even limit its general applicability.

What money symbolises differs between individuals and groups but these symbols are relatively limited in number and stable over time. Hence they can be described and categorised. But rather than ask what psychological characteristics money possesses, it is more fruitful to ask how these characteristics affect behaviour with and toward money. Thus certain coins or notes, either because of their newness, weight or cleanliness, may also be spent before others. Similarly substituting coins for notes may have the effect of stimulating small transactions.

Although it may be possible to draw up an exhaustive list of the major symbolic associates of various types of money, and even document which groups are more likely to favour one symbol over another, a psychological theory of money will only be useful when the symbol is related to behaviour.

Ideally, according to Lea et al. (1987), their early psychological theory of money had three factors:

---

1. Factors associated with the **development** of symbolism. Thus, for particular individuals in particular cultures, shapes, colours and icons have particular value and importance. Hence national differences in the size, colour and iconography of currency. Note how this changes with major changes in government as in the case of Hong Kong, South Africa, the former Soviet Union and Yugoslavia over the past decade.

2. Factors concerning symbolism itself. These are to do with the range and meaning (positive, negative and neutral) attached to all forms of currency from the traditional (coins, notes, cheques) to more modern forms of currency including new works of art which are bought, not for aesthetic pleasure, but as an exclusive source of investment.
3. Factors associated with the **use** of money. For example, why certain types of money are saved and others spent; why some are considered more safe than others, or more personal and more desirable than others; why money is unacceptable as a gift and why casinos use chips rather than cash. Indeed the meaning of money is more observable in the way it is used.

Money is not psychologically interchangeable. It is of value and is a measure of value. It is a complicated symbol imbued by individuals and communities with particular meanings, which in part dictates how it is used by economic forces. It should be acknowledged that individuals display constant and important monetary behaviours. Individuals act on the economy; the collective behaviour of individuals (sometime few in number) shapes economic affairs. On the other hand, a person's economic status and situation in society determines not only how much money they have but how they see that money. We shape our economy and it shapes us. The laws and history of a particular economy (i.e. Western Europe) do affect in small and big ways the conscious and unconscious behaviour of all citizens of that Union.

One of the most fundamental differences between the major social sciences interested in money (anthropology, economy, psychology and sociology) concerns the assumption that people behave rationally and logically with respect to their own money. While econometricians and theorists develop highly sophisticated mathematical models of economic behaviour (always aggregated across groups), these nearly always accept the basic axiom of individual rationality. Psychologists on the other hand have delighted in showing the manifest number of faulty logical mistakes that ordinary people make in economic reasoning. Sociologists and anthropologists have also demonstrated how social forces (norms, rituals, customs and laws) exist that constantly render the behaviour of both groups and individuals *a-* rather than *ir-*rational.

The opposite of rational is impulsive, whimsical, and unpredictable. Economists accept that there are people of limited knowledge, intelligence and insight. And they know that business people with non-rational motives and who make use of non-rational procedures will fail rather than survive. Economic behaviour that reflects human frailty or poor reason is classified as a short-term aberration that has little impact on economic developments in the long run.

The whole rationality issue is a difficult one: doing unpaid work, giving to charity and playing the national lottery may be regarded as irrational. This is often to take a very narrow view of rationality. Clearly work provides many social benefits while gambling is exciting. What the economist often means by rational is behaving in such a way as to maximise income.

There are various synonyms for rationality like optimising or maximising. But as Lea et al. (1987) note " … we have seen that, in an analysis of real human choice behaviour, the rationality assumption is at best unproven, generally unhelpful, and sometimes clearly false" (p. 127). Yet they believe it remains reasonable for economists to use rationality assumptions. However, they do point out that economic psychology's preoccupation with the rationality question is futile. Rather than attempt to define whether an individual's behaviour is rational, maximising or optimising we should shift our attention to what is maximised and why. It is rather pointless being obsessed with the rationality question if this leads researchers to ignore the content of that behaviour.

Essentially the rationality argument can be presented at different levels:

1. The most strict and least acceptable meaning of economic rationality is that people are almost exclusively materially driven and that with both perfect knowledge and cool logic they choose "rationally" material satisfaction. This version has been both theoretically and empirically discredited.

2. The second version is that people nearly always behave rationally with respect to economic situations; societies and individuals supposedly "economise". The trouble with this idea is that although it may be possible to show that in the production and pricing of goods both primitive and modern peoples act rationally, they frequently behave quite irrationally in the exchanging of goods within economical gift-giving. In this sense all individuals and societies are, at once, rational and arational.

3. The third position is to treat rationality as simply a provisional set of assumptions upon which to base a theory or model. Rationality is a form of conceptual simplification that can be revised or rejected if unhelpful or if the data do not fit the theory. Many social scientists would be happy with this level of analysis.

4. The final level of analysis is to treat economic rationality as an "institutionalised value" (Smelser, 1963). This is more than a psychological or sociological postulate but a standard of behaviour to which individuals and organisations hope to aspire. It is a standard to which people may conform or deviate and, hence, contains the concept of social control.

As Katona (1975) noted the real question is not whether the consumer is rational or irrational. Consumers' decisions are shaped by attitudes, habits, sociocultural norms, and group membership. People prefer cognitive short cuts, rules of thumb, routines – they are rarely capricious and whimsical and, for psychologists, never incomprehensible. Likewise, the behaviour of whole groups follows logical patterns that may differ greatly from postulated forms of rational behaviour. In short, the consumer behaves psycho-logically. People get multiple benefits from behaviours involving money such as giving and gambling.

Psychological theories of money neither assume monetary rationality nor rejoice in the countless examples of the ir- and arationality of ordinary people with respect to their money. They have set themselves the task, however, of trying to understand how ordinary people acquire and demonstrate their everyday monetary attitudes, beliefs and behaviours.

The biological psychology of money

The rapid rise of biological psychology over the last 30 years has been dramatic. It has developed theoretically with many evolutionary and sociobiological theories as well as developments in neuroscience.

In a very important paper Lea and Webley (2006) sought a biological perspective on money. They note that money is a "problem for a biological account of human motivation" and may be conceived as a pure creation of culture. In this sense the culture-dominated sciences like sociology offer a very different account to the biological sciences. Their review started from four assumptions:

(1) For humans (but not for other species), money has an extraordinary incentive power, similar to that of other motivators such as food and sex. (2) Whereas the incentive power of food, sex and most other motivators is easily understood in biological terms, that of money is not. (3) A biological explanation of the incentive power therefore needs to be provided because the science of money is still disconnected from the science of life and the gap needs to be bridged. (4) This task has hitherto been neglected. (p. 196)

They proffer two rather different theories to account for the self-evident motivational power of money:

Tool Theory: money is a tool to exchange scarce resources. It is an incentive "only because and only insofar as" it can be exchanged for goods and services that are the strong incentives. Money is instrumental, a means to an end, as recognised by economics. It is a generalised reinforcer: very useful for acquiring practically every material good.

Drug Theory: money affects the nervous system but is a perceptual or cognitive drug like pornography. Money acquires incentive power because it mimics the behavioural, neural or psychological action of a natural incentive. In this sense it is addictive and this may, in part, explain the powerful motivational power that it has.

The Tool Theory explains situations where money gives real but indirect access to rewards; it explains cases where money motivation is a real underlying function whereas that is not the case with Drug Theory. The authors note: " ... if Tool Theory fails, Drug Theory is then the only possible biological theory, and vice versa" (p. 165).

They try to integrate Tool and Drug Theory into other accounts of money motivation. Economic theories tend to be tool theories, while psychological theories tend to be drug theories. Lea and Webley note: " ... money is sought for reasons that go beyond its instrumental function. To varying degrees and in differing ways, therefore, these classic sociological accounts are versions of Drug Theory" (p. 168).

Next they note how so many money research areas support a drug theory perspective:

- **Perceiving coins and the money illusion:** people misperceive coin size because the value of money gives it special status, which interferes with normal perceptual and cognitive processes.
- **Money conservatism:** people resist the changing of their currency though they accept some additional forms of money like credit cards. The reaction of people to the introduction of new, safer, more durable money is emotive rather than calculative and therefore supports Drug Theory.
- **Gifts and money restrictions:** the purchasing of some things like sex or the giving of money gifts is not socially acceptable and seen to be socially and psychologically destructive, which supports Drug Theory.
- **Relationships:** money is a powerful symbol as well as channel of power in relationships, which has a strong drug-like quality.
- **Money status and addiction:** materialism, hoarding, etc., clearly fits the less rational Drug Theory.

In short the evidence is that money has a value and an emotional charge that is above its simple economic use. It is better conceived of as a cognitive drug. Drug Theory, they argue, captures the "parasitic and functionless" quality of money motivation so regularly shown by people.

They conclude with three points:

1. Although money is an efficient tool, and so gains incentive power by enabling us to fulfil a wide range of instincts, a Tool Theory of money motivation is inadequate. The majority of non-economic accounts of money (and even some economic accounts) either take this view or require a more elaborated Tool Theory than is usually assumed. Modern empirical work has uncovered substantial evidence in favour of this conclusion, and we believe that it would be widely if not universally accepted.

2. The inadequacies of Tool Theory can be overcome, and the phenomena that it fails to explain can be integrated, by asserting that money also acts as a drug. That is, we conclude that money derives some of its incentive power from providing the illusion of fulfilment of certain instincts. This argument has formed the core of the present article, and although we believe it is well grounded in the data we have reviewed, it will inevitably be more controversial. In particular, the alternatives of a more elaborate Tool Theory, or an entirely different way of partitioning the possible kinds of theory, cannot be ruled out at this stage, and perhaps they never could be.

3. The incentive power of money depends partly on the illusory fulfilment of the human instincts for reciprocal altruism and object play, though there may well be other instinctive systems that money can also parasitise. This conclusion is more speculative, and is likely to be the most controversial of all. However, insofar as it is persuasive, it would provide the best evidence in favour of the Tool/Drug analysis, since it would show that the analysis has been deployed fruitfully. (p. 175)

They note that the high number of quotes, proverbs and aphorisms about money are both cynical and sceptical, but still about the motivational power of money. Cynical aphorisms assert the fact that money is indeed very powerful, despite many protestations to the contrary, while sceptical aphorisms assert the real limitations about the power of money. People quite clearly believe in a Drug Theory assertion that money is a dangerously powerful force in their lives.

Clearly people are prepared to do or sell almost anything for money. In that sense Lea and Webley (2006) are right that it is a very strong incentive, no doubt with a biological origin.

The economics of money

Most libraries contain hundreds of books with the term money in the title but nearly all are found in economics. There are books on monetary theory; monetary policy; money and capital markets; internal money; money, politics and government policy; and the relationship between money, income and capital. Economists note that money may be analysed according to substance: copper, silver, gold, paper or nothing. The great bulk of money is credited by banks that mobilise securities to circulate money. Further, bank deposits have important merits: they are convenient, entirely homogeneous, and not intrinsically valuable, representing only "money on paper".

As Finn (1992) noted, economists are not so much interested in the meaning of money per se but rather wealth and material prosperity. Wealth can be held in various forms, money being one, and that is what we all want and chase. Economics is the science of the motive to maximise wealth. This is argued to be a primary, pre-eminent and powerful motive for all behaviour.

People accumulate wealth to consume goods and services that increase utility (satisfaction and happiness). Thus the cost of utility can be calculated. The more wealth you have, the more opportunities you have to increase utility. Utility theory supposed it provided a comprehensive view of human decision making. *Homo economicus*: the utility maximiser. This was replaced by rational preference theory.

Finn (1992) summarises the approach of his discipline thus:

> In sum, economists believe that most of the people most of the time will respond positively when they have a chance to increase their wealth because people believe that increased wealth will lead to increased welfare. Similarly, people will change their behaviour to reduce the loss of wealth when any loss is inevitable. Even though the canons of evidence in the discipline do not allow for a scientifically respectable interpretation of the meaning of wealth for individuals, economists proceed with the matter-of-fact point of view that more of nearly every good thing is better than less, and there are very few good things that more wealth is not helpful in attaining. (p. 666)

Whilst there are passionate theoretical debates and policy implications, there is substantial agreement between economists. The following axiomatic points, made by Coulborn (1950) are probably not in dispute:

> [M]oney may be defined as a means of valuation and of payment; as both a unit of account and as a generally acceptable medium of exchange. Money is an abstract unit of account; the "mathematical apparatus" used to express price. It is a common denominator for precision in calculation. Money does have a legal status but the "commercial" idea of general acceptability is vital to any definition of money. Money should be portable, durable, divisible and recognisable. The common unit of account should be of suitable size. Money now no longer needs to be intrinsically valuable.

In a barter economy, ratios of exchange fixed by a rigid custom inhibit economic progress. Money-based systems, unlike barter, generalise purchasing power and make for full satisfaction in exchange. Over time money has imperfections and any durable goods (e.g. gold) may serve as a link between present and future values. Money can mean the loan of money: hence there is a money market where money is borrowed and the price of money refers to the rate of interest at which money is borrowed. There is often a difference between real, nominal, and legal capital. Real capital refers to actual goods and services (i.e. stocks in a warehouse); nominal capital refers to the agreed contemporary values of the real capital; while legal capital is the amount on which companies pay fixed interest and dividends.

Various technical terms refer to monetary groups:

1. **Legal tender:** a lawful form of payment.
2. **Currency:** coins, notes, and the whole tangible media of exchange.
3. **Cash:** anything which is customary in payment, synonymous with medium of exchange, especially coins and notes.
4. **Commodity money:** e.g. gold coins where the metal is equal to the face value (full bodied).
5. **Token money:** usually base metal coins that were once commodity money.
6. **Representative money:** notes that are freely convertible into full-bodied commodity money.
7. **Fiat money:** money that the state says shall be legal tender.
8. **Bank money:** notes and bank deposits issued by individual banks.
9. **Substitute money:** all deposits, including treasury notes, and notes.
10. **Credit:** a belief in payment or repayment; all bank deposits are therefore credits.
11. **Overdrafts:** also a form of credit where people are allowed to draw out more than they deposited.

The functions of money are well known. Money is a medium of exchange: while paper and plastic money are intrinsically worthless, they are guarantees of value that can be used in exchange for goods and services. Money is also a unit of account: we can judge the cheapness or dearness of goods by using money. Third, money is a store of value: unlike perishable goods money does not rot, but it does change value over time, particularly in times of political instability. Finally, money is a standard of deferred payment: buying and selling can take place before a commodity actually goes on to the market (as in future trading).

What, according to economists, are the qualities of **good money**?

First, its **portability**: i.e. it is easily carried. Indeed electronic money or plastic money may be rather too easily moved so that it can elude proper authorities of the law.

Second, good money has **durability**: it stands up to wear and tear. Paper money may last as little as six months because it "wears out", while coins can last 20 to 30 years even with problems of inflation. Coins can be made of anything including plastic but frequently follow the specific symbolism of gold, silver, and bronze.

Third, good money must ensure **recognisability**: it should be immediately recognisable for its exact worth.

Fourth, it needs to be **homogeneous**: one note or coin needs to be as acceptable as any other. Even rare coins, if part of the official currency, can serve in acceptable exchange/payment of debt.

Fifth, naturally, money must be relatively **stable**: the value of money should not vary widely, erratically or unpredictably.

Sixth, it must also be **limited**: the supply of money needs to be controlled, otherwise if too scarce or too plentiful it could seriously change in stability.

Where does money go? How does it circulate: money is earned for producing "real worth" – goods and services (wages, salaries). Money is spent on consuming the goods produced including "necessities", amusements and savings. Money is invested for future prosperity – investments, stocks, etc. Finally there is money management – attempts by the government to control the money system and prevent both depression and inflation. Economists are not interested in the everyday monetary behaviour of individuals. They are always interested in aggregated data and building theories to explain it.

Economic anthropology and primitive money

The anthropologists have undertaken numerous detailed studies of how money is used in different cultures. They often describe what objects are valued and used to barter and the difference between particular types of money. The history of most cultures is the transition from special purpose, socially embedded concepts and uses of money to that which is depersonalised and disembedded, and measure of objects, relations, services and even persons.

They often write about special-purpose money: special for particular purposes, times and people. Modern anthropologists remain interested in money's materiality, what it is made from, as well how particular groups like corporate investors and traders talk about it. For them the symbolism and iconography of money remains very interesting. They are interested in groups that form their own local currency and who expose the taken for granted monetary order.

Maurer (2006) suggested that it is the task of money anthropologists to expose the gap between the economists' cold rational view of money and how it is used and the social, semiotic and arational aspects of modern money usage. Traditionally anthropologists have looked at **primitive** money and the **functional** uses of money in society. One of the more intriguing anthropological contributions has been to describe what constitutes money, and secondly how it is commonly "transacted".

Early studies showed how some tribes fought not with weapons but possessions; how ritualised "gift-giving" has such important meanings. Anthropologists have taken a special interest in how groups evolve complex monetary systems and rules and the functions they fulfil. The use of money is seen as a highly symbolic, ritualised game with implicit and explicit rules.

Unlike psychology, anthropology has long been interested in economics and consumption (Douglas & Isherwood, 1979). Economic anthropology is concerned with the economic aspects of the social relations of persons. Indeed there are standard textbooks on economic anthropology (Dalton, 1971; Herskovitz, 1962; Thurnwald, 1932). Although there have been a number of well-established authorities in this field, Karl Polanyi's work is perhaps the best known. Anthropologists have long been aware that nearly all economic concepts, ideas and theories are based on only one type of economy – industrial capitalism. Some have argued that these modern economic concepts (maximising, supply, demand) are equally applicable to primitive societies, while others are not convinced.

One of the major tasks of economic anthropology is to detect economic universals in human society by sampling the many forms in which they are manifest across cultures: for instance, whereas the deferment of wants, through saving and investing, may be considered good for some cultures, most primitive cultures dictate that resources should be expended on food and shelter.

Thurnwald (1932) suggested that a characteristic failure of most primitive economies is the absence of any desire to make profits from either production or exchange. Various distinctions have been made, such as objects that are treated as treasure and hoarded as such or articles of daily use; whether the object is regarded as capital capable of yielding profit; and also whether the object is the potential source of others of its own kind. Certainly, what is interesting about anthropological studies of money is not only the range of objects used as money but also the fact that primitive money does not fulfil many of the functions that current money does.

Whereas economists seem concerned with only non-social aspects of money, such as its worth, divisibility, etc., anthropologists look at money which is used in *reciprocal and redistributive transactions*, in terms of the personal roles and social context of what occurs. The exchange of whatever serves as money – be it armbands, pigs' tusks, shells or stones – as well as its acquisition and disposition is a structured and important event that often has strong moral and legal obligations and implications which might change various status rights and social roles.

Because money is a means of reciprocal and redistributive payment used fairly infrequently to discharge social obligations in primitive societies, its portability and divisibility are not very important. The introduction of Western-style money does more than just displace indigenous money; it has inevitable repercussions on the social organisation of a people. This is because Western-style money allows both commercial and non-commercial (traditional) payments to be earned with general-purpose money earned in everyday market transactions. Hence patrons, elders and heads of families and clans lose some control over their clients and juniors who can earn their own cash and dispose of it as they wish.

The essence of the anthropological message is this: *money has no essence apart from its uses, which depend on the traditional transactional modes of each culture's economy. Money is what it does and no more.* For Douglas (1967) money rituals make visible external signs of internal states. Money also mediates social experience, and provides a standard for measuring worth. Money makes a link between the present and the future. But money can only perform its role of intensifying economic interaction if the public has faith in it. If faith in it is shaken, the currency is useless. Money symbols can only have effect so long as they command confidence. In this sense all money, false or true, depends on a confidence trick. There is no false money, except by contrast with another currency that has more total acceptability. So, primitive ritual is like good money, not false money, as long as it commands assent.

Thus, whereas economists see the origin of money in terms of commercial issues, anthropologists stress non-commercial origins as in bride payments, sacrificial and religious money, status symbols, as well as the payment of fines and taxes. Certainly money used for non-commercial payments appears to occur before it is used for commercial purposes, suggesting that anthropologists' theories of the origins of money are correct (Lea et al., 1987).

Anthropologists have already emphasised the variety of moneys existing in any culture – that is the number of items that serve as money. Thus great art is now seen as an investment today rather than purely as an aesthetic object. Further, anthropologists have always been sensitive to the symbols of money and the symbolic value of ritual possessions. This observation is always manifest when a country decides to change its currency (coins and notes) even if there is no change in value. Equally, as we see with the introduction of a pan-European currency, the symbols on notes and coins (or lack of them) is a source of much passion and speculation.

The sociology of money

The line between economics, political science and sociology is rarely clear. Just as we have the subdiscipline of economic psychology so there is economic sociology. Early sociologists, such as Herbert Spencer, Emile Durkheim and Max Weber, recognised the sociological implications of the division of labour and how societies try to regulate cooperation and equitable exchange among economic agents by law, customs and codes (Smelser, 1963). Most economic sociology has examined advanced capitalist societies.

Social theorists and political economists like Adam Smith and Karl Marx are happily claimed by sociologists as one of their own. Marx claimed that money transformed *real human and natural faculties* into mere abstract representations. Further, he thought money appeared as a *disruptive* power for the individual and for social bonds. It changed fidelity into infidelity, love into hate, hate into love, virtue into vice, vice into virtue, servant into master, stupidity into intelligence and intelligence into stupidity.

Sociologists do not see economic forces and factors like money supply, fiscal policies, etc. as separate from other social factors. Often economists see individuals and financial institutions as autonomous, free-acting, undersocialised, atomised agents (Baker & Jimerson, 1992) rather than as socialised agents constrained and stifled by social forces. Further, sociologists argue that money has multiple meanings and definitions and is used in many different spheres. "It is not as colourless, neutral, fungible and objective as economists contend. Money is shaped by objective social relations (social structure) and cognitive classifications and evocative meanings (culture)" (Baker & Jimerson, 1992, p. 680).

Baker and Jimerson (1992) have suggested that for the sociologist there are two dimensions that provide a framework to understand the sociology of money. *First,* the **structured** vs. **cultural** perspective. The **structured** perspective concerns money in the interpersonal and regulatory context of exchange. It is about communication and exchange at a personal level and the legal and political mechanisms governing trading and markets. *Second*, there is the **independent** vs. **dependent** variable approach: i.e. money as a cause, catalyst or facilitator vs. money as an effect, consequence or result. Most economists take the independent variable perspective while many sociologists take the dependent variable perspective.

Zelizer (1989) has noted that sociologists are interested in the uses, users, sources, control and allocation of money and all the extra economic factors (i.e. the family) that influence economic behaviour. Sociologists are also interested in the organisation of finance in families, private corporations and the state as well as the role of culture and government in the attempts to control and shape monetary behaviour.

Economic sociologists are also particularly interested in social organisations, be they formal (business, hospitals), informal (neighbourhoods, gangs) or diffuse (ethnic groups). The roles individuals have within them, the behavioural norms that develop, the values they implicitly or explicitly hold, and the structures they impose are all central to the economic sociologists' concepts of institutionalisation.

Sociologists tend to reject materialistic definitions of money, preferring, like anthropologists, to focus on the social relationships that monetary transactions involve. Sociologists reject the economic idea that modern money is general purpose, fulfilling all the possible monetary functions. There exists no form of money that serves all such functions simultaneously. Legal-tender notes are rarely used to store value in practice. Notes and coins represent standard units of value without literally embodying them; indeed, if they did so they would be worth considerably more than their legal-tender equivalents. Cheques, credit cards and bank drafts serve only as means of payment. These different forms of money inevitably fulfil different functions.

Sociologists are interested in control, particularly control of the money supply and attempts to control inflation, deflation and economic depression. They are also interested in monetary networks, which are networks of information. Dodd (1994) notes that there are five factors that must be in place for a network to be defined as such:

First, the network will contain a standardised accounting system into which each monetary form within the network is divisible, enabling its exchange with anything priced in terms of that system.

Second, the network will rely on information from which expectations regarding the future can be derived: money is acceptable as payment almost solely on the assumption that it can be reused later on.

Third, the network will depend on information regarding its spatial characteristics: limits placed on the territory in which specific monetary forms may be used will probably derive initially from measures designed to prevent counterfeiting, although they will eventually refer to the institutional framework governing the operation of a payments system.

Fourth, the network will be based on legalistic information, usually in the form of rules, concerning the status of contractual relationships, which are fleeting and conclusive: to pay with money is literally to pay up.

Fifth, the operation of the network presupposes knowledge of the behaviour and expectations of others. This is usually derived from experience, but can also be sought out and even paid for. Such information is vital in generating trust in money's abstract properties. Monetary transactions are often impersonal, even secretive, and networks need to be able to cope with this. A network is an abstract aggregated concept that reflects the typical sociological level of analysis.

In an excellent, comprehensive paper entitled The Social Meaning of Money, Zelizer (1989) rejects the utilitarian concept of money as the ultimate objectifer, homogenising all qualitative distinctions into an abstract quality. She believes that too many sociologists have accepted economists' assumptions that money per se and market processes are invulnerable to social influences – free from cultural or social constraints.

Yet all sociologists have argued and demonstrated how cultural and social factors influence the uses, meaning, and incidence of money in current society. Zelizer (1989) believes that the extra economic social basis of money remains as powerful in modern economic systems as it was in primitive and anxious societies. Central to sociological (as well as anthropological and psychological) conceptions of money are the following fundamental points.

First, while money does serve as a key rational tool of the modern economic market, it also exists outside the sphere of the market and is profoundly shaped by cultural and social structural factors.

Second, there are a plurality of different kinds of moneys; each special money is shared by a particular set of cultural and social factors and is thus qualitatively distinct.

Third, the classic economic inventory of money's functions and attributes, based on the assumption of a single general-purpose type of money, is thus unsuitably narrow. By focusing exclusively on money as a market phenomenon (the traditional economic view) it fails to capture the very complex range of characteristics of money as a non-market medium. A different, more inclusive understanding is necessary, for certain moneys can be indivisible (or divisible but not in mathematically predictable portions), non-portable, deeply subjective, and therefore qualitatively heterogeneous.

Fourth, the assumed dichotomy between utilitarian money and non-pecuniary values is false, for money under certain circumstances may be as singular and unexchangeable as the most personal or unique object.

Fifth, the alleged freedom and unchecked power of money manifests untenable assumptions. Culture and social structure set inevitable limits to the monetisation process by introducing profound controls and restrictions on the flow and liquidity of money.

Extra economic factors systematically constrain and shape: (a) the *uses* of money, earmarking, for instance, certain moneys for specified uses; (b) the *users* of money, designating different people to handle specified monies; (c) the *allocation* system of each particular money; (d) the *control* of different monies; and (e) the *sources* of money, linking different sources to specified uses.

In order to demonstrate the sociology of special or modern money sociologists have examined domestic money: husbands', wives' and children's money, and how changing conceptions of family life and gender relationships affect how family money is used (this will be examined in some detail later). Domestic or family money is clearly a very special kind of currency. Regardless of its source, once money enters the household its allocation (timing as well as amount) and uses are subject to rules quite distinct from the market. Only changes in gender roles and family structure influence the meaning and use of money. Domestic money usage and attitudes show the instrumental, rationalised model of money and the market economy to be wanting. Money in the home is transformed by the structure of social relations and the idiosyncratic system of each family. Equally institutional, charitable, gift and dirty money all take on unique social meanings.

What sociologists share with anthropologists and psychologists is an interest in the meaning individuals, groups, societies and cultures give to money and how that meaning affects its use. Further, they are particularly interested in how institutions use all forms of money.

Religion and money

At their core, although religions differ a great deal on many issues, they share numerous beliefs about money and materialism. What they preach and what some of their leaders actually do is, of course, another matter. The texts of the three Religions of the Book (Christianity, Islam and Judaism) and those of Hinduism, Buddhism and other eastern religions (Sikhism, Zoroastrianism) were all written in a time of comparative poverty. Yet, like all texts, they are ponderous, metaphoric and often contradictory. As a result they supply excellent material for theological scholars to "decode and interpret" for centuries.

In Christianity there are many references to wealth and riches resulting from (i.e. being the reward for) a good life and "fearing the Lord" (*Job* 42:10–17; *Proverbs* 3:16 and 8:18). Equally there is a theme of *optimality*: the happiness derived from wealth is all about having neither too much nor too little money (*Proverbs* 30:8–9). Further, because wealth is essentially a gift of God, so it belongs to Him.

The Old Testament is clear that wealth is also the *reward of diligence* and hard work. Wealth brings security and protection. But there is also and always the warning (*Psalms* 62:10; *Job* 1:21; *Ecclesiastes* 5:12), essentially that one should never make wealth a principle goal or good; and that the gain of it wrongly or use of it selfishly is to sin against God.

In summary:

- Wealth is no substitute for goodness and righteousness.
- Riches do not last: you cannot take it with you.
- Wealth can encourage a person to ignore both God and his fellow man.

- Wealth can lead to arrogance, pride and hubris: it can damage character and judgement.
- It is the poor, humble and meek that most put their trust in God.
- Wealthy people have a special duty to help and support the poor: to ensure and enshrine principles of social justice.
- Those who oppress the poor to increase their wealth are amongst the most wicked and damned.

The New Testament is full of references to money. Jesus paid taxes to both the government and the temple. Paul was self-supporting and paid all his debts. But there are many references to the dangers of wealth. It is not money itself, but the love of money that is at the root of all evils (*1 Timothy* 6:10). Exploitation, shameful gain, greed and covetousness are all constantly condemned.

Jesus did mix with people of wealth (Nicodemus; Zaccheus) but it is the attitudes of *some* rich people – arrogance, haughtiness and snobbery – that is questioned. Riches are a poor and insecure foundation for life. Further, they are a diminishing asset where "moth and rust destroy, and where thieves break in and steal" (*Matthew* 6:19–21). Certainly, the desire for wealth can blind us to what is important and damage judgement. To spend time and energy in the all-pervasive pursuit of wealth is not to understand the nature of "true riches" (*1 Timothy* 6:7, 6:17–18).

There are various parables concerning wealth, for example the parable of the rich man and Lazarus the beggar whose roles are reversed in the afterlife (*Luke* 16:19–31). The warning is about the consequences for the rich who show lack of concern and awareness of the poor. The rich man is condemned for sins of omission, not commission, for being irresponsible and doing nothing. Further fiscal obligation cannot take the place of personal awareness and gift giving.

Many people will also recall the story of an incensed Jesus clearing the temple of money changers (*Matthew* 21:12–13). The issue was not a deep distrust of the bureau de change, but the wilful exploitation of peoples' credulousness and trust. Worse, the exploitation of another's need is represented.

There is also the parable of the "shrewd manager" (*Luke* 16:1–13), who encouraged others to join him in falsifying accounts. It's a puzzling proverb with four lessons: First, if people put as much effort into their Christian life as they do making money, they would be better for it. Second, money is a means to an end, not an end in itself. Third, a person's conduct in money matters is a simple, sure marker of character: if a person can be trusted with money, he or she can be trusted with anything. Finally, there is room only for one supreme loyalty and that is to God.

There are texts, particularly in *Corinthians*, on the role of giving money away, charitable donations and the like. It is best that giving is *systematic* (i.e. continuous and planned), that it is *proportional* (to income and wealth, as in a percentage) and that it is *universal* among believers: hence tithing. Giving to other believers is symbolic of community. Concern for others can be shown in practical giving.

At the heart of the New Testament message about money, materialism and possessions is the simple question "do I possess my (many) possessions or am I (fundamentally) possessed by them?" It's about the folly of being a slave to material things, luxuries and the supposed "comforts" that they bring. Possessions can lead to possessiveness. Money blinds people to what is important: its acquisition, storage and usefulness is a real test of character. Thus the wealthier a man is, the more he needs God.

Wealth can give one a false sense of independence. People believe it can open all doors and ensure all escape routes. Further, it can cost too much with respect to pride and self-worth – "thirty pieces of silver", where the money you make costs too much. The more you have, the more difficult it may be to leave this world and consider the next one.

There seem to be five simple principles to bear in mind for people of any religion or none. First, did we acquire money in ways that influenced or harmed no one, but enriched and helped the community? Second, is money a master whom we serve, or a friend who can help others and ourselves? Third, do we use our money wisely, judiciously, and in order to help others? Fourth, people are always more important than things, money, machines. Finally, there are times when giving money is not enough; the giving of oneself (time, skills, energy, concern) is the greatest gift of all.

The sacred and the profane

For the economist money is almost profane: it is not treated irreverently or disregarded but it is commonplace and not special. It has no spiritual significance. However, money can be sacred – it is feared, revered, and worshiped. Belk and Wallendorf (1990) point out that it is the myth, mystery, and ritual associated with the acquisition and use of money that defies its sacredness and spirituality.

For all religions, certain persons, places, things, times, and social groups are collectively defined as sacred and spiritual. Sacred things are extraordinary, totally unique, set apart from, and opposed to, the profane world. Sacred objects and people can have powers of good or evil. "Gifts, vacation travel, souvenirs, family photographs, pets, collections, heirlooms, homes, art, antiques, and objects associated with famous people can be regarded as existing in the realm of the sacred by many people" (Belk & Wallendorf, 1990, p. 39). They are safeguarded and considered special, and of spiritual value. Art and other collections become for many people sacred personal icons.

Equally, heirlooms serve as mystical and fragile connections to those who are deceased. They can have more than "sentimental value" and some believe that a neglected or damaged heirloom could unleash bad luck or evil forces.

Unlike sacred objects, profane objects are interchangeable. They are valued primarily for their mundane use value. Sacred objects often lack functional use and cannot, through exchange, be converted into profane objects. Further, exchange of sacred objects for money violates their sacred status, because it brings them into inappropriate contact with the profane realm.

In Western societies money cannot buy brides, expiation from crimes, or (ideally) political offices. The Judeo-Christian ethic is paradoxical on money. People with money acquired honestly may be seen as superior, even virtuous, and removing the desire to accumulate money is condemned. Believers are called on to be altruistic, ascetic, and selfless, while simultaneously being hard working, acquisitional, and, frankly, capitalistic. The sacred and profane can get easily mixed up.

Belk and Wallendorf (1990) also believe that the sacred meaning of money is gender and class linked. They argue that women think of money in terms of the things into which it can be converted, while men think of it in terms of the power its possession implies. Similarly, in working-class homes men traditionally gave over their wages to their wives for the management of profane household needs with a small allowance given back for individual personal pleasures, most of which were far from sacred. Yet in a middle-class house, a man typically gave, and indeed sometimes still gives, his wife an allowance (being a small part of their income) for collective household expenditure.

Money (an income) obtained from work that is not a source of intrinsic delight is ultimately profane, but an income derived from one's passion can be sacred. An artist can do commercial work for profane money and the work of the soul for sacred money. From ancient Greece to twentieth-century Europe, the business of making money is tainted. It is the activity of the nouveau riche, not honourable "old money".

Thus, volunteer work is sacred, while the identical job that is paid is profane. The idea of paying somebody to be a mother or home-keeper may be preposterous for some because it renders the sacred duty profane. But the acts of prostitutes transform a sacred act into a formal business exchange. Some crafts people and artists do sell their services but at a "modest", almost non-going-rate price because their aim is not to accumulate wealth but to make a reasonable income and not become burdened by their work.

Belk (1991) considered the sacred uses of money. A sacred use – for example, a gift – can be "desacralised" if a person is too concerned with price. Sacralising mechanisms usually involve the purchase of gifts and souvenirs, donations to charity, as well as the purchase of a previously sacralised object. The aim is to transform money into objects with special significance or meaning. Money-as-sacrifice and money-as-gift are clearly more sacred than money-as-commodity. Charity giving is a sacred gift only when it involves personal sacrifice and not when there is personal gain through publicity or tax relief. Money used to redeem and restore special objects (e.g. rare works of art, religious objects) also renders it sacred.

Thus, to retain all money for personal use is considered antisocial, selfish, miserly, and evil. To transform sacred money (a gift) into profane money by selling it is considered especially evil. Many people refuse to turn certain objects into money, preferring to give them away. Money violates the sacredness of objects and commodifies them. Equally, people refuse money offered by those who have been voluntarily helped. The "good Samaritans" thereby assign their assistance to the area of the gift rather than a profane exchange. Thus, a gift of help may be reciprocated by another gift.

The argument is thus: the dominant view of money concentrates on its profane meaning. It is a utilitarian view that sees money transactions as impersonal and devoid of sacred money. But it becomes clear when considering the illogical behaviour of collectors, gift-givers, and charity donors that money can and does have sacred meanings, both good and evil. Further, it is these sacred meanings that so powerfully influence our attitudes to money.

Money in literature

The sheer number of references to money by dramatists, poets, novelists and wits has merited a long and comprehensive anthology (Jackson, 1995). The editor points out that such a book is not in itself a study in economics, "though a few of the dismal science's more graceful and pungent prose stylists have earned their place beside the poets" (p. vii). Literature shows well the fantasies, lunacies and dreads which surround ordinary peoples' experience of money. It has been noted that after love and death few subjects have been more attractive to writers than money.

Many people know of Chaucer's crooks and swindlers and Dickens' Scrooge. Writers satirise avarice, highlight the arrogance of the rich, and may howl outrage, disgust and disdain at those who show love of money. Jackson (1995) believes that the modern novel owes much to the concept of money. Novels often describe the following: spendthrifts, gamblers and philanthropists; embezzlers, blackmailers and swindlers; banks and bankers; merchants and wage slaves, financial manias and young provincial men on the make. The novel possesses its characteristic sharp attention to the ways in which the mechanisms of money draw up characters from all levels of society and ease or shove them towards their destinies.

Writers and literature have often been seen as antimaterialist, heroically championing human values against the cold, pitiless calculations of the market. There is the image of the unworldly poet versus the wicked capitalist. This may be more the vision of idealistic readers than pragmatic writers whose frequent economic insecurity keeps them sufficiently worldly minded.

Many writers feel and express the inconsistencies and contradictory values about money in their culture. Thus, art alone for its own sake is an indulgence and a trivial thing, but done for money is somehow cheap and "hackwork". People like to believe that great writers cannot be bought; that the literary conscience ought to resist the temptations of money.

> Most obviously, money and literature are both conventional systems for representing things beyond themselves, of saying that X is Y. A poem asks us to believe that it represents a nightingale or a raven; a coin asks us to believe that it represents a bushel of wheat or a number of hours of labour. Neither money nor writing would have been possible without the human mind's capacity to grasp that one thing may be a substitute for another dissimilar thing, which is to say that both conventions are a product of out ability to make and grasp metaphors. My love is a rose petal; a loaf of bread is a groat.
>
> (Jackson, 1995, p. xiii)

Many writers have reflected on money:

> "Money talks" because money is a metaphor, a transfer, and a bridge. Like words and language, money is a storehouse of communally achieved work, skill, and experience. Money, however, is also a specialist technology like writing; and as writing intensifies the visual aspect of speech and order, and as the clock visually separates time from space, so money separates work from the other social functions. Even today money is a language for translating the work of the farmer into the work of the barber, doctor, engineer, or plumber. As a vast social metaphor, bridge, or translator, money – like writing – speeds up exchange and tightens the bonds of interdependence in any community. It gives great spiral extension and control to political organisations, just as writing does, or the calendar. It is action at a distance, both in space and in time. In a highly literate, fragmented society, "Time is money", and money is the store of other people's time and effort.
>
> (McLuhan, 1964)

As ever, writers' and novelists' observations about people's use and abuse of money are considerably more perspicuous, wry and insightful than the writings of social scientists. Like anthropologists and psychologists, writers of fiction dwell on the symbolism of money, its captivating power and the bizarre things individuals do to acquire it.

Other approaches

The criminology of money

It has been suggested that "money is still seen as a dark force that lies at the root of a pervasive social malaise ... the stories of modern-day criminals, from drug dealers to double-dealing savings and loan executives, are repeatedly told as a warning against the seductive lure of money, and populist politicians warn of the corruption that money breeds in the political system" (Coleman, 1992).

Whilst there are crimes of passion it is generally agreed that the desire for money is the most fundamental motivation, at least for white-collar crime. In societies and groups where economic change is seen as a competitive sport and where monetary wealth is seen as proof of competitive victory, crime can flourish because the impersonal, calculating worldview inhibits the ethical restraints of obligation and responsibility that inhibit criminal behaviour. However, it is clear that **who** steals from **whom** and **why** has different repercussions. Thus, stealing from customers, peers and one's boss at work are perceived very differently. In some organisations there are organised systems of theft. As Coleman (1992) has observed, opportunity influences a lot of money crimes.

The philosophy of money

Philosophers often critique those who write about money. As an example, Wolfenstein (1993) contrasted the views of two great thinkers of the twentieth century and their views on the "conceded" social meanings of money. For Marx money was all about the alienation of labour and the brutal exploitation of workers in the process of producing surplus value, while for Freud it "signifies sadomasochistic relationships" (p. 279). Wolfenstein argues that the true meaning of money is concealed and that various writers have rather strange and fortuitous ways of thinking about it.

The politics of money is concerned with everything that governments do to generate, control, tax and distribute money. Money has always been seen as the chief source of power and influence. Political acts can cause political activity and ensure growth and stability or, indeed, the reverse.

All the great political "isms" – capitalism, socialism, Marxism and communism – have a lot to say about money. Political scientists are interested in how money is converted into political influence. In the West political party lines are often most clearly differentiated on issues of monetary policy. It takes money to get elected and election promises often entail lists of promises about tax and the redistribution of money.

The social ecology of money

This perspective is essentially around scarcity and survival (Walker & Garman, 1992). Money, which provides access to essential goods and services, is about the thriving and survival of people in the market economy. Thus, how individuals, groups, governments and societies choose to spend it is all-important. All allocations involve opportunity costs and attempts to maximise satisfaction.

So, money and time are closely linked: time is invested to yield money, but its purchasing power is reduced over time. Time has money value measured as a wage rate. Therefore people are encouraged to act rationally and thus need to be informed about options, payoffs, benefits, etc. Many factors influence monetary decision making. There are sensible ways to accumulate, protect and allocate money over the lifetime. Thus individual budgeting and family resource management are topics of great interest to those in human ecology.

Behaviourist approaches

Behaviourist research has been concerned with how money becomes a conditioned reinforcement and hence a valued and meaningful object. Research in this tradition has been limited to studies on animals in which animals of various sorts (rats, chimpanzees, cats) perform a task in order to get tokens (poker chips, iron balls, cards), which, like money, can be exchanged for desirable objects such as food. Hence money is valued because it represents or is associated with various desirable objects.

As well as animal studies there is a vast literature on "**token economies**", which is effectively the application of behaviourist "monetary" theories to clinical populations such as mental patients (especially schizophrenics), disturbed adolescents and recidivists. A token economy is a self-contained economic system where clients/patients are paid (reinforced) for behaving appropriately (socialising, working), and in which many desirable commodities (food, entertainment, cigarettes) can be purchased. Thus luxuries (indeed necessities) must be earned (Ayllon & Azrin, 1968).

Numerous studies have shown the benefits of token economies (Ayllon & Roberts, 1974) but they have also received various criticisms on clinical grounds. These include the fact that as there is little comparative research (only a no-treatment control condition) it is difficult to establish whether token economies are better or worse than other conditions; that token economies are often aimed at institutional rather than individual needs; that token economies violate many individual rights in total institutions; and, perhaps most importantly, that conditioned behaviour does not generalise to new environments where the token economy does not operate (Bellack & Hersen, 1980).

4
MONEY AND HAPPINESS

Money won't buy happiness, but it will pay the salaries of a large research staff to study the problem.

Bill Vaughan

I asked for riches, that I may be happy; I was given poverty, that I might be wise.

Anon

Give me the luxuries of life and I will willingly do without the necessities.

Frank Lloyd Wright

When I was young, I used to think that wealth and power would bring me happiness ... I was right.

Gahan Wilson

All I ask is the chance to prove that money can't make me happy.

Spike Milligan

Introduction

It seems perfectly self-evident to many people that money brings happiness: and the more money the more happiness. Indeed it is (or perhaps was) one of the axioms of economics. The question is *how much* money do you need to achieve maximum happiness? There are also issues like *what should you spend your money on* to maximise your happiness? There are questions of things that money can not buy, like health, which we know impacts considerably on happiness. Most people assume that sufficient money is indeed necessary for happiness; but what is sufficient?

In one of the first books in the area Myers (1992) noted:

> More money means more of the good things of life – a trip to Hawaii, a Colorado condo, a hot tub, flying business class instead of coach, a large-screen video system, the best schools for one's children, season tickets to the Philharmonic or the Lakers' games, eating out and eating well, stylish clothes, a retirement free from financial worry, and a touch of class in one's surroundings. Wouldn't you really have a Buick – or better a BMW or Mercedes? Wouldn't you rather have the power and respect that accompanies affluence? Knowing that money is one way that we keep score in the game of life, wouldn't you rather win? And who wouldn't rather have ample security than be living on the edge? (p. 32–33)

Myers and Diener (1996) concluded from data that happiness in the USA remains relatively stable over time, despite the steady increase in average national income. Yet, the University of Chicago's National Opinion Research Centre found that only one in three Americans rated themselves as "very happy" in both 1990 and 1957, despite per-person income increasing from $7,500 to $15,000+ (Myers & Diener, 1996).

There have been doubters and critics. As Schor (1991) put it:

> Do Americans need high-definition television, increasingly exotic vacations, and climate control in their autos? How about hundred-dollar inflatable sneakers, fifty-dollar wrinkle cream, or the ever-present (but rarely used) stationary bicycle? A growing fraction of homes are now equipped with Jacuzzis (or steam showers) and satellite receivers. Once we take the broader view, can we be so sure that all these things are really making us better off? (p. 115)

Campbell, Converse and Rogers (1976) carried out a famous early study of well-being, using an American national sample. When the question was asked directly, money was not rated as important by the majority – it came 11th. Sixteen per cent thought it was very important, compared with 74% for a happy marriage and 70% for being in good health. There was also an indirect measure of what people felt about the importance of domains, correlated with overall life satisfaction. Here money did better, coming third after family life and marriage. So, which conclusion is right? A problem with this study is that the money variable was made rather strong – "A large bank account, so that you don't have to worry about money".

King and Napa (1998) presented people with a number of fictitious persons, varying their income, happiness and meaning in life, and asked how desirable such a life would be. The desirability, moral goodness and expected heavenly rewards were thought to be greatly affected by happiness and meaning in life, while money had either no effect at all or a fraction of the effect of happiness and meaning. Wealth was generally irrelevant for a student sample, but more evident for adults. Curiously students thought that money would influence heavenly rewards, a little, perhaps a result of the Protestant Work Ethic. The money variable was less extreme than in the previous study – the incomes of the fictitious persons varied from $20–30k to over $100k.

We shall see that many, but not all, researchers agree that an income of two to three times the national average is sufficient to maximise happiness.

Happiness and well-being

The word "happiness" means several different things (joy, satisfaction) and therefore many psychologists prefer the term "subjective well-being" (SWB), which is an umbrella term that includes the various types of evaluation of one's life one might make. It can include self-esteem, joy, feelings of fulfilment. The essence is that the person himself/herself is making the evaluation of life. Thus the person herself or himself is the expert here: is my life going well, according to the standards that I choose to use?

It has also been suggested that there are three primary components of SWB: general satisfaction, the presence of pleasant affect and the absence of negative emotions including anger, anxiety, guilt, sadness and shame. These can be considered at the global level or with regard to very specific domains like work, friendship, recreation. More importantly SWB covers a wide scale from ecstasy to agony: from extreme happiness to great gloom and despondency. It relates to long-term states, not just momentary moods. It is not sufficient but probably a necessary criterion for mental or psychological health. The relatively recent advent of studies on happiness, or "subjective well-being", has led to a science of well-being (Huppert, Baylis & Keverne, 2005).

All the early researchers in this field pointed out that psychologists had long neglected happiness and well-being, preferring instead to look at its opposites: anxiety, despair, depression. Just as the assumption that the absence of anxiety and depression suggests happiness is false, so it is true that not being happy does not necessarily mean being unhappy.

Overall, many studies demonstrate positive correlations between income and well-being, with the average reported well-being being higher in wealthier than poorer countries.

There is an extensive philosophic literature on the nature of happiness. From the great Hellenic philosophers through all the great world religions to (relatively) modern political thinkers the question about happiness has been pondered.

Kesebir and Diener (2008) offer a psychological perspective on five fundamental questions:

1. **What is this thing called happiness?** Progress can only occur once concepts are clearly articulated and operationalised. Psychologists have settled on the concept of subjective well-being. That is how individuals see their life conditions and circumstances. It is what people say they experience: it is not (perhaps cannot be) objectively defined.

2. **Can people be happy?** This is in part to do with the contrast between actual and ideal happiness. Pessimists may argue that happiness is a non-achievable illusion, while optimists disagree. As personally defined it is clear most people claim to be happy.

3. **Do people want to be happy?** The answer is of course yes: it is a desirable goal, but itself is not sufficient for a good life. It does not rule out the value for striving for other things.

4. **Should people be happy?** The answer is clearly yes because it is not only the correlate and consequence but also the cause of things like better health, social relationships, and achievements, as well as being associated with prosocial or altruistic behaviour.

5. **How to be happy?** This has been discussed extensively elsewhere but the most important issue concerns the extent to which the major plot of happiness is dispositional and not able to be radically increased.

There are other questions, like "Are there any counterintuitive findings about happiness?" One is that happiness is stable and very much genetically determined. It has been observed that it is no easier trying to become happy than to become taller. Possessions and money have relatively little effect on long-term happiness.

Diener (2000) has defined subjective well-being (SWB) as how people cognitively and emotionally evaluate their lives. It has an evaluative (good–bad) as well as a hedonic (pleasant–unpleasant) dimension.

The *Positive Psychology Centre* at Penn State University has a website dedicated to answering frequently asked questions like "Isn't positive psychology just plain common sense". They note 13 points (abbreviated here) as an example:

- Wealth is only weakly related to happiness both within and across nations, particularly when income is above the poverty level.
- Activities that make people happy in small doses – such as shopping, good food and making money – do not lead to fulfilment in the long term, indicating that these have quickly diminishing returns.
- Engaging in an experience that produces "flow" is so gratifying that people are willing to do it for its own sake, rather than for what they will get out of it. Flow is experienced when one's skills are sufficient for a challenging activity, in the pursuit of a clear goal, when immediate self-awareness disappears, and sense of time is distorted.

- People who express gratitude on a regular basis have better physical health, optimism, progress toward goals and well-being, and help others more.
- Trying to maximize happiness can lead to unhappiness.
- People who witness others perform good deeds experience an emotion called "elevation" and this motivates them to perform their own good deeds.
- Optimism can protect people from mental and physical illness.
- People who are optimistic or happy have better performance in work, school and sports, are less depressed, have fewer physical health problems, and have better relationships with other people. Further, optimism can be measured and it can be learned.
- People who report more positive emotions in young adulthood live longer and healthier lives.
- Physicians experiencing positive emotions tend to make more accurate diagnoses.
- Healthy human development can take place under conditions of even great adversity due to a process of resilience that is common and completely ordinary.
- Individuals who write about traumatic events are physically healthier than control groups that do not. Writing about life goals is significantly less distressing than writing about trauma, and is associated with enhanced well-being.
- People are unable to predict how long they will be happy or sad following an important event.

Positive psychology is the study of factors and processes that lead to positive emotions, virtuous behaviours and optimal performance in individuals and groups. Although a few, mainly "self", psychologists were always interested in health, adjustment and peak performance, the study of happiness was thought to be unimportant, even trivial.

The first books on the psychology of happiness started appearing in the 1980s. Then there came the appearance of a few specialist academic journals but it was not until the turn of the millennium that the positive psychology movement was galvanised into action by significant grant money as well as the research focus of many renowned psychologists. Positive psychology today encompasses considerably more than the study of happiness. There are at least two major journals in this area – *The Journal of Positive Psychology* and the *Journal of Happiness Studies*.

The psychology of happiness attempts to answer some very fundamental questions pursued over the years by philosophers, theologians and politicians. The *first* series of questions is really about definition and measurement of happiness; the *second* is about why certain groups are as happy or unhappy as they are; and the *third* group of questions concerns what one has to do (or not do) to increase happiness.

Most measurements of happiness are carried out using standardised question-naires or interview schedules. It could also be done by informed observers: those people who know the individual well and see them regularly. There is also experience sampling, when people have to report how happy they are many times a day, week or month when a beeper goes off, and these ratings are aggregated. Yet another is to investigate a person's memory and check whether they feel predominantly happy or unhappy about their past. Finally, there are some as yet crude but ever developing physical measures, looking at everything from brain scanning to saliva cortisol measures. It is not very difficult to measure happiness reliably and validly.

Many researchers have listed a number of myths about the nature and cause of happiness. These include the following, which are widely believed but wrong:

1. Happiness depends mainly on the quality and quantity of things that happen to you.
2. People are less happy than they used to be.
3. People with a serious physical disability are always less happy.
4. Young people in the prime of life are much happier than older people.
5. People who experience great happiness also experience great unhappiness.
6. More intelligent people are generally happier than less intelligent people.
7. Children add significantly to the happiness of married couples.
8. Acquiring lots of money makes people much happier in the long run.
9. Men are overall happier than women.
10. Pursuing happiness paradoxically ensures you lose it.

Positive psychology (Linley, 2008; Seligman, 2008) shifts the focus to exploring and attempting to correct or change personal weakness to a study of strengths and virtues. Its aim is to promote authentic happiness and the good life and thereby promote health. A starting point for positive psychology for both popular writers and researchers has been to try to list and categorise strengths and values. This has been done, though it still excites controversy.

Positive psychology has now attracted the interest of economists and even theologians as well as business people. It is a movement that is rapidly gathering steam and converts to examine scientifically this most essential of all human conditions.

Interestingly there is no suggestion that predictors and correlates of happiness in adults are any different from those in children. However, nearly all psychologists acknowledge the importance in early child development of bonding with parents and other adults and developing social skills and social relationships. All researchers have documented the social correlates and predictors of happiness and well-being, particularly the role of parents, sibling and friends (Holder & Coleman, 2007).

Health and wellness are, it seems, systematically related to the age, sex, race, education and income states of individuals. We know the following:

1. Women report more happiness and fulfilment if their lives feel rushed rather than free and easy.
2. Women are more likely than men to become depressed or to express joy.
3. There is very little change in life satisfaction and happiness over the life span.
4. There are social class factors associated with mental health and happiness but these are confounded with income, occupation and education.
5. There is a relationship between health, happiness and income but the correlation is modest and the effect disappears after the average salary level is reached.
6. Better educated people – as measured by years of education – are positively associated with happiness.
7. Occupational status is also linked to happiness with dramatic differences between Classes I and V.
8. Race differences in health and happiness in a culture are nearly always confounded with education and occupation.
9. There are dramatic national differences in self-reported happiness which seem to be related to factors like national income, equality, human rights, and democratic systems.
10. Physical health is a good correlate of mental health and happiness but it is thought to be both a cause and an effect of happiness.

The dark side of happiness

We know intuitively that happiness and well-being are a very desirable state. The positive psychologists and affective scientists have "proved" that people think more clearly and make better decisions when happy. We know happy people build and maintain healthier relationships with others, which brings many benefits. It is clear we are more creative when in a positive state of mind. And there is now very clear evidence of the health-related benefits of being happy. After all that is why it is called "well-being".

But could there be a darker side to happiness? Gruber, Mauss and Tamir (2011) took a leaf out of a book by Aristotle in order to ask four questions:

1. Can there be a wrong degree of happiness?

Is more happiness better, or is there an optimal amount? Are all those injunctions about moderation true? There are quite a few reasons to doubt the "more is better" argument.

2. Is there a wrong time/place for happiness?

Extremely happy people may not have enough experience of setbacks and frustrations. They may be less vigilant about threats of all kinds. When faced with problems we have a flight or fight option. Negative emotions trigger powerful physiological forces that prepare us to confront others. Happiness can make people gullible, naive and inattentive. Showing sadness could engender offers of help. Showing fear, anger and sadness can be very useful in life.

3. Are there inappropriate/wrong/misguided ways to pursue happiness?

The higher one sets the target often the more disappointed and discontented one may become by not hitting it. It has maladaptive outcomes because it sets people up for disappointment. Often the happiness junkies become egocentric and damage their personal relationships. The person in blind pursuit of happiness can be obsessively self-focused, less reflective but also less attentive to others who are, or at least can be, a major source of happiness.

Equally the therapy literature shows that the more people accept, rather than reject, negative feelings, the better they feel. It's like soap in the bath: the more you try to grab it the cloudier the water, the more difficult it is to find.

4. Are there wrong types of happiness?

Are there different flavours of happiness? Can it mean great excitement and great calm? At its base level it is defined as the presence in amount of positivity over that of negativity.

But some things that may in the short term bring happiness to the individual could cause the opposite effect. They may impair social functioning through selfishness. Because of cultural conventions certain happiness-inducing activities should result in embarrassment, guilt and shame. Some cultures value contentment and calm over excitement. Some define happiness more socially than others: personal hedonic experience vs. social harmony.

Happiness, it is argued, comes to those who do not single-mindedly pursue it. It's not healthy to be acutely and chronically happy, cheerful or positive. Some situations require other emotions.

Affluenza

In his book of the above name (which introduced a new, now well-known neologism, Oliver James) a British clinical psychologist, proposed the following theory: increasing affluence in a society, particularly where it is characterised by inequality, leads to increasing unhappiness. The thesis is that modern capitalism makes money out of misery. It encourages materialism but leaves a psychic void. The increasing emotional stress of people in the West is a response to the sick, unequal, acquisitive societies. Just as "dieting makes you fat" so "retail therapy makes you sad". Affluenza is a "rich person's disease"; a corruption of the American dream.

Affluenza comes from *affluence plus influenza*: money makes you sick; capitalism and consumerism are recipes for illness. It is a painful, socially transmitted, and highly paradoxical "disease" that is the result of a false premise. The belief is that wealth and economic success lead to fulfilment, whereas in effect it leads to an addiction to wealth accumulation and the neglect of personal relationships that are the real source of happiness. It is an unsustainable and seriously unhealthy addiction to personal (and societal) economic growth. It is most acute in those who inherit wealth and seem to have no purpose, direction or superego.

The data for the book *Affluenza* came from interviews. The conclusion is that placing a high value on appearance, fame, money and possessions leads to emotional distress. It results in over consumption, "luxury fever", alienation and inappropriate self-medication using alcohol, drugs and shopping to attempt to bring meaning and satisfaction. James (2007) blames many of the problems of modern societies – anxiety, depression, eating disorders, emotional distress, family breakdown, medication, on Affluenza. The emptiness and loneliness many people feel is because they have "traded off" authentic, genuine and intimate relationships for wealth accumulation and consumption.

The vaccine for the virus is a change in lifestyle, but also a change in society. Thus James attacks advertising, which is, in his view, mendacious, misleading and always hyperbolic. He believes women's magazines are the "devil's work". He approves of societies that try to hold affluenza at bay by laws and taxes that increase equality.

The thesis is not new. There are hundreds of religious texts and sermons condemning conspicuous consumption and advocating what we now call "down shifting". Many have argued that materialism leads to a commodification of ourselves and often deprives us of what we most need. The thesis has also been proposed by political thinkers, particularly of the left, who have made many attacks on "selfish capitalism", liberal market-forces ideology and the free market. James' cures look to many like an insupportable model of a brave new world where all sorts of activities/marketing are barred or controlled.

Criticisms have been harsh and many. The book has been accused of being little more than sermonising, sensationalist journalism and ranting cant. A fact-heavy book with a light-weight message. Some reviewers accused the author of being unfamiliar with the research that could both "back up" and challenge his position, and also state that he could be more dispassionate, disinterested and even-handed. He is overly strident about some issues, such as child-rearing. Worse, he makes a number of propositions for a saner, happier society, without sufficient evidence that they would, indeed, work.

It seems all the modern evils are due to affluenza – from a false sense of entitlement to an inability to delay gratification or tolerate frustration, from workaholism to a destruction of the environment. Some have seen the book as little more than a collection of anecdotes about poor little rich boys.

There is also the question about causation: does social and economic inequality cause emotional distress or the other way around? Inequality itself is evil: but this single factor is used to explain everything. Other explanations could also be put forward, such as the rise of secular liberalism as opposed to religious faith or moral and intellectual relativism.

Some attacked the inconsistencies in James' crypto-political agenda. How much state intervention and how much legislation do we need to ensure that people have more balanced expectations and employ money in more appropriate ways? Many accused James (2007) of a select and simplistic reading of his own data. He "cherry picks" both his statistics and his case studies.

However, the thesis of the book has caused enough interest for schools to introduce an Affluenza Discussion Guide with the following sorts of questions:

- **Shopping fever** – How often do you shop? Is it recreation for you? Do you bring a list of what you need and follow it or do you shop by impulse?
- **A rash of bankruptcies** – Have you ever been seriously in debt? What did you do about it? Do you know people who are deep in debt?
- **Swollen expectations** – How do you think new technologies are affecting your life? Do you feel you need to keep up with faster computers and other technologies? Why or why not?
- **Chronic congestion** – Choose a product that you use regularly, and do a "life-cycle analysis" of it – that is, research where it comes from; what it's made of; how long you will use it; and where it will end up.

The Easterlin paradox

Perhaps the most influential work on the relationship between money and happiness can be dated back to the work of Easterlin (1974). He attempted to answer three questions:

- At the individual level, are richer people happier than poorer people?
- At the country level, is there evidence richer countries are happier than poorer ones?
- At the country level, do countries grow happier as they grow richer?

His results are shown here (Figure 4.1) in a well-known, if simplified, graph.

Easterlin found, as predicted, that within a given country people with higher incomes were more likely to report being happy. Although income per person rose steadily in the USA between 1946 and 1970, average reported happiness showed no long-term trend and declined between 1960 and 1970. The differencein international and micro-level results fostered an ongoing body of research. All other measures of happiness, including physiological, measured a similar pattern of results.

In the 40 years since the publication of the Easterlin (1974) finding, numerous researchers have tried to explain the paradox or puzzle, particularly economists. It

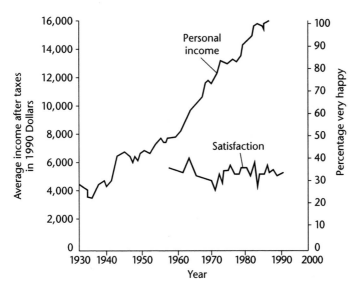

FIGURE 4.1 The evidence for the Easterlin hypothesis

Source: Adapted from Myers (1992).

is the story of diminishing returns on real income. Indeed it may be only that it is a paradox for economists, as other social scientists have never assumed a simple linear relationship between the two. Some have even tried to calculate the effect.

The original idea of the paradox was that cross-sectional data seemed to contradict time series data. At any period of time richer countries had happier people but when you look at trends the relationship disappears. Some suggest the reason is that the market economy puts the relationship under pressure (Ott, 2001).

The Easterlin hypothesis proposes that societal-level increases in income do not lead to corresponding increases in societal happiness up to a point. This research has led to much debate in the area, with many authors suggesting that income does in fact correlate with happiness. Recent investigations by Diener, Ng, and Tov (2009), for instance, concluded that the best predictors of life judgements were income and ownership of modern conveniences, when assessing a population from 140 nations. When looking more closely at this relationship, the authors suggested that self-assessed well-being at an individual level is very strongly predicted by income (Diener et al., 2009). Further, Diener and Biswas-Diener (2002) found substantial correlations, ranging from .50 to .70, between average well-being and average per capita income across nations.

Much research supports this. Recent cross-sectional studies conclude that income and happiness are at least positively related (Diener & Biswas-Diener, 2002; Kahneman, Krueger, Schkade, Schwarz & Stone, 2006).

Malka and Chatman (2003) showed that the relationship between well-being and income varies dependent on participants' extrinsic and intrinsic orientations towards work. Those with more extrinsic work orientation show a stronger relationship between income and subjective well-being.

Interestingly, different payment methods can also impact on the relationship between income and happiness (DeVoe & Pfeffer, 2011). The authors suggest that making time salient will impact upon the link between money and happiness; connecting time and money (paying by the hour) is found to cause individuals to rely more so on income when assessing their subjective well-being.

The evidence seemed clear about the first question. Even after controlling for various other sources of happiness, richer people are happier than poorer people, though the relationship is not really linear.

Faced with various criticisms, Easterlin et al. (2010) updated Easterlin's (1974) analysis using many datasets from developed and developing countries. They showed that over a ten-year period there is no relationship between aggregated subjective well-being and happiness. Thus, as a country experiences material aspirations that go with economic growth, people experience social comparison and hedonic adaptation. They suggest that personal concerns with health and family life are as important as material goods in sustaining happiness. Earlier, Ball and Chernova (2008) did an analysis of over 30 countries and concluded thus:

> (i) Both absolute and relative income are positively and significantly correlated with happiness, (ii) quantitatively, changes in relative income have much larger effects on happiness than do changes in absolute income, and (iii) the effects on happiness of both absolute and relative income are small when compared to the effects of several non-pecuniary factors. (p. 497)

The answer to the second question has exercised the minds of many and now there must be hundreds of papers that have addressed this issue. Essentially the papers fall into three categories:

1. Attempting to explain the data by processes that allow the basic economic utility model to remain

Thus it has been argued that adaptation theory explains these results – that is, that people soon become accustomed to increased wealth and that it therefore shows less effect. It is relative, not absolute income that carries advantage. Economists argue that personal income may be evaluated relative to others – social comparison – or to oneself in the past – habituation (Clark, Frijters & Shields, 2008). The utility function of money is that it brings consumption and status benefits to individuals but if costs and inflation rise and others also experience a rise in income the benefits are not felt.

Boyce, Brown and Moore (2010) tested and confirmed their rank–income hypothesis, which stated that a person's ranked income within his/her comparison group predicted general life satisfaction, whereas absolute income had no effect:

> Our study underlines concerns regarding the pursuit of economic growth. There are fixed amounts of rank in society – only one individual can be the highest earner. Thus, pursuing economic growth, although it remains a key political goal, might not make people any happier. The rank–income hypothesis may explain why increasing the incomes of all may not raise the happiness of all, even though wealth and happiness are correlated within a society at a given point in time. (p. 474)

Another related argument is that increased national wealth has negative as well as positive advantages, such as environmental degradation, crime and unemployment. In fact the data showing income without happiness gets worse if you introduce some of these other country-wealth related variables (Di Tella & McCulloch, 2008).

One argument is all about income inequality rather than absolute income. As America has got richer over the past 40 years the gap has widened between rich and poor, and though it has made poorer groups richer their perception of unfairness and lack of trust has made them less, rather than more happy (Oishi et al., 2011).

Angeles (2011) argued that there is no paradox at all because of two things: first, the data don't show how much happiness has actually increased; and second, many things other than money affect a person's happiness:

> To finalise, we note that our results do not imply that economic growth guarantees a happier nation. Indeed the small magnitude of the effect of income on happiness means that economic growth can be easily overcome by other factors such as the prevalence of marriage, widespread unemployment or public health. There is, however, no reason to be negative about economic growth and suggest its demise as an objective of public policy. Other things being equal, economic growth should have a positive direct effect on average happiness. The most important effects, however, may well be indirect. Economic growth could matter more for its influence on unemployment, family relations and health than for the larger incomes that define it. A good dose of prudence and modesty in policy advice would thus be commendable. (p. 72)

2. A reanalysis of bigger and better datasets

While some studies done in different countries over different time periods have shown broadly similar results (Gardes & Merrigan, 2008), others suggest that if other factors are taken into account the income effect on happiness clearly goes up (Powdthavee, 2010). Some have suggested that the problem lies in the measurement of happiness or well-being. Zuzanek (2013) pointed out differences in affective vs. cognitive and momentary vs. remembered aspects of well-being:

> Real-time or "experienced" well-being is, arguably, a by-product of a balanced time use and a match of respondents' skills and activity challengers that are assisted by but not necessarily determined by income. As the income grows, rising earnings become less important in arriving at life satisfaction and happiness, while the role of other factors contributing to subjective well-being, such as career progression, use of time, work–family balance, health, and lifestyle, increases. In short, time and lifestyle become more precious than money. (p. 10)

Beccheti and Rossetti (2009) also point to the data on "frustrated achievers", who are people whose *improvement* in monetary well-being is accompanied by a *reduction* in life satisfaction – that is, that the cost of pursuing the goal of more money leads to a deterioration in health and relationships. They suggest that up to a third of the population may be considered frustrated achievers.

Graham (2011), who was fascinated by the extensive debate about the Easterlin hypothesis, noted a considerable country effect – people in poorer countries are made happier by money compared to those in richer countries. She concluded:

> The paradox of unhappy growth, meanwhile, suggests that the rate of change matters as much to happiness as do per capita income levels, and that rapid growth with the accompanying dislocation may undermine the positive effects of higher income levels, at least in the short term. ... A mirror image of this paradox at the micro level – the happy peasant and frustrated achiever phenomenon – again suggests that the nature and pattern of economic growth, and in particular instability and inequality issues – can counterbalance the positive effects of higher income levels for a significant number of respondents.
>
> The income–happiness relationship is also mediated by factors such as inequality levels and institutional arrangements, particularly as countries get beyond the basic needs level. The complexity of the relationship – and the range of other mediating factors – seems to increase as countries go up the

development ladder. Rising aspirations and increasing knowledge and awareness interact with pre-existing cultural and normative differences, as well as the extent and quality of public goods, which are in turn endogenous to the cultural and normative differences. At the same time, because global information and access to a range of technologies is now available to countries at much lower levels of per capita income than was previously the case, they have access to the benefits associated with higher income levels, such as better healthcare, quite early on in the development process. (p. 237)

Headey, Muffels and Wooden (2008) examined the data from five developed countries but included wealth/net worth, disposable income and consumption as measures of money. They argued that wealth confirms economic security, which must lead to well-being. Their data showed much clearer evidence of the effect of changing financial circumstance on well-being: in short "that money matters more to happiness than previously believed" (p. 81).

Equally some have shown that money does increase happiness. Gardner and Oswald (2006) traced lottery winners who they compared to a control group who did not win any money. They found the winners went on to exhibit significantly better psychological health compared to those who did not win. Similarly Frijters, Haisken-DeNew and Shields (2004) showed that after the unification of Germany there was a clear and sustained increased in the life satisfaction of East Germans attributable to their increased wealth and freedom.

3. To question whether happiness itself is a good thing

Gruber et al. (2011) have proposed that there may be a wrong degree and time for happiness, wrong ways to pursue it and wrong types of happiness. In this sense it is not even a really desirable goal. Similarly Gandelman and Porzecanski (2013) have noted that in most countries happiness inequality is less than income inequality and therefore not really related to the pecuniary dimensions of life.

This research has led to much debate in the area, with many authors suggesting that income does in fact correlate with happiness. Recent investigations by Diener and Tov (2009), for instance, conclude that the best predictors of life judgements were income and ownership of modern conveniences when assessing a population from 140 nations. When looking more closely at this relationship, the authors suggest that self-assessed well-being at an individual level is very strongly predicted by income (Diener et al., 2009). Further, Diener and Biswas-Diener (2002) found substantial correlations, ranging from .50 to .70, between average well-being and average per capita income across nations.

Much research supports this. Recent cross-sectional studies conclude that income and happiness are at least positively related (Diener & Biswas-Diener, 2002; Kahneman et al., 2006).

Happiness causes success

Whilst most of the research has concentrated on the literature that looks at the (causal) effect of income/money on happiness/well-being at the individual/group level there is also research that suggests dispositional happiness brings success in part measured by money.

Indeed, Boehm and Lyubomirsky (2008) reviewed cross-sectional, longitudinal and experimental evidence that happy people earn more money. Happy people experience and show more positive emotions that others like and that leads to career success. Happy people seem more job engaged; are more favourably rated by others; obtain more social support; are less likely to be made redundant; are better at customer service and sales; and report more job satisfaction. The authors note that happiness is not the only resource which brings job success but it is often one that is overlooked.

Similarly Diener and Chan (2011) used seven types of evidence in a long review to show that (causally) higher happiness/subjective well-being leads to better health and longevity. They suggest that the data imply that high well-being can add four to ten years to your life. As health is a major predictor of work success it is clear how happiness can, through the moderating effect of physical and mental health, lead to great wealth.

Happiness or life evaluations?

Diener, Ng, Harter and Arora (2010) investigated the impact of money on one's evaluations of one's life. They suggest that life evaluations were closely related to income and the ownership of material goods, yet people's positive emotional feelings were most related to psychosocial factors, including the ability to count on others, as well as to learn new things. It may be that in Myers and Diener's (1996) early study "happiness" was not defined as precisely as the assessment of life evaluations vs. emotional feelings as in more recent research. The authors based their assessment of happiness on data from the National Opinion Research Centre (Niemi, Mueller & Smith, 1989). Current research therefore suggests that income predicts some aspects of satisfaction and happiness, but not all (see Table 4.1).

Other variables

What other factors influence (mediate and moderate) the relationship between wealth and happiness? We know that all sorts of factors have been shown to be reliably related to subjective well-being, including gender, age, health, race, education, religious affiliation, marital status, etc. Various factors have been investigated:

- **Age.** One study showed that after controlling for various relevant factors there was a positive association between income and happiness for young (18–44) and middle-aged (45–64) people, but not for older (over 65) individuals (Hsieh, 2011). Money may buy happiness but clearly more for younger than older people.

TABLE 4.1 Income as a predictor of happiness and well-being

Study	Assessing income vs. well-being	Scale used to measure	Findings
Caporale, Georgellis, Tsitsianis & Yin (2009)	Life satisfaction	European Social Survey (ESS): "All things considered, how satisfied are you with your life nowadays? Please answer using this card, where 0 means extremely dissatisfied and 10 means extremely satisfied."	The results provide clear evidence of a strong significant relationship between income and life satisfaction. An increase in income from the base band (€7–120) to the next income band raises the expected value of life satisfaction score by 0.27 points, while the movement to the middle income band (€350–460) increases life satisfaction by 0.71 points. A move to the highest band (> €2,310) improves the score by 1.08 points.
DeVoe & Pfeffer (2011)	Well-being	"If you were to consider your life in general these days, how happy or unhappy would you say you are, on the whole" – very happy, fairly happy, not very happy, not at all happy	The association between income and happiness was entirely absent for non-hourly workers, but was significantly positive for hourly workers.
Diener & Tov (2009)	Life judgements and emotions	The Gallup World Poll	Life judgements were best predicted by income and ownership of modern conveniences. The best predictors of emotions were social and personal factors.
Easterlin, McVey, Switek, Swangfa & Zweig (2010)	Life satisfaction	The World Values Survey (WVS): "All things considered, how satisfied are you with your life as a whole these days?" Dissatisfied (1) – Satisfied (10).	For a worldwide sample of 37 countries with intermittent life satisfaction data (1–10 scale) for periods ranging from 12 to 34 years up to 2005, there is no significant relation between the improvement in life satisfaction and the rate of economic growth.

TABLE 4.1 (continued)

Study	Assessing income vs. well-being	Scale used to measure	Findings
Kahneman & Deaton (2010)	Emotional well-being and life evaluation	Life evaluation – Cantril's Self-Anchoring Scale: "Please imagine a ladder with steps numbered from 0 at the bottom to 10 at the top. The top of the ladder represents the best possible life for you, and the bottom of the ladder represents the worst possible life for you. On which step of the ladder would you say you personally feel you stand at this time?" Rate your current life on a ladder scale: 0 "the worst possible life for you" and 10 "the best possible life for you." Questions about emotional well-being had yes/no response options and were worded as follows: "Did you experience the following feelings during a lot of the day yesterday? How about _____." Each of several emotions (e.g. enjoyment, stress) was reported separately.	More money does not necessarily buy more happiness, but less money is associated with emotional pain. Above a certain level of stable income, individuals' emotional well-being is constrained by other factors in their temperament and life circumstances. The data suggest that $75,000 is a threshold beyond which further increases in income no longer improve individuals' ability to do what matters most to their emotional well-being.
Oishi, Kesebir & Diener (2011)	Well-being	Three-point happiness item on the GSS: "Taken all together, how would you say things are these days – would you say that you are very happy, pretty happy, or not too happy?"	Participants were on average happier at times of relative national income equality than of relative national income inequality. However, income inequality of the year was unrelated to the mean happiness of the middle, upper-middle and top income group. The negative link between income inequality and happiness was only applicable to low-income individuals.

- **Work.** To earn more money takes time and sacrifice. To acquire more money means to sacrifice quality, time, and effort, which in turn leads to reduced happiness. Kaun (2005) has argued that much income-generating time is ill-spent because it comes at the cost of companionship and connection to the community, which is essential to human satisfaction. Pouwels, Siegers and Vlasblom (2008) make the same point: money has to be earned; that takes time. Working hours have a negative effect on happiness.
- **Physical health.** Chronic ill-health has an impact on one's ability to work for money and also one's subjective well-being. However, as Rijken and Groenewegen (2008) showed, money may not bring happiness but it does help affect social deprivation and loneliness, which are related to life satisfaction, happiness and well-being.
- **Individualism and autonomy.** In a big meta-analysis Fischer and Boer (2011) found that individualism, not wealth, was a better predictor of well-being. Individualism promotes and permits affective and intellectual autonomy. People are encouraged to pursue affectively pleasant experiences; to cultivate and express their own directions, ideas and passions; and find meaning in their own uniqueness – all of which encourage happiness.
- **Social comparisons.** If a person is in the habit of comparing themselves with others they tend always to express less satisfaction (McBride, 2010).
- **Face-consciousness.** The idea of "face" or presenting a positive, favourable social image is very important in many Asian countries. Zhang, Tian and Grigoriou (2011) showed that people can be assessed on the extent to which they are face-conscious and that the more face-conscious a person is, the more powerful an effect his/her financial situation has on his/her happiness. For the face-conscious a poor financial situation can dramatically decrease life satisfaction and increase negative moods.
- **Higher order needs.** If money can fulfil a person's particular higher order needs it will bring about happiness. These include the need for autonomy, competence and relatedness (Howell, Kurai & Tam, 2013).

Diener and Oishi (2000) have noted that people have a "malleable" desire for material goods and services and that, on average, they are happier when they get them. Wealthy societies seem to gain little from extra wealth. They concluded:

> If wealthy societies are reaching the postmaterialistic point where added goods and services enhance SWB very little, we may be at a critical crossroads in terms of public policy and individual choices. People in wealthy nations feel an increasing time shortage, and yet many are working even longer hours than before. People seek a level of material wealth undreamed of by earlier generations, and make sacrifices in time and personal relationships to

attain it. However, despite the picture of a "good life" presented in the media and in advertising, people may want to reassess their priorities. To the extent that individuals or societies must sacrifice other values to obtain more wealth, the pursuit of income is not likely to be worth the costs. After World War II, people had no computers or televisions, indoor plumbing was not taken for granted, and many people had ice boxes rather than refrigerators. Yet, people report being about as happy as they are now. Thus we must question then whether we need a trip to Antarctica, a larger home with more bathrooms, and a high-status automobile to be truly happy. Certainly if these items require us to make sacrifices in self-growth, leisure time, and intimate relationships, they may interfere with happiness rather than enhance it. As long as people want more goods and services, they will tend to be somewhat dissatisfied if they do not get them. Thus, the educational challenge is to convince people that other pursuits may sometimes lead to greater fulfilment than does the pursuit of more money. (p. 18)

When people do not get love and support from others and are money-seeking it can lead to their avoiding attachments to others and thus to more pain. Zhou and Gao (2008) have argued that anticipation of (all) pain heightens the desire for social support and the desire for money because the former is a primary psychological buffer against pain, and the latter a secondary one.

Hacker and Pierson (2010) highlight that in recent years in the USA there has been growing income inequality among social classes, with researchers suggesting that this may be linked to happiness. Oishi et al. (2011) assessed survey data from between 1972 and 2008, coming to the conclusion that Americans were on average happier in years when national income was more equal. The authors explained the inverse relation between income inequality and happiness through feelings of fairness and general trust.

Similarly, Helliwell (2003) described how, despite many findings showing that well-being and income correlate (Diener & Biswas-Diener, 2002), when factors such as quality of government, human rights and health are controlled, these correlations drop substantially. Helliwell (2003) proposes that instead of income being the main predictor of well-being, "people with the highest well-being are those who live where social and political institutions are effective, where mutual trust is high and corruption is low" (p. 355).

Such findings suggest that the relationship between money and happiness is not simple and linear but is in fact impacted by numerous variables (see Table 4.2).

Is there a limit?

Frey and Stutzer (2002) propose that above a moderate level of income (in the US $10,000 per capita income) individuals only experience minimal increases in

TABLE 4.2 Impacts on the money/happiness relationship

Impacting variable	Why?
National income change	Increasing income in well-off societies results in smaller rises in well-being than those experienced as a result of income increases in poor nations (Hagerty & Veenhoven, 2003).
	The income–well-being correlation in the USA was reported to be .13 (Diener, Sandvik, Seidlitz & Diener, 1993), compared to .45 in the slums of Calcutta (Biswas-Diener & Diener, 2001).
Governance	Diener, Diener, and Diener (1995) report that human rights in nations correlate with average well-being.
	Nations with democratic governments score high on individual well-being (Donovan & Halpern, 2003).
	Effective and trustworthy governance correlates with the well-being of nations (Helliwell, 2003).
Religion	Religious people are suggested to experience greater well-being on average than non-religious people (Diener, Suh, Lucas, & Smith, 1999).

well-being. Diener and Seligman (2012) further investigated this "limit" and analysed nations with per capita GDP above US$10,000. The correlation between well-being and income was only .08. This confirms the suggestion that once a moderate level of income is achieved, well-being can only be predicted minimally.

Interestingly, Diener and Seligman (2012) looked further into this issue. The authors presented a table comparing life satisfaction between a number of groups of people from around the world. Respondents from the Forbes list of the 400 richest Americans scored highly – supporting previous correlations between income and well-being. However, the Maasai of East Africa were nearly equally satisfied. The Maasai people are highly traditional, with no electricity or running water, and live in huts made of dung. These results thus imply that luxury is not necessary in order to achieve well-being. Interestingly, however, slum dwellers in Calcutta, and the homeless in California, are less happy with their lives. This suggest that physical needs and desires may be a crucial moderator of the impacts of income on well-being.

Overall, many studies demonstrate positive correlations between income and well-being, with average reported well-being being higher in wealthier than poorer countries.

Diener and Oishi (2000) have noted that people have a "malleable" desire for material goods and services and that on average they are happier when they get them. Wealthy societies seem to gain little from extra wealth.

Money and pain

Pain comes in many forms, such as physical pain, social exclusion pain, and monetary loss pain. Mikulincer and Shaver (2008) state that while money can act as a pain buffer among people who do not get love and support from others, money seeking can lead to people avoiding attachments to others and thus to more pain. Social support and money alleviate pain, while the loss of those two factors results in an upsurge of pain awareness.

The argument is that money is a shield and a painkiller. It has been shown to activate dopaminergic pathways and has actually been used as a substitute for drugs in certain programs. Activated brain areas of anticipator monetary loss are similar to those of physical pain. Money can be used to distance and buffer people when they buy certain products like sex. People from broken, conflicted, poor and unsupportive families overemphasise the power of money. Similarly, pain-prone people crave money to cope with their anxiety concerning competence, safety and self-worth.

Likewise, if money buffers pain, when people are primed with money ideas they seem less likely to seek out social support. Money is activated when social support fails.

What to buy to increase happiness?

In an interesting twist to the money–happiness debate three researchers suggest it has to do with the way people spend their money (Dunn, Gilbert, & Wilson, 2011). Because people don't know the basic scientific facts about what brings about and sustains happiness they spend it unwisely. They suggest eight pieces of advice for spending money right to increase happiness:

1. Buy experiences not things. This is not about the acquisition of material goods but the participation of social experiences. Possessions like a big car should be defined in terms of what it can do, rather than in terms of something one has.
2. Help others instead of yourself. Giving to others in terms of gifts, donations, but also in terms of volunteering brings benefits as all benefactors know. It is called prosocial spending and brings many rewards.
3. Buy many small pleasures instead of a few big ones. It is the frequency not the intensity of pleasure that is important. This reduces the hedonic treadmill problem of adaptation. Novelty, surprise and joy are the result of breaking up or segmenting small pleasures. Frequent fleeting pleasures are more important than sporadic and prolonged experiences.
4. Buy less insurance. People over-estimate their vulnerability to negative events. People have efficient coping systems and defence mechanisms that help them overcome all sorts of issues of loss. Insurance, warranties, exchange policies, are therefore not money well spent.
5. Pay now and consume later, not the other way around. This is partly because the anticipation of pleasure brings "free" happiness. Thinking about future events triggers stronger emotions than thinking about past events: i.e. anticipation is more powerful than reminiscence. Also,

instant gratification choices are often about vices. Anticipating future purchases can create uncertainty and the possibility of choice.

6. Think about what you're not thinking about: happiness is in the details. Look at the small things when you buy experiences.

7. Beware of comparison shopping: this can be distracting as [shoppers] do not focus on what aspects of purpose bring happiness but rather only the attributes that distinguish one product from another. Doing comparison shopping tends to make people over-estimate the hedonic pleasure of one purchase over another.

8. Follow the herd instead of your head: others' ratings are helpful because they often say what made them happy or show the joy (or lack of it) non-verbally.

What difference does it make to prime "time" vs. priming "money"? Mogilner (2010) found a dramatic difference – if you prime people to think about time they spend more of it with friends and family and less time working, while if you prime money people work more and socialise less, both of which decrease happiness: "simply increasing the relative salience of time (vs. money) can nudge someone to spend that extra hour at home rather than at the office, there finding greater happiness" (p. 1353).

Various studies have shown how priming "time vs. money" changes the evaluation of time (DeVoe & Pfeffer, 2007). Recently Pfeffer and DeVoe (2009) showed that people primed to think of their own time in terms of money were less willing to volunteer their time.

Indeed, this observation has been substantiated in economic studies such as that of Becchetti, Trovato and Iondono-Bedoya (2011), who showed that wealth increases material assets but not social assets and that richer people tend to have fewer social contacts and relationships, which are a key ingredient in happiness.

In another priming study, Bijleveld, Custers and Aarts (2011) primed people by high or low value coins and showed how this prompted them to concentrate more strongly on their task and details, which actually reduced their performance.

Another priming study looked at how money priming affected mating preferences. Yong and Li (2012) primed Singaporean males and females with large and small sums of money. They found, as predicted, that males but not females raised their minimum requirements for a date after being primed with large resources. Thus, make men feel they have large resources through simple priming and they seek out "better quality" mates in terms of attractiveness.

In an imaginative study, Yang, Wu, Zhou, Mead, Vohs and Baumeister (2012) primed either "clean" or "dirty" money. It has been established that priming cleanliness activates higher moral standards. They argued that handling literally dirty money, which may have a chequered past of shady characters and dirty deeds, activates a "dirty self" and selfish goals. They were able to show in seven experiments that handling dirty money in fact encouraged people to cheat others:

> One might have thought that handling dirty money would make people less enamoured of money, because people do not want to have dirty things. We consistently found the opposite: the dirty money participants were most prone to make decisions that brought them the most money, regardless of interpersonal considerations of fairness and reciprocity. We assume this is not because dirt made money more desirable. Rather, our findings suggest that dirty money reduced the subjective appeal and relative power of the values of fairness and reciprocity, evoking instead selfish notions of exploitation and greed. Dirty money did not make people actually dislike fairness, but when it came to trading off fairness against greed, people who had handled dirty money tended to choose greed.
>
> All these results are consistent with the assumption that many people have ambivalent attitudes toward money, characterised by two different sets of associations. Clean money evokes the positive benefits of money for facilitating fair trade, cultural progress, and the capacity to marshal resources to tackle personal and social problems. In contrast, dirty money may evoke the many crimes, abuses, and shady dealings that have throughout history marked the often illicit pursuit of personal financial gain at the expense of others. (p. 15)

Hansen, Kutzner and Wanke (2012) found that money primes ideas of personal strength and resources. They demonstrated experimentally that money primes affect consumers' evaluations of products on the basis of product descriptions. Money primes seem to encourage people to focus on the primary features of an advertised product.

Money and happiness

The data tend to show the following: when individuals of different wealth are compared in terms of their well-being, richer ones are on average happier. However, the effect of money on happiness is very small, expressed by a correlation of about .13, which accounts for a very small part of the variation in happiness. A major exception to this is that the effect of money is greater for poor individuals, and for poor countries, while there is very little effect for those on average incomes or above. The explanation for this pattern of results is that poor people and those in poor countries spend their money on more essential commodities, like food. The effect is also greater for those keen to be rich and have material possessions. Comparison with the income or possessions of others is more important than the absolute amount received: people do not want to have less than others, especially when the differences are thought to be unfair.

Health and mental health are affected by money more than happiness is. This is not due to spending money but to having better health-related behaviour and better coping styles, which are parts of class subcultures. There are two important causes of unhappiness – marital break-up and unemployment. Both are more common for poorer individuals; however this is not due to having less money.

5

MONEY ATTITUDES, BELIEFS AND BEHAVIOURS

An advantage of being rich is that all your faults are called eccentricities.

Anon

I don't wake up for less than $10,000 a day.

Linda Evangelista

I get so tired listening to one million dollars here, one million dollars there, it's so petty.

Imelda Marcos

The advantage of a classical education is that it enables you to despise the wealth that it prevents you from achieving.

Russell Green

Introduction

All languages are rich with slang words associated with money: *Bacon, Beans, Brass, Bullets, Bunce, Buttons, Cabbage, Charms, Chips, Clink, Coconuts, Corn, Crap, Dingbats, Dirt, Dough, Ducats, Filthy Lucre, Gilt, Gingerbread, Gravy, Grease, Greenbacks, Hardware, Honey, Iron, Juicem Junk, Kopecks, Lettuce, Lolly, Loot, Lucre, Manna, Mazuma, Moolah, Muck, Nuggets, Peanuts, Pieces, Push, Pony, Readies, Rivets, Rocks, Rubbish, Salt, Sand, Sauce, Shekels, Spondulicks, Spus, Stuff, Sugar, Swag, Trash, Wad* ... and many more.

These reflect, in part, our different attitudes to money. There is considerable interest in how and why people have such different attitudes to money and the consequences thereof (Blaszczynski & Nower, 2010).

All researchers and speculators have remarked how people get caught up in the psychological alchemy that transforms cash into objects, services, and fantasies.

Many are fascinated by how parents and cultures influence the development of an individual's personal money meanings (Sato, 2011). "People bearing psychological money scars have lost their connection with the original purpose and use of bank notes" (Forman, 1987, p. 2).

The extent to which money is imbued with psychological meaning is clearly apparent from the following quote by Wiseman (1974):

> One thinks of kleptomaniacs, or of the women who drain men of their resources, to whom money, which they are always striving to take away, symbolizes a whole series of introjected objects that have been withheld from them; or of depressive characters who from fear of starvation regard money as potential food. There are too those men to whom money signifies their potency, who experience any loss of money as a castration, or who are inclined, when in danger, to sacrifice money in a sort of "prophylactic self-castration". There are, in addition, people who – according to their attitudes of the moment towards taking, giving or withholding – accumulate or spend money, or alternate between accumulation and spending, quite impulsively, without regard for the real significance of money, and often to their own detriment. There is the price that every man has, and the pricelessness of objects, and the price on the outlaw's head; there are forty pieces of silver and also the double indemnity on one's own life.
>
> Behind its apparent sameness lie the many meanings of money. Blood-money does not buy the same thing as bride-money and a king's ransom is not the same kind of fortune as a lottery prize. The great exchangeability of money is deceptive; it enables us to buy the appearance of things, their physical form, as in the case of a "bought woman", while what we thought we had bought eludes us. (pp. 13–14)

For both modern and ancient peoples, money has a magic quality about it. The alchemists, whose ultimate blend of magic, religion and science failed, still held the power of fascination for money. Most people believe, according to pollsters and clinical psychologists dealing with money problems, that many of their everyday problems would be solved if they had significant amounts of money. The myths, fables, and rituals surrounding money have increased with modern society and there is a formidable money priesthood – from accountants and actuaries, to stockholders and friendly/building societies.

Money ethics

Tang (1992, 1993, 1995) and colleagues (Tang, Furnham & Davis, 1997; Tang & Gilbert, 1995) have done a lot of empirical work on what he called the Money Ethic Scale (MES). Tang believes attitudes to money have an *affective* component (good, evil), a *cognitive* component (how it relates to achievement, respect, freedom) and a *behavioural* component. He set out to develop and validate a clear, straightforward, multidimensional scale. He started with 50 items tested on 769 subjects, which he reduced to 30 easy statements which had five clear factors. The questions and the labels given to the factors are set out in Table 5.1.

Various hypotheses were tested and confirmed. Thus the ability to budget money was correlated with age and sex (female). High-income people tended to think that money revealed one's achievements (hypothesis 3) and was less evil, while young people were more oriented to see money as evil.

Table 5.1 Factor loadings for the Money Ethic Scale

Factor 1: Good	*Factor 2: Evil*
1. Money is an important factor in the lives of all of us	15. Money is the root of all evil
2. Money is good	4. Money is evil
17. Money is important	21. Money spent is money lost (wasted)
46. I value money very highly	32. Money is shameful
24. Money is valuable	19. Money is useless
36. Money does not grow on trees	37. A penny saved is a penny earned
27. Money can buy you luxuries	
14. Money is attractive	
45. I think that it is very important to save money	
Factor 3: Achievement	*Factor 4: Respect (self-esteem)*
5. Money represents one's achievement	20. Money makes people respect you in the community
9. Money is the most important thing (goal) in my life	31. Money is honourable
8. Money is a symbol of success	25. Money will help you express your competence and abilities
3. Money can buy everything	12. Money can bring you many friends
Factor 5: Budget	*Factor 6: Freedom (power)*
47. I use my money very carefully	11. Money gives you autonomy and freedom
48. I budget my money very well	7. Money in the bank is a sign of security
43. I pay my bills immediately in order to avoid interest or penalties	29. Money can give you the opportunity to be what you want to be
	30. Money means power

Note: N = 249.
Source: Tang (1992).

High Protestant Ethic subjects (PEs) reported that they budgeted their money properly and tended to see money as evil and freedom/power. High Leisure Ethic individuals (LEs) were more oriented to see money as good and less as evil, achievement, and freedom/power. Also, as predicted, economic and political values were positively associated with achievement respect/self-esteem and power. Social and religious values were negatively correlated with achievement and power.

Tang and Gilbert (1995) found that intrinsic job satisfaction was related to the concept that money is symbolic of freedom and power, while extrinsic job satisfaction was related to the notion that money is not an evil. They found that (mental health) workers with self-reported low organisational stress tended to believe money was inherently good. Further, those that claimed they budgeted their money carefully tended to be older, of lower income, higher self-esteem, and low organisational stress. As before, those who endorsed Protestant Work Ethic values tended to think money represented an achievement and was inherently good.

Using a shortened version of the scale Tang (1995) found that those who showed a highly positive attitude to money expressed strong economic and political values but not religious values; and they tended to be older with lower pay satisfaction. Thus, those who value money seem to have greater dissatisfaction, no doubt because of the perceived inequity between pay reality and expectations. Tang (1995) argued that those who endorse the money ethic are usually motivated by extrinsic rewards, and are most interested in and satisfied by profit or gain, sharing bonuses and other contingent payment methods of compensation. People who endorse the money ethic are clearly materialistic and sensitive to monetary rewards.

Tang et al (1997) did a cross-cultural analysis of the short MEQ comparing workers in America, Britain and Taiwan. After controlling for age, sex, and educational levels, American workers thought "Money is Good" and that they "Budget Money well". They had the highest scores on the Short Money Ethic Scale, organisation-based self-esteem, and intrinsic job satisfaction. Chinese workers had the highest endorsement of the Protestant Work Ethic, the highest "Respect for Money" score, yet the lowest intrinsic job satisfaction. British workers felt that "Money is Power" and had the lowest extrinsic job satisfaction.

Tang and Kim (1999) found that money ethic related to organisational citizenship behaviour, job satisfaction and commitment in a group of American mental health workers. Tang, Chen and Sutarso (2008) have suggested that the love of money leads to unethical behaviour but that this is moderated by Machiavellianism and the perception of others' integrity. In numerous studies he and colleagues have shown that love of money per se is not powerfully related to unethical behaviour, except where it is moderated or mediated by other factors (Tang & Liu, 2011).

None of these findings are counterintuitive and Tang has demonstrated empirically what many have observed: the successful economics of SE Asia are highly materialistic, stressing hard work and economic rewards. In one study

Luna-Arocas and Tang (2004) identified four money profiles: Achieving Money Worshippers, Careless Money Admirers, Apathetic Money Managers and Money Repellent Individuals.

Money locus of control

How do you make money and become rich? Is it a matter of hard work or chance, ability and effort versus fate and good fortune? Does fortune favour the brave? Are you captain of your ship and master of your fate? Or is the only way to become rich to win the lottery or be left money by a relative?

There is an extensive literature on locus of control that concerns people's belief (generalised expectancy) that outcomes are within their control. **Internals** believe that they are captains of their ship; masters of their fate; while **externals** believe it is powerful forces and other people as well as plain chance that influences behaviour.

There are numerous locus of control scales focusing on such issues as health. However, few have been devised to measure money beliefs. Furnham (1986) devised an economic locus of control scale, but more recently Steed and Symes (2009) devised an internal wealth locus of control scale. They tested and confirmed a simple but important hypothesis: those who believed they were more in control of their wealth took part in more wealth-creation behaviour.

Thus, locus of control seems to have self-fulfilling properties. Those who believe they can manage and increase their money do so; while those who believe wealth creation is a matter of chance leave it to fate.

The structure of money attitudes

Social psychologists and psychometricians have been particularly interested in measuring attitudes to money (Luft, 1957). Rim (1982) looked at the relationship between personality and attitudes towards money: stable extraverts seemed more open, comfortable and carefree about their money than unstable introverts. Personality variables seem, however, to be only weak predictors of money attitudes and behaviour.

Wernimont and Fitzpatrick (1972) used a semantic differential approach (where 40 adjective pairs were rated on a 7-point scale) to attempt to understand the meaning that different people attach to money. In their sample of over 500 Americans they used such diverse people as secretaries and engineers, nursing sisters and technical supervisors. Factor analysis revealed a number of interpretable factors, which were labelled *shameful failure* (lack of money is an indication of failure, embarrassment and degradation), *social acceptability*, *pooh-pooh attitude* (money is not very important, satisfying or attractive), *moral evil*, *comfortable security*, *social unacceptability* and *conservative business values*. The respondents' work experiences, sex and socioeconomic level appeared to influence their perceptions of money. For instance employment status showed that employed groups view money much more positively and as desirable, important and useful, whereas the unemployed seemed to take a tense, worrisome, unhappy view of money.

Other researchers have attempted to devise measures of people's attitudes towards money. Rubinstein (1980) devised a money survey for *Psychology Today* to investigate readers' attitudes and feelings about money, to get an idea of its importance in their lives, what associations it evokes and how it affects their closest relationships. Some of these questions were later combined into a "Midas" scale but no statistics were presented.

The free-spenders were classified by statements such as: "I really enjoy spending money"; "I almost always buy what I want, regardless of cost" and reported being healthier and happier than self-denying "tight wads". Those who scored high in penny-pinching had lower self-esteem and expressed much less satisfaction with finances, personal growth, friends, and jobs. They also tended to be more pessimistic about their own and the country's future, and many reported classic psychosomatic symptoms like anxiety, headaches, and a lack of interest in sex. Although over 20,000 responses were received from a moderately well distributed population, the results were only analysed in terms of simple percentages and few individual difference variables were considered.

Rubinstein's (1980) data did reveal some surprising findings. For instance, about half her sample said that neither their parents nor their friends knew about their income. Less than a fifth told their siblings. Thus, they appeared to think about money all the time and talked about it very little, and only to a very few people. Predictably, as income rises so does secrecy and the desire to cover up wealth. From the extensive data bank it was possible to classify people into money contented (very/moderately happy with their financial situation), neutral and money discontented (unhappy or very unhappy with their financial situation). The two differed fundamentally on various other questions (see Table 5.2).

It seemed that the money contented ruled their money rather than let it rule them. When they wanted to buy something that seemed too expensive, for example, they were the most likely to save for it or forget it. The money troubled, in contrast, were more likely to charge it to a credit card. Note, too, how the money troubled appeared to have many more psychosomatic illnesses.

Rubinstein also looked at sex differences. Twice as many working wives as husbands felt about their income "mine is mine". Indeed, if the wives earned more than their husbands over half tended to argue about money. Contrary to popular expectation, the men and women assigned equal importance to work, love, parenthood, and finances in their lives. The men, however, were more confident and self-assured about money than the women. They were happier than the women are about their financial situation, felt more control over it, and predicted a higher earning potential for themselves.

There were interesting and predictable emotional differences in how men and women reacted to money (Table 5.3).

Surveys such as Rubinstein's give a fascinating snapshot of the money attitudes, beliefs, and behaviours of a particular population at one point in time. It is a pity,

Table 5.2 The money contented and the money troubled

	Money contented*	Money troubled*		Money contented*	Money troubled*
Has inflation substantially altered your way of living in the past year?			*I think most of my friends have:*		
Yes, a great deal	5%	40%	More money		
Yes, somewhat	26%	45%	than I do	17%	59%
No, not very much	46%	12%	About as much		
No, not at all	22%	2%	money as I do	42%	32%
Over my head	0%	12%	Less money than		
			I do	41%	9%
Relative to your present income, how deeply in debt are you?			*There always seem to be things I want that I can't have*		
Enough to feel			Strongly agree	7%	50%
uncomfortable	4%	44%	Agree	35%	42%
Not much	37%	26%	Disagree	37%	7%
Very little or not at all	59%	17%	Strongly disagree	20%	2%
None	24%	6%			
What are your major fears?			*Which of the following have bothered you in the past year?*		
Not having enough			Constant worry		
money	10%	63%	and anxiety	7%	50%
Loss of a loved one	43%	56%	Fatigue	24%	49%
Not getting enough out	19%	52%	Loneliness	16%	47%
of life			Feeling worthless	6%	34%
Not advancing in career	14%	40%	Headaches	10%	33%
Becoming ill	41%	51%	Insomnia	10%	28%
			Feeling guilty	6%	26%
			Weight problems	13%	25%
			Lack of interest		
			in sex	12%	25%
			Feelings of		
			despair	4%	24%

Note: *Since respondents were asked to circle all that apply, percentage sums sum to more than 100%.
Source: Rubinstein (1980).

however, that these results were not treated to more thorough and careful statistical analysis. Others, however, have concentrated on developing valid instruments for use in psychological research in the area.

Yamanchi and Templer (1982), on the other hand, attempted to develop a fully psychometrised *Money Attitude Scale (MAS)*. A factor analysis of an original selection of 62 items revealed five factors labelled *Power–Prestige, Retention Time, Distrust,*

TABLE 5.3 Money associations and gender

	Women*	Men*
In the past year, can you recall associating money with any of the following?		
Anxiety	75%	67%
Depression	57%	46%
Anger	55%	47%
Helplessness	50%	38%
Happiness	49%	55%
Excitement	44%	49%
Envy	43%	38%
Resentment	42%	31%
Fear	33%	25%
Guilt	27%	22%
Panic	27%	16%
Distrust	23%	25%
Sadness	22%	20%
Respect	18%	19%
Indifference	16%	16%
Shame	13%	9%
Love	10%	13%
Hatred	8%	7%
Spite	9%	8%
Reverence	2%	5%
None	2%	5%

Note: *Since respondents were asked to circle all that apply, percentages sum to more than 100%.
Source: Rubinstein (1980).

Quality and *Anxiety*. From this a 29-item scale was selected, which was demonstrated to be reliable. A partial validation – correlations with other established measures such as Machiavellianism, status concern, time competence, obsessionality, paranoia and anxiety – showed that this questionnaire was related to measures of other similar theoretical constructs. Most interestingly, the authors found that money attitudes were essentially independent of a person's income.

Gresham and Fontenot (1989) looked at sex differences in the use of money using the MAS. They did not confirm the factor structure, finding different but similar factors labelled *Power–Prestige* (use money to influence and impress), *Distrust-Anxiety* (nervous about spending and not spending money), *Retention-Time* (money behaviours which require planning and preparation for the future) and *Quality* (purchasing of quality products as a predominant behaviour). Clear sex differences were found on all but the retention-time factor. Unexpectedly, despite many views to the contrary, females, more than males, seemed to use money as a tool in power struggles. Also, women were more anxious about money in general than men and also tended to be more interested in the quality of products and services that they bought.

Medina, Saegert and Gresham (1996), in a cross-cultural study, looked at Mexican Americans vs. Anglo-Americans' attitudes to money using the MAS. After a useful review of the literature they formulated and tested four cross-cultural hypotheses: compared to Anglo-Americans, Mexican Americans will have lower Power/Prestige and Retention-Time, but higher Distrust-Anxiety and Quality scores. Mexican Americans had lower Retention-Time and Quality scores. The authors suggest that the way Mexican Americans are discussed in the Hispanic consumer behaviour literature must be called into question. However, it does become clear that different ethnic and national cultures do hold different attitudes towards money and presumably related behaviours regarding such things as saving, spending and gambling. Attitudes to time and fate (control) are clearly important cultural correlates of attitudes to money.

McClure (1984) gave 159 American shoppers a 22-item questionnaire about money: spending habits, perceived control over finances, importance of money to one's life, preferences about monetary privacy, and conflict resulting from money. He also administered three personality tests. He found that extraverts tended to be more extravagant and less stingy than introverts. People with strong feelings of control over their money reported less general anxiety and tended to be more extroverted. Neurotic introverts considered money more important in their lives and were more private about it compared to stable introverts. Despite clear links to personality, the results showed the attitudes measured in the questionnaire were unrelated to demographic differences of gender, education, occupation or religion.

Prince (1993) was interested in the relationship between self-concept, money beliefs and behaviours. He found themes in the questionnaires such as envy, possessiveness, and non-generosity. Money envy was shown to be associated with negative beliefs about other people and their money as well as personal values expressing possessiveness.

Furnham (1984) conducted a study which had three aims: (i) to develop a useful, multifaceted instrument to measure money beliefs and behaviours in Britain; (ii) to look at the relationship between various demographic and social/work beliefs and people's monetary beliefs and behaviours; and (iii) to look at the determination of people's money beliefs and behaviours in the past and the future. He asked the following questions:

1. I often buy things that I don't need or want because they are in a sale or reduced in a sale, or reduced in price.
2. I put money ahead of pleasure.
3. I sometimes buy things I don't need or want to impress people because they are the right things to have at the time.
4. Even when I have sufficient money I often feel guilty about spending money on necessities like clothes, etc.
5. Every time I make a purchase I "know" people are likely to be taking advantage of me.

6. I often spend money, even foolishly, on others but grudgingly on myself.
7. I often say "I can't afford it" whether I can or not.
8. I know almost to the penny how much I have in my purse, wallet or pocket all the time.
9. I often have difficulty in making decisions about spending money regardless of the amount.
10. I feel compelled to argue or bargain about the cost of almost everything that I buy.
11. I insist on paying more than my (our if married) share of restaurant, film, etc. costs in order to make sure that I am not indebted to anyone.
12. If I had the choice I would prefer to be paid by the week rather than by the month.
13. I prefer to use money rather than credit cards.
14. I always know how much money I have in my savings account (bank or building society).
15. If I have some money left over at the end of the month (week) I often feel uncomfortable until it is all spent.
16. I sometime "buy" my friendship by being very generous with those I want to like me.
17. I often feel inferior to others who have more money than myself, even when I know that they have done nothing of worth to get it.
18. I often use money as a weapon to control or intimidate those who frustrate me.
19. I sometimes feel superior to those who have less money than myself regardless of their ability and achievements.
20. I firmly believe that money can solve all of my problems.
21. I often feel anxious and defensive when asked about my personal finances.
22. In making any purchase, for any purpose, my first consideration is cost.
23. I believe that it is rude to enquire about a person's wage/salary.
24. I feel stupid if I pay more for something than a neighbour.
25. I often feel disdain for money and look down on those who have it.
26. I prefer to save money because I'm never sure when things will collapse and I'll need the cash.
27. The amount of money that I have saved is never quite enough.
28. I feel that money is the only thing that I can really count on.
29. I believe that money is the root of all evil.
30. As regards what one buys with money I believe that one only gets what one pays for.
31. I believe that money gives one considerable power.
32. My attitude towards money is very similar to that of my parents.

33. I believe that the amount of money that a person earns is closely related to his/her ability and effort.
34. I always pay bills (telephone, water, electricity, etc.) promptly.
35. I often give large tips to waiters/waitresses that I like.
36. I believe that time not spent in making money is time wasted.
37. I occasionally pay restaurant/shop bills even when I think I have been overcharged because I am afraid the waiter/assistant might be angry with me.
38. I often spend money on myself when I am depressed.
39. When a person owes me money I am afraid to ask for it.
40. I don't like to borrow money from others (except banks) unless I absolutely have to.
41. I prefer not to lend people money.
42. I am better off than most of my friends think.
43. I would do practically anything legal for money if it were enough.
44. I prefer to spend money on things that last rather than on perishables like food, flowers, etc.
45. I am proud of my financial victories – pay, riches, investments, etc. – and let my friends know about them.
46. I am worse off than most of my friends think.
47. Most of my friends have less money than I do.
48. I believe that it is generally prudent to conceal the details of my finances from friends and relatives.
49. I often argue with my partner (spouse, lover, etc.) about money.
50. I believe that a person's salary is very revealing in assessing their intelligence.
51. I believe that my present income is about what I deserve, given the job I do.
52. Most of my friends have more money than I do.
53. I believe that my present income is far less than I deserve, given the job I do.
54. I believe that I have very little control over my financial situation in terms of my power to change it.
55. Compared to most people that I know, I believe that I think about money much more than they do.
56. I worry about my finances much of the time.
57. I often fantasise about money and what I could do with it.
58. I very rarely give beggars or drunks money when they ask for it.
59. I am proud of my ability to save money.
60. In Britain, money is how we compare each other.

The results show six clear factors labelled thus: (1) *Obsession* (items 28, 43, 45, etc.); (2) *Power/Spending* (items 3, 16, etc.); (3) *Retention* (items 7, 9, etc.); (4) *Security/ Conservative* (items 14, 55, etc.); (5) *Inadequate* (items 27, 32); and (6) *Effort/Ability* (items 51, 53, 54).

Predictably, older, less well-educated people believed their early childhood to be poorer than that of younger, better-educated people, reflecting both the average increased standard of living and the class structure of society. Overall there were few differences in the subjects' perception of money in the past, but a large number regarding money in the future. Older people were more worried about the future than younger people, possibly because they had greater financial responsibility with families, children and mortgages. Richer people were more concerned about the future than poorer people. Politically conservative (right-wing) voters believed that the country's economic future was bright, while Labour (left-wing) voters and those with high alienation and conservative social attitudes believed that it would get worse.

Hanley and Wilhelm (1992) used the Furnham (1984) measure to investigate the relationship between self-esteem and money attitudes. They found, as predicted, that compulsive spenders have relatively lower self-esteem than "normal" consumers and that compulsive spenders have beliefs about money that reflect its symbolic ability to enhance self-esteem.

They note:

> Descriptively, the findings of this study show that there are significant differences between a sample of compulsive spenders and a sample of "normal" consumers on five of the six money attitude and belief dimensions under study. Compulsive spenders reported a greater likelihood than "normal" consumers to be preoccupied with the importance of money as a solution to problems and to use money as a means of comparison. Additionally, compulsive spenders were more likely to report the need to spend money in a manner which was reflective of status and power. In contrast, the compulsive spenders were less likely than "normal" consumers to take a traditional, more conservative approach to money. Compulsive spenders were more likely to report that they did not have enough money for their needs, especially in comparison to friends. Finally, compulsive spenders reported a greater tendency, than did "normal" consumers, to feel a sense of conflict over the spending of money. (p.16–17)

Baker and Hagedorn (2008) used two scales – the MAS and MBBS – to get a meaningful and reliable four-factor measure to look at attitudes to money (see Table 5.4). They found predictable correlations. Participant income was negatively associated with frugality-distrust and anxiety; education was negatively correlated with frugality-distrust, anxiety and power–prestige; gender was negatively

TABLE 5.4 Four-factor measure of attitudes to money

Factors	Attitudes
F1: "Power–prestige"	I use money to influence people to do things for me. I admit I purchase things to impress others. I own nice things in order to impress others. I behave as if money were the ultimate success symbol. I sometimes boast about how much money I have. I spend money to make myself feel better.
F2: "Retention-time" or "planning-savings"	I do financial planning for the future. I put money aside on a regular basis for the future. I save now to prepare for my old age. I keep track of my money. I follow a careful financial budget.
F3: "Distrust" or "frugality–distrust"	I argue or complain about the costs of things I buy. It bothers me when I discover I could have bought something for less. After buying, I wonder if I could have paid less elsewhere. I automatically say I can't afford it, whether I can or not. When I buy, I complain about the price I paid.
F5 (F4 in replication): "Anxiety"	It's hard for me to pass up a bargain. I am bothered when I have to pass up a sale. I spend money to make myself feel better. I get nervous when I don't have enough money. I show worrisome behaviour when it comes to money.

Source: Baker and Hagedorm (2008).

correlated with power–prestige and frugality distrust; while age was strongly negatively correlated with all factors except planning/saving.

Earlier Lynn (1991) also used some of the items from Furnham's (1984) scale to look at national differences in attitudes to money over 43 countries. He argued that various studies have shown that people respond with greater work effort when they are offered financial incentives. It is probable, however, that people differ in the importance they attach to money and therefore in the degree to which they will work harder in order to obtain it and it may be that there are national differences in the strength of the value attached to money.

People from more affluent countries attach less value to money. The sex differences show a general trend for males to attach more value to money than females. The male scores are higher than females in 40 of the nations, and only in India, Norway and Transkei was this tendency reversed. A possible explanation for this sex difference is that males generally tend to be more competitive. There were also high correlations between the valuation of money and competitiveness across nations. The results were not dissimilar from related American studies (Rubinstein, 1980; Yamanchi & Templer, 1982).

Attitudes towards money are by no means unidimensional: factor analytic results yielded six clearly interpretable factors that bore many similarities to the factors found in Yamanchi and Templer (1982), such as power, retention and inadequacy, as well as the hypothetical factors derived from psychoanalytic theory (Fenichel, 1947). Whereas some of the factors were clearly linked to clinical traits of anxiety and obsessionality, others were more closely related to power and the way in which one obtains money. Also, some factors more than others proved to be related to the demographic and belief variables: obsession with money showed significant differences on sex, education and income, and all the belief variables (alienation, Protestant work ethic, conservatism), whereas the inadequacy factor revealed no significant differences on either set of variables. These differences would not have been predicted by psychoanalytic theory. It should also be noted that feelings of alienation did not discriminate very clearly, thus casting doubt on a narrowly clinical approach to money beliefs and attitudes.

Wilhelm, Varese, and Friedrich (1993) found that money beliefs contribute more to an individual's financial satisfaction than their perception of financial progress. They found:

> For both males and females money attitudes are significant contributors in predicting current financial satisfaction. The money belief of "Effort" is especially important for males, having the strongest relative contribution across both objective indicators of financial wellbeing and other money beliefs. The money belief of "Retention" is negatively associated with financial satisfaction for males and is the third strongest predictor. Thus, for males, financial satisfaction is increased as they possess a belief that they deserve what they earn and a belief free from associating guilt with the spending of money. A similar relationship between money beliefs of "Retention" and "Effort" and financial satisfaction exists for females. In addition, for females the money belief of "Spend" was also a significant predictor of financial satisfaction suggesting that in addition to the absence of guilt related to the spending of money, females are more financially satisfied if they also have the belief that money can be used to feel good. (p. 196)

Lim and Teo (1997) used three established money scales to devise their own scale, which had eight factors:

1. **Obsession:** concern or preoccupation with thoughts about money (solve problems, achieve goals).
2. **Power:** money is a source of power because it offers autonomy and freedom.
3. **Budget:** the ability to budget, be prudent, seek bargains.
4. **Achievement:** money is a reflection of achievements, success and ability.
5. **Evaluation:** money is a standard of evaluation and comparison with others.
6. **Anxiety:** the extent to which people worry about money and are defensive about the topic.
7. **Retention:** difficulties about making decisions and being cautious and insecure about money.
8. **Non-generous:** a reluctance to give money to beggars, charity or others.

There were few sex differences but some indication that there was some difference between those with and without an austerity or hardship mindset:

People who had experienced hardship tended to view money as a form of evaluation probably because they had experienced being looked down upon when they were in desperate need of money. Similarly, the "hardship" group experienced more financial anxiety than the "no hardship" group, probably because they have undergone the emotional and psychological distress associated with financial deprivation. Consequently, they tend to see money as a means of comparison or evaluation. (p. 377)

Rose and Orr (2007) argued that the literature suggested four dimensions:

1. **Status:** the tendency to perceive money as a sign of prestige. Money is used to impress people.
2. **Achievement:** the tendency to perceive money as a symbol of one's accomplishments. Money is valued as a sign of success.
3. **Worry:** the tendency to worry excessively about money. Money (or the perceived lack thereof) is a source of anxiety.
4. **Security:** the tendency to save and value money for its ability to provide a sense of safety or well-being. Money is important because it provides money for the future (p. 746).

They then developed and tested a scale with these four items (Table 5.5). They note that these dimensions are stable and measurable but not necessarily exhaustive. Further, they note these symbolic meanings relate to both personal values and specific consumer behaviours.

TABLE 5.5 Four dimensions of money

Construct	Item
Worry	I worry a lot about money.
	I worry about my finances much of the time.
	I worry about not being able to make ends meet.
	I worry about losing all my savings.
	The amount of money I save is never quite enough.
Status	I must admit that I purchase things because I know they will impress others.
	I sometimes buy things that I do not need or want in order to impress people.
	I own nice things in order to impress others.
	I sometimes "buy" friendship by being very generous with those I want to like me.
Achievement	Money is a symbol of success.
	I value money very highly as a sign of success.
	A high income is an indicator of competence.
	Money represents one's achievement.
	I believe that the amount of money that a person earns is closely related to his/her ability.
Security	Saving money gives me a sense of security.
	It is very important to me to save money for the future.
	Doing financial planning for the future provides me with a sense of security.
	I prefer to save money because I am never sure when things will collapse and I will need the cash.
	It is very important to me to save enough to provide well for my family in the future

Source: Rose and Orr (2007).

This measure has been used by others such as Keller and Siegrist (2006), who empirically derived four types and looked at their stock investments:

1. Safe players
Safe players place high value on their personal financial security and on saving. They tend to be cautious in financial matters, planning most purchases carefully and large purchases intensively. They are thrifty and keep exact records of spending ...

Safe players associate money with success, independence, and freedom. They are more interested in and self-confident about their handling of money than the open books and money dummies types [see types 2 and 3 below]. Safe players have a negative attitude about stocks, the stock market, and gambling, and they do not like to disclose information about their personal finances.

2. Open books
Open books are more willing to disclose information about their personal financial situations to others, but otherwise have little affinity for money. They have a low obsession with money, low interest in financial matters, and little self-confidence about handling money. They have a negative attitude toward stocks, the stock market, and gambling. Financial security and saving money have medium importance to them, but in comparison to safe players, the importance is low.

3. Money dummies
People in the money dummies group also have a low affinity for money, a low obsession with money, and little interest in financial matters. They have a negative attitude toward stocks and gambling ...

However, compared to safe players and open books, money dummies do not believe it is unethical to profit from the stock market. Savings and financial security are not as important to money dummies as they are to safe players. Money dummies do not like to reveal information about their personal financial situations.

4. Risk-seekers
The risk-seekers group has the most positive attitude toward stocks, the stock market, and gambling. Risk-seekers tolerate financial risk well, and would invest higher sums of money in securities. For risk-seekers, securities are not associated with loss or uncertainty ...

Risk-seekers associate money with success, independence, and freedom. They have more interest in money and more self-confidence in handling money than any of the other types. Predictably, they find financial security and saving less important than the other segments. Risk-seekers do not like to disclose information about their personal financial situations. (pp. 91–92)

One of the most recent attempts to develop a money beliefs measure was that of Klontz et al. (2011), who tested their 72-item scale on 422 individuals. They hypothesised that there were eight dimensions but their analysis revealed four. These were labelled **Money Avoidance**, **Money Worship**, **Money Status** and **Money Vigilance**. They found many correlates of these money attitudes. They were eager to tease out what they called the four money scripts:

Money avoidance. Money avoiders believe that money is bad or that they do not deserve money. For the money avoider, money is often seen as a force that stirs up fear, anxiety, or disgust. People with money avoider scripts may be worried about abusing credit cards or over-drafting their checking account; they may self-sabotage their financial success, may avoid spending money on even reasonable or necessary purchases, or may unconsciously spend or give money away in an effort to have as little as possible in their control. (p. 12)

Money worship. "More money will make things better" is the most common belief among Americans. Individuals who subscribe to this notion believe that an increase in income and/or financial windfall would solve their problems ... money-worshipping money scripts may be associated with money disorders including compulsive hoarding, unreasonable risk-taking, pathological gambling, workaholism, overspending, and compulsive buying disorder. (p. 14)

Money status. "Money is status" scripts are concerned with the association between self-worth and net-worth. These scripts can lock individuals into the competitive stance of acquiring more than those around them. Individuals who believe that money is status see a clear distinction between socioeconomic classes ...

Money vigilance. For many people, money is a deep source of shame and secrecy, whether one has a lot or a little ... People who are secretive with their money may be developing financial behaviours that are unhealthy for their financial future. For example, individuals who hide money under their mattress are guaranteeing themselves a rate of return less than inflation leading them to insufficient preparation for retirement and perhaps their children's college education. (p. 15)

Medina et al. (1996) have tabulated some of many money questionnaires developed by researchers and the possible factors that influenced them. This is a very useful table (updated here in Table 5.6) for the future researcher in the area. It also demonstrates the psychometric interest in money attitudes over the last 25 years. What it shows is that there are a number of different questionnaires to choose from if one is interested in research in the area. The choice of questionnaire should probably depend on three things: (i) what one is interested in measuring and the precise dimensions of most concern; (ii) the psychometric properties of the questionnaire, specifically reliability and validity; and (iii) practical considerations like the length of the questionnaire and its country of origin.

What this table does not show, however, is the factor structure of each questionnaire and the overlap. Many have similar dimensions related to such things as obsession with money; concern over retaining it; money as a source of power, etc.

Table 5.6 Empirical studies: methodological characteristics and demographic and personality factors that do and do not influence money attitudes

Empirical studies	Scale used	Sample	Subjects	Location	Factors that influence money attitudes	Factors that do not influence money attitudes
Wernimont and Fitzpatrick (1972)	Modified Semantic Differential (MSD)	533	College students, engineers, religious sisters, etc.	Large US Mid-Western city	Work experience, socioeconomic level and gender	
Yamanchi and Templer (1982)	Money Attitude Scale (MAS)	300	Adults from different professions	Los Angeles and Fresno, CA		Income does not affect money attitudes
Furnham (1984)	Money Beliefs and Behaviour Scale (MBBS)	256	College students	England, Scotland and Wales	Income, gender, age, and education	
Bailey and Gustafson (1986)	Money Beliefs and Behaviour Scale	NA	College students	US South-Western city	Gender	
Gresham and Fontenot (1989)	Modified Money Attitude Scale	557	College students and their parents	US South-Western cities	Gender	
Bailey and Gustafson (1991)	Modified Money Beliefs and Behaviour Scale	472	College students	US South-Western city	Sensitivity and emotional stability	
Hanley and Wilhelm (1992)	Money Beliefs and Behaviour Scale	143	NA	Phoenix, Tucson, Denver, and Detroit	Compulsive behaviour	
Tang (1992)	Money Ethic Scale (MES)	769	College students, faculty, managers, etc.	Middle Tennessee city	Age, income, work ethic, social, political, and religious values	
Bailey and Lown (1993)	Money in the Past and Future Scale	654	College students, their relatives and other professionals	Western US States	Age	

Table 5.6 *(continued)*

Empirical studies	Scale used	Sample	Subjects	Location	Factors that influence money attitudes	Factors that do not influence money attitudes
Tang (1993)	Money Ethic Scale (MES)	68 and 249	College students	Taiwan		
Wilhelm, Varese and Friedrich (1993)	MBBS	559	Adult Americans	USA	Gender, financial progress	
Bailey et al. (1994)	MBBS	344, 291, and 328	Employed adults related to college students	USA, Australia, Canada	Geographical location	
Lim and Teo (1997)	MBBS, MAS	200	Students	Singapore	Gender differences	
Roberts and Sepulveda (1999)	MAS	273	Adults	Mexican		Compulsive buying
Masus et al. (2004)	MBBS	290	Students from Korea, Japan, USA	Asian and American	Culture	
Ozgen and Bayoglu (2005)	Money in the Past and Future Scale	300	Turkish students	Ankara, Turkey	Gender, age, family type	
Burgess (2005)	Modified Money Attitude Scale	221	Urban South African	Major metropolitan cities	Values and culture	
Engelberg and Sjoberg (2006)	MAS	212	Swedish students	Sweden	Emotional intelligence	
Tatarko and Schmidt (2012)	MPPS	634	Adults	Russian	Social capital	
Christopher et al. (in press)	MPPS	204	Students	American	Materialism	

Note: NA = Not Available.
Source: Adapted from Medina, Saegert, and Gresham (1996).

Over the years money attitudes as measured by these scales have been related to many variables. For instance, Engelberg and Sjoberg (2006) hypothesised and found that those who were more *emotionally intelligent* were less money oriented. In a later study using the same Swedish students, Engelberg and Sjoberg (2007) found that obsession with money was linked to lower levels of *social adjustment*. Roberts and Sepulveda (1999) were interested in Mexican versus American attitudes to money and how they affected *compulsive buying* and consumer culture. They found that attitudes to saving and money anxiety predicted compulsive buying. Christopher, Marek and Carroll (in press) found a predicted link between money attitudes and *materialism*.

One study looked at the relationship of money attitudes and "*social capital*", defined as the resources a person embeds in social relationships and which benefit them. Tatarko and Schmidt (2012) found that the more social capital a person had, the less obsessive – beliefs about its power, need to retain it, feelings of insecurity and inadequacy – they were with money. The authors argue that social capital provides social support and that when people do not have it they try to compensate by accumulating financial capital.

In a study in South Africa, Burgess (2005) found money attitudes were related to values. This power–prestige was related to low benevolence, self-transcendence and security. One study looked at the factors that determined the money (financial resources) *parents transferred* to their children. Hayhoe and Stevenson (2007) found that parental money attitudes and values were one of the most important predictors along with parental resources and family relationships.

On the other hand Chen, Dowling and Yap (2012) found that money attitudes were not related to gambling behaviour in a group of student gamblers.

Two recent studies on money attitudes are worth considering. Furnham, Wilson and Telford (2012) devised and tested a simple four-factor Money Attitude Scale: money as security, freedom, power and love (Table 5.7). They found enough evidence of the validity of the scale. Men believed money was more associated with power. As in previous studies they found education and political orientation clearly linked to money attitudes.

Von Stumm, Fenton-O'Creevy and Furnham (2013) used this measure and others to test over 100,000 British adults. They found that associating money with power was positively associated and associating money with security was negatively associated with adverse financial events like bankruptcy, the repossession of house or car and the denial of credit:

Table 5.7 The items for the Money Attitudes scale

Statement	Mean	SD	Factor			
			1 (22.6%)	2 (12.7%)	3 (8.8%)	4 (8.3%)
1. Relative to my income I tend to save quite a lot of money	2.70	1.22		.71		
2. If I don't save enough money I get very anxious	2.69	1.19		.69		
3. I'd rather save money than spend it	2.91	1.09		.75		
4. It is important to have savings, you never know when you may urgently need the money	4.17	0.88		.62		
5. With enough money, you can do whatever you want	3.36	1.26			.79	
6. The main point of earning money is to feel free and be free	3.46	1.14			.77	
7. There are very few things money can't buy	2.70	1.33			.60	
8. If I had enough money, I would never work again	2.29	1.33	.60			
9. The best thing about money is that it gives you the power to influence others	2.11	1.19	.62			
10. Money is important because it shows how successful and powerful you are	2.23	1.18	.73			
11. You can never have enough money	2.65	1.36	.59			
12. I have always been inspired by powerful tycoons	2.13	1.25	.71			
13. I often demonstrate my love to people by buying them things	2.75	1.20				.80
14. I am very generous with the people I love	3.69	0.99				.80
15. The best present you can give to someone is money	1.53	0.81	.61			
16. Money can help you be accepted by others	2.52	1.17	.57			

Note: 1 = strongly disagree, 5 = strongly agree.

Money attitudes were here largely independent of income and education. Viewing money as a power tool, a safety blanket, a way to receive and share love, or as an instrument of liberation had little to do with one's financial means. Money attitudes were not much related to financial capability, except for security, which was positively associated with three capabilities (i.e. with making ends meet, planning ahead, and staying informed). This suggests that people with a money-security attitude are also more capable of managing their resources than those who do not associate money with security.

Power and security attitudes contributed most consistently to the odds of experiencing adverse financial events, albeit in opposite directions: while higher power was associated with an increase in risk, security was associated with a decrease. It is plausible that people who associate money with power try to demonstrate the latter by purchasing status symbols that are possibly beyond their means. Higher power was especially associated with the risk for car repossession: power-oriented individuals may purchase overly expensive vehicles to signal higher social status but fail to keep up with the repayments. (p. 348)

Measuring economic beliefs

Money beliefs are embedded in mere general economic beliefs. But there remains a paucity of good instruments about for the assessment of economic beliefs. Although there exist a number of questionnaires to measure conservatism and authoritarianism, they all attempt to measure *general* social attitudes. Furthermore, these tests have been criticised on numerous grounds including the fact that, first, often all scores go in the same direction and, second, many of the items are vague, ambiguous or culture specific. As a result investigators have attempted to develop short, accurate and simple measures that are reliable, valid and economical (Wilson & Patterson, 1968).

Furnham (1985a) set about developing a new measure of economic beliefs. The rationale for this test was based on that of Wilson and Patterson's (1968) catch phrase "measure of conservatism", which has been shown to be very successful (Eysenck, 1976; Wilson, 1975):

The solution proposed here then, is to abandon the propositional form of item and merely present a list of brief labels or catch-phrases representing various familiar and controversial issues. It is assumed that in the course of previous conversation and argument concerning these issues, the respondent has already placed himself in relation to the general population, and is able to indicate his "position" immediately in terms of minimal evaluation response categories. This item format is an improvement in so far as it reduces the influences of cognitive processes task conflict, grammatical confusion and social desirability. (Wilson & Patterson, 1968, p. 164)

Although this format may have the disadvantage of being "caught in time" and in constant need of being updated (Kirton, 1978), as well as revealing a unitary score from a multidimensional inventory (Robertson & Cochrane, 1973), it clearly has many advantages because it is quick and reduces response sets.

A large pool of items was obtained by Furnham from various sources including party-political pamphlets and manifestos, textbooks of modern British politics and questionnaires on political beliefs and outlooks. From a large pool of items 50 were selected to form the basis of the scale. Approximately half of the items represented left- and half right-wing politico-economic views, thus controlling the response-category bias. Careful examination of the data reduced this list to the 20 items set out in Table 5.8. Further, as predicted, these items did discriminate those of widely different political beliefs.

The Economic Belief Scale measures economico-political beliefs. Money and related issues are clearly politically related and this short scale attempts to measure how "left-" or "right-wing" people vary with respect to their economic beliefs. The percentage of people who hold left-/right-wing economic beliefs changes

Table 5.8 The Economic Beliefs Scale: instructions, items, format and scoring

Economic beliefs

Which of the following do you favour or believe in?
Circle *Yes* or *No*. If absolutely uncertain circle "*?*"
There are no right or wrong answers; do not discuss these; just give your first reaction. Answer all items.

1. Nationalisation	Yes ? No	11. Strikes	Yes ? No
2. Self-sufficiency	Yes ? No	12. Informal black economy	Yes ? No
3. Socialism	Yes ? No	13. Inheritance tax	Yes ? No
4. Free enterprise	Yes ? No	14. Insurance schemes	Yes ? No
5. Trade unions	Yes ? No	15. Council housing	Yes ? No
6. Saving	Yes ? No	16. Private schools	Yes ? No
7. Closed shops	Yes ? No	17. Picketing	Yes ? No
8. Monetarism	Yes ? No	18. Profit	Yes ? No
9. Communism	Yes ? No	19. Wealth tax	Yes ? No
10. Privatisation	Yes ? No	20. Public spending cuts	Yes ? No

Note: Scoring. Odd items score Yes = 3, ? = 2, No = 1; even items score Yes = 1, ? = 2, No = 3. The higher the score the more economically left-wing (socialist) the beliefs.

over time often as a function of socio-political conditions. Whilst the psychometric validity of the scale has been demonstrated it does not, as yet, appear to have been used in money-related research.

Unconscious and conscious finance

Two groups of professionals claim to offer to help people with their money problems: financial planners and therapists. The one deals with the conscious and the rational; the other with the unconscious and irrational. Some try the combination of the two. Thus Kahler and Fox (2005) talk about **interior** and **exterior** finance. The former is the emotional intuitive aspects of money beliefs and behaviours and the latter the cognitive and logical aspects. The aim is to uncover (and challenge) the former to enable it to become integrated with the latter. This confronts the pain of the repressed but making the unconscious conscious is insufficient to ensure financial health, neither is being given knowledge and instruction into the working of the financial worker. Both need to occur.

The idea is that hidden, unconscious beliefs have powerful consequences. We all have numerous, powerful, unconscious "money scripts", which are "partial truths" passed down by parents and relations. It is a pointless waste of energy to try to apportion blame or indeed to feel guilty. The exercise should be to confront and challenge money scripts. Kahler and Fox (2005) list two dozen of these.

The idea of maladaptive money scripts is that some money behaviour leads to some negative emotion and the way to avoid pain is to develop an unconscious script, which may have had short-term protective functions but soon becomes seriously maladaptive. The argument is that people medicate – behaviourally or chemically – to avoid this pain. Medicating behaviours include compulsive spending or saving, hoarding or even workaholism, while food, alcohol and drugs act as chemical "medicines" to dull pain.

The money scripts are not necessarily bad or wrong but have been a way of coping with particular circumstances. The idea is to deal with the psychic pain and to use the energy as a tool for change. Kahler and Fox (2005) note: "Our experience shows the only way to dissolve an emotion is to accept it and experience it" (p. 57). Like all therapists they believe that people have to look at, confront and, where necessary, change the "shadows" or their interior relationship with money, which is the most difficult part of the whole financial integration process. Avoiding, ignoring or medicating painful (money) emotions does not work in the long run.

There are many ways of confronting interior finance voices, demons and handicaps: journalising or diarising money behaviours and thoughts; individual or group therapy; discharging anger. The authors note various blockers to releasing the "authentic energy" or confronting one's personal interior finance issues. These "interior blocks" include financial dependency and victimhood; financial co-dependency; fear; shame; guilt. They recommend forgiveness and letting go.

Having confronted and possibly "cured" internal financial issues it becomes possible to move on to exterior finance issues like day-to-day money management and the elimination of debt. This includes the usual things around designing a sensible spending plan and a future investment and insurance plan. Kahler and Fox conclude with advice on how to find and work with advisors as well as therapists. They suggest the following seven questions that you might usefully ask a potential therapist:

1. What are the characteristics of your typical client?
2. What is your education?
3. What is the process you use? What is a typical session like?
4. What type of "interior work" have you done on yourself?
5. What is your relationship with money? What are your money scripts?
6. What is your engagement agreement or treatment plan?
7. How do you charge for your services?

Materialism

Materialism is the importance a person attaches to possessions and the ownership and acquisition of material goods that are believed to achieve major life goals and desired status such as happiness. Possessions for the materialist are central to their lives, a sign of success and a source of happiness.

Materialism is seen as an outcome and driving force of capitalism that benefits society because it drives growth. However, there can be negative social consequences like economic degradation. Further, materialism for certain individuals can increase their sense of belonging, identity, meaning and empowerment. We are what we own. Others argue that the ideology of materialism is misplaced and leads to individual and social problems like compulsive buying, hoarding, and kleptomania. Materialism is really about self-enhancement (Kilbourne & LaForge, 2010).

Certainly societal attitudes to materialism vary over time with secular and religious authorities often clashing. Many early Greeks, Medievals and Romantics condemned materialism, arguing that the pursuit of possessions interfered with the pursuit of the good. This idea has been confirmed by Promislo, Deckop, Giacalone and Jurkiewicz (2010), who showed that materialism increased work–family conflict. Materialistic workers were more prepared to let their work interfere with their family.

Research in this area suggests a model something like that shown in Figure 5.1.

Other factors have been shown to play a part. Thus Flouri (1999) showed peer influence was important in determining adolescents' materialistic attitudes along with parental communication, parental materialism and religious beliefs. Perhaps the easiest way to understand materialism is to see how it is measured by psychologists. Consider the items of the well known, and much used, Materialism Values Scale (Richins & Dawson, 1992).

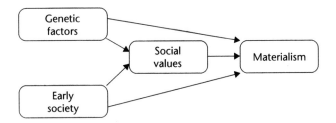

FIGURE 5.1 Materialism and work–family conflict

Others have developed scales for use with children, like Schor's (2004) Consumer Involvement Scale, which has three dimensions: *Dissatisfaction* ("I feel like other kids have more stuff than I do", "I wish my parents earned more money"); *Consumer Orientation* ("I care a lot about my games, toys and other possessions", "I like shopping and going to stores"); and *Brand Awareness* ("Brand names matter to me", "Being cool is important to me"). Using this scale Bottomley, Nairn, Kasser, Ferguson and Ormrod (2010) found that the more materialistic children were, the lower their self-esteem, the more conflict they had with parents and the more engaged they were in consumer society.

Indeed, most studies of those who hold strong materialistic values show negative psychological correlates. For instance Dittmar (2005) showed that the greater the discrepancy between a person's perceived actual and ideal self the more they take part in compulsive behaviour as a form of identity seeking.

Some researchers have looked at the relationship between materialism and money-related behaviour. Tatzel (2002) developed a typology to describe the two:

1. **Value seekers:** materialists who were **tight** with money. These were bargain hunters, collectors who saved to spend.
2. **Big spenders:** materialists who were **loose** with money. They were debt prone, exhibitionists who "thingified" experience.
3. **Non-spenders:** non-materialists who were **loose** with money. They were generous people who spent for recreation and self-development.

More recently Christopher et al. (in press) showed materialism in American students was positively related to feelings of inadequacy about money and the tendency to use money as a means of self-aggrandisement.

Numerous studies have been undertaken on materialism, which is defined as the importance and value people attach to worldly possessions. Different societies at different times have expressed very different attitudes to materialism. The ancient Greeks and the nineteenth-century Romantics were against the pursuit of material goods because they believed it "interfered" with the pursuit of the good. Thus, some see it as associated with envy, possessiveness and non-generosity while others see it relating to happiness and success – self-control and success versus spiritual emptiness, environmental degradation and social inequity. This is why "post-materialism" is seen as a good thing. Equally there is the emergence of the new materialists who buy goods for durability, functionality and quality and who have an ambiguous, even hypocritical attitude to issues.

Tatzel (2003) has noted the "consumer's dilemma" with respect to materialism: we are told it is psychologically unhealthy and morally wrong to be preoccupied with money and materialism *yet* consuming is attractive and it *seems* that having more money and possessions would make life better.

There are positive and negative social and individual consequences (Kilbourne & LaForge, 2010). For some, materialism is associated with societal wealth growth and a high standard of living found in capitalist societies. For others it has harmful consequences for society, leading to inequality, exploitation, and general diminished well-being.

Consumption, some argue, is good for the development of identity, a sense of belonging and meaning. Others point to the evidence of reduced well-being among those who are most materialistic and the data on compulsive buying.

There is disagreement also about the correlates of materialism. Some studies suggest males are more materialistic than females – others the opposite. Equally, the data on age, education and income correlates of materialism are unclear.

There are many measures of materialism. Richins and Dawson (1992) suggest that those measures have three dimensions:

1. **Acquisition centrality:** acquisition as central to life; a way of giving meaning and an aim of daily endeavours.
2. **Pursuit of happiness:** the possession of things (rather than relationships or achievements) as an essential source of satisfaction and well-being.
3. **Possession-defined success:** judging the quality and quantity of possessions accumulated as the index of success: he who dies with the most toys wins.

They also note the difference between instrumental and terminal materialism. The former is a sense of direction where goals are cultivated through transactions with objects, providing a fuller unfolding of human life, while the latter is simply the aim of acquisition. They devised the following simple 18-point scale:

Success
I admire people who own expensive homes, cars, and clothes.
Some of the most important achievements in life include acquiring material possessions.

I don't place much emphasis on the amount of material objects people own as a sign of success.*
The things I own say a lot about how well I'm doing in life.
I like to own things that impress people.
I don't pay much attention to the material objects other people own.*

Centrality
I usually buy only the things I need.*
I try to keep my life simple, as far as possessions are concerned.*
The things I own aren't all that important to me.*
I enjoy spending money on things that aren't practical.
Buying things gives me a lot of pleasure.
I like a lot of luxury in my life.
I put less emphasis on material things than most people I know.*

Happiness
I have all the things I really need to enjoy life.*
My life would be better if I owned certain things I don't have.
I wouldn't be any happier if I owned nicer things.*
I'd be happier if I could afford to buy more things.
It sometimes bothers me quite a bit that I can't afford to buy all the things I'd like.

Note: Those items with an asterisk are reversed or anti-materialistic questions.

Rickins and Dawson also tested and confirmed various hypotheses such as the idea that materialists are selfish and self-centred and more dissatisfied and discontent with life.

Bottomley et al. (2010), who studied materialism in 11- to 15-year-olds, found three identifiable dimensions: material dissatisfaction; consumer orientation; and brand awareness. Further, they found materialism linked to television and computer usage, negative attitudes to parents, lack of time doing homework and household chores, and lower self-esteem. As has been found before they noticed that a materialist orientation is generally associated with less generosity, caring less about other people, having more conflictual relationships with people and treating others in more objectifying ways.

Tatzel (2002) divided people into four groups based on high/low materialism and tight/loose with money. The value seeking, bargain hunting, tight-with-money materialist does price comparisons and saves to spend. The exhibitionistic, trend conscious, debt-prone big spender is a loose-with-money materialist.

On the other hand there are two low materialist types: the tight-with-money, price averse saver with an ascetic lifestyle, and the generous, recreative, experiencing loose-with-money type.

Tatzel concludes that the underlying goal of all materialism is to overcome insecurity by attaining social prestige, which is driven by total extrinsic materialism.

Many studies have addressed the origin of materialism. Flouri (1999, 2004) provided evidence of a relationship between poor parenting (mother's lack of involvement), a child's behavioural and emotional problems and materialism. Certainly the data suggest that early family environments are very important predictors of the adolescent's materialism.

Similarly, Promislo et al. (2010) found evidence that a family's materialistic views affect the work–family conflict leading to individuals valuing money more than people.

Financial risk taking

We all, on a daily basis, take risks: with our health, wealth and safety. Some people seem to be risk takers in all aspects of their lives. Why are some people more likely to be risk takers than others? Is it due to their sex and age? While there is evidence for "risk taking" as a personality style trait there is also evidence that people may be rather inconsistent with respect to their health and wealth. They might be cautious in one area but carefree in another.

Some people talk about *risk tolerance* – the extent to which a person chooses to risk experiencing a less favourable outcome in the pursuit of a morally favourable outcome. Others call it *risk-preference* or even more directly the "fear/greed trade off".

More importantly, what they say about their approach to risk and their actual risk-taking behaviour may be *rather different*. That is, a serious risk taker may not think of him/herself as risky but "well-informed", "adventurous" or "bold". Whilst this **disparity** or **disconnect** may in part be a function of boasting it may equally be down to people not knowing their real taste for risk.

Because of its obvious importance there is a great deal of serious academic work on personal financial risk taking. Many studies have sought to explore the personal factors that determine an individual's risk tolerance or appetite. The results of studies show education, income and wealth are positively associated with financial risk taking (but only slightly), while age and number of dependents is negatively associated with risk taking (only slightly). The big difference is sex: males are more likely to take risks.

For example, one big study done in Australia (Hallachan, Faff & McKenzie, 2004) surveyed over 16,000 people and found **seven** factors all related to risk tolerance: gender, age, number of dependents, marital status, tertiary education, income and wealth. They found that those who were more risk tolerant (i.e. more prone to financial risk taking) were:

- Males more than females.
- Married more than unmarried people.
- Better rather than less well educated.
- High income rather than low income.
- Higher net-wealth vs. lower net-wealth.
- Younger rather than older.

They were particularly interested in the relationship between age and gender, which showed that older people were much less financially risky. After the age of 50, people seem to be generally much less risky. Also, the very rich tend not to be as risky as many "highish" income earners.

Many studies have found that women are much less financially risky than males. Indeed, women engage in less risky (and aggressive) behaviour and are more risk averse in many aspects of their lives. Many have attributed this *to evolutionary factors*. "For females the low-risk, steady-return investment in parenting effort often yields highest returns, whereas for males, the higher risk investment in mating effort produces a higher expected pay off" (Eckel & Grossman, 2002, p. 282).

One study asked whether it was gender-roles or sex differences themselves: that is, was it masculinity and femininity more than biological gender? It showed that it was a person's masculinity, more than their biological sex, which was related to risk taking. The researchers suggested that younger, better-educated businesswomen were more likely to be more assertive and independent (as well as richer and more experienced with money) and therefore more likely to take financial risks (Meier-Pesti & Penz, 2008). They also pointed out that masculine over-confidence and under-estimation of financial risk may be particularly misplaced.

Another study looked at a person's general financial well-being as a function of their knowledge about the world of finance (Shim, Xio, Barber & Lyons, 2009). The idea is that a person's background and values predict their financial knowledge and attitudes, which in turn affect their financial behaviour, including risk taking.

Indeed, financial knowledge itself is highly related to financial risk taking. One study showed that because men have better financial knowledge than women, they tend to be greater risk takers (Wang, 2009). However, the relationship between objective and subjective knowledge (what they really knew and what they thought they knew) was not that strong. Some were *poorly calibrated* – that is they were greatly over- or under-confident about their real knowledge. Interestingly, it was a person's subjective knowledge (that is their opinion/beliefs about their knowledge) that was most closely related to their risk-taking behaviour (not their actual knowledge).

For many people it is harder to grow or even keep safe the money they have. Increasingly, after years of proven probity, banks seem less safe places to store your money. The crash of 2008, the Euro crisis, and state intervention to nationalise banks have meant that many people see banks as insecure and interest rates are so low that they try to find other ways to protect their money. People get asked: pensions or property: which is the best investment (for your current money)?

There is also what is perceived to be both more complex and more risky, namely the investment in **stocks** and **bonds**, or indeed other things like various schemes that have become discredited. People at the peak of their income earning ability – around 45–65 years – often think ahead to retirement. Changes in social security systems as well as to financial services industries have meant that many have taken an interest in the stock market.

There are many big questions here but two are of particular interest:

1.   Why invest in the market at all?
2.   Why choose one particular investment over another?

These ideas are of course linked. They are not only interesting academic questions but they are also important for those who want to segment the investor market. Even the most orthodox economists now seem able to admit that these decisions are not based on rational analyses.

Over the years researchers have looked at various factors that they thought possibly important: a person's politics and values, their general attitudes to money and to risk as well as their sex, age and occupational status. For example, in one study Keller and Siegrist (2006) examined eight possible factors:

Attitudes to financial security: budgeting, importance, etc.

Attitudes toward stock investing: positive, willing, excited vs. negative, uncertain, cautious.

Obsession with money: symbolic as well as functionally very important to them personally.

Perceived immorality of the stock market: the ethics of what some call casino capitalism.

Attitudes toward gambling: positive vs. negative.

Interest in financial matters: general awareness and beliefs they can handle their money better.

Attitudes toward saving: happy and proud to be a saver vs. negative.

Frankness about finances: to what extent they disclose their actual situation to acquaintances, friends and family.

In their study of over 1,500 Swiss adults, Keller and Siegrist found as noted earlier through cluster analysis that they could differentiate quite clearly four types of investor:

Safe players: cautious, playful, thrifty, record keeping and slightly obsessed. They are self-confident, secretive and tend to avoid the stock market, which they see as gambling.

Open books: they tend to be less obsessed, interested or self-confident about their investing.

Money dummies: they are negative and not very concerned about financial security.

Risk seekers: they find profiting from the stock market least unethical and have an appetite for, and tolerance of, risk. They seek stock market investment as a means to freedom, independence and success.

The authors found in their study that each type differed in their possession of investment portfolios, their buying and selling of securities, their risk tolerance in pursuit of capital, their responses to fluctuations and their sensitivities to ethical issues.

Leiser and Izak (1987) argued that a culture with high inflation – such as Israel in the 1980s – leads to people having changing attitudes to their coinage. They found that it was the attitude of the public to a given coin that best predicted what they called the money-size illusion. Further, the biases in estimated sizes remained even after the coin was withdrawn.

The introduction of a new coin offers interesting and important opportunities for research. One example was the introduction of the Euro in 2002. Numerous studies were done such as those by Jonas et al. (2002), who showed how the size and denomination of the currency changing (i.e. German Deutschmarks, Italian lira) had a powerful anchoring effect on what people thought about their new currency.

We know that, despite what economists say money is not strictly fungible at least from the perspective of users. They do not treat all money the same: clean money is kept longer than dirty or damaged money. Rarer coins and notes are horded. In some countries the currency is a form of art. Favoured pictures and colours are spent less quickly than those notes or coins that people do not find as pleasing. Those who design money have to think carefully about the symbolic features in money such as colour and what people and images appear on the currency.

Some indication of this issue could be seen in the 2013 debate in Great Britain as to whom they should have on their bank notes. It was argued that they too often showed "dead white males" and that great female leaders, scientists and writers were underrepresented. Hence the call and vociferous debate on the design of bank notes.

These issues equally apply to credit cards which are often very carefully designed and coloured to indicate the wealth of the owner. Black is often the most "valuable", followed by gold, then silver, then perhaps the corporate colour of the organization (bank) issuing them.

Thinking about money

Few would disagree with the proposition that everybody has a fairly complex set of attitudes to the abstract concept of money as well as actual currency. Money is clearly symbolic and imbued with moral and emotional meaning. These attitudes clearly play a role in how people use money – whether they are compulsive savers or profligate spenders, whether it includes pain or pleasure and whether it is sacred or profane. What is abundantly clear is that money is far from value free and that few people are dispassionate, disinterested, economically rational users of money.

Researchers in the area have attempted through self-report questionnaires to understand the basic structure of money attitudes. Over the past 25 years many different instruments have been constructed and psychometrically examined which have purported to investigate the fundamental dimensions underlying money attitudes. While there remains no agreement on the basic number of factors or how they should be described, it is possible to see that some overlap. For instance, many of the measures show attitudes about power, prestige and spending, where money is seen as something one can use to influence and impress others. Also, most of the measures found evidence of a retention factor, which is concerned with saving, investing and carefully planning the use of money.

As well as self-report questionnaires that attempt to measure attitudes to money, there has also been some work on more specific concepts like money ethics or more general concepts like economic beliefs. What these studies show is that money attitudes are inextricably linked with such things as political beliefs and voting intentions.

Those who wish to research this area have a large choice of measures to use. Some are better psychometrised than others and there is a large overlap between them.

6

UNDERSTANDING THE ECONOMIC WORLD

An economist is an expert who will know tomorrow why the things he predicted yesterday didn't happen today.

Evan Esar

Undermine the entire economic structure of society by leaving the pay toilet door ajar so the next person can get in free.

Taylor Meade

Today the greatest single source of wealth is between your ears.

Brian Tracy

Education costs money: but then so does ignorance.

Sir Claus Moser

If it's free, it's probably not worth a damn.

Don Stepp

Introduction

This chapter examines the economic beliefs and behaviours of young people, concentrating specifically on two things: stage-wise theories about the development of economic ideas; and research into the development of specific economic concepts like profit and interest rates. It looks at when and how young people come to understand how the economic world works. It is, in essence, the developmental psychology of money.

Many studies have looked at how young people acquire, think about, and use money. They have shown age but also sex, family structure and school success factors (Meeks, 1998; Mortimer, Dennehy, Lee & Finch, 1994). Some have been experimental studies that have looked at such things as when and why children share money (Leman, Keller & Takezawa, 2008) or give money away to charities (Knowles, Hyde & White, 2012).

Webley, Burgoyne, Lea and Young (2001) noted that the transition from economic child to economic adult is often sudden, violent and bewildering, which may account for the relatively poor understanding in young people of how the world of money works. They are faced with choices like staying in education, going into the labour market or going into claimancy. They are also confronted with issues like marriages and mortgages, which require a steadily increasing time horizon.

Until recently there has been comparatively little research on the economic beliefs and behaviours of young people (Berti & Monaci, 1998; Furnham, 1999a, 1999b, 2008; Furnham & Lunt, 1996; Thompson & Siegler, 2000). Even less has been done on *how* knowledge and beliefs are acquired as opposed to the *content* of the knowledge base (Berti & Bombi, 1988). Furthermore, it has not been until comparatively recently that researchers have looked at young people's reasoning about economic issues such as consumption, saving, marketing and work-related knowledge.

What is special about economic understanding is that it forms the basis of the understanding of power in society and the concepts/ideology a child develops are therefore of concern to educationalists and politicians (Webley, 1983). The need to relate to the economic structure of any particular society – an idea more radically expressed by Cummings and Taebel (1978) – and the importance of characterising a child's environment (e.g. exposure to own economic experience) are therefore aspects that might distinguish the development of economic concepts from others. Social values and ideology are intricately bound up with the latter and not the former and can influence understanding profoundly. It is, quite simply, impossible to understand the concept of poverty or wealth without understanding the structure of society and the concept of inequality. In this sense the socioeconomic status of the family and the culture in which a young person grows up should have a big impact on when and how they acquire economic understanding.

The development of economic ideas and concepts in children

There is a long and patchy history of research into the development of economic ideas in children and adolescents (Leiser, Sevon & Levy, 1990; Roland-Levy, 1990). Lunt's (1996) review into children's economic socialisation falls into three phases: *First*, there was a small amount of descriptive work that established that children had a clearly developing understanding of economic life. *Second*, researchers attempted to map descriptions of children's comprehension of economic matters onto Piaget's theory of the stages of cognitive development, producing classic stage-wise theories. *Third*, an attempt is being made to introduce social factors into the explanation of the development of economic understanding. This "third wave" shows that there has been a burgeoning of research in economic socialisation since the mid-1980s and even more so over the past five years.

Although there have been a variety of studies that have claimed to support the Piagetian view about the development of economic concepts in the child these studies have found different numbers of stages. This might be due to several reasons: the age ranges of the subjects were different; the number of subjects in each study was different (sometimes perhaps too small to be representative); or there was variation in the precision of the definition of stage boundaries.

Table 6.1 shows that there is disagreement about the number of stages, points of transition and content of understanding at each stage.

Note, also, that researchers have rather "given up" on this approach of trying to specify the stages children go through in getting to understand all, or even specific concepts.

These stages suggest though that the child's understanding of *different* economic concepts always advances simultaneously, which is clearly not the case. Stage-wise theories appear to have a number of implicit assumptions: the sequence of development is fixed; there is a specific end-state towards which the child and adolescent inevitably progresses; some behaviours are sufficiently different from previous abilities that we can identify a child or adolescent as being in or out of a stage.

There is increasing criticism of the cognitive stage-wise approach. Dickinson and Emler (1996) argued that economic transactions take place between people in a variety of social roles and there is no clear and simple domain of economic knowledge separate from the broader social world into which the child is socialised. Different social groups possess different economic knowledge. Knowledge about wealth lags in development. They suggest that there are systematic class differences so that working-class children emphasise personal effort as the basis of wage differentials, whereas middle-class children recognise the importance of qualifications. They argue that these differences in attribution bring about a self-serving bias that acts to justify inequalities and therefore reinforces the status quo of socially distributed economic resources. In this sense social class determines understanding which maintains the system.

TABLE 6.1 Dates, samples and stages found in studies of the development of economic understanding

Author	Year	Subject	Age range	Stages
Strauss	1952	66	4.8–11.6	9
Danziger	1958	41	5–8	4
Sutton	1962	85	Grade 1–6	6
Jahoda	1979	120	6–12	3
Burris	1983	96	4–5, 6–7, 10–12	3
Leiser	1983	89	7–17	3

Source: Furnham and Argyle (1998).

Leiser and Ganin (1996) reported a study of the social determinants of economic ideology and revealed a complex relation between demographic, social and psychological variables. Increased economic involvement was related to support for free enterprise. Middle-class adolescents supported a version of liberal capitalism, whereas the working classes were most concerned about inequality. Thus the social conditions influence the system of financial allocation within the household, which then creates consumers with particular orientations towards the economy, which in turn reproduces the existing social organisation of the economy.

The questions here are: by what age can you assume that young people (children and adolescents) have a *good grasp* of economic reality? When can they be considered (by all practical measures) *responsible economic agents*? When should we expect them to be economically literate?

The development of economic thinking

Although numerous studies of children's understanding of different aspects of the economic world have been carried out, it appears they have concentrated on some topics rather than others (Berti & Bombi, 1988). For example, relatively few studies exist on young people's knowledge of betting, taxes, interest rates, the up and down of the economy (boom, recession, depression, recovery, etc.) or inflation, though the recent work of Thompson and Siegler (2000) may be an exception.

Money

Children first learn that *money is magical*. It has the power to build and destroy and to do literally anything. Every need, every whim, every fantasy can be fulfilled by money. One can control and manipulate others with the power of money. It can be used to protect oneself totally like a potent amulet. Money can also heal both the body and the soul. Money opens doors; it talks loudly; it can shout but also whisper. Most importantly its influence is omnipresent.

Children's first contact with money (coins and notes and more recently credit cards) often happens at an early age (watching parents buying or selling things, receiving pocket-money, etc.) but this does not necessarily mean that, although children use money themselves, they fully understand its meaning and significance. For very young children, giving money to a salesperson constitutes a mere ritual. They are not aware of the different values of coins and the purpose of change, let alone the origin of money, how it is stored or why people receive it for particular activities.

Pollio and Gray (1973) carried out one of the first studies conducted with 100 subjects, grouped at the ages of 7, 9, 11, 13 and college students, on "change-making strategies" and found that it wasn't until the age of 13 that an entire age group was able to give correct change. The younger subjects showed a preference for small value coins (with which they were more familiar) when making change, whereas the older ones used all coins available.

Berti and Bombi (1979) interviewed 100 children from 3 to 8 years of age on where they thought that money came from. At **level 1** children had no idea of its origin: the father takes the money from his pocket. At **level 2** children saw the origin as independent from work: somebody/a bank gives it to everybody who asks for it. At **level 3** the subjects named the change given by tradesmen when buying as the origin of money. Only at **level 4** did children name work as the reason. Most of the 4- to 5-year-olds' answers were in **level 1**, whereas most of the 6- to 7- and 7- to 8-year-olds' were in **level 4**. The idea of payment for work (level 4) thus develops out of various spontaneous and erroneous beliefs in levels 2 and 3 where children have no understanding of the concept of work yet, which is a prerequisite for understanding the origin of money.

Berti and Bombi (1981) later singled out six stages: Stage 1: No awareness of payment; Stage 2: Obligatory payment – no distinction between different kinds of money, and money can buy anything; Stage 3: Distinction between types of money – not all money is equivalent any more; Stage 4: Realisation that money can be insufficient; Stage 5: Strict correspondence between money and objects – correct amount has to be given; Stage 6: Correct use of change. The first four stages clearly are to be found in the preoperational period whereas in the last two, arithmetic operations are successfully applied. Abramovitch, Freedman, and Pliner (1991) found that 6- to10-year-old Canadian children who were given allowances seemed more sophisticated about money than those who were not.

Despite these studies there is a lot we do not know: for instance how socioeconomic or educational factors influence the understanding of money; when children understand how cheques or credit cards work and why there are different currencies. Are they becoming more or less sophisticated with regard to money concepts?

Prices and profit

There are a number of prerequisites before children are able to understand buying and selling. A child has to know about the function and origin of money, change, - ownership, payment of wages to employees, shop expenses and shop owners need for income/private money, which altogether prove the simple act of buying and selling to be rather complex. The question is why are similar products differently priced? What does price actually indicate about a product? Who decides the price of products?

When do children comprehend the laws of supply and demand? Webley & Nyhus (2006) reviewed the studies in this area and showed that by the age of 10 children began to understand that pricing was influenced by supply and demand, motivation and morality of salespeople, and product packaging. They note that studies have shown that the social context (country, economic system) clearly influences a person's understanding because market economies afford more opportunities to understand issues.

Furth (1980) pointed out four stages during the acquisition of this concept: (1) no understanding of payment; (2) understanding of payment of customer but not of the shopkeeper; (3) understanding and relating of both the customer's and the shopkeeper's payment; and (4) understanding of all these things. Jahoda (1979), using a role-play where the child had to buy goods from a supplier and sell to a customer, distinguished between three categories: (1) no understanding of profit – both prices were consistently identical; (2) transitional – mixture of responses; and (3) understanding of profit – selling price consistently higher than buying price.

Berti, Bombi, and de Beni (1986) pointed out that the concepts about shop and factory profit in 8-year-olds were not incompatible. They showed that through training children's understanding of profit could be enhanced. Both critical training sessions stimulating the child to puzzle out solutions to contradictions between their own forecasts and the actual outcomes, and ordinary tutorial training sessions (information given to children) that consisted of similar games of buying and selling, proved to be effective.

In a study with 11- to 16-year-olds, Furnham and Cleare (1988) also found differences in understanding shop and factory profit. Only 7% of 11- to 12-year-olds understood profit in shops, yet 69% mentioned profit as a motive for starting a factory today, and 20% mentioned profit as an explanation for why factories had been started. Young children (6 to 8 years) seemed to have no grasp of any system and conceived of transactions as simply an observed ritual without further purpose. Older children (8 to 10 years) realised that the shop owner previously had to buy (pay for) the goods before he could sell them. Yet, they do not always understand that the money for this comes from the customers and that buying prices have to be lower than selling prices. They thus perceive of buying and selling as two unconnected systems. Not until the age of 10 to 11 are children able to integrate these two systems and understand the difference between buying and selling prices.

When and how do young people think about the free provisions of services? Davies and Lundholm (2012) questioned 78 young people aged 11 to 23, using a qualitative approach. They concluded:

> Previous research focusing on students' explanation of prices has consistently categorised conceptions in terms of: (i) demand; (ii) supply; and (iii) supply and demand. To some extent our data are consistent with this broad classification. We found instances where individual students and groups of students argued a case for the provision of a good or service for free: (i) only in terms of merit or equity (demand-side argument); (ii) only in terms of costs of production (supply-side argument); and (iii) in terms of a balance between demand- and supply-side arguments. In our case the demand-side argument is expressed only in terms of "need" rather than ability to pay. The relationship between conceptions expressed by an individual regarding "what ought to be the price" and "what causes price" remains an issue for future research. For example, are conceptions of "what ought" in terms of "need" associated with conceptions of "what is" in terms of "demand". (pp. 86–87)

Because of the obvious political implications of the ideas of profit and pricing it would be particularly interesting to see not only when (and how) young people come to understand the concepts but also how they reason with them. It is equally important to investigate when young people understand how competition (or lack of it in monopolies) affects profit, the pressure of shareholders for profits and the moral concept of profiteering.

Market forces

One of the most fundamental of all economic concepts is that of market forces: supply and demand. The central question is when do children understand the fundamental point that excess supply (over demand) forces prices down, while excess demand over supply forces prices up.

There have certainly been few studies in the area: Berti and Grivet (1990) examined the understanding of market forces in 8- to 13-year-old Italian children. They found that children understood the logical effect of price charges on purchases before they understood the effects of supply and demand on prices. Younger children (8 to 9 years) confused economic and moral issues, seeing price changes as designed to help poor people. People were not seen as profit maximisers.

Later American studies by Siegler and Thompson (1998) and Thompson and Siegler (2000) threw further light on this issue. They found that children understood the laws of demand before those of supply. They noted that (inevitably) the direct links between cause and effect are understood before indirect ones and that positive correlations are understood before negative ones. They also noted that there is more fallacious thinking – that more sellers would lead to more sales.

In two studies of 64 Israeli, 6-, 8-, 10- and 12-year-olds, Leiser and Halachmi (2006) first played a barter game with children. They argued that young children understand, give and take by 3 to 4 years old, but they do not understand money concepts like buy, spend and sell. Hence it may be possible to demonstrate that even young children grasp the basic concept but not in monetary terms. They provide wonderful examples of what they actually did in their study:

Football cards: Demand, barter

In Ido's class, the kids collect soccer players cards, and sometimes they exchange cards amongst them. The children in his class like Revivo best(which one do you like best?). During every recess, Ido and Shmulik swap cards (point) – Ido gives Shmulik a card with Revivo on it and Shmulik gives him in return three regular cards.

During the last recesses, they met children from the other class (point) and they too want to swap with Ido, and to get Revivo cards. Now both

Shmulik, and the other children are all around Ido, and each one of them wants Ido to exchange the Revivo cards with him.

Will Ido now receive more regular cards for the Revivo card, or fewer regular cards, or will he get just like before?

Hints:
1. How will Ido decide with whom to swap his card?
2. Will the children agree to give him five cards if he asks them?
3. If one other child offers five regular cards for the Revivo card, will other children also be ready to offer more cards to Ido?

Chocolate balls: Demand, money

This (point) is Naama. Naama is a very good cook. She especially likes to prepare delicious chocolate balls. Yoav (point) loves chocolate balls, and always comes to buy chocolate balls from Naama. He pays 2 Shekel for every chocolate ball.

Little by little, the children in the neighbourhood heard about the tasty chocolate balls that Naama makes. They too came to buy chocolate balls (point).

Now all the children are in front of Naama, and they all want to buy chocolate balls from her. Will the price of chocolate balls go up or down, or will it stay the same?

Hints:
1. If there remains only one chocolate ball, and all the children cry: "I want it, I want it!", whom will Naama give it to?
2. If one chocolate ball is left and all the children want to buy it, will Naama be able to ask 5 shekel for it?
3. If Yoav decides that he is willing to pay 5 shekel for the ball, will other children offer more money for the ball?

They found, to their surprise, that children found the questions about money actually easier than those involving barter. However, they did find, as predicted, that the understanding of market forces did go up with age. Children also found demand-change questions easier than supply-change questions.

In a second study children were also asked if the buyer would be pleased by the change. Again they found demand-change questions easier to understand. Interestingly the authors also found evidence of confusion between moral and economic issues. They note:

Why then is the effect of change in demand easier to understand than that of changes in supply? We offer the following explanation. From the point of view of the child, it is the seller who sets the price. This is what overtly happens in buying situations children are familiar with: the buyer asks "how much?" and the seller quotes a price. If demand increases, the seller can exploit the situation and raise the price. Conversely, if demand drops, the seller can try to ask for less. The type of causality involved here is the simplest of all: a deliberate decision ... When there is a change in supply, however, the buyer is not in a symmetric status, and cannot simply declare a different price: it is still the seller who decides, as far as the child is concerned. The buyer can walk out, of course, but the seller sets the price. The customers are not altogether powerless, though: If there are more suppliers, more buyers may decide to try to shop elsewhere, demand will slacken and the seller, sensing this, may decide to lower the price to lure them back. Thus while the increased supply enables the buyers collectively to put pressure on a price, this is a form of aggregate causality that is more complex, and harder for the child to fathom. (pp. 14–15)

Banking

There has been a surprisingly large number of studies on children's understanding of the banking system. Jahoda (1981) interviewed 32 subjects of the ages 12, 14, and 16 about banks' profits. He asked whether one gets back more, less or the same as the original sum deposited and whether one has to pay back more, less or the same as the original sum borrowed. From this basis he drew up six categories: (1) no knowledge of interest (get/pay back same amount); (2) interest on deposits only (get back more; repay same amount as borrowed); (3) interest on loans and deposits but more on deposit (deposit interest higher than loan interest); (4) interest same on deposits and loans; (5) interest higher for loans (no evidence for understanding); and (6) interest more for loans – correctly understood. Although most of these children had fully understood the concept of shop profit, many did not perceive the bank as a profit-making enterprise (only one quarter of the 14- and 16-year-olds understood bank profit).

Ng (1983) replicated the same study in Hong Kong and found the same developmental trend. The Chinese children were more precocious, showing a full understanding of the bank's profit at the age of 10. A later study in New Zealand by Ng (1985) confirmed these additional two stages and proved the New Zealand children to "lag" behind Hong Kong by about two years. Ng attributed this to socioeconomic reality shaping (partly at least) socioeconomic understanding. This demonstrated that developmental trends are not necessarily identical in different countries. A crucial factor seems to be the extent to which children are sheltered from, exposed to, or in some cases even take part in economic activity. In Asian and some African countries quite young children are encouraged to help in shops, sometimes being allowed to "man" them on their own. These commercial experiences inevitably affect their general understanding of the economic world. This is yet another example of social factors rather than simply cognitive development affecting economic understanding.

Takahashi and Hatano (1989) examined the understanding of the banking system of Japanese young people aged 8 to 13. Most understood the depository and loan functions but did not grasp the profit-producing mechanism. First, opportunities for children to take part in political and economic activities are very limited. Second, children are not taught about banking in schools. Third, humans do not have any "pre-programmed cognitive apparatus" to understand human organisations. Finally, banks themselves do not attempt to educate consumers in what they do.

Berti and Monaci (1998) set out to determine whether third grade (7- to 8-year-old) children could acquire a sophisticated idea about banking after 20 hours' teaching over a two-month period. It was a before and after study that taught concepts like deposits, loans, interests, etc. They concluded:

> While the notion of shopkeepers' profit was successfully taught to third graders who already possessed the prerequisite arithmetic skills in only one lesson, in the present study it took 20 hours to teach the notion of banking at the same school level. Should this notion be retained in a third grade curriculum nevertheless? Or should that great amount of time be more profitably spent teaching children more fundamental skills, such as writing and arithmetic? Considering the key role of the bank in the economic system, and the pivotal role of the children's widespread misconceptions of banking in supporting their misconceptions of other economic institutions, we think that children's understanding of banking should be promoted as early as possible. Further, it should not be forgotten that some of the hours needed to teach banking were in reality spent on arithmetic exercises, which allowed children to practice operations which in any case they would have had to practice (even if not calculating for exercising arithmetic skills meaningfully). (p. 269)

It would be of particular interest to examine the understanding of children in certain Muslim countries that consider usury a sin. It is also interesting to know whether children can differentiate between banks, building societies, merchant banks, offshore banks, etc. Recent political issues around banks and bankers have indeed had an effect on children's knowledge about, or attitudes to, banks and bankers.

Possession and ownership

The topic of possessions and ownership is clearly related to both politics and economics but has been investigated mainly through the work of psychologists interested in economic understanding. Berti, Bombi, and Lis (1982) interviewed 120 children of ages 4 to 13 to find out children's knowledge about: (a) ownership of means of production; (b) ownership of products (industrial and agricultural); and (c) ownership of product use. Children's ideas about ownership of means of production develop through the same sequences but at different speeds. The notion of a "boss-owner" seem to occur at 8 to 9 years for the factory, 10 to 11 years for the bus and 12 to 13 years for the countryside, perhaps due to the fact that 85% of the subjects in the study had had no direct experience of country life.

Cram and Ng (1989) in New Zealand examined 172 children of three different age groups (5/6, 8/9, 11/12 years) about their understanding of private ownership by noting the attributes the subjects used to endorse ownership. Greater age was associated with an increase in the endorsement of higher level (i.e. contractual) attributes and in the rejection of lower level (i.e. physical) attributes, but there was only a tendency in the direction. Nearly 90% of the youngest group rejected "liking" as a reason for possessing, which increased to 98% in the middle and oldest groups, whereas the differences on the other two levels were more distinct. This indicates that, surprisingly, 5- to 6-year-olds are mainly aware of the distinction between personal desires and ownership.

Concepts relating to means of production seem to develop similarly to those of buying and selling. They also advance through phases of no grasp of any system, to unconnected systems (knowledge that the owner of means of production sells products but no understanding of how he gets the money to pay his workers) and to integrated systems (linking workers' payment and sales proceeds), depending on the respective logic–arithmetical ability of the child. Although these concepts seem to follow the same developmental sequence, it cannot be said whether, to what extent and how, the same factors (experimental, maturation, educational) contribute to the development of each concept.

Taxation

While there have been various books on adults' beliefs and behaviours with respect to tax of all forms (Berti & Kirchler, 2001; Lewis, 1982; Webley, Levine & Lewis, 1991), there is almost no data on children's and adolescents' understanding. An exception is the studies that were part of the "Naïve Economics Project" designed by Leiser et al. (1990), which had only one question (out of 20) on tax. It was "What would happen if there were no more taxes?" and the multiple-choice options were: (a) don't know; (b) good – people would have more money; (c) bad – no public services; and (d) aware of both positive and negative aspects. Researchers from different nations, including Algeria, America, Austria, Denmark, France, Poland and Yugoslavia, reported on their findings.

Results are not strictly comparable as they used different-aged children and reported their results quite differently.

For instance, Lyck (1990) interviewed 164 Danish children and found 11% of 8-year-olds, 30% of 12-year-olds, 86% of 14-year-olds and all parents understood the concept of tax (from this question). He noted:

> The word tax in Danish (*skat*) means (1) treasure, (2) darling and (3) tax. Denmark has a large public sector, large public expenditures, and high personal income tax rates (50–68%). It was surprising that many children did not know about taxes and public goods. In Denmark, few taxes are "earmarked" and are in this way invisible and maybe difficult to grasp. Almost all of the small children thought "tax" always meant "treasure" and some "darling". Older children thought it was rent or other expenses. Among adults and the children with knowledge of taxes, an overwhelming majority found tax rate reductions to be bad because less public goods would be available (25 of 30 adults). (p. 587)

Kirchler and Praher (1990) interviewed thirty 8-, 11- and 14-year-old Austrian children. They found that one third of the children thought that abolishing all taxes would not be a good idea. Older children especially were aware of the utility of taxes and believed that abolishing them would have negative and positive consequences (13%, 53% and 86% of the respective age groups). Young children either said abolishing taxes would be good (37%, 37% and 10% of the respective age groups) or were unable to answer (50%, 10% and 3%). These results do suggest, however, that by 14 years Austrian children have a reasonable grasp of the concept of tax. In America, Harrah and Friedman (1990) interviewed similar groups of American children. They found 56% of 8-year-olds said (a) and 44% (b), while for 11-year-olds, 20% said (a) 46% (b) and 30% (c). Most of the 14-year-olds (60%) said (c) while 33% said (d). These results suggest that American children are perhaps less familiar with or sympathetic to the concept of taxation compared to Austrian children.

Wosinski and Pietras (1990) studied around 90 Polish children in the specified age groups. They found both 8- and 11-year-olds very ignorant of tax. The middle group thought about positive (33%) as well as negative (35%) consequences of tax abolition, and pointed out some disadvantages for the government and for the whole nation (59%). These explanations were found among 37% of the older children. Forty-three per cent of the 14-year-old subjects mentioned positive consequences, but saw short-term consequences such as the abolition of tax for people.

Roland-Levy (1990) compared the responses of comparable groups of 8- to 11-year-old Algerian and French children (118 in total) and found the French children better understood the purpose of taxes and that they had a more mature economic reasoning.

Furnham (2005) interviewed 60 children aged 10/11, 12/13 and 14/15 divided by both sex and socioeconomic status about their knowledge of taxation. The results demonstrated clear age-related trends but fewer gender or social class trends. At the age of 14 to 15 years old adolescents still do not all fully comprehend the nature and purpose of taxation. Indeed, it is in this area of economic understanding that young people seem most ignorant. Knowledge of tax grows with age yet even the majority of the 15-year-olds did not have a full understanding of the question with respect to age. This raises two further central questions: (1) by what age are children/adolescents able to fully grasp the principle of tax? and (2) what experiential factors (i.e. schooling, shopping) are likely to facilitate that understanding?

Furnham (2005, p. 711) considered:

What are the substantive economic implications of this research? First that attitudes to taxation (and subsequently votes about tax-related issues) are probably related to the understanding of the principles of taxation which are acquired relatively late by adolescents. Tax avoidance and evasion are serious economic issues and no doubt relate to many factors including a full understanding of the history and function of taxation. For many young people the experience of being taxed comes as a nasty shock for which many are very unprepared. Further understanding of tax results not only from cognitive maturation and general understanding of how social institutions work but also primary and secondary socialisation (at the home and the school) but also exposure to tax in the local economy. Thus, having sales tax or VAT added on to advertised shop prices no doubt makes young people more aware at least of the presence of the tax which they maybe motivated to investigate. Equally to educate young people in the economic as well as ethical and moral function of taxation seems an important step in their grasp of socio-political realities.

In another study Furnham and Rawles (2004) asked 240 university applicants to a premier British university (mean age 18.83 years) to complete an anonymous 14-item open-response questionnaire concerning knowledge of, and attitudes to, taxation. Responses suggested considerable ignorance of facts (such as different types of taxation and the amount paid on fixed incomes) but general acceptance of taxation systems. Most knew about the government's role in taxation and what taxation revenue was spent on. They were in favour of income tax but few could list other taxes or knew precisely the percentage of taxation people at different income levels paid. Various direct quotes from the free-response items are listed below to illustrate the range and richness of response. Results suggest that university students remain fundamentally ignorant about the purpose, functions and legislation concerning taxation. Implications for both education and politics are considered:

1. What does the word taxation mean to you?

There were many very varied answers to the question. Some participants (60%) attempted to answer the questions in terms of the purpose and function of taxation while others offered a personal (mainly negative) view on taxation. Overall the answers to the first question showed that the respondents certainly understood the basic premise of the concept of taxation. Some attempted to answer the question by providing a technical definition while others injected a certain amount of levity.

2. Do people in other countries pay tax?

The response was 91.7% "yes" (correctly), 1.3% "no", 3.9% "don't know". Around a quarter attempted to qualify their answer by pointing out the circumstance where people are not required to pay (i.e. insufficient income; country superstructure too weak).

3. Who decides how much tax people have to pay?

The vast majority gave the correct answer, i.e. "The Government" (91.6%). The remainder were either wrong (i.e. "The Treasury") or did not know the correct answer (8.4%).

4. What does the government mainly spend our tax money on?

Table 6.2 shows examples of the tabulated results for this question. What is perhaps most interesting is that fewer than a quarter of the participants nominated such things as defence. In all, 19.8% listed four or more answers, 29.4% three, 19.7% two, 18.5% one and 12.6% none. Around a quarter of the sample expressed various cynical beliefs about government spending.

5. Apart from income tax can you list other taxes people have to pay?

In all, only 12% of the respondents were able to list four or more taxes, 19.3% listed three, 31.1% two, 28.6% one and 8.0% were unable to list any tax at all.

6. Do you think tax is a good thing or a bad thing?

The results were 75.8% "good", 6.4% "bad", 14.8% "both", and 3.0% "don't know".

7. When do you think people have to start paying tax?

The correct answer was given by 45% of the respondents and 21% gave a partially correct answer. Thus 34% either did not or could not answer, or got it wrong.

Table 6.2 Percentage of participants nominating the 11 'issues' on which government spends taxation money

	Government spends taxation on:	Participants' responses (%)
1	Health	61.2
2	Education	54.0
3	Defence (arms/military)	24.5
4	Public works	24.3
5	Transport (roads)	23.3
6	Social security	20.7
7	Emergency services (ambulance)	10.5
8	Civil Service (government salaries)	10.1
9	Criminal justice system	3.0
10	Asylum seekers	1.7
11	Implementing legislation	1.3

Source: Furnham and Rawles (2004).

Table 6.3 Percentage of participants specifying taxes (other than income tax) that (British) people have to pay

	Other taxes people have to pay	Participants' responses (%)
1	VAT	58.6
2	Council tax (rates/poll tax)	41.4
3	Car/Road tax	38.1
4	National Insurance	20.3
5	Inheritance tax (death duties)	19.4
6	Import/Excise tax	7.2
7	Stamp duty	6.8
8	Corporation tax	5.1
9	Airport tax	2.5
10	Capital gains tax	2.1
11	London congestion charge	2.1
12	Windfall tax	1.3

Source: Furnham and Rawles (2004).

8. Is it against the law to avoid paying tax?

In all 77.3% said "yes", 10.3% "yes" but specifying particular exceptions, 11.2% said they did not know and 1.3% said "no".

9. If a person has a job with an annual salary of £12,000 (or £1,000 per month) what percentage income tax do they have to pay?

The mean answer was 8.80% (SD = 9.5%), with 36.3% of the respondents putting "don't know", 16.5% putting "10%", 11.4% putting "20%" and the remainder everything from 1% to 45%.

10. If a person has a job with an annual salary of £24,000 (or £2,000 per month) what percentage income tax do they have to pay?

The mean answer to this question was 12.15% (SD = 11.97). Again around a third (37.3%) said they did not know while 8.5% of the respondents said "10% of income"; 14% said "20%" and 5.1% said "30%".

11. If a person has a job with an annual salary of £36,000 (or £3,000 per month) what percentage income tax do they have to pay?

Just under 40% (39.4%) said they did not know. The spread of the guesses was wider in this question: 5.1% of participants said "10%", 7.2% said "20%", 4.2% said "25%", 5.5% said "30%" and 13.1% said "40% of their income". The lowest estimate was 2% and the highest 60%.

12. What is VAT?

There were essentially three responses to the question. First, 27.8% gave a simple definition of the term VAT, while 38.4% gave a full explanation of the term. In all 33.3% gave either a wrong explanation or none at all.

13. What is inheritance tax?

Only 14.3% of the participants gave a good explanation, while 42.7% were judged to be basically right. In all, 42.2% either had answers missing or were wrong.

14. What is stamp duty?

Only 9.1% of the participants got this correct, while 73% noted that they did not know or left the question blank.

Children and young people clearly remain ignorant about many aspects of taxation, until they receive their first pay cheque with tax deducted.

Poverty and wealth

Why are some people rich and others poor? There have been over 20 studies on the young (Baguma & Furnham, 2012). They tend to show that there are typically three types of explanations for poverty: (1) voluntaristic/individualistic, suggesting it is people's choice; (2) structural/societal, suggesting that it is caused by social factors; and (3) fatalistic/chance, suggesting that fate is the main cause. This, of course, raises the question as to what is the definition of poverty. The results showed that all sorts of factors, like a young person's age, education, gender and culture, influenced their beliefs.

Leahy (1981) asked 720 children and adolescents of four age groups (5/7, 9/11, 13/15, 16/18 years) and four social classes to describe rich and poor people and to point out the differences and similarities between them. Adolescents perceived rich and poor as different kinds of people who not only differ in observable qualities but also in personality traits. Lower-class subjects tended to refer more to the thoughts and life chances of the poor, taking their perspective, and upper-middle-class subjects tended to describe the traits of the poor, perceiving them as "others".

Stacey and Singer (1985) had 325 teenagers of 14½ and 17 years from a working-class background complete a questionnaire, probing their perceptions of the attributes and consequences of poverty and wealth, following Furnham (1982). Regardless of age and sex, all respondent groups rated familial circumstances as most important and luck as least important in explaining poverty and wealth. With internal and external attributions for poverty and wealth rating moderately important, these findings differ slightly compared to Leahy's (1981) results, as here adolescents clearly thought sociocentric categories to be more important than the other two.

Wosinski and Pietras (1990) discovered in a study with 87 Polish subjects of ages 8, 11 and 14 that the youngest had in some aspects (e.g. the definition of salary, the possibility of getting the same salary for everybody, the possibility of starting a factory) better economic knowledge than the other groups. They attributed this to the fact that these children were born and had been living under conditions of an economic crisis in Poland. They had experienced conditions of shortage, increases in prices and inflation, and heard their family and TV programmes discuss these matters.

Again it seems that socioeconomic concepts shape the speed of acquisition of economic concepts. This is particularly the case of wealth and poverty that is often featured in children's storybooks.

Saving

Parents are often very eager to encourage their children to save (see section on pocket money below). Sonuga-Barke and Webley (1993) argued that children's behaviour and understanding of saving, like all economic behaviour, are constructed within the social group and are fulfilled by particular individuals aided by institutional (particularly school) and other social factors and facilities.

Researchers need a child-centred view of economic activity, examining children as economic agents in their own right, solving typical economic problems such as resource allocation.

There have been comparatively few studies on children's saving (Ward, Wackman & Wartella, 1977). Webley and colleagues have done pioneering research in this area (Webley et al., 1991). Sonuga-Barke and Webley (1993) believe that saving is defined in terms of a set of actions (going to the counter and depositing money) made in relation to one or other institution (bank or building society), but is also a problem-solving exercise; more specifically it is an adaptive response to the income constraint problem. Children have to learn that there are constraints on spending and that money spent cannot be re-spent until more is acquired. Thus, all purchases are decisions against different types of goods; different goods within the same category; and even between spending and not spending.

In a series of methodologically diverse and highly imaginative experimental studies, Sonuga-Barke and Webley (1993) found that children recognise that saving is an effective form of money management. They realise that putting money in the bank can form both defensive and productive functions. However, parents/banks/building societies don't seem very interested in teaching children about the functional significance of money. Yet young children valued saving because it seemed socially approved and rewarded. Saving is seen and understood as a legitimate and valuable behaviour not an economic function. However, as they get older they appear to see the practical advantage in saving.

Some countries, like Japan, show a high rate of personal saving compared to others. The welfare state, the inter-generational transfer of money and the inability to postpone gratification have all been suggested as reasons for poor saving in Britain. There remains a good deal of research to be done to establish when, how and why adult saving habits are established in childhood and adolescence.

Furnham (1999b) examined the saving and spending habits of young British people aged 11 to 16 years. Nearly 90% of the respondents claimed to have a regular source of income, the vast majority of which (70%) came from pocket money (around £2.50, or $3.75, per week). Most respondents (80%) noted that their parents would not give them more money if they spent it all, confirming their middle-class status. Just less than three quarters (72.5%) claimed that they lent money to friends, but just over half (54.25%) claimed that they borrowed money from friends. The most commonly cited reason for saving (71.1%) was to buy something special. About two thirds (66.5%) said they had a bank account (though it may well be in their parent's name), and most of those that did not simply reported that they had not got around to opening one. A quarter, in fact, reported that they intended to open a new bank account in the forthcoming year, though there is no way of checking that. Of those who already had a bank account, just over a third (37.9%) reported having it for more than four years.

When asked why they had opened a bank account, five reasons seemed most important: (1) to keep money safe; (2) to earn interest on money; (3) because their parents opened it for them; (4) because their parents advised them to open it; and

(5) because there were special offers for young people opening bank accounts. Nearly 80% of the respondents held accounts at one of the big four banks in Great Britain. About a fifth of the respondents had changed banks for a variety of reasons. Visits to banks were relatively infrequent (once or twice a month). Curiously, the respondents reported withdrawing money more frequently than depositing it, presumably because they deposited comparatively large amounts and withdrew small amounts.

In an interesting experimental study Otto, Schots, Westerman and Webley (2006) were able to show saving strategies in 9- and 12-year-olds. Between the ages of 9 and 12 years (British) children learn to deal with bank accounts and bank facilities in a functional way. Indeed, they found that 12-year-olds frequently made use of a deposit facility in a bank to avoid temptation.

Commercial communications

One of the most politicised of all the academic questions in economic socialisation concerns the understanding of advertising. Most of this debate inevitably concerns television advertising. The central question is simply at what age are children able to: (a) understand the difference between a commercial and the programme; (b) understand the aim or purpose of that commercial. The issue is couched in terms around gullibility and exploitation.

Smith and Sweeney (1984) set out what they consider to be the seven principal concerns of extreme consumerists regarding children and television advertising:

1. Children under the age of seven years do not understand the persuasive intent of television advertising and are therefore vulnerable to this medium;
2. Advertising to children creates unrealistic purchasing requests and leads to family tensions;
3. If the product is advertised, then the child must be paying more for it in order to offset advertising costs;
4. Television creates a demand for "junk" food, and so teaches the child poor nutritional standards;
5. Products advertised to children are by nature bad or harmful;
6. The advertising industry fails to control its own practices through responsible self-regulation;
7. Nothing positive is gained by advertising to children and nothing would be lost if further constraints or bans were introduced.

For all children the family models, sanctions and approves television watching. As a consequence, the effects of advertising (and all programmes) differ depending upon whether and how the family discusses economic issues.

The effects of advertising are a function of what the child brings to the advertising, not only what it brings to the child. In order to examine the efficacy of advertising to children it is important to establish a number of elementary, obvious, but clinically important facts:

- Do children pay attention to commercials?
- Can and do children distinguish between commercials and other programmes?
- Do children understand the purpose of the commercial or the intention of the advertiser?
- Do children correctly interpret the content of the commercial?
- Can children remember commercials?
- Do children's viewing/reading habits more than their knowledge, values or attitudes predict purchasing preference?

Research appears to indicate that:

- Although there are no clear figures about it, children are exposed to thousands of commercials a year.
- Attention to commercials is not simply a matter of watching or not; there can be various degrees of attention to the commercial.
- The degree of attention has an important influence on the other factor of the information processing in advertising and the effects of TV advertising.
- If children's attention to an ad is low, the effects of the ad will be low.
- The opposite is by no means true: if attention to an ad is high, the effects of the ad can vary from high to low. Attention is a necessary but not sufficient requirement for having an effect.
- Children's degrees of attention to commercials will actually depend on various characteristics related to the *message*, the *child* and the *viewing environment*.
- Younger children (i.e. until approx age 7) usually like commercials and pay much attention to them; older children show a greater loss of attention when ads are coming on.

De Bens and Vanderbruaene (1992, p. 68) summarising their exhaustive review noted:

Younger children like commercials very much; older children, on the contrary, showed a greater loss of attention when commercials came on. A majority of six- to eight-year-old children were found to distinguish commercials from programmes, and by age ten nearly all children could do so. Most children of age eight had a medium understanding of advertising intent. Younger children as well can understand the intent of commercials, but this will largely depend on influences exercised by their parents, peers, school, and by their cumulative exposure to advertisements. Understanding commercial intent proved to be important for developing "cognitive defences" against commercials, due to an increase in the child's scepticism towards the commercial messages.

The child's memory for a certain commercials is influenced by child-related factors such as age, cognitive development, advertising-related factors (content, usual features, slogans, music ...) and external factors (such as the viewing environment). The influence of TV commercials on children's consumption behaviour is not greater than that of other factors.

Chan and McNeal (2006) looked at 1,758 Chinese children aged 6 to 14 years. They essentially tested two models: the cognitive development model, which simply states that understanding of commercial communication develops as children age, vs. the social learning model, which suggests that learning from parents and television itself are the primary determinants of advertising literacy. The former was more important though results did indicate that in the case of girls, household income and exposure to television all impacted in a significant way on advertising literacy.

Pensions

Do young people understand the benefits of, and need for, pensions? Do they think it is an unimportant issue or one only worth considering when one is older? There is very little in the social science literature on pensions. Piachaud (1974) studied pension attitudes of 1,200 people in order to discover people's opinions on the adequacy of pensions, how much they believed pensions should be and whether they would be willing to pay for higher pensions. Over 90% of the respondents thought that pensions were inadequate (35% actually labelling them "very inadequate") and 80% of all those questioned were willing to be worse off so that pensions could be increased. Also, the people questioned as to how much they thought the state pensions should be gave an answer that was almost double the pension at the time, with the 18- to 24-year-old age group wanting the highest pension. The study showed that although people wanted larger pensions, they were not fully willing to pay for them. Currently the basic state pension provides less than 14% of earnings of pension-age Britons (Webley et al., 2001).

Furnham and Goletto-Tankel (2002) studied the beliefs of 452 16- to 29-year-old Britons. They asked various open-ended questions like:

• At what age are people entitled to receive the state (old age) pension?

- How much do you think they receive per week for a full basic state retirement pension?
- Imagine a person wants to receive £300 per week (today's money) when they retire in 20 years. How much do you think they would have to put into a private scheme per month to receive this?

The students believed in the need for a private pension, agreeing that the state pension was not at all adequate, which is exactly what Piachaud (1974) found over 25 years ago. Such trends in attitudes appear to be ingrained in the British populace. The youths found the topics of pensions and life assurance boring and not worthy of considering at this point in their lives, owing to the fact that they were not considering taking out either a pension scheme or life assurance.

Of particular interest were the results that showed that those that wish to save money believe that private pensions are quite confusing and that state pensions are a legal right and something that may be necessary in old age. These young people all believed that state pensions were unsatisfactory at present (the same results as found by Piachaud, 1974) and likely to get worse, and all agreed that they would need occupational and private pensions if they were to live comfortable lives when retired.

Clearly this is an under researched issue. A central question is whether students understand the meaning as well as the mechanisms of private and state pensions. Currently many seem ignorant, weary and fatalistic about the whole issue.

Life assurance

When do young people understand the concept and, indeed, the practice of life assurance? There appears to be almost no published literature to date on people's understanding of, or attitudes towards, life assurance. An exception is the paper by Economidou (2000), who looked at 203 British adults' decisions on whether to insure or not to purchase insurance. Those who were positive about insurance tended to be more future-orientated and believed in the necessity of it, while those with negative views tended to be more present-orientated and non-attached to possession. Older, richer respondents with children tended inevitably to be more positive to all types of insurance (health, life, flight, home contents).

In Britain, but not the USA, there is a distinction between life assurance and insurance. The difference is that for assurance the idea is that one insures against a certain fact (death) although the timing is uncertain, while for insurance one insures against an event that might happen but which one wants covered by a policy.

Furnham and Goletto-Tankel (2002) questioned over 450 British 16- to 21-year-olds on the topic. They asked questions like:

- What does life assurance mean to you?
- What happens at the end of a life assurance policy?
- What is an endowment policy?
- What is an annuity? When does it pay out?

They were also asked to fill out an attitude questionnaire. Higher scores indicated higher agreement. The analysis showed that the items seemed to factor into five themes.

The researchers found that understandings of savings, pensions and life assurance were significant predictors concerning the attitudes towards the three economic issues. Understanding of life assurance best predicted positive attitudes towards saving, whereas understanding of pensions predicted negative attitudes towards saving behaviour. This suggests that those with a greater understanding of life assurance both save money more regularly and think of saving as being positive. This may be because those with such understanding think more about long-term benefits of saving, and see it as a rewarding and socially acceptable goal (Sonuga-Barke & Webley, 1993).

Overall the findings seem to suggest that young people were ignorant about and not interested in life insurance, which they saw as an issue they only needed to deal with later in life.

Other issues

Children's understanding of various other issues has been examined. Thus Diez-Martinez, Sanchez, and Miramontes (2001) looked at Mexican adolescents' (12 to 17 years) *understanding of unemployment*. They were interested in how they responded to parents, relatives and friends being unemployed. They examined particularly the adolescents' individual and social explanations for the cause of unemployment. They found, as predicted, comprehension of the phenomena of unemployment to be related to age, cognitive ability and social origin of the young people.

Two studies on Black and White South African children soon after the end of Apartheid are of particular interest (Bonn, Earle, Lea & Webley, 1999; Bonn & Webley, 2000). The researchers' interest was in studying a particular society, choosing rural, urban and semi-urban groups that had seen big race differences in wealth and very different opportunities for social mobility. Some of their answers as to the origin of money were unique: Whites, God, the bank, Nelson Mandela, factories or gold mines. The poorest rural children had the weakest understanding of money or banking. Yet the researchers showed that as children got older their ability to integrate and understand economic concepts grew, irrespective of their particular social background.

It seems easier for young people to identify individual causes than social causes. Older children identified poor training/experience, conflicts with boss/colleagues, punctuality and absenteeism. They also understood better that people become unemployed because their companies go broke, their products don't sell, there are not enough working opportunities, or because of government economic policies, currency devaluation and the introduction of new technology. As children get older they begin to appreciate how social forces influence individuals' economic behaviour.

Learning about money

The importance of how and when children and adolescents begin to understand money and the working of the economy cannot be underestimated. Research on what young people (children and adolescents) know about and do with money is clearly important not least because of their increasing purchasing power. Their ideas and understanding are affected by motivation and social experience. Whilst the former is not easy to influence, the latter is. Various groups are interested in increasing the monetary literacy and sensible behaviour of young people.

Studies have shown how economic understanding is acquired gradually and often goes through recognisable stages. However, personal experiences are shaped by gender, social class, and ethical and national culture, and these often powerfully modify how, and when, young people acquire monetary understanding. Thus, whereas in many aspects of cognitive development children from the First (developed, Western) World seem to be more advanced than comparably aged children from the Third (developing) World, the reverse is often true of economic and monetary understanding. This is primarily due to children from the developing world having to be much more involved in day-to-day economic activity. Five-year-olds may sell fruit while their parents are away and soon acquire knowledge of change.

Social and economic understanding seems to lag behind understanding of the physical world. Similarly, there seems to be less research on the former than the latter. There are jobs in the public understanding of science: perhaps we need to do as much research on the scientific understanding of the public!

7

ECONOMIC SOCIALISATION AND GOOD PARENTING

Children are rarely in the position to lend one a truly interesting sum of money. There are, however, exceptions, and such children are an excellent addition to any party.

Fran Lebowitz

In bringing up children, spend on them half as much money and twice as much time.

Anon

No matter how bad a child is, he is still good for a tax deduction.

American proverb

Introduction

This chapter concerns how young people come to acquire their money beliefs and behaviours at home, school and work. It concerns how parents try to educate and socialise their children into becoming economically responsible citizens and how that can go badly wrong. Certainly the growth in books for researchers, practitioners and parents suggests that there is considerable interest in how, why and when young people acquire a working knowledge of the economic world. One obvious other factor that must account for this rise in interest is the increasing spending power of young people. Many questions remain about young people from rich, First World countries. For instance, are they becoming more or less materialistic (Rinaldi & Bonanomi, 2011)?

How, when, and where do young people acquire their economic knowledge and money beliefs and behaviours? The role of parents is self-evidently important. Parents' lifestyle, values, parenting style and child-rearing attitudes are important.

They model delay of gratification, future orientation, conscientiousness and the value of saving. They not only model behaviour but also discuss, guide and try to induce certain good habits as they see them.

To do this research requires having large longitudinal samples representative of the population traced over time. Some has been done, such as the work of Webley and Nyhus (2006), who used Dutch data and found, indeed, that parental behaviour, like discussing financial matters, as well as their own values, did have a predictable but weak impact on their children's later behaviour. Clearly many factors impact on a person's money beliefs and behaviours.

Children are economic agents and do have an autonomous economic world, sometimes called the playground economy. They swap and trade "goods" of value to them, a practice sometimes discouraged by schools and parents. Webley and Nyhus (2006) believe that by adolescence, children's understanding of economic situations is "broadly comparable" to that of adults.

Studies have examined and found evidence of sex differences in how young people are socialised with respect to money and their resultant attitudes (Rinaldi & Giromini, 2002). Even in gender-sensitive countries like Norway, researchers have found that girls and boys have divergent preferences and spending patterns. Brusdal and Berg (2010) found the role of parents crucial in the understanding and consumption patterns of their children. They conclude:

> How family members keep, use, and discuss money is not a minor issue. Money is a tool for well-being, for it enables the purchasing of commodities to satisfy individual needs. It is up to the adults of the family to choose the best practice in managing their income and expenditures. This is a matter of financial capability: there is no single model of behaviour, but each family has to find the way that is the most appropriate for it.
>
> Careful money management is certainly a good way to avoid quarrels. It is therefore extremely important, especially in blended families, to pay attention to money management. That requires various capabilities of the family members. Well-informed and financially capable adults are able to make good decisions for their families and to thereby increase their economic security and well-being. (p. 5–6)

Parental involvement and motivation

Inevitably parents have a big impact on their children's monetary behaviour. This depends on how either parent controls the family budget (Kenney, 2008); how much parents are happy to spend on their children's primary and secondary education (Mauldin, Mirmura & Uni, 2001); parental divorce, stability and conflict (Eldar-Avidan, Haj-Yahia & Greenbaum, 2008); and the amount of time fathers spent with their children (Medvedovski, 2006). One study showed a direct link from maternal and paternal job insecurity to the money anxiety and management of their children (Lim & Sng, 2006). This was seen as evidence of spilt-over theory.

Parental modelling and direct teaching about money can have both positive and negative consequences. Solheim, Zuiker and Levchenko (2011) showed parental style was important. They found in some families that it was an openly discussed issue whereas in others things were kept secret, while in others still it was very clearly a course of conflict and stress. They found three "socialisation pathways" leading to different money management outcomes:

> One outcome could be characterised as positive and effective; students who observed that their parents saved and managed their money taught them the importance of saving and money management. Another ultimately effective pathway could be characterised as negative; students observed negative ramifications of their parents' inability to save or manage their money. Contrary to what we might expect, this negative model resulted in students' resolve to not repeat their parents' mistakes. A third pathway also started out with negative saving or management modelling, but the outcome was also negative; like their parents, students were currently neither saving or managing well. (p. 107)

Many studies have looked at the intergenerational transmission of consumer attitudes, behaviours and values. Family structure and climate impact directly on children's consumerism. That is, the quality of a child/adolescent's relationship with their parent is primarily related to their money management practices.

Clinical studies on compulsive buyers have pointed to conflicted families that could be over protective, indifferent and emotion denying, rejecting or perpetually in a state of power play. It has been shown that some parents use gifts and money as inadequate substitutes for encouragement and affection, which in turn leads to unhealthy "pathological" consumption in children (Fabian & Jolicoeur, 1993).

Developmentalists have shown for a long time that parental involvement during childhood is a good predictor of a child's adjustment and well-being as well as their educational and occupational mobility. But does it lead to better financial management? This question was addressed by Flouri (2001) in a study of over 2,500 14- to 18-year-old British adolescents. It examined their family structure, socioeconomic status and parental involvement as well as their money management. Results confirmed the hypothesis: *low parental involvement was significantly associated with poor money management.* However, that association was weaker if the young person experienced family disruption. It is concluded that familial climate appears to be uniquely important in a wide range of adolescent behaviours.

Webley and Nyhus (2006) used Dutch data to compare the future orientation, conscientiousness and saving of 16- to 21-year-olds with that of their parents. They found, as predicted, that parental behaviour and values did systematically impact on those of their children. They suggest that the mechanisms for this intergenerational transmission of beliefs and behaviours are modelling of behaviour, frequent discussions and guidance about money-related issues, attempts to instil good money habit formation and independence training. At the heart of the issue is thinking about the future and planning for it.

What sort of parents teach their children the economic values of thrift and saving? Indeed, it has been suggested that parents care less about teaching thrift than teaching various other virtues. In fact there is longitudinal literature in support of the well known post-modernist view that materialist values are being replaced by post-materialistic values like a need for belonging and self-esteem.

Anderson and Nevitte (2006) quote various sources of evidence that support the idea that virtues like thrift and saving are on the decline: that people no longer identify saving with morality and that the stigma attached to bankruptcy has significantly reduced. People thought it much more important to teach tolerance than thrift. The authors note that thrift implies wise money and resource management, which leads to savings behaviours, which in turn is linked to debt.

Some see rising debt being caused by economic factors. On the *supply side* there is increasing access to capital from credit suppliers and relaxation in credit laws leading to lower interest rates, more competition for borrowers and many deferred payment schemes. On the demand side there are economic changes in recessions with high unemployment leading to bankruptcy. There have also been changes in the law – with regard to insurance and social security – which it is argued reduce moral hazard and encourage more risk.

But psychologists and sociologists talk of the culture of thrift, frugality and saving, which is the result of parents' schooling and general social pressure. In their study Anderson and Nevitte (2006) found three things. *First*, they found that those who cannot do, teach. That is, those parents who did not save or were in debt were more likely to choose thrift as something they believed they should teach their children. *Second*, education is a strong predictor of the priority parents place on the value of teaching thrift. Therefore more educated parents educate their children more. *Third* as parents get older they stress this thrift education more. The results seem to concur with many other studies, which suggest that money beliefs and behaviours are passed on by parents to children.

What motivates parents to give money to their children? In a typical economic analysis Barnet-Verzat and Wolff (2002) considered three theoretically based hypotheses for this intergenerational transfer of money: altruism, exchange and preference shaping. We know that parents who emphasise prosocial and general altruistic values tend to give more money and try more often to meet the perceived needs of their children. But this can also been seen as a salary in exchange for the completion of household tasks. It is also used to shape behaviour such as when money is given for school grades attained.

In their study of over 3,000 French families, Barnet-Verzat and Wolff (2002) attempted to test the various hypotheses. However, they did recognise two problems. The *first* was that parents often have multiple motives – not just one single, primary motive. The *second* is that the exchange hypothesis may equally be difficult to test because reciprocities both immediate and delayed are often rather difficult to detect. They argued that one could simply ask the question of parents themselves but that motivational data is best seen in actual behaviour.

Their careful econometric analysis showed that everything depends not on the size of the transfer but its regularity. Regular payments look more like exchange (the buying of children's services) while irregular payments are more like altruistic gifts. Family size as well as age, education and income of the family were systematically and logically related to pocket money motives. Richer parents gave more one-off gifts. Parents with more education and more professional jobs were more punctual and regular in their giving. Parents are more likely to buy their children's help/labour as the size of their family increases. Richer parents with fewer children are more likely to use pocket money to reward school results.

Clearly, family size is an important variable because it directly affects parents' costs, but there are also issues around fairness and ensuring children all get treated equally. What is particularly interesting about studies such as this is that they examine what parents actually do as opposed to what they say they do. Some parents feel pressured to start pocket money systems; others seize it as an excellent educational opportunity. Clearly their ideas and motives are complex. Further, they are inevitably constrained by various economic and social factors from doing what they might like to do.

Many have observed that children who have, and get, everything they want neither understand money nor respect those who gave it to them. Parents, it is argued, can set up for themselves potential time bombs in the way they socialise their children.

Allowances, pocket money and family rules

Parents attempt to educate their children about money by providing a good example and instruction. But most of all they develop allowance or pocket-money systems that they believe will teach their children important lessons with regard to pocket money. It is a well-researched topic and there are many books for parents that provide suggestions and rules that are supposedly beneficial. Parents have many motives when setting up and putting into practice their pocket-money allowance system. They use it as an incentive to do things, to demonstrate their altruism, and also to try to shape their children's preferences (Barnet-Verzat & Wolff, 2002, 2008).

Furnham (2001) showed that parents' education, income and political beliefs, as well as their own attitudes to money, affected their pocket money beliefs and behaviours. Those parents who were "money smart" and believed in the socialising power of pocket money were most strict, showing "tough love" with respect to money and how it was spent. Pocket-money studies done in different countries have obviously shown different results but there are clear trends. For instance, it seems to be the case that (perhaps paradoxically) children from lower socioeconomic status families get more pocket money than those in higher social class families (Scragg, Laugesen, & Robinson, 2002). There remain consistent differences in how children are treated with respect to money and the "lessons" they learn (Ruspini, 2012).

Until recently there has been little academic research in this area and most of the information comes from marketing studies. In Britain, for example, a regular survey of pocket money has been carried out by Bird's Eye Walls (Table 7.1). This reveals that the average pocket money per week in 2,000 was £3.10, that it increases with age, that boys get on average slightly more than girls and that the highest rates of payment are in Scotland, where average payments are almost half as much again as in the south-west of England. Though in some years pocket money has gone up by less than the rate of inflation and in other years by more, overall it was 25% higher in 1989 than it would be if it had simply kept pace with inflation since 1975.

In 2009 the average 10-year-old received £2.70 and the average 15 year old £5.66 per week. However, when you add pocket money, presents of money, and money earned, this goes up to £7.50. Nevertheless, young people claimed to save £4.25 for specific goods and experiences (Children's Mutual, 2010). By the end

Table 7.1 Children have a large disposable income: consider the British data from the Walls' annual survey, in the last century

Year	TOT	Boys	Girls	Age:5–7	Age: 8–10	Age:11–13	Age: 14–16
1982	£1.75	£1.72	£1.77	£1.14	£1.40	£2.09	£2.42
1983	£1.51	£1.66	£1.43	£0.78	£1.16	£1.68	£2.60
1984	Unknown	Unknown	Unknown	Unknown	Unknown	Unknown	Unknown
1985	£1.85	£1.94	£1.74	£0.96	£1.07	£1.91	£3.51
1986	£1.94	£2.02	£1.86	£0.91	£1.24	£2.23	£3.41
1987	£2.20	£2.19	£2.20	£0.84	£1.21	£2.28	£4.58
1988	£2.08	£2.13	£2.01	£1.00	£1.54	£2.36	£3.51
1989	£2.71	£2.73	£2.69	£1.24	£1.61	£2.80	£6.05
1990	£3.54	£3.23	£3.85	£1.29	£1.90	£3.53	£9.16
1991	£3.96	£4.11	£3.81	£1.48	£2.35	£4.01	£9.20
1992	£3.86	£4.11	£3.59	£1.27	£2.49	£4.28	£8.51
1993	£4.15	£4.28	£4.03	£1.67	£2.72	£4.04	£9.77
1994	£4.30	£4.52	£4.08	£1.98	£2.63	£3.95	£9.60
1995	£4.18	£4.08	£4.28	£2.14	£2.34	£4.30	£8.90
1996	£4.85	£4.51	£5.26	£2.41	£2.81	£4.32	£10.57
1997	£4.49	£4.31	£4.67	£2.07	£2.59	£4.41	£10.25
1998	£5.73	£6.65	£4.66	£2.41	£3.13	£5.46	£13.06
1999	£5.48	£5.47	£5.49	£2.53	£3.62	£5.25	£11.55
2000	£6.09	£6.08	£6.09	£3.12	£4.04	£6.27	£12.10

Source: Adapted from Walls (2000).

of 2011 the average 15-year-old received £8.35 per week. A press release from the Halifax Pocket Money Survey of 2011 noted the following:

- Young people spend more than they claim to receive (£110 vs. £83).
- In all 60% said that they did not need more money to be happy.
- They still live in a cash society: 85% get paid in cash, 6% online.
- In all, 90% said that they wanted to learn more about money.
- In 2011 only 12% thought that they would have no debt at age 25.
- Around a third saved for their long-term future.
- Around a quarter earned their own money through a part-time job.
- Around two thirds keep a good track of their money.
- 33% of girls and only 24% of boys said that money worried them.
- 58% of girls compared to 43% of boys said they worried about not having enough money for the future.
- Girls were more likely to say that they would get into future debt.
- They preferred to learn about money from experts.

Another British study of over 7,500 children and adolescents under 18 hit the headlines because it was claimed that average pocket money had hit £1,000 per year.

In a report called MoneySense, the British-based RBS Group reported on a research panel of 50,000 12- to 19-year-olds who were followed over five years (2007–2011). Their report makes interesting reading.

Lewis and Scott (2003) used a polling company to look at what British parents did themselves to encourage financial literacy in their children and what role they believed schools should play in economic socialisation. All the children were younger than 16 with 50% below 10 years. They were also interested in parental determinants of those beliefs. That is, to what extent did factors like parental sex, age, income, social class and education impact on their attitudes and behaviours?

The researchers found the parents engaged in a wide range of activities. Some parents even taught their children about shares. The two factors that related most closely to their behaviours were the social class of the parents and the age of the children. In short, middle-class parents (I & II) did most while white working-class parents (III & IV) did least finance-related educational activities in the home. Table 7.2 reflects the data.

They were also asked what role they believed schools should play. Clearly the parents were very enthusiastic that schools should play a role in encouraging economic literacy. Examination of the various parental and child factors showed that only one factor played a consistent part; this was the social class. Fewer working-class parents (unskilled or semi-skilled) compared to other occupations felt the need for schools to teach economic competency.

To a large extent one could see these results as depressing and in part accounting for the (non-genetic) transfer of money attitudes and behaviours across generations.

Table 7.2 The proportion of respondents who believe schools should teach 11 finance-related topics at secondary school, and levels of significance for the logistic regression analyses with the seven background variables

Finance-related activities	Yes (%)	Significant predictors
Careers/getting a job	84	Social class
Managing personal finances	71	Social class
Lessons about how a bank operates	67	Social class
Practical lessons (i.e. opening a bank account)	62	Social class
Understanding the use of credit and debit cards	61	Social class
Understanding borrowing and interest rates	60	Social class
Economics/about the economy	57	Social class
Managing the household finances	56	Social class
Banking over the Internet	35	Social class
Purchasing products or services over the Internet	27	Social class
Borrowing over the Internet, via banks and loan companies	24	Age of respondent

Source: Lewis and Scott (2003).

Middle-class parents believe in, practice and prefer schools to get involved in economic socialisation or what they no doubt call something like sensible money attitudes and practice.

Lewis and Scott (2003) noted that what they called personal finance education in schools needs to be "sensitive" to the social backgrounds and financial experiences of the pupils lest children from an "excluded" background feel further separated.

Certainly, children in both primary and secondary schools arrive with a set of beliefs and practices part determined by their and their parents' abilities but also their direct and deliberate socialisation. Just as working-class parents read to their children less than middle-class parents so they try to instil economic knowledge less consistently. It is surprising that they do not even abrogate that responsibility to schools more than middle-class parents. One obvious question is who best to target if one hopes to improve the financial literacy of young people: parents, schools or the young people themselves. Inevitably the answer is all three but the first and most probably most important target must be parents.

American studies show that around three quarters of ninth graders (15-year-olds) received an allowance (Mortimer et al., 1994). They also show that the allowance is a form of salary, as American parents demand some work performance for the receipt of allowance money. French surveys paint a similar picture but also reveal that parents report giving much lower amounts than children report receiving, essentially because parents focus only on pocket money whereas children count all money they receive (Micromegas, 1993). This gives an idea of when pocket money may be an important socialising agent since it constitutes 100% of the income of French 4- to 7-year-olds but only 14.5% of the income of 13- to 14-year-olds (half of French 14-year-olds work regularly).

Studies on pocket money/allowances

Over fifty years ago, Prevey (1945) studied 100 American families' practices in training their adolescents about money. They concluded that boys were provided with experiences that are more valuable in training children in the use of money than girls. They found parent practices in training children in the use of money tended to be positively related to later ability to utilise financial resources in early adulthood. Later money habits were clearly related to parental practice of encouraging earning experiences and discussing family financial problems and expenses with high-school-age children.

Marshall and Magruder (1960) found that children's knowledge of money is directly related to the extensiveness of their experience of money – whether they are given money to spend; if they are given opportunities to earn and save money – and their parents' attitudes to, and habits of, money spending. However, they did not find that children had a greater knowledge of money if parents gave an allowance; neither will children given opportunities to earn money, have more knowledge of money use than children lacking this experience.

In a later study Marshall (1964) found that there was no difference in financial knowledge and responsibility between children given an allowance and those not given an allowance (allowance and non-allowance children did not differ in mean scores on any of the ten measures of financial knowledge and responsibility). Parents who gave their children allowances differed in other practices and in attitudes about money from parents who handle the problem of providing spending money for their children in other ways.

Abramovitch et al. (1991) investigated how spending in an experimental store was affected by children's experience of money. Their participants (aged 6, 8 and 10) were given $4 either in the form of a credit card or in cash to spend in an experimental toy store that offered a variety of items priced from 50 cents to $5. They were allowed to take home any unspent money. Children who received an allowance spent roughly the same amount in the cash and credit card condition ($2.32 vs. $2.42), but those who did not receive an allowance spent much more with a credit card ($2.82) than when they only had cash ($1.76). After they had finished in the store the children were given a pricing test in which they had to say how much familiar items (e.g. running shoes, television) cost; children who received an allowance scored higher on this test, as did the older children. These results suggest that receiving an allowance may facilitate the development of monetary competence.

Though the limited evidence does suggest that allowances are effective, it seems as if parents make only limited use of their potential as a vehicle for economic socialisation. Sonuga-Barke and Webley (1993) focused specifically on whether parents used pocket money to teach children about saving. They found that, for most parents, pocket money was seen as money to be spent, not money to be saved. Though there were some half-hearted attempts to foster saving (e.g. by parents offering to match any money saved by the child) this opportunity was rarely taken up.

Newson and Newson (1976) carried out an extensive study of over 700 7-year-olds. They found that most of their sample could count on a basic sum of pocket money, sometimes calculated on a complicated incentive system. Some children appeared to have been given money that was instituted for the express purpose of allowing the possibility of fining (confiscating); others were given money as a substitute for wages; while some had to "work" for it. Over 50% of the sample earned money from their parents beyond their regular income but there were no sex or social differences in this practice. The authors did, however, find social-class differences in children's unearned income and savings.

Furnham and Thomas (1984a) found that older British children received more money and took part in more "economic activities" such as saving, borrowing and lending. Class differences were also apparent: working-class children received more money but saved less than middle-class children. Middle-class children also reported more than working-class children that they had to work around the house for their pocket money and tended to let their parents look after the pocket money that they had saved.

Furnham and Thomas (1984b) investigated adults' perceptions of the economic socialisation of children through pocket money. Mothers turned out to be more in favour of agreeing with children in advance on the kinds of items pocket money should cover, more in favour of giving older children pocket money monthly, and also more in favour of an annual review of a child's pocket money than fathers. It is possible that this is due to the tendency for women, both at work and in the home, to have greater contact with children and therefore a better understanding of their capabilities.

Miller and Yung (1990) found, contrary to adult conceptions, no evidence that American adolescents understand pocket money to be an educational opportunity promoting self-reliance in financial decision making and money management. Most adolescents saw pocket money as either an entitlement for basic support or earned income. The authors argue that the significance of allowances for adolescents is not the receipt of money per se but how the conditions of receipt are evaluated, the extent of work obligations, and monetary constraints on the amount, use, and withholding of income. In families pocket money and allowances are systematically related to all other areas of socialisation.

Feather (1991) in Australia found the amount of pocket money provided was related quite naturally to the child's age, but also with the parents' belief about the need to foster a strong and harmonious family unit. For the older children, parents saw independence training and meeting the child's needs as more important factors and there was some evidence of the difference between mothers and fathers. The parents' work ethic did not affect the amount they gave yet there was evidence that pocket money is bound up with other parental values and practices.

In Canada, Pliner, Freedman, Abramovitch and Darke (1996) were concerned with the allowance system of household allocation. They conducted a number of experiments comparing children who received an allowance with those who did not. The children who received an allowance were found to be better able to make use of credit and to price goods. These skills also increase with age and it appears that the allowance system brings forward the acquisition of consumer skills. Pliner et al. suggest that the allowance system works because it engenders a relationship of trust and expectation that requires the child to become financially "literate" and experienced.

Another Canadian study looked at 81 white, middle-class, two-parent intact families and the family practices associated with allowances (Kerr & Cheadle, 1997). The parents believed that the allowance system taught money management, saving and independence, and that one has to work hard for rewards. Their system meant 80% agreed that children could get extra money for extra work but that money was not for school grades or good conduct. Allowances were chore-related. Around two thirds of parents said they would stop allowances once their children were working. They also imposed some restrictions on what could be done with allowances (required to save, and not purchase certain goods).

In France, Lassarres (1996) found that the best allocation strategy is the giving of allowances paired with discussions of the family budget. The mechanism that makes the allowance system so effective is the possibility it affords for discussions about financial matters within the family. Lassarres suggested various reasons why parents' allowances change as the child develops. The allowance is an attempt to control the increasing demands made by the child. Thus, a straightforward pocket money system is often the first thing to be introduced, which then gradually evolves into a full allowance system that includes a variety of obligations on both parties.

Three British studies examined the issue of pocket money and allowances. Furnham (1999a) found that most British parents (91%) were in favour of starting some weekly based system for 6-year-olds, with the amount of money increasing linearly over time. The greatest increase was found to occur between 7 and 10 years, and the least between 15 and 18 years. Around three quarters of the sample believed allowances should be given weekly, and that children should be encouraged to save and take on a part-time job. Parents had consistent ideas about rules and responsibilities associated with the allowance system they established, and how it educated their children in to the world of money.

Furnham and Kirkaldy (2000) replicated the above study on 238 German adults and compared their results to those of Furnham (1999a). The results were overall similar. In all 91% of British and 99% of Germans believed in the early introduction of pocket money: the British favoured starting at 6.73 years, the Germans at 6.40 years. Identical numbers (62% from both groups) thought they knew the "market rate" for their children's pocket money: that is the average amount given to children of that age.

Furnham (2001) reflected more specifically on individual difference factors associated with parental allowance beliefs. Previous studies have concentrated on demographic and national differences. This study focused on three types of parental individual difference variables in addition to demographic differences. Many of the attitudinal questions asked in the studies by Furnham (1999a, 1999b) and Furnham and Kirkaldy (2000) served as the dependent variables.

The following results (Table 7.3) are taken from a recent British survey of over 500 parents (Milner & Furnham, 2013).

TABLE 7.3 British parents' beliefs

Part 1: Recommendation	Yes (%)	No (%)
Provide children with tools to save money (e.g. transparent piggy banks)	97.4	2.6
Play with real or fake money: count, stack, guess the cost/value of things	94.4	5.6
Describe the difference between needs and wants (food vs. ice-cream; medicine vs. a CD player)	97.2	2.8
Encourage coin identification and change calculations at home and in shops	97.4	2.6
Start pocket money as early as 3 to 4 years old	38.2	61.8
Make pocket money related to behaviour (i.e. specific chores completed appropriately and on time – gardening, cleaning, tidying) with the aim of them eventually becoming responsible for their own jobs and job charts	84.5	15.5
Explain why they cannot have certain items they ask for (e.g. it costs too much, the money ran out)	98.2	1.8
Use coins to rehearse arithmetic problems	89.5	10.5
Try to help them divide money into spend and save piles regularly and wisely	88.0	12.0
Take them shopping and explain the decision making behind your purchasing behaviour	81.5	18.5
Discuss contents, values, options of different goods when shopping particularly in supermarkets	84.0	16.0
Let them watch your money transactions, i.e. how to receive, calculate, query change	85.6	14.4
Explain and set up a budget for childhood money (lunch, bus fare, school trips, breakages)	75.7	24.3
Introduce the concept of "citizen of the household" and what responsibilities this entails (e.g. sharing, giving, honesty)	75.8	24.2
Get them into banking; formal savings. Explain how banks work. Go to the bank, read leaflets and open an account (s) with them	92.6	7.4
Let them read about their investments, e.g. bank statements/share certificates if they have any	81.2	18.8
Encourage them to have a (big) long-term savings goal	84.5	15.5
Show them family bills (food, rent, insurance) and explain them fully	68.3	31.7
Explain and model charity giving and encourage your child to do likewise	82.5	17.5
Establish rules for what happens to "gift money" from others at Christmas, birthdays, etc.	68.2	31.8
Explain issues like tipping, tolls, tokens, consumer rights, value-for-money, comparative shopping	78.0	22.0

Part 1: Recommendation	Yes (%)	No (%)
Buy and explain consumer magazines and how they work	28.9	71.1
Watch and/or read television commercials together and analyse them for motive, product value and technique	50.8	49.2
Explain tax (income and VAT) and tax your children's pocket money (say 10%) to have a family tax where the whole family both contributes and decides how to spend it. Family meetings should be called to discuss this	35.5	64.5
Lay down rules (with explanations) for borrowing, lending and trading both within and outside the family	64.7	35.3
Explain the use of verbal and written contracts about money related issues (e.g. payback after loans)	71.0	29.0
Establish rules/policies about breakages, money found on the street, mistaken over/under payments, shoplifting	88.5	11.5
Encourage, model and educate the use of debit and credit cards	78.7	21.3
Encourage personal and internet banking. Discuss and calculate interest with them	71.7	28.3
Direct debit pocket money into their accounts, perhaps as a standing order	53.3	46.7
Make them personally and totally responsible for their own bills – especially clothes, mobile phones, computers	66.0	34.0
If you loan them money agree and stick to reasonable repayment terms (period, interest)	73.7	26.7
Charge them board if they have an income from part-time work	41.9	58.1
Help them save wisely, i.e. discuss where best saving conditions are likely to be found	94.5	5.5
Encourage regular, sensible, thoughtful budgeting	94.0	6.0
Explain the stock-market and together play with a set amount (e.g. £100) by starting a portfolio, even at 13 or 14 years old	37.1	62.9
Show and explain family insurance policies, schemes and payments	51.9	48.1
Explain the concept of a will and the details of yours specifically with respect to financial implications	65.6	34.4
Discuss your income and how you spend it honestly	61.3	38.7
Encourage smart consumerism: keeping receipts, knowing rights, understanding shop sales, knowing store return policies, reading the labels	89.1	10.9
Discuss entrepreneurship and opportunities to supplement income	78.1	21.9
Encourage your child to do part time (Saturday) jobs	88.9	11.1
Ask for evidence of their budgeting plans and decision making	47.7	52.3

Source: Milner and Furnham (2013)

Quizzing your children

This was a multiple choice "situational test" that required respondents to indicate how they would behave in a range of money-related situations with their children. The test had clearly been devised as a self-assessment quiz but the results from this study showed both a normal distribution and a satisfactory internal reliability. In essence the test measured how "sensible" parents were with regard to their children and came at the beginning of a book that attempted to teach children to be better informed about money.

The results showed that the higher participants scored on this test the more they approved of parental involvement in the economic socialisation of their children; they believed more in stressing regularity but were less "liberal". "Money-smart" parents clearly believed that it was their responsibility to model monetary behaviour and to discuss with their children such things as advertisements, buying decisions, and family budgeting. On the other hand they did not endorse the views that pocket money should not be based on chores or that it should never be withheld. This may be seen as an example of what the book called "tough love".

These are the first six items:

1. Your 7-year-old daughter loses the $5 she got for her birthday from her Aunty Mary. You:
   a. Ask Aunt Mary to send another $5.
   b. Tell your child she should have put the money in the bank.
   c. Let her do chores to make up the $5.
   d. Tell your child she should have been more careful.

2. Your 14-year-old son has been saving half of his allowance and money earned from neighbourhood jobs. Now he wants to use the money to buy a $200 compact disc player. You:
   a. Allow him to buy it.
   b. Offer him your old turntable instead.
   c. Tell him there's no way he can touch his savings.
   d Buy it for him.

3. You usually pay $40 for your son's sneakers. Now he wants a pair of $200 inflatable high-tops. You:
   a. Chip in the $40, and let your child come up with the balance.
   b. Say "I'll buy a $40 pair, or you can still wear your old ones."
   c. Buy them, because "everyone else has them."
   d. Buy yourself a pair, too (everyone else has them!).

4. Your daughter has mowed your lawn since she was 12. Now 14, she wants to make money by mowing neighbours' lawns. She also wants to be paid to do your lawn. You:
   a. Say "Okay, and go ahead and use our mower and gas."
   b. Hire a neighbour's kid to do your lawn.
   c. Tell her to forget it because mowing your lawn is her job.
   d. Say "Use our mower and pay for the gas you use. We'll pay you half of what you charge neighbours."

5. You're trying to teach your 16-year-old about the stock market. She invests her own money in a stock you selected. It loses money. You:
   a. Make up the loss.
   b. Hire a neighbour's kid to make future stock picks.
   c. Say "That's how the market works. Too bad."
   d. Share the loss with her, and help her figure out what to do with the remaining stock.

6. Your 15-year-old daughter gets an allowance for which she is expected to help out around the house. She has ceased to help. You:
   a. Hire a neighbour's kid to help clean the house.
   b. Stop the allowance altogether.
   c. Continue to pay until the child turns 18.
   d. Tie the amount and payment of the allowance more closely to chores accomplished.

Advice for parents

Educationalists have been interested in economic understanding in children for a very long time (Bas, 1996, 1998; Goodnow, 1996, 1998; Goodnow & Warton, 1991; Gunter & Furnham, 1998). Indeed, there are a stream of papers going back to the turn of the century that concern themselves with children and money (Dismorr, 1902; Kohler, 1897). There has been a vigorous research interest in such things as children's knowledge of money and work experience since then (Mortimer & Shanahan, 1994; Witryol & Wentworth, 1983). Because of the perceived importance of children and adolescents understanding the economic world, there are a number of books and articles aimed at both young people and their parents (Estes & Barocas, 1994; Gruenberg & Gruenberg, 1993).

For instance, in a book subtitled "A smart kid's guide to savvy saving and spending", Wyatt and Hinden (1991) claim to provide a perfect "hands on introduction to managing money". Rendon and Krantz (1992) aimed their book specifically at teenagers. It explains such things as: the difference between capitalist and socialist economies; the nature of inflation and recession; how the stock market works (what causes highs and lows); and the government's role in the economy. They believe various factors affect young people's attitudes toward money. These include: whether they have more, less, or the same amount of money as other people in their community; how close they live to people who have either a lot less or a lot more money than they do; how much they hear about people who have either a lot less or a lot more money than they do; whether their parents' current money situation is very different from the one they (their parents) grew up with; and how they – and their family – feel their situation compares with the situations of many people they see on television, the movies, or in their textbooks.

There are also a number of interesting books on money specifically for parents. Davis and Taylor (1979) wrote *Kids and Cash* for "parents who ... want answers about allowances ... want their kids to earn and save money ... believe a job teaches responsibility ... are interested in preparing their children for the realities of the adult world". They believe all children need to learn money skills like: *Spending Money* (understanding concepts like scarcity, price differentials and the necessity of choices); *Budgeting* (planning and keeping to money plans); *Saving* (the importance and benefits of postponement of gratification); *Borrowing* (the concepts and costs of borrowing); *Earning Money* (by such things as selling ability, learning to take risks, understanding the competition).

They stress the importance of the allowance/pocket money system to teach children about the value of money and the basis of responsibility. They argue that parents use five systems that do not work:

1. Money is given when needed: irregular, unplanned, capricious.
2. Commission system: effectively a pay for work done system.
3. Allowances tied to responsibility: money conditional upon chores done.
4. Allowance with no strings: paid regularly without responsibilities.
5. Allowance with no strings: but supervised spending.

They also attempt to give good advice to parents about how to educate their children through allowances by following quite specific rules.

Godfrey (1994, 1996) sets out to help parents teach their children the value and uses of money. The author, a banker who founded a children's bank, suggests that a school-aged child should be told that they are a "Citizen of the Household" and 15% of his/her allowance should go into tax. They also need to give 10% to charity. Further, if they save they should be given interest on savings. Family meetings should discuss, openly and honestly, economic affairs. A written agenda and a log should be kept. Issues might include product testing the purchases of major items, vacation planning, charity and gift giving. It is also recommended that there is a pool of family money, called the family bank, and the family as a whole should discuss how it is administered and the money spent. Further, the family bank should have an explicitly stated credit policy: hence if a child borrows product money ahead of time they have, say, three weeks to pay it back … with interest.

As children get older their household jobs become harder and they should be taught that they have to be responsible for these jobs. The message to be given is that children, as citizens of the household, should volunteer to do chores and odd jobs. As children get older and they borrow, lend and trade, they can be taught the importance of verbal contracts, negotiation and the general rules of trading. Also, the family and community values on breakages, shoplifting, etc., need to be discussed along with consumer affairs. For instance, it is proposed that pre-adolescents are taught the following simple, but important, consumer concepts: get the best buy for the best price; make sure you know the store's policy; don't forget to keep receipts; shop during sales; know your rights. In the teenage years, the Citizens of the Household concept can be extended to other concepts, such as curfew. Further, they need to be taught good practice about credit cards, and budgeting, as well as starting a financial portfolio.

There are many books giving parents advice. There is overall agreement but some important differences. They are clear about what you should and should not do. Bodnar (1997), whose book is subtitled "Teach your kids sound values for wiser savings, earning, spending and investing", suggests 10 things *not* to teach your children:

1. Ignoring the whole topic: because of embarrassment, fear or ignorance not discussing money openly and honestly;
2. Indulging your children: for guilt or shame or any other problem;
3. Sending mixed messages: about saving and spending, waste and profligacy, research and impulsivity;
4. Being inconsistent: setting money rules and then breaking them;
5. Not setting up a system at all: instituting early rules;
6. Using verbal platitudes instead of practices: being cynical and sarcastic rather than giving good advice;
7. Failing to educate and listen: answering their questions, giving good answers;
8. Reliving your childhood: not understanding about the changes in the current cost of things;
9. Informational overload: the opposite of 1, by not understanding when, why and what to say;
10. Complaining about your job: making the world of work seem unpleasant or slavery.

Gallo and Gallo (2002) have written various books to help middle–class to millionaire parents raise financially responsible children. They note that most parents feel they want their children to be better financially educated than themselves but they are not sure precisely what to do. Their messages about how to become a financially intelligent parent are neither new nor counterintuitive but they are eminently sensible. Thus, they argue that parents need to be able to say **No** and **Enough** as important parts of money education. They note that financially clueless parents argue about or don't ever talk about finance generally. They recommend eight things to do:

1. Encourage the work ethic so that children become industrious and feel competent. The message should be **do** your best, rather than **being** best.
2. Be clear, open and consistent in your money stories and messages. Be sure not to make money issues a source of anxiety, argument or silence. Talk about how you acquired, use and manage money.
3. Encourage reflective thinking about money, which is concerned with thinking about alternatives, good choices and avoiding impulsivity. It can be modelled by talking about good and bad purchases; about alternative options in spending money; and whether those decisions should be made alone or after consultation.
4. Model gifting by becoming a charitable family. This helps children think about less fortunate others and one's need to help. It must involved overcoming inertia and developing a reward and recognition programme for others.
5. Teach financial literacy, which is about modelling and education through pocket money and allowance to make decisions, and saving, spending and general day-to-day money management. Teaching about jobs, investments and entrepreneurship is also encouraged.
6. Use money to support and reward your values. This involves distinguishing between money for self-worth vs. money for self-fulfilment. It should warn against excess, bragging and waste.
7. Moderate your extreme money tendencies, such as the usual money pathologies: shop till you drop; pay cash for everything; agonise over unbalanced accounts; fret about going to the "poorhouse"; rack up big debts and act as if money can buy love. If others say they find your money beliefs and behaviours irksome it may be time to do something.
8. Engage in difficult financial discussions by discussing with children how much money people in the family make, what things are worth, and what money is owed. It is suggested parents "share their struggles" and each tell their own money stories.

The idea is to integrate financial issues with all other aspects of parenting – to use everyday "money moments" to educate about money and life skills.

Bodnar (1997) in a long, practical, self-help book, with the subtitle "Teach your kids sound values for wiser saving, earning, spending and investing", offers simple but important tips. She specifies *golden rules for fending off fights*:

For richer or poorer, in good times and bad, it's possible for spouses to avoid, or at lease defuse many of the most common disputes about money by adding the following resolutions to your vows:

- *Talk about money openly and matter-of-factly:* Silence is not golden and could lead to unpleasant surprises later.
- *Settle the issue of joint versus separate checking accounts:* Either system will work if you both accept it. Or both of you could chip in to fund a third kitty for household expenses.
- *Designate which spouse will pay bills, balance the cheque-book and handle investments.* Whether you pool your money or keep separate accounts, someone has to do the financial housekeeping.
- *Know where your money is:* Even if your spouse is the numbers whiz, you can't afford to tune out. Touch base periodically so you know how much you owe on your credit cards and how much is in your retirement accounts.
- *Don't begrudge your spouse small indulgences.* Each of you should have some money to spend with no explanations needed.
- *Consult with each other on purchases of, say, $500.* That counts as a big indulgence and your partner deserves a say.
- Don't criticise your spouse about money in front of others. Talk openly, but talk privately.
- Coordinate your responses when your kids ask for something, so they don't play one parent against the other. If Mum says no, Dad says no.
- *Discuss your goals regularly, preferably at a time when you're not under the gun to solve a money problem.* Even when you keep separate accounts, you need to coordinate financial plans, if you hope to retire together. (p. 22)

Clearly the growth of these books is an indication of the importance of this issue to parents who want advice in how best to instil good monetary habits and understanding.

Just as there are numerous books for parents on how to bring up financially literate and educated children, so there are books for young people themselves. Self (2007) has written an engaging and useful book aimed at teenagers. Money he notes is not boring. There are some "simple but useful" maxims like:

- The only boring thing about money is not having enough of it.
- Having enough money has less to do with how much money you earn, and more with how you manage your money.
- People who don't manage their money work longer and harder, live somewhere "less nice" and have less to spend on things they want.
- The sooner you start managing your money, the richer you will be.
- Think of money as a friend; respect it and look after it.
- Have a long, medium and short-term money plan about earnings, savings, things to sell.
- Make sure you don't get ripped off by selling scams and learn about careful shopping.
- Get to grips with relevant money concepts like percentages, simple and compound interest, inflation, capital and income as well as gearing.
- Get to grips with banking terminology and issues like standing orders, direct debits, debit cards, overdraft facilities, online and phone banking.
- Plastic is not fantastic: have a debit card not a credit card. And beware of store cards that are often not good value.
- Shop around when borrowing and remember: when you borrow you are giving away.
- Find out how tax works and know the difference between income tax, national insurance, value added tax, capital gains tax.
- Know your entitlements to state benefits.
- You can't avoid paying tax, but you can make sure you do not have to pay more than you have to.
- Borrowing has two costs: interest and lost opportunity to do something else with the money.
- If lenders believe you might take your loan/debt elsewhere they will often agree to a better deal.
- Learn about investments: how much to invest, how long to tie up your money.

Teaching economic theory

Parents, governments and educators are interested in teaching economic literacy. This is more than just teaching economic concepts like opportunity costs, marginal utility and marginal analysis (Salemi, 2005). It is well established that financial knowledge relates to how people invest their money (Wang, 2009).

There are many media shows and newspaper sections devoted to money management. Financial experts offer advice to help people develop better money habits. This is nearly always a two-stage process. One is about adopting sensible habits of investing, saving and spending. The second is about recognising the psychological factors that drive poor money decisions and habits. It is usually a matter of taste and expertise concerning which is covered most. Some researchers have examined how one might even teach primary and kindergarten students through the use of stories and their own literature (Rodgers, Hawthorne, & Wheeler, 2006).

Others have tested college students' actual literacy. Chen and Volpe (1998) tested students with the following examples of questions:

Your net worth is

a. the difference between your expenditures and income.
b. the difference between your liabilities and assets.
c. the difference between your cash inflow and outflow.
d. the difference between your bank borrowings and savings.

The returns from a balanced mutual fund include

a. interest earned on cash in the fund.
b. dividends from common stock in the fund.
c. interest earned on the bonds in the fund.
d. capital gains from stocks and bonds in the fund.
e. all of the above.

They found that the participants got just over half (53%) correct. Also non-business majors, females, those with lower socioeconomic status, those under 30 and those with little or no work experience did worst.

One Italian study asked whether there were sex differences in financial literacy and money attitudes. Rinaldi and Todesco (2012) tested 1,635 12- to 14-year-olds and found no sex differences in financial literacy but there were sex differences in money attitudes. Compared to girls, boys assigned the role of money in achieving happiness higher, were more pro-investment oriented and had higher self-confidence in managing their money.

One recent study of over 100 Korean adolescents attempted to determine which of various possible factors best predicted their financial literacy: father's education, monthly household income, their personal allowance, their main source of financial knowledge, or whether or not they possessed a bank account (Sohn, Joo, Grable, Lee & Kim, 2012).

However, the "money smarts" (or money style) test was a logical predictor in each of the significant regressions (Bodnar, 1997). This was a multiple choice "situational test" that required respondents to indicate how they would behave in a range of money related situations with their children. The test had clearly been devised as a self-assessment quiz but the results from this study showed both a normal distribution and a satisfactory internal reliability. It is quite clear that "Money-smart" parents care a lot about their children's knowledge and use of money. They seem to feel it is their duty to educate their children into the economic work and that one of the best ways of doing this is through discussion and modeling the behaviours that they want their children to follow.

Inevitably these parents are likely to be well educated and financially privileged though this may not necessarily have always been the case. Indeed there is anecdotal stories about very rich people who are either very strict or very lax with the financial education of their children. Some are very clear that it is very easy to spoil children which teaches them very little about the economic world and provides a very poor basis for independence and success in life.

Childhood-related money problems

It has been suggested by many therapists that money problems originate in childhood. Matthews (1991, pp. 227–228) provides a checklist that may help identify this:

1. Were your parents extremely secretive about money matters? Are you still in the dark regarding how much money your parents have (or had)?
2. Did your parents argue about money frequently?
3. Do you collude with any other family members to keep certain financial information from other members?
4. Do you believe you have "absorbed" a fear of poverty from your parents, though you've never been in real financial danger?
5. Do you feel like a fraud when you are in the company of your family, even if the rest of the world considers you a bona fide success?
6. Do you find yourself frequently complaining about financial mistreatment by a parent or sibling?
7. Is one of the siblings in your family the designated "success", while others seem unable to unwilling to succeed economically?
8. Do you sometimes conceptualise your financial actions (spending, saving, etc.) in terms of "being good" or "being bad"?
9. Do your parents use money to reward and punish you even now when you are an adult?
10. Do your parents send you money unexpectedly and expect certain prescribed gestures of affection in return?
11. Is it difficult for you to image outdoing your parents financially?
12. Do you frequently find yourself acting exactly the opposite way with money as your parents (e.g. do you spend flagrantly where they scrimp avidly)?
13. Was there any type of compulsive behaviour in your family of origin, e.g. alcoholism, drug use, overeating?
14. Was it "understood" in your family that money was a male domain?
15. Do you notice that money is used to communicate the same emotional messages in your marriage as it did in your family of origin?

The issue about money is that if parents appear to be "conflicted" by money their children sense it. Children and adolescents are highly sensitive to inconsistency and hypocrisy. They can see that their parents have unresolved issues or disagreements about money. They can detect when some issues always lead to heated arguments and are therefore best avoided. Openness about money is also related to ideology like religion which can complicate the issue even more.

Psychoanalysts point out that some children respond to parental messages by doing the precise opposite. One can find this with money: financially over-cautious parents spawn profligate and imprudent children. Other children attempt to outdo or exaggerate the financial behaviours of their parents. Some people appear completely indifferent to money and unworldly. A common theme running through their money attitudes is that they do not deserve it. Inevitably, those who believe they do not deserve a fair financial return for their labours will not receive it.

Yet, as well as early and later childhood experiences, inevitably cultural values and habits describe *and* prescribe money-related behaviour. Societal values dictate what is rich and what is poor; how money should be made; on what one's disposable income should be spent; who are monetary heroes and anti-heroes. Schools formally and informally socialise children into financial attitudes and habits. Equally, the media tends to reinforce culturally acceptable money values and habits, which naturally appear a little bizarre to cultured travellers. All societies also have their messages about money sacrificing, donations and gifts to others.

The following are money messages that adults reported getting from their parents:

- If I tell somebody how little I earn then they will view me differently.
- My friendships are threatened if I start earning a lot more or a lot less money.
- My father worried, but did not talk, about money the whole time.
- My mother cheered herself up by shopping.
- My parents insisted on having separate bank accounts.
- Nobody told me the real financial status of our family.
- I was often ashamed about how comparatively poor we were.
- Most fights between my parents involved money.
- Our family had lots of money secrets.
- I was shocked to find, later in life, my beliefs about our family's poverty/ wealth were completely wrong.
- My parents were more concerned about the places I worked rather than the money I earned.
- My father prided himself on being a "good provider" for his children.
- I was told my pocket money was a privilege not a right.
- My father gave gifts not to symbolize love but to provide substitutes for it.

Healthy, happy, economically knowledgeable parents beget children who (hope-fully) understand economic reality and act both responsibly and wisely when it comes to money. All parents make errors, but there are simple rules about bribery, inconsistency and secrecy that can help matters.

There are well known stages in thinking development when children are able to understand about specific money concepts (profit, budget, interest) and to acquire skills. Often they know more about where babies come from than how bank interest or the free-market work.

Adults, some in therapy for money-related problems, but also those with few money worries, easily recount messages they got from their parents. These may be implicit or explicit, but they remain powerful determinants of the adult's thinking and emotions around money.

Parents can do sensible things for themselves and their children. These include buying enough insurance, saving for their retirement and their children's education, making (and where appropriate revising) a will and enjoying their money. It is unwise to think of yourself as or behave as if you are an accountant, a social worker, a manager or a genie. Your job is simply to educate and model the behaviour that you want.

Poor little rich kids

There is no shortage of books written by therapists on the psychology of affluence and the problems it brings. Hausner (1990) proposed a nine-point plan to help parents raise what she called "The Children of Paradise" – namely children from prosperous families.

O'Neill (1999) notes that the "monied class" often find themselves in a "golden ghetto" where this select group are separated from the majority. Children in the golden ghetto get isolated and marginalised from most people in society. They can feel discriminated against by envious others with whom they feel uncomfortable. She argues that the idea that affluence is synonymous with happiness as a "persistent and pernicious cultural myth" (p. 50).

O'Neill believes that the psychological dysfunctions of affluence are: absentee, workaholic parents and distrust of others – and these can easily get passed on. Equally, sudden wealth (acquired through inheritance, lottery wins) can create a false sense of entitlement, a loss of motivation and increasing intolerance of frustration. Inheriting money can damage self-esteem, worth and confidence because the inheritors are not sure if they could have made it on their own or whether people treat them differently because of their money. They never know the answers to such questions as: "Did I succeed?" or "Did my money buy success?"; "Do they love me because of who I am?" or "because I am rich"; "Is he merely a gigolo after my money?" or "Is this true love?" Indeed, society is often highly ambivalent towards the wealthy – exhibiting wealthism, hence the idle rich. There is abundant evidence of anger, envy and resentment of the rich.

O'Neill argues that family wealth founders have a "never enough" mentality that can reflect addictive or compulsive elements. It is also often driven by a narcissistic need to be special.

Poor little rich kids – once made popular by the cartoon Richy Rich – often report "empty childhoods" with missing parents, a sense of lack of love and low self-esteem. Their special privileges can lead to social and emotional isolation from others their own age and hence difficulty interacting with them. This can lead to shame. More interaction with surrogate caretakers (tutors, nannies) means they often have problems with personal identity. They don't identify with their parents or pick up their values and beliefs. They can and do experience a sense of emotional abandonment or, worse, emotional incest where the parent gratifies their own unmet needs for emotional intimacy at the expense of the child's needs and emotional security.

Hence isolated and confused children are easily prone to anxiety and depression because of the void many feel by being deprived of parental attention, care and love. Also, according to O'Neill (1999), because affluent children experience so little "healthy frustration" and so few setbacks, as well as having most experiential and material desires fulfilled, they develop unrealistic expectations as well as a lack of personal accountability. This can lead to the "perennial child" syndrome. As a consequence they seem very poor at forming, maintaining and thriving in intimate relationships.

Financial disparity can lead to many relationship issues. The most well known and acceptable is rich men having trophy wives. It is more problematic for a woman who has great wealth. O'Neill argues that rich children feel guilt but particularly shame when they realise how many poor people there are. Their coping strategies are either to donate large sums to charity or "shut out" poor people from their lives who remind them of their wealth. Rich people do not understand the cause of their discontent and disconnect because of the myths surrounding money and hence they project or displace their feelings of anger, resentment and fear onto others, so jeopardising having healthy relationships, which reduces shame. "Strategies to hide wealth are often unconscious efforts to keep feelings of shame at bay" (p. 151). Money can be a tool of humiliation to both those who don't have it and those that do.

As a consequence O'Neill (1999) has various recommendations to help prevent rich children from developing full-blown Affluenza:

- Reduce the emphasis on externals (appearance, possessions, achievements) and make the home environment accepting, supportive and eager to reward uniqueness.
- Dismantle the false sense of entitlement. Children must not feel special, deserving and entitled to anything they want.
- Teach gratification delay and the ability to tolerate frustration. Impatience and demands for instant gratification need to be controlled. Children need to experience and know how to handle boredom, disappointment and failure.
- Diffuse affluent cultural and family expectations of getting ever richer, keeping the dynasty alive.
- Separate money and love. Money should never be a substitute for love and attention.

She calls it preventative medicine: immunising children from Affluenza and demystifying the wealth taboo. She offers a simple 12-point plan, including the following (1999, pp. 169–170):

1. Have close friends who are not wealthy; raise children where they make friends with a mix of people; encourage contact (e.g. through volunteering) across class lines.

2. Communicate with young adults about money issues such as resentment, envy, trust, being open about money or not, making loans and gifts, power differences, and dependence. Acknowledge that even a small trust fund makes their financial life quite different from peers who have no such cushion.

3. Teach children the ways that money and class can create difference between people (e.g. people will have different expectations of what their lives will be like) but that having wealth does not make people better or worse than others. Show them ways they can act out of concern for injustice, rather than guilt for their advantages.

8

SEX DIFFERENCES, MONEY AND THE FAMILY

Marriage is like a bank account. You put it in, you take it out, you lose interest.

Irwin Corey

Millionaires are marrying their secretaries because they are so busy making money they haven't time to see other girls.

Doris Lilly

Women prefer men who have something tender about them – especially legal tender.

Kay Ingram

Money speaks, but it speaks with a male voice.

Andrea Dworkin

Introduction

Are there sex differences in attitudes toward money? What is the role of money in families? How do spouses and partners "come to an arrangement" about their money? To what extent could one call some families healthy and adapted with respect to their money and others troubled and maladaptive?

There are often family issues to resolve like: who makes the money outside the home and who does the domestic work? Who controls the money and the expenditure? How is money used on the extended family? How does one make decisions about inheritance?

This area of research is mainly the work of sociologists, who have taken great interest in marriage, the family and how things have changed over time.

Psychologists have also been interested in the pathological nature of some money beliefs and behaviours that originate in family dynamics.

It has been shown that many deep-seated money beliefs and behaviours can be traced to early socialisation in the family. Families develop explicit and implicit norms and behaviours with respect to money: who controls it; when and how it is talked about; how it is distributed and spent. There are all sorts of patterns of income control and expenditure (Pahl, 1995). Sometimes the husband or wife manages all family finances, giving the other partner some allowance. In some families, expenditure decisions about certain issues (finance, transportation, holidays) are done by one partner though the other has the financial control. Education, social class, and personal values dictate which system people adopt and when and how they change over time.

Many families develop a domestic economy where "jobs" are distributed, often according to gender stereotypes. Partners often develop an equity or exchange theory concept where they come to agree a fair exchange of money or activities. Yet, disagreeing over money is a common and chronic source of marital conflict for many couples (Furnham & Argyle, 1998).

Money and time spent on children has always been an important issue. For some Third World countries children are seen as an investment, a pension, or a source of support in old age. The issue of money in the extended family is an important one. Some people work unpaid on the family business. Grandparents do childcare and other relatives "help out". Some expect monetary rewards or to be left money in a will. Inheritance is a big issue in families. It is now much more about the transfer of property rather than titles. This chapter will examine how couples deal with money, money in families and the "hot topic" of sex differences with respect to money.

Money in couples

Different couples often have very different money beliefs, behaviours and "arrangements". Some maintain separate bank accounts, others only have shared accounts; still others have both. Some argue a great deal over money, others do so very seldom. Because of the taboo nature of money, couples often experience surprise at the beliefs and preferences of their partner. While it may be that people assortatively mate with respect to physical attractiveness, education and occupation, it does not seem to be the case with respect to money. Thus, misers marry spendthrifts, and the money carefree marry the money troubled. Indeed it may be that opposites attract: spenders are attracted to savers (but not necessarily vice versa). When over-spending spendthrifts marry under-spending tightwads one may expect sparks. Divorce lawyers say that money differences are often a cause of marital problems as well as a powerful weapon with which to beat each other up as part of the divorce settlement.

Vogler, Lyonette and Wiggins (2008) looked at different couple management systems: where either the male or the female managed all the money; where they pool money and jointly manage; where there is a partial pooling (to pay for collective expenditure); and where there are completely independent management systems. Interestingly, they found that when either men or women made autonomous spending decisions, both were less satisfied with family life, indeed life in general.

Some have, to outsiders, very odd arrangements whereby the one "pays" the other a stipend or allowance. The issues are about whom, how, when, and why people in couples generate, manage and control money. This is in part a function of whether people live in a nuclear versus a blended family. Shapiro (2007), a couple therapist, has argued that discussing money openly is crucially important for all couples and that it is an indicator of acceptance, adequacy, acknowledgement, commitment, competence and security.

To some extent money arrangements are a function of whether couples are "moderns" (both earn to save), "innovators" (wives earn more than husbands) or "conventionals" (husbands earn more than wives) (Izraeli, 1994).

There are different "explanations" for the way couples do money management (Yodanis & Lauer, 2007): it depends who generates/makes the money; the overall family income; the gender ideology in the couple; the relationship characteristics (co-habiting, married, previously married); the cultural/societal practices. The control over money is an indication of power as well as hard work. Usually the more equal the resource contribution, the more shared the management strategies.

In a study focusing on money, power, praise, and criticism, and what they called "the economy of gratitude", Deutsch, Roksa and Meeska (2003) provided empirical evidence to conclude thus:

Gender certainly still counts when people count their money. First, men and women feel differently about the money they earn. Second, women are praised more than men for earning money, although on average they earn less money than men do. Third, women feel more appreciation from husbands for earning income than husbands feel from wives. Fourth, men's and women's absolute and relative incomes affect the economy of gratitude differently. Finally, the relation between income earned and parenting doesn't work the same way for men and women.

Men have stronger negative and stronger positive feelings about their incomes than women do. It is not surprising that men feel more positively about the money they earn because they do earn more than women. However, if money were gender neutral, we would expect that women would be more embarrassed about their incomes, given that they earn less than men. That's not the case. The link between masculinity and money seems to leave men more vulnerable to feelings of embarrassment than women are. (p. 301)

There is plenty of empirical and anecdotal evidence that money is among the major sources of marital (and relationship) arguments. People in relationships often have different financial management strategies and beliefs about how to allocate resources within the household. Arguments occur over children, chores and money given to children as well as gift giving. One study found that the wife's income (resource availability), followed by children in the home, followed by the differences in age and income (i.e. power) between husband and wife were the stronger predictors of money arguments (Britt, Huston & Durband, 2010).

Spouses differ in their gifting preferences as well as appetite for financial risk. Further, when resources are low, conflict tends to be high. In other words couple net worth is a powerful correlate of conflict, as is the general financial debt situation. The higher the constraints on the household finances, the more arguments tend to occur. The data show that couples who keep records, and discuss and share goals argue less. One study found that spouses did not rate money as the most frequent source of marital conflict in the home; however, compared to non-money issues, marital conflicts about money were more pervasive, problematic, recurrent and unsolved (Papp, Cummings & Goeke-Morey, 2009). Papp et al. noted:

> We found that couples attempting to resolve money conflicts may be particularly likely to face a self-defeating cycle, in which they explicitly attempt to problem solve, yet experience greater negativity and use of non-productive tactics as important and threatening money issues resurface (e.g. monthly bills) and remain unsolved. Although other relationship issues may recur (e.g. chores), it may be easier for couples to agree to disagree or avoid matters that do not incur external consequences such as steeper financial penalties. Another possibility is that money is more closely tied to underlying relational processes, such as power, touching many aspects of individual and couple functioning or feelings of self-worth or self-esteem, perhaps especially for men. Additional research is needed to disentangle the meaning of money conflicts for couple relationships and broader family wellbeing. (p. 100)

In a recent economic study Britt et al. (2010) distinguished between the time/ effort spent arguing and the topic of those arguments. They found that being a money arguing couple is more a function of communication than either the resources available or the power distribution (who earns the most). It's more about communication patterns than money per se. Later they found that while money arguments in marriage are an important indicator of relationship satisfaction, they do not predict divorce (Britt & Huston, 2012).

Family dynamics are in part revealed by how finances are dealt with. Child and adolescent psychiatrists see a family's financial planning, values and history as a "window on understanding family myths and dynamics" (Jellinek & Berenson, 2008, p. 250).

Money and families

Many commentators have noted that "children are getting younger", especially in the economic sense. They have a lot more money than their parents did at their age and are hence much more active in the market place. Hence parents are becoming more concerned about helping their children with their financial decisions and management.

Lewis (2001) commented on the Nestlé sponsored research into *Money in the Contemporary Family*. It was an in-depth study of over 650 British parents carefully selected to represent all the social classes. The researchers found that 43% taught their children very little about money but that these were primarily older and lower social class parents. Yet the data revealed that modern parents are better at teaching their children than they believe their parents taught them. Thus 35% said that they were taught a fair amount about money, but 55% said that they taught a fair amount about money. Inevitably this could be misreporting through memory distortion, dissimilation or attempts to present themselves in a very positive light.

They were asked, "What, if any, of the following do or did you do for your children?" The following were in the top ten mentioned:

Piggy bank	62%
Pocket money	58%
Encourage to set up bank account	46%
Money games	46%
Short-term savings	37%
Discuss money matters	37%
Play Monopoly	36%
Encourage shopping around	32%
Pay for chores	29%
Encourage long-term savings	26%

Economic socialisation in the home appears to be much less common among parents from social grades D&E (semi and unskilled) or with lower household incomes. Piggy banks are still a particular favourite of those from the A&B (professional and semi-professional) groups. Involving children in household accounts was rare (9% of parents overall), but those from the AB social groupings are more likely to involve their children in this activity (21%).

Only one third (34%) of Ds and Es in this representative sample give their children pocket money. Interestingly three in ten parents paid their children regularly for doing household chores, which rises to more than two fifths among parents from C2 households.

Parents were asked what they thought schools should be teaching children. More than half of parents stated that eight of the 11 alternatives provided should be taught to their children at school. Careers (81%); managing personal finances (67%); managing household finances (59%); understanding the use of credit and debit cards (58%); and lessons on how a bank operates (57%) proved the most popular. Majorities also favoured practical lessons, for example, opening a bank account (54%), understanding borrowing and interest rates (52%) and understanding the economy as a whole (51%). Also, one fifth or more of parents endorsed the teaching of banking (31%), purchasing (25%) and borrowing (22%) over the Internet.

The eagerness for schools to become involved in the teaching of financial matters was generally more likely among ABCs than among C2, Ds and Es. Schooling in managing finances (73%), lessons about how a bank operates (62%) and lessons on such things as how to open an account (59%) were found to be more popular among parents who claimed that they had no credit card debt. Thus, it seems that those who had been more financially successful were more eager to have this taught to their children.

Parents were asked when they believed their eldest daughter or son would become financially independent and when the respondents themselves became financially independent from their families. The average predicted age of financial independence for daughters was 19.4 years, rising to 20.7 years for those from an AB background and to 20.5 years for respondents who had themselves been through higher education. For sons, the average predicted age for financial independence was 19.3 years. The predicted age is found to be higher among ABC1s and for parents who currently have a son in higher education. Parents say they became financially independent at an earlier age than predicted for their sons or daughters (18.2).

Ideally it would be most advantageous to have this sort of data collected over time and across regions and countries so that one could trace changes in parents' beliefs and practices with respect to their children. Researchers on topics like childhood health are equally interested in acquiring this longitudinal and comparative data to try to understand life trajectories.

Money is certainly a hot issue in families. There may be a dark, pathological side to money in families as well. It is an umbilical cord for young people who struggle for separation from their parents. Children can learn to use money both to rebel and to exact retribution. Parents in turn can use money to both reject and hold on to their children. Families can have money secrets.

Newcomb and Rabow (1999) assessed the familial experiences of 605 students in relation to money, and considered their current beliefs and attitudes towards money. The authors concluded that parents have differing practices and expectations for children of different genders with regard to their future earnings. For instance, sons more than daughters communicated that their parents expected them to know how to save their earnings. Sons were found to be engaged in monetary discussions earlier than females, and highlighted that they received less financial support than their female counterparts did. Consequently, males and females differed in their evaluations of money in relation to themselves and others, with males valuing it more positively than females. Men perceived those who earned money as being rational and responsible, with money making them feel happy and in control, whereas women had more conflicting, negative thoughts towards money. Women were more fearful of finances and did not have a clear awareness of investing options. Such detailed research confirms the belief that differing socialisation is experienced in males' and females' childhoods. Differing training with regard to money results in differing beliefs with regard to money in later life, in respect to aspects such as the self, others, and finances. Danes and Haberman (2007) recently confirmed such suggestions. The authors found many differences in socialisation between genders, including that female teens received more money from their parents than did males, with males spending and saving more money.

Interestingly, it is not only parents who treat male and female children differently with respect to their monetary education. Hira and Lobil (2006) investigated the roots of adults' financial support in their childhoods. The report concluded that males were the recipients of more assistance and advice from teachers and other adults regarding their money management and investment decisions. Furthermore, female children have been found to receive more money management advice from their mothers, where males' main source of information was reported as being from their fathers.

Madares (1994) gave advice as to what parents can do for their children. She argued that parents reward (and punish) their children with money, power, love and recognition. At school they can gain recognition, power and love, but not usually money. "The meaning of money and how to obtain it is taught in the family ... In our families, children learn to save, negotiate for money, work for money, be stingy and be generous ... we can use money to elevate or patronise a child" (p. 43). Parents' gifts, she argues, can create artificial needs in children; gifts given and taken away can become very emotionally charged. Indeed, relationships can be commoditised by the exchange of money or goods.

An important issue is the quality and quantity of strings attached in the business of giving. The anxious, over-indulgent parent who abhors the possibility that their child may in any way be deprived gives everything children need (and want). They make it difficult for their children to become independent from their parents. Others do the opposite but this can make children feel neglected, unloved and insecure with (paradoxically) the same result – difficulty in separating from parents.

This leads to the problem of motivation – the *real* motivation of giving. The parent giver and child receiver may have very different interpretations about the reason for the gift. Parents give money because of their obligations, but also through love (generosity), guilt, or for favours (companionship, chores). Parents have the power to give or withhold. Children, argues Madares (1994), need to develop a power-base. This could be based on achievements, or love.

There is often a *quid pro quo* or *tit for tat* subtext with regard to money in families. If a child believes parents give out of guilt not generosity they may feel resentful. Some children learn the dark arts of extortion from guilt-ridden parents. Part of the problem lies in what is, and is not, negotiable. What is given by right, by obligation, and what as part of exchange? Is pocket money a right or a privilege?

Children, argues Madares (1994), correctly need to be clear about:

> • What belongs to the whole family and thus cannot be withheld as punishment.
> • What really belongs to the parents but can be used and enjoyed by everyone if they follow certain rules or achieve certain targets.
> • What belongs to the child and cannot be taken away for punishment.

So the television belongs to the whole family, though toys belong to the child. Doing badly at school many mean less or no television viewing but it does not mean removals of prizes, toys or expulsion from one's room or indeed the whole family.

Next there is the issue of family accounting: that is, the implicit rules of fairness of giving and receiving in families. The problem of family accounting is that accounts are never really audited and never really closed. Indeed, they can be passed on from one generation to the next. There is no open, tangible, book keeping in most families. So it is probably healthy to make explicit the rules by which money is distributed. Is money given out of entitlement, or love, or obedience, or respect, or sporting/academic success? Families might have an annual finance day where all financial issues are discussed and plans are made. It must be made clear who has decision power in financial matters. There must be time lines. At a certain time accounts are closed and not revisited. The whole matter is at an end.

Certainly, studies of "money troubled" adults show clearly that the heart rules them more than the head when it comes to their money. Indeed, many of their troubles originated from "lessons" learnt as a child about money. The family is the primary socialisation unit. Teaching economic literacy, good money management and sensible saving and spending should be a parental priority.

Wealth in families

Collier (2006) also wrote a book called *Wealth in Families* to help families talk and think about their wealth and its effects. He suggests asking a few questions such as:

- What are your family's true assets?
- How wealthy do you want your children to be?
- Do you feel you have responsibility to society?
- Can your family make just decisions around money, philanthropy and legacy?

Substantial wealth, whether it is inherited or made, often transforms wealth holders. It can give a sense of empowerment and freedom but it also brings burdens. For wealthy parents the question is always how to provide financial security for all their children while ensuring that they achieve their potential: how to use money to help rather than hinder. The issue is how much they **should** receive not how much they **could** receive.

There is no simple answer to the question of **how much** is an appropriate financial inheritance. A round million or more? A percentage of one's wealth? Should it be left in complex, legally binding networks of trusts and foundations to attempt to ensure that the wealth is passed to succeeding generations? Then the question is **when** to transfer a substantial inheritance to one's heirs: sooner versus later; at some birthday; or with strings attached?

There is also the issue of **what form** the inheritance should take: a trust with careful strings attached? That will restrict their freedom to take risks, to make mistakes and actually to learn about money.

Last, there is the issue of how much to **tell** children. Should the issue be a secret or discussed openly and honestly with all family stakeholders?

Collier (2006) introduces the idea of **financial parenting**. It is financial education to preserve family wealth. There are some simple principles: set a good example; provide consistent guidance; allow children to make mistakes; use mentors. Further, he provides "age-appropriate" recommendations of what to do.

Rich and poor fathers

The whole area of economic socialisation was electrified by a book published a decade ago. Kiyosaki (1997), who likes to be known as a person "who teaches people to become millionaires", wrote a best seller called *Rich Dad, Poor Dad*. It pushes the message of teaching financial literacy very heavily. It is also heavily autobiographic.

The Poor Dad in the story is based on Kiyosaki's highly educated real father, who was the head of the education department in the state of Hawaii. Late in his career the father took a stand on principle against the governor of Hawaii. This led directly to this Poor Dad losing his job, and his inability to find comparable work ever again. Because he had never learned to handle money, he fell into debt.

In contrast to this character is Rich Dad, who is the father of Kiyosaki's best friend. He dropped out of school but became a self-made multi-millionaire regardless of his poor start in life. The Rich Dad insisted that the boys learn to make money work for them to avoid spending their whole lives working for money.

The author argues that the rich think differently in how they define simple words like assets and wealth, and how they fund their luxuries. He defines an asset as any item which produces income (such as rental property, stocks or bonds) and a liability as anything that produces expense (such as one's own home, new widescreen TV, exercise machine, new garden tractor, motorcycle, computers, processed foods, swing sets, barbeque grill, tools, letting your property run down and a new car every two years).

He further argues that the poor buy worthless items that they think are assets, which do not earn anything and may have no market value. He notes that wealth is measured as the number of days the income from your assets will sustain you, and financial independence is achieved when your monthly income from assets exceeds your monthly expenses. He gives various tips (i.e. choose friends carefully, pay yourself first, etc.).

The book makes various interesting and challengeable assumptions. It defines things as assets only if they generate cash flow. The rich acquire them. It argues that rich people work to learn things that make money over and over again. It is an argument for knowledge – working not labouring. There are strong arguments to create intellectual property and then market it. It also has a puritan streak because it argues that rich people are more likely to be frugal than spendthrift.

Kiyosaki (1997) argues that rich people pay off their debts and then start investing in assets that generate revenue. Like all successful and popular books, Kiyosaki's has its critics and detractors. What is important, however, is the interest caused in economic socialisation. The idea is that the "financial philosophies" of parents have a direct and dramatic impact on the economic behaviour and success of their children. Inevitably this has fuelled an interest in the teaching of sound economic principles in both the school and the home.

Because of the massive popularity of the book, a whole series of spin-offs occurred. Naturally it attracted attention and criticism. Criticisms include that the book is full of exaggerations and fabrications. Some point out that it gives almost no useful concrete advice while others lament the quality of advice that it gives as well as the fact that it seems to downplay the importance of formal education. Critics have argued that the tax dodges are little more than tax delays and that Kiyosaki misrepresents the (American) tax system.

Nevertheless, the central message has been heard very clearly. The book has sold in its millions all over the world, probably more to those who want to become rich themselves rather than to those who want to educate their children more successfully.

Parental socialisation

There is also an empirical literature on this topic. Parents are known to shape the money or saving attitudes of their children (Clarke, Heaton, Israelsen, & Eggett, 2005; Hilgert, Hogarth & Beverley, 2003), attitudes toward credit (Norvilitis et al., 2006) and gathering of financial information (Lyons, Scherpf & Roberts, 2006). Lyons et al. (2006) confirm the influence of parents on their children's monetary behaviour and attitude, with a study finding that 77% of high school and college students had requested financial information from their parents. Pinto, Parente and Mansfield (2005) demonstrate how influential parents are on their children's monetary behaviours, finding a significant negative relationship between amount of information learned from parents and credit use; the more information provided by parents regarding credit, the lower outstanding balance carried by students with credit cards.

The impact of the family on knowledge regarding money and views towards money seem to decline with age (Churchill & Moschis, 1979). The authors found that family communication regarding purchasing behaviours declines with age, whereas discussion with friends increases over time. Thus, parental influence with regard to spending decreases through life and peer influence increases.

Despite how influential parents have been found to be in shaping their children's money attitudes, contradictory research has found those in Western cultures to be reluctant to discuss finances with their children due to how taboo the topic is. For instance, Danes (1994) found that parents considered the discussion of some financial issues off limits regardless of the child's age – including revealing family income, and disclosing family debt. Despite how reluctant many parents are toward discussing financial matters with their children, they have a large influence over the ways their children are socialised into society (Bandura, 1989).

Financial socialisation refers to the learning of knowledge about money and managing finances, as well as developing skills including banking, budgeting and saving (Bowen, 2002). Parents have been found to be a key source of children's monetary socialisation, through observation of their parents' practices and by including children in financial practices (Beutler & Dickson, 2008; Pinto et al., 2005). So, although parents may not explicitly discuss financial issues, children learn from their parents through observation. Beutler and Dickson (2008) highlight the importance of financial socialisation, proposing that the failure to adequately socialise young people for later financial roles is costly to both society and the individual personally.

Despite the proposition that many families are uncomfortable about discussing monetary matters, opposing research suggests that parents have a direct influence on their children's financial values through direct teaching, reinforcement and purposive modelling (Moschis, 1985). A recent study by Solheim et al. (2011) concluded that there are multiple pathways through which families influence a child's financial attitudes and behaviours, including parental "coaching" – "emphasising the importance of sound money practices as well as instilling a sense of responsibility for effectively managing financial resources" (p. 108) – as well as observations of parents' saving and management of money. This suggests that children's money habits are in fact influenced by both the discussion of monetary behaviours (despite the highlighted stigma attached to this) and through observing parents' actions and choices.

Sex differences in money grams

The idea of money grams is the idea that parents give frequent, short and urgent messages to their children about money. These are not always intentional. Children notice how and when their parents talk about money, discussions about how much to spend on certain goods, as well as their approval and disapproval about how others spend money. They are particularly sensitive to conflicting messages sent by different parents: the strict mother and the indulgent father; the saver and the spender; the parent happy to discuss any aspect of money and the parent who finds the whole issue difficult and embarrassing.

Table 8.1 Money grams

Statement	Yes (%)	No (%)
20. Do you think about your finances all the time?	23	77
4. Do you lie awake at night trying to figure out a way to spend less money and save more, even though you are already saving money?	18	82
1. Do you find yourself worrying about the spending, using, or giving money at all times?	38	62
16. Are you increasingly anxious about whether you can pay your bills each month?	15	85
9. Are you constantly puzzled about where your money goes or why there is none left at the end of each month?	27	73
17. Do you spend money on others but have problems spending it on yourself?	36	64
15. When you ask for money, are you flooded with guilt or anxiety?	32	69
2. Are you inhibited about talking to others about money, particularly about your income?	35	65
14. Do you spend a large proportion of your free time shopping?	14	86
3. Do you buy things you don't really need because they are great bargains?	43	57
18. Do you buy things when you feel anxious, bored, upset, depressed, or angry?	27	73
19. Are you reluctant to learn about practical money matters?	11	89
11. Do you refuse to take money seriously?	14	86
13. Do you often gamble and spend large sums on bets?	3	97
10. Do you use money to control or manipulate others?	5	95
6. Do you regularly exceed the spending limit on your credit cards?	9	91
7. Does gambling make you feel a burst of excitement?	16	84
8. Would you walk blocks out of your way to save a bus fare you could easily afford?	38	62
5. Do you hold on to or hoard your money?	24	76
12. Do you resent having to pay the full price for any item when you shop?	37	63

Source: Forman (1987)

In most cultures women have had much less opportunity than men to handle significant sums of money. Pocket money and allowances are negotiated with the father by boys, though girls may be encouraged to charm their fathers into opening their wallets. Hence some girls come to believe that financial wheeling and dealing is a masculine activity and shun all money matters for fear that it renders them somehow less feminine. On the other hand, if boys equate having, spending and "flashing" money with masculinity they can feel very inadequate in the company of others with money, or overspend that which they don't have as a means of making a statement about their "male assets". These sex differences, however, may be on the decline.

Gresham and Fontenot (1989) found sex differences in: (1) using money to influence and impress; (2) nervousness about spending money; and (3) purchasing quality products as a predominant behaviour. The study suggests that women are more anxious about money than are males, and tend to be more interested in the quality of the products they are purchasing than their male counterparts, supporting much previous literature. Yet, interestingly, females were found to use money as a tool in power struggles more so than males, contradicting previous research. Gender differences have been established in boys' and girls' spending habits, and in what they choose to spend their money on (Brusdal, 2004; Wilska, 2005). Studies looking into these differences suggest that males consume products related to physical activities, such as sports, whereas girls consume products related to using their bodies for fashion and style (Drotner, 1991).

There is evidence that some parental economic training "backfires" as the psychoanalysts would predict. That is, that parental training designed to bring about a very specific outcome (being a cautious saver) leads the child to react to parental concerns and forcefulness by doing the exact opposite.

There is also the conundrum of different children in the same family having very different attitudes to money. This may be due to the different personalities of the children, parental changes in childrearing or that children are highly influenced by their peers. Thus, it is possible to have spenders and savers in the same family as well as those who are very concerned about money while others appear strikingly carefree about how they deal with their money.

Money pathology in men and women

Do men place more importance on money than women? Furnham (1998) considered the differing attitudes that males and females have toward money and concluded that females regarded money as being of less importance than did males.

Sabri, Hayhoe, and Goh (2006) researched the area further, again discovering differing monetary attitudes between males and females. The authors concluded that males and females differ in their attitudes towards money with regard to obsession and power. Males were more likely to demonstrate obsessive and power attitudes towards money than females. These findings are supported by Lim and Teo (1997), who also found that men are more likely than women to associate money with being a source of power, and felt more anxiously about their finances. The differing importance that the genders place on their money can be demonstrated, with Zuo (1997) finding that males prefer to earn more than their wives, and not to rely on their wives' incomes.

Despite men being found to place greater emphasis on money, women have been shown to have more of an emotional relationship with money (Gresham & Fontenot, 1989). Money pathologies can result from emotional attachment to money, leading to impulsive buying, compulsive spending and inability to demonstrate financial self-control (Verplanken & Herabadi, 2001). Women have been shown to be more associated with money pathologies than are men, with

Furnham and Okamura (1999) finding that females are more prone to compulsive spending, for instance.

There are varying explanations for women's propensity towards money pathologies – a current suggestion being the influence of the menstrual cycle. Much research highlights the fact that females are found to be more rational post-ovulation, and to act more impulsively, demonstrating anxiety and irritability, during pre-menstrual phases (Baca García, Díaz Sastre, de Leon, & Saiz Ruiz, 2000).

Interestingly, Hanashiro, Masuo, Kim and Malroutu (2004) found that women spend more money when they are frustrated. Pine and Fletcher (2011) investigated the relationship between the menstrual cycle and spending, concluding that impulsive spending was significantly different across menstrual phases. Spending was found to be less controlled and more excessive for women further through their cycle in the urethral phase. The authors associate this finding with women also reporting mood swings, increased irritability, impaired memory and concentration at this time in their menstrual cycle. Such experiences led to women spending more money than intended, as well as more regularly spending money that was unplanned and on impulse. Almost two thirds of women in the sample in the luteal phase had made a purchase on impulse.

It may be suggested that such impulsive spending is not detrimental (Wood, 2005), and does in fact form part of normal behaviour. However, when considering the women in Pine and Fletcher's (2011) study, 57% had spent over £25 more than they had needed to, with 28% of these buyers later feeling remorseful about this.

Studies investigating spending habits have suggested that males choose to spend their money on different items. Drotner (1991) investigated differences in purchases between the sexes, and concluded that males are more likely to consume products related to physical activities and sport, whereas girls prefer to purchase items used to enhance their image.

Women are generally considered to enjoy shopping more than males. This stereotype has been empirically tested and proven by Dittmar and Drury (2000) who found that women attach more significance to shopping than males do. One reasoning behind this is that females are found to relate their sense of self more closely with shopping than males do.

Do women have a special, unique and particularly problematic relationship with money? Ealy and Lesh (1998) believe they do and started running workshops for women to look at their money issues. Their aim was to confront two fundamental fallacies: money defines you and is part of your self-worth; and money earned should and does powerfully affect relationships.

They quoted various studies and surveys, which, for instance, showed:

- Young (American) women fear money more than learning about handling it later, they work less and receive more financial support from their parents than their male counterparts.
- Only 11% of women vs. 25% of men in a nationwide poll were rated as "very knowledgeable" concerning their investments.

- Women worry more (29% vs. 17%) about money and differently – men worry more about losing face, and paying the mortgage, while women worry about day-to-day issues.
- Women work fewer years and are less well paid than men. Hence they accumulate less and have less retirement provision.

Ealy and Lesh begin their workshop in the familiar money messages way, asking about parental beliefs and behaviours with respect to money. They also enquire into the cultural, religious and education-based messages the participants received.

They believe that (Western) society sends two strong and contradictory messages to women:

1. Women don't have to bother learning about how to manage money because their/a man will gladly and competently take care of all that. This leads women into never asking for a fair salary, never learning about investments and being uncomfortable talking about money.
2. Possession of wealth comes only at a very high price: true happiness does not come from money, and interest in money will exact a painfully high price in terms of relationships and personal security.

They believe that women assume a dependent relationship with money when they approach all money dealings from one or all three basic beliefs: I should not have to; I do not want to; I cannot. All lead to a sense of helplessness and powerlessness. Further, beliefs about dependency become self-fulfilling, hence the importance of education and empowerment to reduce the feelings of anxiety. Related to this is the fear of success; the "meek is better" message that it is unfeminine and unladylike to be powerful *and* economically successful. This leads to a failure to achieve potential, and lowered self-esteem and self-confidence.

Ealy and Lesh (1998) also talk about sneaky but persuasive fears such as "money = security". This, they argue, leads to the belief that any relationship is better than no relationship. This belief may be rooted in family history. They also may stay in unhealthy, poorly paid and deeply unsatisfying working situations for the same reason. It is the fear of dependency, homelessness, and being a burden that leads some women to stay in bad relationships, bad jobs, and bad families because they believe their only security comes from the money they receive by staying where they are.

For women, money can also be an addiction or a treadmill to nowhere. It has a drug-like quality for various reasons: people spend an inordinate amount of time thinking about how to obtain it, so much so that we neglect ourselves and our relationships in the process. Further, we compromise ourselves in getting it.

Women may be particularly prone to **compulsive** or **emotional spending** that is used to comfort, vent feelings, even "feel more alive". Shopping sprees may be a way to get back at an unresponsive partner or parent. It may be an unacknowledged manifestation of anger, fear or hurt. Say it with spending not flowers. For some women compulsive spending is very simply a substitute for a direct, honest, explicit expression of anger. Yet it keeps the spender unbalanced and diverts the focus of energy from even greater unhealthy behaviour.

The opposite of compulsive spending is **guilty spending**, which is rooted in the mentality of scarcity. It is "not enough theory", where women can spend money (quite happily) on others but not themselves. It is based on faulty assumptions like, "I only have value when I give to others or put myself last".

Money can also facilitate the avoidance of intimacy. People are never ready for a relationship until they have made enough money, or else they substitute money for intimacy but believe it is a bad bargain.

Ealy and Lesh (1998) argue that women also get unhelpful messages about money from financial institutions. Women do not take sufficient control of their finances. Ignorance leads to fear which leads to paralysis. Avoidance behaviours are aimed to spare women from making scary decisions and taking risks. The recommendations are clear and self-evident:

- Rewrite the "can't, don't, shouldn't" money message
- Redefine your relationship with money by
  - Taking the (negative) emotion out of the issue
  - Working to understand money
- Resolve to take charge of your money life now.

After becoming more self-aware and empowered with respect to money it is easier to make better decisions: how and when to save it or give it away; how to charge for work; and how much to pay others. "Staying clear with yourself about your motivations for charitable giving, about pricing your work, and honouring other women's work will move you toward a more positive relationship with money" (p. 132).

The workplace is often a source of money issues. Women may prefer a better work–life balance than men; women may trade off extrinsic for intrinsic rewards more than men. Finding "joyful" work and co-workers they like and respect are important, as is work that bolsters self-esteem.

Finally, Ealy and Lesh (1998) point out how important it is for women to teach their daughters about money to ensure they get messages about empowerment, courage and capability as opposed to fear, inability and disempowerment. The idea is to give girls the tools (early on) to make money knowledge (and comfort) an integral part of their lives; to encourage saving wisely, awareness of career options and understanding of how money can and should operate healthily in relationships.

Conclusions

Tolstoy famously noted that, "All happy families are alike; each unhappy family is unhappy in its own way". He may have been right with regard to money. Children can grow up in a money healthy and happy home where money is not a taboo topic or a source of argument and tension among parents or children. People from all cultures and with very different amounts of money "have issues" with their and their family's money. Cultural, religious and value differences often influence how boys and girls are treated differently with regard to how they are expected to acquire, store, and share their money.

9

MONEY MADNESS

Money and mental health

We can tell our values by looking at out chequebook stubs.
Gloria Steinem

Money, like vodka, turns one into an eccentric.
Anton Chekhov

Where money talks, there are few interruptions.
Herbert Prochnow

When you've got them by their wallets, their hearts and minds will soon follow.
Fern Naito

Introduction

Many philosophers, journalists and playwrights have written about the irrational, immoral and bizarre things that people do with, and for, money. Newspapers, magazines and television programmes frequently focus on compulsive savers and hoarders (who live in poverty but die with literally millions in the bank) or impulsive spenders (who utterly recklessly "get rid of" fortunes often obtained unexpectedly). The former are compelled to save money with the same urgency and vengeance that the latter seem driven to gamble with it (see Chapter 2 on millionaires).

Robbery, forgery, embezzlement, kidnapping, smuggling and product-faking are all quite simply money motivated. Money, indeed, does make the world go round. There is no obvious biological drive to amass wealth and get rich, yet the "purposeless drive" appears to be one of the most powerful known to man. Money is both intoxicating and inflaming, and the fairy-tale dream of acquiring great riches appears to have affected all cultures for all time (see the tool and drug theory).

Journalists, like clinicians, are fascinated by fairly regularly occurring cases where otherwise normal people behave completely irrationally with respect to money. Typical cases are people who spend money they know they don't actually have; or those who scrimp and save, leading chronically deprived lifestyles when they do not have to. Incredible arguments and acrimony over money can strain and break friendships and marriages, and cause very long-lasting family feuds. Money clearly represents different things to different people, and it can have tremendous psychological power.

Money is frequently discussed socially – tax rates, cost of living, price of property – but remains a taboo topic. Celebrities and even "ordinary mortals" seem happier to talk about their sex lives and mental illnesses long before their monetary status, salary or frequent financial transactions. Secrets about money matters are not surprising in our society but this is not so in all cultures. In the openly materialistic cultures of South East Asia, enquiries into others' and open discussion of one's own financial affairs seems quite acceptable. It is often denied, overlooked or ignored in courtship and argued about constantly during marriage, and is the focus of many divorce proceedings. Contested wills between different claimants can turn mild-mannered, reasonable human beings into irrational bigots.

There are all sorts of reasons why money remains a taboo subject. Various theories have been put forward to explain this:

- Rich people, who dictate etiquette, eschew discussing their money lest the poor figure out how to get it for themselves. Or because friends and relatives might want it or become envious of it.
- It is superstitious to talk of money: it means it could be taken away.
- Boasting about money could encourage envious others to inform tax authorities.
- If money is associated with food, avoiding discussing it reduces hunger, need, greed and vulnerability.
- If money is associated with filth in the eyes of the people, shunning discussing it can be a way of fending off feelings of shame.
- On some levels we know our attitudes to money reveal a lot about us which we would rather keep private.

In a recent study of over 100,000 Britons, Furnham, Fenton O'Creevy and von Stumm (2013) found the following responses (Table 9.1) to a number of questions considered to be possible indicators of money pathology (Forman, 1987).

Nearly half of the items showed that 30% or more of the respondents did say "yes", an indication of the how widespread money fears and anxieties are.

This chapter is particularly focused on the pathological meaning and use of money. It is, curiously, an area of research with a plethora of interesting and unusual case studies but a paucity of theory or indeed good empirical research.

Table 9.1 Money pathology of the British people

Items	Yes(%)	1	2	3	4
Do you resent having to pay full price for any item when you shop?	51.5				.67
Do you use money to control and manipulate others?	4.5				
Would you walk out of your way to save a bus fare you could easily afford?	35.3				
Do you hold onto, or hoard your money?	35.2				
Do you buy things when you feel anxious, bored, upset, depressed or angry?	33.7				
Do you buy things you don't really need because they are great bargains?	33.1				
Do you spend a large proportion of your free time shopping?	12.1				
Are you reluctant to learn about practical money matters?	9.4				
Do you refuse to take money seriously?	9.1				
Do you regularly exceed the spending limit on your credit card?	4.7				
Are you constantly puzzled about where your money goes or why there is none left at the end of each month?	23.0				
Do you find yourself worrying about the spending, using or giving of money all the time?	4.8				
Are you increasingly anxious about whether you can pay your bills each month?	18.5				

Source: Furnham, Wilson and Telford (2012)

Anthropologists, social psychologists, sociologists and theologians have all suggested possible explanations for money pathology. They have tended to stress three factors as playing a major role in pathology:

1. **Early learned experience:** Growing up in poverty, economic recession or clear economic comparative difficulty has been suggested as a motive for some individuals to be driven to secure, in both senses of the word, large sums of money.

2. **Intergroup rivalry:** The concept of **pity** by the rich for the poor and the **envy** and **hatred** of the rich by the poor provide plenty of opportunity for intergroup conflict. Threats to security, status, reputation and ego can act as powerful forces as well as a psychological threat to attempt to control money.

> 3. **Ethics and religion:** Feeling guilt about money and being personally responsible for the poor is at the heart of many religions. The self-denial, self-depreciation and guilt associated with certain puritan sects has often been invoked for the strange behaviour of individuals taught that too much money acquired "too easily" or displayed too ostentatiously is sinful.

However, there exists no well-formulated articulate theory of individual differences with respect to money. That is with the exception of psychoanalysis.

The psychoanalysis of money

The psychoanalysts have been writing about money for over 100 years. Borneman (1973) collected and assessed this disparate literature. It is a literature peppered with expressions like anal, eroticism and sadism.

Biographers have speculated about how Freud's personal life influenced his views on the topic (Warner, 1989). Freud's obsession with "sliding back into poverty" and his obsessive compulsive behaviour have been cited as influential in his theory. Some case studies consider issues such as how patients use money in therapy to express unconscious desires. An example is Rothstein's (1986) work on a banker who used money as an expression of transference love and attempts at seduction.

In an essay entitled "Character and Anal Eroticism", Freud (1908) argued that character traits originate in the warding off of certain primitive biological impulses. In this essay he first drew attention to the possible relationship of adult attitudes to money as a product of eroticism. In fact he later wrote, "Happiness is the deferred fulfilment of a pre-historic wish. That is why wealth brings so little happiness; money is not an infantile wish."

Many psychoanalytic thinkers, such as Fenichel (1947) and Ferenczi (1926), have developed these notions. The latter described the ontogenic stages through which the original pleasure in dirt and excreta develops into a love of money. Freud (1908) identified three main traits associated with people who had fixated at the anal stage: orderliness, parsimony and obstinacy with associated qualities of cleanliness, conscientiousness, trustworthiness, defiance and revengefulness.

Parental behaviour, it is argued, in this phase can cause obsessive-compulsive behaviour. Further, children will parent as they were parented. Hence rigid vs. permissive, premature vs. delayed "potty training" can have long-lasting effects. The anal character retains childhood ambivalence and inhibitions towards money.

O'Neill, Greenberg, and Fisher (1992) found evidence that those with anal personalities characterised by obstinacy, orderliness and parsimony enjoyed toilet humour more than non-anal types, so providing modest evidence for the theory. According to the theory, all children experience pleasure in the elimination of faeces. At an early age (around 2 years) parents in the West toilet-train their children, some showing enthusiasm and praise (positive reinforcement) for defecation, others threatening and punishing a child when it refuses to do so (negative reinforcement). Potty- or toilet-training occurs at the same stage that the child is striving to achieve autonomy and a sense of worth.

Often toilet-training becomes a source of conflict between parents and children over whether the child is in control of its sphincter or whether the parental rewards and coercion compel submission to their will. Furthermore, the child is fascinated by and fantasises over its faeces, which are, after all, a creation of its own body. The child's confusion is made all the worse by the ambiguous reactions of parents who, on the one hand, treat the faeces as gifts and highly valued, and then, on the other hand, behave as if they are dirty, untouchable and in need of immediate disposal. Yet the children who revel in praise over their successful deposits come to regard them as gifts to their beloved parents to whom they feel indebted, and may grow up to use gifts and money freely. Conversely, those who refuse to empty their bowels except when they must later have "financial constipation".

Thus, the theory states quite explicitly that if the child is traumatised by the experience of toilet-training, it tends to retain ways of coping and behaving during this phase. The way in which a **miser** hoards money is seen as symbolic of the child's refusal to eliminate faeces in the face of parental demands. The **spendthrift**, on the other hand, recalls the approval and affection that resulted from submission to parental authority to defecate. Thus, some people equate elimination/spending with receiving affection and hence feel more inclined to spend when feeling insecure, unloved or in need of affection. Attitudes to money, then, are bimodal; they are either extremely positive or extremely negative.

Evidence for the psychoanalytic position comes from the usual sources: patients' free associations and dreams. Freudians have also attempted to find evidence for their theory in idioms, myths, folklore and legends. There is also quite a lot of evidence from language, particularly from idiomatic expressions. Money is often called "filthy lucre", and the wealthy are often called "stinking rich". Gambling for money is also associated with dirt and toilet-training: a poker player puts money in a "pot"; dice players shoot "craps"; card players play "dirty-Girty"; a gambler who loses everything is "cleaned-out".

Psychoanalytic ideas have inspired a good deal of empirical work (Beloff, 1957; Grygier, 1961; Kline, 1967). Although there are a number of measures that have been constructed to measure dynamic features, Kline (1971) developed his own test of the anal character. This scale has been used in Ghana as well as Britain and has attracted a good deal of research. For instance, Howarth (1980, 1982) found the anal scale quite separate from measures of neuroticism or psychoticism. However, O'Neill (1984) found anality related to various Type A characteristics like time consciousness and obstinacy, which suggests they may be difficult to treat.

Table 9.2 A test of the anal character

1.	Do you keep careful accounts of the money you spend?	(Yes/No)
2.	When eating out, do you wonder what the kitchens are like?	(Yes/No)
3.	Do you insist on paying back even small trivial debts?	(Yes/No)
4.	Do you like to think out your own methods rather than use other people's?	(Yes/No)
5.	Do you find more pleasure in doing things than in planning them?	(Yes/No)
6.	Do you think there should be strong laws against spending?	(Yes/No)
7.	There is nothing more infuriating than people who do not keep appointments?	(Yes/No)
8.	Do you feel you want to stop people and do the job yourself?	(Yes/No)
9.	Do you think most people do not have high enough standards in what they do?	(Yes/No)
10.	Do you make up your mind quickly rather than turn things over for a long time?	(Yes/No)
11.	Do you think envy is at the root of most egalitarian ideals?	(Yes/No)
12.	Do you like to see something solid and substantial for your money?	(Yes/No)
13.	Do you easily change your mind once you have made a decision?	(Yes/No)
14.	Do you disagree with corporal punishment?	(Yes/No)
15.	Do you regard smoking as a dirty habit?	(Yes/No)

Source: Kline (1971).

Borneman (1973) notes how various money issues are related to childhood eating and defecating behaviour:

- **Ingesting**: this is about acquiring and buying. This partly explains the monetary associations with food. People take enormous pleasure in the acquisition (money, property, possessions), which is the faecal aspect of the enterprise.
- **Digesting**: food is an investment that leads to profit.
- **Withholding of excrement**: this is linked to saving, parsimony and collecting. Fixation at the retentive phase leads to irrational collecting.
- **Expelling the faeces**: this is linked to spending, selling and producing. This is the psychology of **loss**, squandering and surrender, but also of fun.

Most interestingly, Borneman (1973) is deeply critical of Kaufman (1956), whose essay he chooses to include in his anthology. He accuses Kaufman of trying to help patients by adapting to their society's culture. He is deeply critical of the assumption that money can be used as a means to encourage both socially desirable and socially undesirable behaviour because of the socio-political association of desirability.

Psychoanalysis is at its best in the observation of contradictions and patterns, in providing a plausible if non-commonsensical explanation for odd, irrational behaviour that brings people pain and distress. It is at its worst when it pathologises and tries to explain everything.

Compulsive buying

Television programmes have made the whole issue of compulsive buying better understood. There are a number of popular terms for pathological compulsive buying: shopaholism, consuming passions, retail therapy, acquisitive desire, overspending, and affluenza. The very early literature referred to *oniomania* or buying mania, considered an impulse pathology characterised by excessive, impulsive, uncontrollable consumption. It has been linked (genetically) to other impulse disorders like gambling, alcoholism and binge eating.

There is recent evidence of biological disorders of neurotransmitters that may in part account for the behaviour (the "highs" and "rushes" felt). The psychological factors identified concern the gaining of approval and recognition, the bolstering of self-esteem and escaping into a fantasy where people feel important and respected. There are also sociological and cultural forces that actually encourage the behaviour.

Most compulsive shoppers are middle- or lower middle-class females. There are many forms of this "odd behaviour pattern". Some buy every day; others in response to negative life events. Some buy for themselves; others for family and friends. Many buy things they don't need or ever use, which seem to lose their meaning after the purchase is made. Most purchases are clothes, jewels, electronic equipment, or collectables.

It has been argued that compulsive spending is a serious and growing problem because of increasing production of goods around the world linked to increased wealth and the ease of credit. Next, people compare themselves to a much wider circle than they did in the past. Previously "keeping up with the Joneses" just meant the neighbours, but television and other media have made reference point groups bigger and richer.

Benson (2008) noted that compulsive buying has now been recognised as a common, and serious, social problem. She noted that many overshoppers feel they have to keep their compulsion secret, lest they are condemned as narcissistic, superficial and weak willed.

People overshop to feel better about themselves or more secure. It may be a distraction helping them avoid other important issues. It can be a weapon to express anger or seek revenge. It may be a vain attempt to hold on to the love of another. It may be a balm used to soothe oneself or repair one's mood. It may be an attempt to project an image of wealth and power. It may be a way of trying to fit into an appearance-obsessed society. Equally, it may be a response to loss, trauma or stress. It could be the lesser evil compared to being addicted to alcohol, drugs or food. It could also be a way of trying to feel more in control or finding meaning in life.

Benson (2008) asked the obvious question: What are you shopping for? She poses the following hypotheses. Do you overshop to:

- Feel better about yourself or more secure – blocking pain, feelings of failure?
- Avoid dealing with something important – delaying, repressing actions?

- Express anger or seek revenge – punishing spouse, parents, friends, children?
- Hold on to love – to prevent abandonment, hold on to people?
- Soothe yourself or repair moods – to "drug" yourself with uppers and downers?
- Project an image of wealth and power – to boost self-esteem, self-worth?
- Fit into an appearance-obsessed society – to project youth, success, etc.?
- Reduce stress, loss and trauma – a relief valve, a compensating balm?
- Be a lesser evil – preventing something even more "destructive"?
- Feel more in control – where you can best "self-manage" your life?
- Finding meaning in life and deny death – solve existential dilemmas?

As usual parental socialisation is implicated:

- Parents who themselves were abused/neglected give gifts to compensate.
- Parents who "earn" their love through particular achievements often have children who feel emotionally undernourished.
- Parents who don't give time, energy or love to indicate the child is secure, valued, loved and important leave them feeling neglected and empty – a void which they seek to fill by shopping.
- Families that suffer financial reversal experience lowered self-esteem believing the latter to be exclusively associated with the quality and quantity of possessions that can be bought.
- Families that have a feeling of both or either emotional and financial impoverishment seek to alleviate this feeling with objects.
- Families that give no financial guidance to their children.

Benson (2008) sets out to describe typical "triggers" which she divides into five categories:

1. **Situational:** sales signs, magazine ads, bad weather.
2. **Cognitive:** feeling guilty, deserving a reward, rationalisation.
3. **Interpersonal:** buying after a fight, attempting to impress peers, nice salesperson.
4. **Emotional:** feeling excited, sad, lonely, stressed, or even euphoric.
5. **Physical:** as a substitute for eating, after drinking alcohol.

She then lists typical aftershocks, which can be financial (calls from creditors; poor credit rating; massive overdrafts), relationship-based (secretiveness; fights; clutter), emotional (depressed; ashamed; angry), work-based (lowered performance; long hours; stealing), physical (headaches; sleeping problems), to do with personal development (wasted time; fewer holidays), or spiritual (lost community spirit; mismatch of values and lifestyle).

Benson (2008) recommends keeping a journal and developing a shopping autobiography to understand how, when and why one shops, as well as "conducting a motivational interview" with oneself. The six shopping questions are: Why am I here? How do I feel? Do I need this? What if I wait? How will I pay for this? Where will I put it? This should include a "matrix", which is a simple short-term/ long-term, if I shop/if I don't shop audit. She suggests people develop a shopping pattern checklist that covers things like *when* you shop; *where* you shop; *with whom* you shop; *for whom* you shop; how you acquire *something you want*; *what kinds* of goods/services/experiences you buy/acquire; what is your shopping *signature/style* is; how you *give permission* to yourself to overshop.

It is partly an attempt to get to a person's "scripts": to make them more self-aware about their behaviour so that they can change it. It is also about finding alternative behaviours for "self-fondness, self-care and self-respect" as well as fulfilling fundamental needs. The underlying message is: before you go shopping, understand what you are shopping for and attempt to counteract the pressure to consume.

Next there is the issue of becoming financially fit. This includes learning how to save, buying much less using credit cards, learning how to budget and checking on spending by categories. Benson recommends shopaholics look carefully at *what* precisely they are shopping for. Is it self-kindness, self-care or self-respect? If so are there useful, better alternatives that do not involve shopping? This also involves countering, demagnetising or resisting the pull and pressure to consume. This means avoiding danger zones, reducing exposure, resisting social pressure and creating better alternatives. It also involves *mindful* shopping: shopping with a plan. Also, getting used to returning, reselling and recycling. She also recommends a form of cognitive behavioural therapy to challenge distorted thinking.

Family dynamics can influence compulsive shopping where, for instance, parents attempt to control, placate, or dominate others with gifts. Equally some give little financial guidance.

Therapists like Benson (2008) attempt to "demagnetise" people and help them resist the need to buy, consume and spend. She advises people to avoid their danger zones (places they are likely to overspend), reduce their exposure to advertisements and choose a creative, smarter alternative for meeting material needs. Part of the strategy is to learn to resist social pressure from; salespeople, neighbours/comparison groups, significant others (family and friends), and children. The aim is to make people mindful about shopping. It encourages them to shop with a plan that includes reviewing purchases as well as plans for returning, reselling and recycling.

Cognitive behaviour therapy can be used to discourage overspending. Thus, people are warned about all-or-nothing (black/white) thinking; overgeneralisation (all/never); dwelling on single negative thoughts; jumping to (too hasty) conclusions; catastrophisation; denial; emotional vs. rational reasoning; labelling; having inappropriate "should" statements; and personalisation. The idea is to challenge then change distorted thinking, to adopt the language of spirituality rather than materialism and to count your blessings.

The emotional underpinning of money pathology

The Freudians have suggested that many money-linked attitudes disguise other powerful emotions. Many Freudians rejoice in the paradox whereby some outward, visible behaviour disguises or masks the opposite motive or desire. Thus, pity towards the poor may in fact disguise hatred, racial prejudice, and feelings of threat. Threat of physical violence or political clout with attempts to legally or illegally remove the wealth and concomital status, reputation or ego of the well-to-do is a powerful motive. The poor are a psychological and economic threat to the latter because they may be prepared to work for very low wages, and can easily be stigmatised and victimised as dirty, dishonest, and worthy of their fate.

One emotion frequently associated with money is **guilt**. This has been associated with Puritan values of asceticism, denial and anhedonia (Furnham, 1990). Puritanism preaches the sinfulness of self-indulgence, waste and ostentatious consumption. Values such as conscientiousness, punctuality, thrift and sobriety made people with these beliefs or this socialization guilty not about the acquisition, but more the spending of money. It is not antagonistic to the concept of money or receiving equitable rewards for hard work, but Puritanism opposes money gained too easily (i.e. gambling, inheritance) or dishonestly or sinfully, and, particularly money that is frivolously spent.

Guilt about money (or indeed anything) can cause a sense of discomfort, dishonesty, unhappiness, even self-loathing. This guilt may be consciously felt and steps made to reduce it. Goldberg and Lewis (1978) believe that money guilt may result in psychosomatic complaints, transferred to feelings of depression. Psychoanalysts have documented cases of the fear of affluence in those schooled in the Puritan ethic. The basis of this fear is apparently loss of **control**. Money controls the individual: it dictates how and where one lives; it can prescribe and proscribe who are friends and associates; and it can limit as much as liberate one's social activities. The Puritan ethic focuses on limits and the conservation of such things as time, money, resources, even emotions. If money were in super abundance there would seem little, certainly less, reason to exercise any control over it. In this sense one could lose the need for control. Maintaining control – over physical factors and emotions – provides a person with the illusion of a sense of security.

Psychoanalysts believe that one reason for those who suddenly become rich being unable to deal with their wealth is because they lack the self-discipline and, of course, actual experience to handle it. "Where controls have not been internalized and realistic self-discipline has not evolved, the individual is dependent upon external controls to provide a sense of security" (Goldberg & Lewis, 1978, p. 75). Large amounts of money seem to imply for many individuals that one can use it irrespective of the consequences, and this uncontrolled behaviour creates anxiety. Paradoxically if the money dries up or disappears, order and security are restored to life. Further, if people have made sudden and dramatic changes to their life, getting rid of the money and all it bought may mean a return to normality.

As well as arousing guilt money can represent security. Studies of the self-made, very rich in America have shown a much greater than chance incidence of these rich people experiencing early parental death, divorce, or other major deprivation (Cox & Cooper, 1990). Psychoanalysts believe that they, in adulthood, set out to amass so much money that they will never be stranded again. Having had to assume adult responsibilities at an early age, they may have felt the need to prove to themselves and others their lack of need for dependence on parents. The desire to amass wealth, therefore, may be nothing more than a quest for emotional, rather than physical security.

Money-greed for psychoanalysts may relate more to orality than anality (Goldberg & Lewis, 1978). They point here to terms like "bread" and "dough" referring to money. The money-hungry person who seeks and devours money with little regard to social etiquette reacts to money as a starving person does to food. This behaviour, it is said, derives from a deprived infancy.

As we shall see, psychoanalytic writers have tried hard to categorise people in terms of the underlying dynamics of their money pathology. To psychoanalysts and other clinicians from diverse backgrounds money has psychological meanings: the most common and powerful of which are **security**, **power**, **love**, and **freedom** (Goldberg & Lewis, 1978).

Security

Emotional security is represented by financial security and the relationship is believed to be linear – more money, more security. Money is an emotional life-jacket, a security blanket, a method to stave off anxiety. Evidence for this is, as always, in clinical reports, archival research and the biographies of wealthy people. Yet turning to money for security can alienate people because significant others are seen as a less powerful source of security. Building the emotional wall around themselves can lead to fear and paranoia about being hurt, rejected or deprived by others. A fear of financial loss becomes paramount because the security collector supposedly depends more and more on money for ego-satisfaction: money bolsters feelings of safety and self-esteem.

Goldberg and Lewis (1978) specify several "money-types" that all, consciously or not, see money as a symbol of security. They provide typical "case history" data for the existence of these various types though they offer little quantitative rather than qualitative research findings.

a. **Compulsive savers**: for them saving is its own reward. They tax themselves and no amount of money saved is sufficient to provide enough security. Some even become vulnerable to physical illness because they may deny themselves sufficient heat, lighting, or healthy food.

b. **Self-deniers**: self-deniers tend to be savers but enjoy the self-sacrificial nature of self-imposed poverty. They may spend money on others however (though not much) to emphasise their martyrdom. Psychoanalysts point out that their behaviour is often a disguise for envy, hostility, and resentment towards those who are better off.

c. **The compulsive bargain hunter**: money is fanatically retained until the situation is "ideal" and then joyfully given over. The thrill is in out-smarting others – both those selling and those paying the full price. The feeling of triumph often has to validate the irrationality of the purchase which may not really be wanted. But they get short changed because they focus on price not quality.

d. **The fanatical collector**: obsessed collectors accumulate all sorts of things, some without much intrinsic value. They turn to material possessions rather than humans as potential sources of affection and security. They acquire more and more but are reticent to let any go. Collecting can give life a sense of purpose and help to avoid feelings of loneliness and isolation. Objects are undemanding and well-known collections can bring a sense of superiority and power.

Power

Because money can buy goods, services and loyalty it can be used to acquire importance, domination and control. Money can be used to buy out or compromise enemies and clear the path for oneself. Money and the power it brings can be seen as a search to regress to infantile fantasies of omnipotence. Three money-types who are essentially power-grabbers, according to the psychoanalytically oriented Goldberg and Lewis (1978), are:

a. **The manipulator:** These people use money to exploit others' vanity and greed. Manipulating others makes this type feel less helpless and frustrated, and they feel no qualms about taking advantage of others. Many lead exciting lives but their relationships present problems as they fail or fade due to insult, repeated indignities or neglect. Their greatest long-time loss is integrity.

b. **The empire builder:** They have (or appear to have) an overriding sense of independence and self-reliance. Repressing or denying their own dependency needs, they may try to make others dependent on them. Many inevitably become isolated and alienated particularly in their declining years.

c. **The godfather:** They have more money to bribe and control so as to feel dominant. They often hide an anger and a great over-sensitivity to being humiliated – hence the importance of public respect. But because they buy loyalty and devotion they tend to attract the weak and insecure. They destroy initiative and independence in others and are left surrounded by second-rate sycophants.

As Goldberg and Lewis (1978) note, the power-grabber felt rage rather than fear as a child, and expresses anger as an adult. Security collectors withdraw with fear, power-grabbers attack. Victims of power-grabbers feel ineffectual and insecure, and get a pay-off by attaching themselves to someone they see as strong and capable. They may therefore follow "winners" particularly if they have enough money.

Love

For some, money is given as a substitute for emotion and affection. Money is used to buy affection, loyalty and self-worth. Further, because of the reciprocity principle inherent in gift giving, many assume that reciprocated gifts are a token of love and caring.

a. **The love buyer**: many attempt to buy love and respect: those who visit prostitutes; those who ostentatiously give to charity; those who spoil their children. They feel unloved not unlovable and avoid feelings of rejection and worthlessness by pleasing others with their generosity. However, they may have difficulty reciprocating love, or their generosity may disguise true feelings of hostility towards those they depend on.

b. **The love seller**: they promise affection, devotion, and endearment for inflating others' egos. They can feign all sorts of responses and are quite naturally particularly attracted to love buyers. Some have argued that forms of psychotherapy are a love buyer–seller business transaction open to the laws of supply and demand. The buyers purchase friendships sold happily by the therapist. Love sellers gravitate to the caring professions.

c. **The love stealer**: the kleptomaniac is not an indiscriminate thief but one who seeks out objects of symbolic value to them. They are hungry for love but don't feel they deserve it. They attempt to take the risk out of loving, and being generous, are very much liked but tend only to have very superficial relationships.

Overall, then, it seems that whereas parents provide money for their children **because** they love them, parents of potential love dealers give money **instead** of love. Because they have never learnt to give or accept love freely they feel compelled to buy, sell, or steal it. The buying, selling, trading and stealing of love is for Freudians a defence against true emotional commitment, which must be the only cure.

Freedom

This is the more acceptable, and hence more frequently admitted, meaning attached to money. It buys time to pursue one's whims and interests, and frees one from the daily routine and restrictions of a paid job. There are two sorts of autonomy worshippers:

a. **The freedom buyers**: for them money buys escaping from orders, commands, even suggestions that appear to restrict autonomy and limit independence.

They want independence not love – in fact they repress and hence have a strong fear of dependency urges. They fantasise that it may be possible to have a relationship with another "free spirit" in which both can experience freedom and togetherness simultaneously. They are frequently seen as undependable and irresponsible, and can make those in any sort of relationship frustrated, hurt and angry.

b. **The freedom fighters**: they reject money and materialism as the cause of the enslavement of many. Frequently political radicals, drop-outs or technocrats, they are often passive-aggressive and attempt to resolve internal conflicts and confused values. Camaraderie and companionship are the main rewards for joining the anti-money forces. Again idealism is seen as a defence against feeling. There may be a large cost if the person gets involved with cults.

An underlying theme is that dependency on other people and on the world early in life was perceived as a threatening rather than a rewarding experience. This typology is based on clinical observations and interpreted through the terminology of a particular theory. For some, this may lead to interesting hypotheses that require further proof either by experiment, or at least evidence from a much wider normal population.

Marketing people have used this typology to suggest that salespeople could both listen for and use words that trigger or prime people so as to reveal their particular associations with money. Thus:

* **Security**: Anxiety. Consistent. Consolidate. Deadlock. Fear. Foundation. Get what you pay for. Guarantee. Impact. Insurance. Life cover. Loss. Protected. Reassurance. Reliable. Risk-averse. Rooted. Saving. Safety net. Sturdy. Trust. Volvo.
* **Power**: Action. Aggressive. Appetite. Caddy. Champagne. Double-digit. Eagle. Empire. Envy. Gold standard. Growth. High-octane. Investment. Outperform. Porsche-performance. Proud. Risk. Status. Secret weapon. Serve. Thirst. Top of the class.
* **Love**: Bereavement. Child. Chocolates. Cradle. Diamonds. Disney. Divorce. Education. Family. Happiness. Home. Honeymoon. Inheritance. Joy. Love Bug. Marriage. Nest egg. Nurture. Partner. Provide. Red. Roses. Soulmate. Teddy bear. VW Beetle.
* **Freedom**: Adventurous. Around the world. Break free. Dream. Emerging markets. Exploring. Flexible. Free as a bird. Free-thinking. Gamble. Hunting. Impulsive. Independence. Maverick. Multinational. Off-road. Off the beaten track. Opportunity. Passport. Retirement. Roulette. Shackles. Trailblazer. Travel. Virgin sands. Visa.

Researchers at Mountainview Learning in London attempted to help bankers understand how to understand their clients attitudes to money using the fourfold classification system.

Psychotherapists believe that money beliefs and behaviours are not isolated psychic phenomena but are integral to the person as a whole. People who withhold money may have tendencies to withhold praise, affection or information from others. People who are anxious about their financial state may have something to learn about a fear of dependency or envy. Therapists attempt to help people understand their money madness. Money can become the focus of fantasies, fears and wishes, and is closely related to denials, distortions, impulses and defences against impulses.

Money can thus be associated with:

> Armour, ardour, admiration, freedom, power and authority, excitement and elation, insulation survival and security, sexual potency, victory and reward.
>
> Thus, money may be perceived as a weapon or shield, a sedative or a stimulant, a talisman or an aphrodisiac, a satisfying morsel of food or a warm fuzzy blanket ... so having money in our pockets, to save or to spend, may provide us with feelings of fullness, warmth, pride, sexual attractiveness, invulnerability, perhaps even immortality. Similarly, experiencing a dearth of money may bring on feelings of emptiness, abandonment, diminishment, vulnerability, inferiority, impotency, anxiety, anger and envy. (Matthews, 1991, p. 24)

For psychoanalytically inclined clinicians the money personality is part pleasure-seeking, frustration-avoiding *id*, part reasonable and rational *ego*, part overseeing, moral, *super ego*. This accounts for the oft-reported but curious paradox of seeing people lethargic and depressed after a major win and elated, even virtuous, after financial depletion.

Rather than typologies of money madness, Matthews (1991) sees attitudes to money on a *continuum* from mild eccentricities with subtle symptoms through moderate money neurosis to full-blown money madness. Again, her data is obtained from treating patients and running workshops with all the limitations that that implies. Further, she believes that money attitudes and behaviours are influenced by the emotional dynamics of early childhood; interaction with families, friends, teachers and neighbours; cultural and religious traditions; and, more, by modern technology and by the messages in the mass media.

Matthews (1991) has observed that many money disorders are learned from "family disorders". The message families send about money are, however, simultaneously overt and covert, and often paradoxical, inconsistent and confusing. Parents can, and do, express their feelings toward their children through money, for example by reinforcing good habits or success at school.

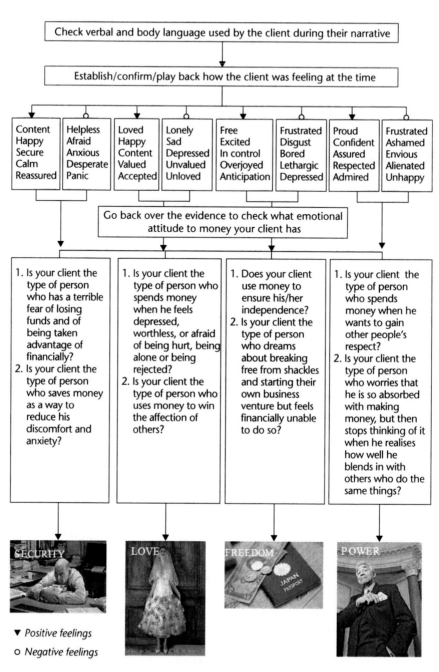

Check verbal and body language used by the client during their narrative

Establish/confirm/play back how the client was feeling at the time

Content Happy Secure Calm Reassured	Helpless Afraid Anxious Desperate Panic	Loved Happy Content Valued Accepted	Lonely Sad Depressed Unvalued Unloved	Free Excited In control Overjoyed Anticipation	Frustrated Disgust Bored Lethargic Depressed	Proud Confident Assured Respected Admired	Frustrated Ashamed Envious Alienated Unhappy

Go back over the evidence to check what emotional attitude to money your client has

1. Is your client the type of person who has a terrible fear of losing funds and of being taken advantage of financially?
2. Is your client the type of person who saves money as a way to reduce his discomfort and anxiety?

1. Is your client the type of person who spends money when he feels depressed, worthless, or afraid of being hurt, being alone or being rejected?
2. Is your client the type of person who uses money to win the affection of others?

1. Does your client use money to ensure his/her independence?
2. Is your client the type of person who dreams about breaking free from shackles and starting their own business venture but feels financially unable to do so?

1. Is your client the type of person who spends money when he wants to gain other people's respect?
2. Is your client the type of person who worries that he is so absorbed with making money, but then stops thinking of it when he realises how well he blends in with others who do the same things?

SECURITY   LOVE   FREEDOM   POWER

▼ Positive feelings
○ Negative feelings

FIGURE 9.1 A strategy to understand typologies

Source: Reproduced with permission from Mountainview Learning, London.

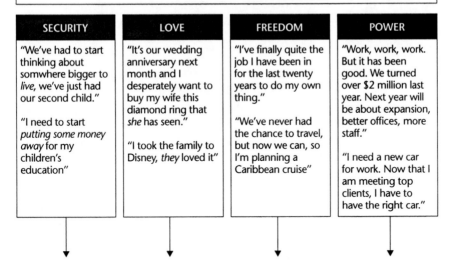

"I need to know a bit about you. Can I ask you to just tell me about what has been going on in your world the last year. Tell me your story"

SECURITY	LOVE	FREEDOM	POWER
"We've had to start thinking about somewhere bigger to *live*, we've just had our second child." "I need to start *putting some money away* for my children's education"	"It's our wedding anniversary next month and I desperately want to buy my wife this diamond ring that *she* has seen." "I took the family to Disney, *they* loved it"	"I've finally quite the job I have been in for the last twenty years to do my own thing." "We've never had the chance to travel, but now we can, so I'm planning a Caribbean cruise"	"Work, work, work. But it has been good. We turned over $2 million last year. Next year will be about expansion, better offices, more staff." "I need a new car for work. Now that I am meeting top clients, I have to have the right car."

FIGURE 9.2 Questions to determine type

Source: Reproduced with permission from Mountainview Learning, London.

Matthews (1991) believes there are a host of reasons why people run so easily into debt. People may buy too many things to boost their capacity for self-esteem or to try and fulfil a fantasy they have about themselves. Some may overdebt out of an unconscious desire to impoverish themselves, or to get rid of their money because on some level they find it loathsome. Alternatively they may overdebt because they feel unfulfilled and frustrated in some significant aspect of their lives and because spending temporarily takes their mind off their sense of emptiness and unhappy circumstances. People may overdebt because compulsive behaviour of one sort or another runs in their family or as a reaction against a family of origin where thriftiness was excessively prized. People may overdebt to try to keep up with their peers, or because they are unable to resist media messages which instruct them to "shop till we drop."

Matthews (1991) also speculates about the *"pack-thinking"* (conformity of views) of investors who play stock markets and whose greed and belief in eccentric experts can lead to spectacular monetary successes and failures. For these economic shamans, the stars and superstitions appear to play a major role in a highly capricious and unpredictable world. Many behave quite irrationally to allay feelings of uncertainty and insecurity about financial matters.

Forman (1987) argued that of all the neuroses, the money neurosis is most widespread. Like all neurotic processes it involves unresolved conflict associated with fear and anxiety that may relate directly to maladaptive, self-defeating, irrational behaviour. Money cannot buy love and affection, personal states of mind like inner peace, self-esteem or contentment, or particular social attributes like power, status or security. Forman believes too many people have a simple equation like money equals love or self-worth, or freedom, power or security.

In his book Forman (1987) describes five classic neurotic types:

1. The **miser** who hoards money. They tend not to admit being niggardly, have a terrible fear of losing funds, and tend to be distrustful, yet have trouble enjoying the benefits of money.
2. The **spendthrift** who tends to be compulsive and uncontrolled in their spending and does so particularly when depressed, feeling worthless and rejected. Spending is an instant but short-lived gratification that frequently leads to guilt.
3. The **tycoon** who is totally absorbed with money making, which is seen as the best way to gain power status and approval. They argue that the more money they have, the better control they have over their worlds and the happier they are likely to be.
4. The **bargain** hunter who compulsively hunts bargains even if they are not wanted because getting things for less makes them feel superior. They feel angry and depressed if they have to pay the asking price or cannot bring the price down significantly.
5. The **gambler** feels exhilarated and optimistic taking chances. They tend to find it difficult to stop even when losing because of the sense of power they achieve when wining.

Forman considers in some detail some of the more fascinating neuroses associated with everyday financial and economic affairs like saving, paying insurance and taxes, making a will, using credit cards. He does not speculate directly on the relationship between those various money complexes, appearing to suggest that they are all related to the same basic pathology. He developed a forced-choice (ipsative) questionnaire and a way for people to self-diagnose. The idea is that if one agrees with the majority of items in any one section one may have that pathology.

The literature on the emotional underpinning of money problems is certainly fascinating. Written by therapists mainly from a psychoanalytic background it also has severe limitations. There is clearly overlap between various different systems or descriptions and there is no agreement on typologies or processes. More importantly, there is little collaborative empirical evidence for many of the points made. While it is possible that many of these concepts and processes are correctly described, we need disinterested, empirical evidence demonstrating the validity of these writings. We do not need to know how widespread these pathologies are in the general population. Indeed, it is striking from the (scant) sociological and epidemiological research on money how common money pathology is, not the reverse. There is also no evidence on the incidence of these pathologies in the population as a whole, nor whether therapy (of any sort) cures these problems. Long on speculation and short on evidence, this area of research warrants good empirical studies to examine these ideas.

Treating pathology

Goldberg and Lewis (1978) argue that psychotherapists see money madness as of secondary importance. They also note that the different money types, not unnaturally, seek out therapists that fulfil their particular needs. Thus, those concerned with authority will seek out a less conventional therapist, while the security collector will be attracted to the least expensive therapist in the local market. Because (nearly) all therapists charge money for their services (though there is not necessarily any relationship between cost and quality of treatment), entering psychotherapy means spending money on oneself. Yet money remains a relatively taboo subject between therapist and client. Clearly all therapists need to understand the shared meaning attached to payment and non-payment for services throughout the course of therapy. Also, paying shows commitment.

Psychotherapists believe that money beliefs and behaviours are not isolated psychic phenomena but integral to the person as a whole. People who withhold money may have tendencies to withhold praise, affection or information from others. People who are anxious about their financial state may have something to learn about a fear of dependency or envy. Therapists attempt to help people understand their money madness. Money can become the focus of fantasies, fears and wishes, and is closely related to denials, distortions, impulses and defences against impulses.

Forman (1987) considered a range of therapies that he believes may be successfully used to help those with money neurosis, though of course the therapies may be applied to many other psychological problems. First, he notes how **cognitive behaviour therapy** may address negative attitudes. Self-defeating thoughts are characterised by self-blame, guilt, unresolved anger, and low self-esteem. They are riddled with distortions, including *overgeneralisations* (in which a single negative event is seen as a never-ending pattern of defeat), *arbitrary conclusions* (in which one thought does not follow from another), and *black and white thinking* (in which everything is all or nothing).

The first step is developing a contract for how the patient will behave – the rewards and penalties for compliance and non-compliance with objectives. Next is the task of uncovering automatic, money-related thoughts and attitudes. The third step is to recognise the harmful effects of these thoughts, and then to replace them by healthy thoughts on the subject. The final step is to change behaviour in line with the new healthy thoughts.

Another recommended therapy is **de-stressing or systematic relaxation**, which is an attempt at stress inoculation. The idea, somewhat tenuous, is that money neurosis is exacerbated by stress. Next psychoanalysis is recommended which also has set steps.

Assertiveness training is also recommended to help some people turn down unreasonable money requests in a way that does not let them or the requester feel uncomfortable. Various other therapies are considered including "thought-stopping therapy" and role playing. Alas this eclectic approach to therapy has little or no evidence to support it, nor a full explanation of the processes at work.

Paying for psychotherapy

It has been observed that, since Freud, many psychoanalysts have argued that patients do not get well *unless* they pay for their treatment. Robertiello (1994) firmly rejects this thesis, noting that not only has he given free treatment but that he lent patients large sums of money and even paid a patient "to come to sessions to get him past a resistance in which he projected his own problems with money onto me" (p. 36).

Therapists have written about money in analysis: how they "charge" their patients. Unlike sex and death, money does seem to remain a taboo subject. Haynes and Wiener (1996) have pointed out that the analyst's complexes and practices about money can clash badly with those of the client, causing particular problems. The agreement about fees, the presentation of bills, charging for cancellation, the increases of fees, can all present problems. Do higher fees mean better work? Yet payment is received for work in progress which cannot guarantee results. Therapists' fees confirm their self-esteem, professional status and belief in efficacy. Thus, when this is challenged by patients, therapists have to confront their own attitudes to money and then negotiate that meaning with the patient. Again it is asserted that self-knowledge and insight is the best cure.

Indeed, a whole book has been dedicated to the topic of fees in psychotherapy and psychoanalysis (Herron & Welt, 1992). The idea is that conflicts about money can be a serious source of tension, misunderstanding and ill will. Of course, the Freudians see money as a vehicle for favourite concepts like transference and counter-transference. Other issues include therapists' unhealthy, pathological greed, where they use the defence mechanism of reaction formation to deny their entitlement to an adequate fee, and "healthy" greed, where the fee is a normal entitlement to the position, role and task performed. Money it is argued can help therapist and patient understand the therapeutic boundaries of treatment.

Herron and Welt (1992) note that the patient's fee restricts both the entrance to and continuance of therapy. They talk of getting the "dosage" right given the economic situation of the client and the type of therapy they are receiving. They argue that there are emotional and financial issues regarding the fees that both client and therapist need to confront honestly. Issues need to be discusses early and frankly so that expectations are made clear. There is conflict but it needs to be discussed.

The psychoanalysts have also looked at the heads and tails of money: its good and bright side vs. its bad and dark side (de Mause, 1988). Hence the interest in how the word gold (in German) is related to guilt in English and how gift and poison are related. The psychoanalysts are interested in how people manipulate their bad feelings by "injecting" (projective identification) into objects. Feelings of despair, rage, guilt, need for love, are too dangerous to experience consciously and are injected into money, which becomes a poison container. Thus, groups have poison-cleaning acts like sacrifices to purify people of bad feelings. The argument is that banks often look like temples and bankers become sacrificial priests who have to handle poison money.

Therapists "lease their time". Freud argued that charging a fee for therapy was much better than giving it for free for three reasons (Dimen, 1994):

---

1. Free treatment stirs up resistance: erotic transference in young women, pattern transference in young men, both of whom rebel against the obligation to feel grateful.
2. It pre-empts counter-transference of the therapist who may come to resent the patients' selfishness and exploitativeness.
3. It is more respectable and less ethically objectionable to the pretence of philanthropy. It acknowledges openly the therapist's interests and needs.

It is interesting to note that Freud wrote about and worried about the adequacy and unevenness of his income from therapy. He had a "pervasive, if intermittent, focus on money" (Dimen, 1994, p. 77). He felt greed and cynicism toward some rich patients and benevolent and paternalistic condescension to poorer patients. Yet he argued therapy was a bargain because it restored health and economic efficiency.

Many professionals charge for their time (doctors, lawyers). Their mental labour fee is a sign of their professional status and an index of authority, privilege and power. It is important that psychotherapy is bought and sold under conditions that heal and not ones of "dis-ease".

In a reflective and self-critical piece Dimen (1994) notes how analysts are so uncomfortable with their own feelings of need and greed that they treat it exclusively as a problem for the patient. "Indeed, analysts' dystonic relation to their own dependence may constitute the biggest single counter-resistance in regard to money" (p. 76). She wonders whether, if financial uncertainty unsettles analysts, financial security may render them smug. Do money worries make analysts feel unsafe, and thence less confident and competent?

Analysts want to see themselves as beneficent purveyors of good rather than involved in commerce. They sell their services to make a living. Dimen (1994) asks the reasonable question of how an analyst might feel and react if they learnt that a patient had lost their job or come into a great deal of money.

Like others before her Dimen makes the distinction between sacred and profane money or between special purpose money and general purpose money. The one can be a sign of love, the other of hate. The idea is that the very powerful, close, intense relationship between analyst and client is paid in cold, hard, general-purpose cash and this threatens to change that relationship.

Therapists have written about money issues with interesting case studies. Barth (2001) discussed four case studies where she used "money-talk" to discuss and negotiate separateness and connectedness in therapeutic relationships:

> In matters of money, questions about fees, insurance arrangements and payment style, for example, can lead to significant information about issues of dependency, deprivation, envy, longing, connecting, and other aspects of relationship – both within and outside of the therapeutic interaction. (p. 84)

She notes that in many relationships money is about power. It can lead to feelings of deprivation and vulnerability. She also notes the two issues that money issues raise: managed care (our attitudes to medical providers) and gender issues.

Three positions on paying for therapy

1. It is beneficial to therapeutic outcomes

Seeing a therapist involves an explicit or implicit contract. You "buy" expertise, help, advice. But are therapy patients buying love or friendship and how does that influence the relationship?

Many people argue that psychotherapy should be available for those in need of treatment for their mental disorder, funded by the NHS. However, Herron and Sitkowski (1986) propose that some fee is necessary in order for psychotherapy to be effective. Paying increases a sense of worth and commitment. Things given free are often seen as worthless. They note that therapists have conflict over fees. The two interesting questions in this area are (1) how, when and why does the fee affect the outcome (if at all), and (2) how can or should we interpret patients' payment style and methods (timing, cash vs. cheque). Research by Menninger and Holzman (1973) concludes that there is a connection between successful psychotherapy and a client making a sacrifice (being the fee paid to the therapist).

Langs (1982) agrees that paying a fee has a beneficial impact on the outcome of therapy, but suggests that this is due to a fee providing a stable boundary for the patient and therapist, as opposed to it being beneficial due to money's **sacrificial** effect.

Davis (1964) proposed a further explanation for the benefits recorded as a consequence of paying for therapy, incorporating cognitive dissonance theory (Festinger, 1957). Davis suggests that paying a fee for therapy adds to the dissonance created by the effort required to engage in psychotherapy. This leads to increased motivation for the patient to achieve the goals set in therapy in order to remove the dissonance.

2. It is detrimental to therapeutic outcomes

Despite such propositions, Schofield (1971) takes a contrasting view, stating that "I have been unable to observe any systematic difference in my approach, in how hard I work, or how responsive my clients are as a function of whether they are receiving 'free' or expensive therapy" (p. 10).

Yoken and Berman (1984) conducted a study confirming this view, with volunteers being randomly assigned to either a fee or no-fee counselling session. After the treatment session all participants reported reduced levels of symptoms and distress. Yet interestingly, the no-fee treatment group were found to benefit from greater symptom reduction than the fee-paying individuals, completely contradicting research suggesting paying for therapy enhances the outcomes. Interestingly, those paying for treatment had greater expectations of its results, but these did not materialise. Pope, Geller and Wilkinson (1975) support this finding in a study of 434 patients assigned to one of five fee-assessment categories (no payment, welfare, insurance, scaled payments, full fee) based on the individual's ability to pay. The study concluded that fees had no significant effects on outcome, appointments or attendance.

Reasonings behind the beneficial effects recorded as a result of free treatment have been offered by numerous authors. Yoken and Berman (1984) suggest that in a no-fee environment a patient's therapist is regarded as more caring, which is received positively by clients and facilitates positive changes. Alternatively, it may be that those paying fees have higher expectations of treatment (as found in Yoken & Berman's 1984 study), which results in them underestimating the beneficial effects of therapy in self-reports following treatment.

However, in Pope et al.'s (1975) study the therapists were not directly affected by fee payment, as the centre employed them and paid them regardless of each client's payment. Similarly, in Yoken and Berman's (1984) study therapists were unaware of what clients were paying. Pope et al. (1975) proposed that fee payment has been found to improve outcomes in past research due to service providers' needs being met, as opposed to the patient benefiting from sacrifice or cognitive dissonance. Mayer and Norton (1981) considered this, and reached the conclusion that therapists involved in billing and collecting fees improve clinical practice. Such findings suggest that fees have an impact on the clinical relationship through impacting the therapist as opposed to the patient.

3. It does not impact the outcome of therapy

Shipton and Spain (1981) reviewed research in the area in the hope of coming to a sound solution to this debate, yet their review was inconclusive, suggesting that there was limited evidence that fees did or did not impact on the outcome of therapy.

Neither therapists nor patients often talk about their personal income or financial resources. On the other hand therapists often report how many patients dream and fantasise about money. Some, like Freud, note associations with dirt and faeces, others with semen and love. Feuerstein (1971) noted that some therapists say patients lie about their money (underestimate their income) in the hope of having their fee reduced. He notes "in a profession devoted to uncovering the truth and to making conscious what is unconscious, the frequent lack of openness or awareness in this area is disturbing" (p. 100).

Clearly therapists who work in institutions as opposed to those who work privately have different attitudes and behaviours with respect to fees. It has been noted that some corporate therapists do not report sessions and invoice clients or departments, expressing their rebellion against and resentment toward authority.

One issue is the sensitivity and compassion of therapists and their identification with the economic plight of patients. Somehow fees seem to go against the whole humanitarian ideals of therapists and the enterprise of healing.

There are all sorts of issues for the therapist. First, they know that there is a strong subjective belief that worth and price are linked. If you charge little you are seen to be of less skill, efficacy, and helpfulness. Next, there is the issue of charging patients not according to their needs but their income. Some ponder on the fact that if they know some patients are paying much less than others that they treat them differently.

Moore (1965) noted that some patients deliberately go into debt and thus assume a regressive, dependent and masochistic relationship.

Self-help books

There is no shortage of books that purport to help you "discover your Midas Touch" (Teplitsky, 2004). They differ less in tone and promise than context. The idea is that one needs to confront a few issues, and follow a few steps to acquire (lots of) money. Some offer to teach the "secrets" of acquiring wealth/prosperity. Many ignore socio-political and economic impediments to wealth acquisition.

Many of these books attempt to explain how one's money beliefs and behaviours are unhelpful. They suggest faulty financial strategies – often blamed on family – need to be very directly confronted. They are the result of the psychological residue of early family life and what Marx would call "fake consciousness". Many dwell on dependency issues as well as bad habits.

They like to confront cultural myths like money bringing happiness, only the wicked prospering, there is a secret to making money. Many of these books, as Teplitsky (2004) observes, offer bits of sensible advice. These include:

1. **Positive thinking** – a sort of attribution therapy.
2. **Affirmation** – avoiding words like "no, not, none, never, neither, nor" and affirming one's ability and values.
3. **Visualisation** – coming up with positive mental images of money making.

4. **Recording dreams** – these may unconsciously help or hinder the acquisition of money.
5. **Radiate wealth** – visualise, but don't actually act, dress, speak, spend, and think like a wealthy person.
6. **Self-hypnosis and meditation** – which is about relaxing and clearing your mind of clutter.

Other metaphysical approaches, including prayer, are suggested.

There are money guides for people to help them "overcome" their money troubles. One such is by Middleton and Langdon (2008) and is simply entitled *Sort Out Your Money*. The advice is nearly always sound and straightforward: learn sensible shopping; avoid impulse buying; shock yourself by using cash.

There are a surprising number of popular books that are essentially self-help treatises about money. Most are short, non-technical, and non-research-based books by coaches, consultants and therapists. They fall roughly into three categories. The **first** sort are therapeutic as can be seen in the title of the book. Thus, in a book called *Money is Love*, Wilder (1999) chose the subtitle *Reconnecting to the Sacred Origins of Money*. She talks of "freeing the energy" by talking, writing and praying about money. Her aim and promise on the cover is that "you can reconnect with the sacred origins of money, and direct the flow of money through your life and the world on a current of love, joy, goodwill and abundance".

DeVor (2011), a "Master Certified Money Coach", in her self-published book subtitled *A Guide to Changing the Way You Think About Money* also offers a mix of financial advice and therapy. She notes the emotional associations of money, how important it is to do an honest net financial worth audit and how to move from the **scarcity** zone (negative emotions associated with money) to the **abundance** zone (positive feelings). This abundance–scarcity dimension is how we think about and use our money. Her therapy is to keep an "Abundance Journal", which examines what, and how much, people spend money on **and** how they feel about it.

The **second** sort of book is not about therapy and repair so much as helping you become rich, which, indeed, other books suggest you shouldn't aim to achieve. Price (2000), in a book called *Money Magic*, chose as a subtitle *Unleash Your True Potential for Prosperity and Fulfilment!* Like others she maintains that we all have a "money biography", which leads us to being one of several money types:

- **The innocent**: trusting, indecisive, dependent, apparently happy-go-lucky, but really fearful and anxious.
- **The victim**: resentful, unforgiving, addictive, emotional, past-oriented and seeking to be rescued.
- **The warrior**: confident, calculating, driven, competitive, disciplined, wise, discerning and successful.

- **The martyr**: secretive, manipulative, self-sacrificious, passive-aggressive, disappointed.
- **The fool**: restless, impetuous, optimistic, undisciplined, overly generous.
- **The creator/artist**: detached, non-materialistic, passive, internally motivated.
- **The tyrant**: oppressive, aggressive, secretive, materialistic, critical and judgemental.

We have to first identify the type we are, then our "money shadow", which is the part of us that is disowned, hidden and secret. Thereafter we are encouraged to identify our true net worth. This allows us to clean our financial house and see money as a creative flow. The rewards of self-insight and money health are abundance and prosperity. This process involves prayer, forgiveness, and "reconnection with your spiritual self". You have to change your habits and consequently are given tips such as: create a gratitude list, create an altar in your home consisting of anything that represents what you value most in life.

Another book in this genre is subtitled *Building Wealth from the Inside Out* by Casserly (2008), who offers financial therapy. The book is summarised essentially at the beginning, by encouraging what is called "Affirmations for Wealth Building". These include: "I choose to recognise my emotions behind money", "I choose to face my current financial reality", and "I choose to follow my desired financial roadmap and let that guide me out of my current financial reality". The chapters explain the strategies such as "3: Breaking away from your inherited beliefs"; and "7: Facing your financial reality". The process is familiar: confront your demons, examine your family, work personal and financial life and break away from your "inherited beliefs".

Casserly also lists types, which she calls financial personalities. These are: Hoarders, Spenders, Saboteurs, Givers, Controllers, Planners, Carefree Butterflies and Attractors. The therapy is to find your financial blind spots and to choose to change. The treatment involves eradicating the "crabs in your bucket" − namely the people who hold you back and keep you off track. You need to face your financial dark side as well as build and renovate your portfolio.

The **third** type of book is for those interested in global or regional wealth and welfare. An example is that by Twist (2003) who notes: "Money is the most universally motivating, mischievous, miraculous, maligned and misunderstood part of contemporary life" (p. 7). Later: "Money itself isn't the problem. Money itself isn't bad or good. Money itself doesn't have power or not have power. It is our interpretation of money, our interaction with it, where the real mischief is and where we find the real opportunity 'for self-discovery and personal transformation'" (p. 19).

Twist's (2003) book is full of stories. She suggests that too many of us are made unhappy by a *"scarcity mindset"* that has toxic myths: there is not enough, more is better, that is just the way it is. She believes our "life sentences" or personal truths, called by others money-grams, can haunt us and render us deeply unhappy and unsatisfied. The opposite of the scarcity mindset is the "*sufficiency mindset*", which is the path to happiness. It is the very old philosophy of to have or to be.

Twist argues that money is like water; better when it flows. Also that what you appreciate appreciates. "If we tend the seeds of sufficiency with our attention, and use our money like water to nourish them with soulful purpose, then we will enjoy the bountiful harvest" (p. 142). Also, "Money carries our intentions. If we use it with integrity, then it carries integrity forward. Know the flow – take responsibility for the way your money moves into the world" (p. 224).

Popular books on money are remarkably similar despite their rather different styles. They mix common sense, psychotherapy insights and non-materialist philosophy. The message is essentially that many of us have deep, unhelpful emotional associations with respect to money. This, together with poor financial knowledge and planning, leads to personal misery. Further, for most of us in the West our materialist culture encourages thinking and behaviour that leads to unhappiness not happiness. The solution is to be aware of your emotional use of money, to think about it and use it differently. To a large extent it is cognitive behaviour therapy supported by the teachings of many of the world's great religions on the folly of materialism.

10

MONEY AND MOTIVATION IN THE WORKPLACE

Most people work just hard enough not to get fired and get paid enough money not to quit.

George Carlin

If you don't want to work, you have to work to earn enough money so that you won't have to work.

Ogden Nash

The most efficient labour-saving device is still money.

Franklin Jones

He made his money the really old-fashioned way. He inherited it.

A. J. Carothers

Introduction

It comes as a surprise to many people that most psychology textbooks that deal with work (that is business, occupational, organisational, industrial, work psychology) are unlikely to refer to money at all. It is not in the index of most work psychology books. Money, per se, is usually seen as one of many rewards for work done, and in itself not particularly important. It is classified as an intrinsic reward.

To the layperson, and especially the supervisor, who finds it difficult to motivate his/her staff to work harder, it is a crucial and powerful motivational tool: the ultimate carrot. Yet, psychological research has consistently suggested that where money has motivational power it is nearly always *negative*. If you pay people at market rates and equitably, money, it is argued, has little motivational force.

We know that the relationship between salary and job satisfaction is very weak (correlations usually around $r = .15$); that the relationship between pay itself and pay satisfaction is not much higher (around $r = .25$); that focusing on money rewards can act to demotivate people; and that after a salary around twice the national average (£50,000 or $75,000) there is little or no increase in levels of well-being and happiness.

There is substantial evidence that, beyond a reasonable level, the *absolute* amount of pay is not as important to well-being as the *comparative* amount. In any society salary is an index of status and prestige, and there is an obvious disparity in this relationship. Pay is a form of *social approval*. Low pay indicates low skills and less important work to most people. Strikes for more money are often as much about desire for respect as they are about salaries (Lindgren, 1991). As we can see in divorce courts, money becomes a symbolic compensation for hurt feelings. Equally, pay differentials, as we shall see, are imbued with as many psychological as economic factors.

Psychologists cite support for their relative disregard of money as a motivator from surveys in which workers were asked which factors were most important in making a job good or bad; "pay" commonly came sixth or seventh after factors such as "security", "co-workers", "interesting work", and "welfare arrangements". This has been confirmed in more recent surveys, which have found that pensions and other benefits are valued more than salary alone. In short: *Money is important but not that important relative to other factors.*

The central question is how, when, for whom and, most importantly, why money acts as a motivator or demotivator at work.

Intrinsic and extrinsic motivation

Some jobs and some tasks are intrinsically satisfying. That is, by their very nature they are interesting and pleasant to do. They can be enjoyable for a wide variety of reasons and much depends on the preference, predilections, and propensities of individuals who presumably choose them.

There are those who work without pay. The existence of voluntary work (e.g. that done by children and home-makers) makes it clear that money is not the only reason for working. There are also people who do not need to work, but still do so. Of those who win lotteries, 17% stay in full-time work afterwards (Smith & Razzell, 1975). For some it is because they enjoy their work, as in the cases of scientists and other academics, but this is not the only reason. There are also a lot of people in full-time work who are already so rich that they do not need any more money, so presumably are working for some other reason.

Intrinsic satisfaction implies that merely doing the job is, in itself, its own reward. Therefore, for such activities no reward and no management should be required. The activity is its own reward. But the naive manager might unwillingly destroy this ideal state of affairs.

Take the case of the academic writer scribbling at home on a research report. The local children had for three days played extremely noisily in a small park near his study and, like all noise of this sort, it was highly stressful because it was simultaneously loud, uncontrollable and unpredictable. What should be done? (1) Ask (politely) them to quieten down or go away. (2) Call the police or the parents if you know them. (3) Threaten them with force if they do not comply. (4) All of the above in that order.

The wise don did none of the above. Unworldly maybe, but, as someone whose job depended on intrinsic motivation, the academic applied another principle. He went to the children on the fourth morning and said, somewhat insincerely, that he had very much enjoyed them being there for the sound of their laughter, and the thrill of their games. In fact, he was so delighted with them that he was prepared to pay them to continue. He promised to pay them each £1 a day if they carried on as before.

The youngsters were naturally surprised but delighted. For two days the don, seeming grateful, dispensed the cash. But on the third day he explained that because of a "cash flow" problem he could only give them 50p each. The next day he claimed to be "cash light" and only handed out 10p. True to prediction the children would have none of this, complained and refused to continue. They all left in a huff promising never to return to play in the park. Totally successful in his endeavour, the don retired to his study, luxuriating in the silence.

This parable illustrates a problem for the manager. If a person is happy (absorbed in a state of flow) doing a task, for whatever reason, but is also "managed" through explicit rewards (usually money), the individual will tend to focus on these obvious, extrinsic rewards, which then inevitably have to be escalated to maintain satisfaction. This is therefore a paradox: reward an intrinsically motivated person by extrinsic rewards and he/she is likely to become *less* motivated because the nature of the motivation changes. Unless a manager can keep up the increasing demands on the extrinsic motivator (i.e. constant salary increases) the person usually begins to show less enthusiasm for the job.

The use of reinforcers – i.e. paying people – is often counterproductive when the task is intrinsically interesting. That is, intrinsic motivation decreases with extrinsic rewards. Deci and Ryan (1985) demonstrated 30 years ago that reinforcement of progressively improved performance produced no loss (or gain) of intrinsic interest.

Some activities are rewarding because they satisfy curiosity, some because they produce an increased level of arousal. Deci (1980) proposed that intrinsic motivation is increased by giving a sense of mastery and competence, through the use of skills, and also by a sense of control and self-determination by autonomy to choose how the work is done. Both of these factors have been found to increase motivation. In addition to the enjoyment of competence, leisure research shows that people often enjoy the sheer activity, e.g. of dancing, music, or swimming, though they enjoy these things more if they are good at them (Argyle, 1996).

Experiments with children showed that if they were given external rewards for doing things that they wanted to do anyway, intrinsic motivation decreased. However, later research with adult workers has found that pay or other extrinsic rewards can increase intrinsic motivation, for example if the external rewards also give evidence of individual competence (Kanfer, 1990).

The most controversial work in this area suggests not only that intrinsic motivation is far preferable to extrinsic motivation, but also that extrinsic rewards are actually demotivating. The most powerful and popular advocate of this is Kohn (1999) who suggested that rewards can only create temporary compliance, not a fundamental shift in performance.

Kohn offers six reasons why this seemingly backward conclusion is, in fact, the case:

1. **Pay is not a motivator** – While the reduction of a salary is a demotivator, there is little evidence that increasing salary has anything but a transitory impact on motivation. This was pointed out 50 years ago. Just because too little money can irritate and demotivate does not mean that more money will bring about increased satisfaction, much less increased motivation.

2. **Rewards punish** – Rewards can have a punitive effect because they, like outright punishment, are manipulative. Any reward itself may be highly desired, but by making that bonus contingent on certain behaviours, managers manipulate their subordinates. This experience of being controlled is likely to assume a punitive quality over time. Thus, the withholding of an expected reward feels very much like punishment.

3. **Rewards rupture relationships** – Incentive programmes tend to pit one person against another, which can lead to all kinds of negative repercussions as people undermine each other. This threatens good teamwork.

4. **Rewards ignore reasons** – Managers sometimes use incentive systems as a substitute for giving workers what they need to do a good job, like useful feedback, social support, and autonomy. Offering a bonus to employees and waiting for the results requires much less input and effort.

5. **Rewards discourage risk taking** – People working for a reward generally try to minimise challenge and tend to lower their sights when they are encouraged to think about what they are going to get for their efforts.

6. **Rewards undermine interest** – Extrinsic motivators are a poor substitute for genuine interest in one's job. The more a manager stresses what an employee can earn for good work, the less interested that employee will be in the work itself. If people feel they need to be "bribed" to do something, it is not something they would ordinarily want to do.

This literature essentially says this: one can distinguish between intrinsic motivation to partake in some activity out of sheer enthusiasm, joy or passion and extrinsic motivation which involves offering a range of incentives to do an activity rather than the activity itself. The intrinsically motivated worker is therefore easier to manage, happier and possibly more productive. More controversially it has been suggested that extrinsic rewards like money can actually decrease joy and passion and even productivity in the long run. Of course, all jobs are a combination of both: some are done "just for the money" because the tasks are so unintrinsically motivating.

Monetary incentives, effort and task performance

It is axiomatic for many people that monetary incentives and rewards motivate people to work harder and better to achieve better performance. But some theories actually suggest the opposite because monetary rewards are all extreme, which often decreases intrinsic motivation and satisfaction leading over time to decreased effort and performance. Equally, some have argued that money is associated with negative emotions, which in turn has a negative impact on effort. Still others suggest that (some) monetary incentives may increase effort and performance up to a point but after that lead to a decrease. The data, however, are far from clear partly because of the complexity of the issue and the many factors involved.

The model in Figure 10.1 is a simplified version of that of Bonner and Sprinkle (2002), who pointed out some of the many factors involved in this relationship.

One fundamental feature of the theory is the idea that the reason for the **highly equivocal evidence** that incentives affect performance in a simple, positive and linear way is that there are many intervening variables that affect that relationship. These include person variables (the abilities, personality and motivation of individuals); task variables (like demands and complexity); environmental factors (group, organisational factors) and the incentive schemes (individual vs. group, monetary vs. non-monetary).

FIGURE 10.1 Money and performance

Banner and Sprinkle consider each of these relationships in turn:

1. **Effort leads to performance**.
   a. The first issue is the *direction* of the effort. If the incentive is for quality vs. quantity or vice versa it will certainly direct the type of effort put in. Often this leads to the law of unintended consequences where strategies backfire.
   b. The second is the *duration* of the effort. One issue is the time period over which the incentive contract is established. The longer the period, usually the higher the sustained effort.
   c. The third is the *intensity* of effort, which measures the amount of attention (cognitive resource) devoted to a task. Money can increase short-term intensity though it can also bring about fatigue and stress.
   d. The fourth is *strategy development*, which is concerned with the plan, strategy or habit developed by the individual given their perception of the reward situation.

2. **Motivation variables**. Four theories are relevant here.
   a. **Expectancy theory.** This suggests that people hold theories about pay for performance levels and the value of the pay. Pay for performance works if people see the clear, just relationship between their effort and outcome performance *and* really value the associated money.
   b. **Agency theory.** This suggests that people are self-interested and rational and risk averse. The amount of effort is related to the perception that it leads reasonably to performance that very directly relates to financial well-being.
   c. **Goal-setting theory.** Here personal goals are the stimulant of effort. Specific, challenging, self-set goals have most motivational power. Monetary incentives can shape new goals and get people to be committed to them.
   d. **Self-efficacy theory.** This posits a self-regulatory mechanism, which is the belief about one's ability to perform a specific task. It affects the tasks that a person chooses to do and their emotional state while doing those tasks. Incentives increase interest in the task, and thence effort and in turn skill, which increases self-efficacy beliefs.

One crucial person variable is the skills (including knowledge) of the individual and where, when and how they have to bring those to the task to achieve an output that is rewarded by money. Clearly people need the skill to perform a task otherwise increased effort will have limited results. Often increased effort cannot compensate for lack of skill.

A fair day's wage: Equity and relative deprivation

The issue that is consistently debated in this area is that of perceived *fairness*. However, fairness is a relative concept: what is fair for the giver (allocator) may not be fair for the receiver. Questions arise about specific issues: should you pay for the job or performance on the job; and should you pay for talent or effort?

Equity theory, borrowed by psychologists from economics, views motivation from the perspective of the social comparisons that people make among themselves. It proposes that employees are motivated to maintain fair, or "equitable", relationships among themselves and to change those relationships that are unfair, or "inequitable". Equity theory is concerned with people's motivation to escape the negative feelings that result from being treated unfairly in their jobs once they have engaged in the process of *social comparison*.

Equity theory suggests that people make social comparisons between themselves and others with respect to two variables – *outcomes* (benefits, rewards) and *inputs* (effort, ability). Outcomes refer to the things that workers believe they and others get out of their jobs, including pay, fringe benefits or prestige. Inputs refer to the contributions that employees believe they and others make to their jobs, including the amount of time worked, the amount of effort expended, the number of units produced, or the qualifications brought to the job. Equity theory is concerned with outcomes and inputs as they are *perceived* by the people involved, *not* necessarily as they actually are, although that in itself is often very difficult to measure. Not surprisingly, therefore, workers may disagree about what constitutes equity and inequity on the job. Equity is therefore a subjective, not objective, experience, which makes it more susceptible to being influenced by personal factors.

Equity theory states that people compare their outcomes and inputs to those of others in the form of a ratio. Specifically, they compare the ratio of their own outcomes/inputs to the ratio of other people's outcomes/inputs, which can result in any of three states: *overpayment, underpayment* or *equitable payment*.

- **Overpayment inequity** occurs when an individual's outcome/input ratio is *greater than* the corresponding ratio of another person with who that individual compares himself/herself. People who are overpaid are supposed to feel *guilty*. There are relatively few people in this position.
- **Underpayment inequity** occurs when an individual's outcome/input ratio is *less than* the corresponding ratio of another person with whom that individual compares himself/herself. People who are underpaid are supposed to feel *angry*. Many people feel under-benefited.
- **Equitable payment** occurs when an individual's outcome/input ratio is *equal* to the corresponding ratio of another person with whom that individual compares himself/herself. People who are equitably paid are supposed to feel *satisfied*.

According to equity theory, people are motivated to escape the negative emotional states of anger and guilt. Equity theory admits two major ways of resolving inequitable states (Table 10.1). *Behavioural* reactions to equity represent things that people can do to change their existing inputs and outcomes such as working more or less hard (to increase or decrease inputs), or stealing time and goods (to increase outputs). In addition to behavioural reactions to underpayment inequity, there are also some likely *psychological* reactions. Given that many people feel uncomfortable stealing from their employers (to increase outputs), or would be unwilling to restrict their productivity or to ask for a salary increase (to increase inputs) they may resort to resolving the inequity by changing the way that they think about their situation. Because equity theory deals with perceptions of fairness or unfairness, it is reasonable to expect that inequitable states may be redressed effectively by merely *thinking* about their circumstances differently. For example, an underpaid person may attempt to *rationalise* the fact that another's inputs are really higher than his/her own, thereby convincing himself/herself that the other's higher outcomes are justified.

How people will react to inequity depends on how they are paid. If they are paid by the time they are there they can reduce the rate of work, but if they are on piece work they may reduce the quality of work. Similarly, a salaried employee who feels overpaid may raise his/her inputs by working harder, or for longer hours or more productively. Likewise, employees who lower their own outcomes by not taking advantage of company-provided fringe benefits may be seen as redressing an overpayment inequity. Overpaid persons (few though they are!) may readily convince themselves psychologically that they are really worth their higher outcomes by virtue of their superior inputs. People who receive substantial pay rises may not feel distressed about it at all because they rationalise that the increase

Table 10.1 Reactions to inequity

Type of inequity	Type of reaction	
	Behavioural	*Psychological*
Overpayment inequity (guilt): $1 < O$	Increase your inputs (work harder), or lower your outcomes (work through a paid vacation, take no salary)	Convince yourself that your outcomes are deserved based on your inputs (rationalise that you work harder, better, smarter than equivalent others and so you deserve more pay)
Underpayment inequity (anger): $1 > O$	Lower your inputs (reduce effort), or raise your outcomes (get pay increase, steal time by absenteeism)	Convince yourself that others' inputs are really higher than your own (rationalise that the comparison worker is really more qualified or a better worker and so deserves higher outcomes)

Source: Furnham and Argyle (1998)

is warranted on the basis of their superior inputs, and therefore does not constitute an inequity.

Research has generally supported the theory's claim that people will respond to overpayment and underpayment inequities in the ways just described. An American study by Berkowitz, Fraser, Treasure, and Cochrane (1987) found that the strongest predictor of pay satisfaction was current inequity (- .49). Equity theory says that people seek fair distribution of rewards in relation to "inputs", which can include amount of work done, ability, etc., and will be discontented and leave the situation if this cannot be achieved, or they may try to increase equity in other ways such as by more absenteeism or stealing from their employers. What is seen as equitable depends to a large extent on comparisons. Brown (1978) found that industrial workers would choose a lower salary if it meant that they would receive more than a rival group.

As one might expect, equity theory has its problems: how to deal with the concept of negative inputs; the point at which equity becomes inequity; the belief that people prefer and value equity over equality. Nevertheless, the theory has stimulated an enormous literature that partially addresses itself to the issue of motivation and money's role in it.

Compensation: Pay satisfaction and job satisfaction

A great deal of research has been dedicated to the question many people think is self-evident: the relationship between pay and job satisfaction. While people are happy to acknowledge the fact that pay/salary/money is *but one* "reward" for work, it is considered by far the most important. Pay satisfaction is a core component of job satisfaction but there are a whole host of other factors (relationships at work, autonomy on the job, physical working conditions) that also play a part.

There are various dimensions to pay satisfaction that are interrelated: pay level, pay rises, benefit level and pay structure/administration (Williams, McDaniel & Ford, 2006). Further, various factors are related to pay satisfaction, like worker money attitudes (Thozhur, Riley & Szivas, 2006), race, gender, income and also pay equity comparisons (Tang, Tang & Homaifar, 2006).

Most studies have examined pay satisfaction in those of average as well as low pay. Some have shown self-evident findings such as the idea that personal attitudes to pay actually influence pay satisfaction (Thozhur et al., 2006).

One important study looked at the evidence for the relationship between seven factors: age, gender, education, tenure, salary grade, and job classification as well as actual salary/wage (Williams et al., 2006). There were two particularly interesting findings from this analysis. The *first* was how low the correlations were, indicating little or no relationship between things like gender and tenure and different types of pay satisfaction over various different samples. The *second* was that all the higher correlations were negative: thus older people were less satisfied with pay rises and structure; education and pay structure; salary grade and pay rise satisfaction. The authors believe the results suggest that older people may be less satisfied with pay because their expectations for the reward of service were not met. Similarly, the higher paid may be less happy because they too had higher expectations of the things that they received.

There are various dimensions to pay satisfaction that are interrelated: pay level, pay rises, benefit level and pay structure/administration (Williams et al., 2006). Further, various factors are related to pay satisfaction, like worker money attitudes (Thozhur et al., 2006), race, gender, income and also pay equity comparisons (Tang et al., 2006). Most studies have examined pay satisfaction in those of average as well as low pay. Some have shown self-evident findings such as the idea that personal attitudes to pay actually influence pay satisfaction (Thozhur et al., 2006).

For instance, Dulebohn and Martocchio (1998) showed that pay satisfaction was related to how fair people saw pay procedures to be, how fairly they thought pay was distributed, their understanding of the system, their commitment to the organisation, how effective they thought the pay-plan was, the extent to which they identified with their group, as well as the actual amount of money they received. Others have shown that the pay-performance process is mediated by other factors. Thus, Gardner, Van Dyne and Pierce (2004) showed that pay level affects self-esteem, which in turn affects performance. That is, pay signals to a person the extent to which the organisation values him/her and those feeling they are highly valued become better performers.

Dozens of researchers have done small-scale (relatively few people) studies correlating pay and satisfaction at any one point in time. It is possible to summarise this extensive research effort:

- Nearly all studies find a positive relationship between pay and job satisfaction but it is small ($.10 < r < .20$). Pay is not a strong factor in job satisfaction: external rewards are relatively ineffective in driving motivation, performance and satisfaction.
- Most studies concentrate on pay, not general job satisfaction.
- Other factors like a person's personality, ability and values appear to influence (i.e. mediate or moderate) the relationship between pay and satisfaction.
- Pay satisfaction is not primarily determined by simply how much one gets (i.e. absolute monetary reward).
- There are theories (i.e. self-determination theory) that suggests that over time, money rewards are demotivating and dissatisfying because they undermine perceived autonomy and well-being.

In a recent large-scale meta-analysis of 92 different samples, Judge, Piccolo, Podsakoff, Shaw and Rich (2010) found a correlation of $r = .15$ between pay level and job satisfaction, and of $r = .23$ between pay level and pay satisfaction. They concluded:

That the jobs which provide these things are little satisfying to individuals is, at first blush, surprising. Both within and between studies, level of pay had little relation to either job or pay satisfaction. This indicates that within an organisation, those who make more money are little more satisfied that those who make considerably less. Moreover, relatively well paid samples of individuals are only trivially more satisfied than relatively poorly paid samples. (p. 162)

One explanation they give relates to adaptation theory – the idea that pay increases are very quickly "spent" psychologically and therefore lose their satisfying value. This is not to say that pay is not motivating, but rather it is just one of the factors that is related to satisfaction.

There is a danger of taking far too great an individualistic perspective on this issue. That is, the idea that people have considerable latitude to influence their work-related effect and performance to achieve greater monetary rewards. Those who look at this issue from an organisational perspective ask the question: which comes first; pay (and general job) satisfied people or organisational performance?

Schneider, Hanges, Smith and Salvaggio (2003) found, as predicted, a positive relationship between company/organisation success and employee attitudes (satisfaction). Most importantly they found that it was organisational performance that drove employee satisfaction, not the other way around. It is frequently assumed that satisfaction drives productivity but their data showed the opposite, which led them to develop a testable model that went thus:

1. High performance work practices (as a function of organisational structure/management) lead to production efficiency.
2. Production efficiency leads to superior financial performance of the company.
3. Superior financial performance (often) leads to increased pay and benefits as well as the enhanced reputation of the organisation, all of which increases satisfaction with pay and security and overall satisfaction because of the attractiveness of the organisation.
4. This in turn leads to what is called organisational citizen behaviour, or people's general respect and help for one another in the organisation, which feeds into production efficiency and the virtuous circle.

The results in this area show that pay is weakly related to job satisfaction, which is determined by many factors. Further, it is clear that the assumption that satisfaction leads to (causes) productivity is too simple as there is evidence that in certain circumstances the direction of causality goes the other way.

Reward systems

Every job has an inducement/incentive and hopefully an agreement between inputs (amount of work) and outputs (e.g. pay). This wage–work bargain is in fact both a legal and a psychological contract that is often very poorly defined (Behrend, 1988).

> For instance: what about bonuses, currently a highly debated topic. The concept is derived from the Latin "bonum" meaning a good thing. The idea of a bonus is not unlike performance related pay. There are two types of pay – base pay or salary vs. "variable" pay, which may be a one-off and related very specifically to financial performance over a time period.
>
> Thus it could be argued that bonuses are cheaper and more efficient than trying to influence pay structures to make pay effective. Thus one can have a company with the CEO on a £/$100,000 base and a 75% bonus programme with middle managers on £/$50,000 with 50% and supervisors on £25,000 with 25%. This system can keep internal comparators stable on say a 1:20 ratio, meaning that the highest paid in any organisation gets 20 times the lowest.

Organisations determine pay by various methods, including: historical precedents, wage surveys and job evaluations (using points). They have to benchmark themselves against the competition so as to meet or exceed the market rate (Miner, 1993). Certainly, it is believed that monetary rewards are better at improving performance than such things as goal setting (management by objectives) or job-enrichment strategies.

Should men be paid more than women; doctors more than nurses; newsreaders more than airplane pilots? What factors are relevant in determining fair pay? The list may include the following:

- **Demographic** – sex, age, race;
- **Status** – education, job experience, job knowledge;
- **Work-output** – quality and quantity of work;
- **Job related** – job complexity, impact, responsibility and working conditions.

There is a rich literature on what professionals and lay people think about pay systems (Hogue, Fox-Cardamone, & Du Bois, 2011). Nearly everyone is paid – in money – for work. But organisations differ widely in how money is related to performance. The question of central interest to the organisational psychologists is the power of money as a motivator. There are several ways of doing this:

1. **Piece work:** Here workers are paid according to how much they produce. It can only be judged when workers are doing fairly repetitive work where the units of work can be counted.
2. **Group piece work:** Here the work of a whole group is used as the basis for pay, which is divided between them.
3. **Monthly productivity bonus:** Here there is a guaranteed weekly wage, plus a bonus based on the output of the whole department.
4. **Measured day work:** This is similar except that the bonus depends on meeting some agreed rate or standard of work.
5. **Merit ratings:** For managers, clerical workers and others it is not possible to measure the units of work done. Instead their bonuses or increments are based on merit ratings made by other managers.
6. **Monthly productivity bonus:** Managers receive a bonus based on the productivity of their departments.
7. **Profit-sharing and co-partnership:** There is a guaranteed weekly wage, and an annual or twice yearly bonus for all based on the firm's profits.
8. **Other kinds of bonus:** There can be a bonus for suggestions that are made and used, and there can be competitions for making the most sales, finding the most new customers, not being absent, etc.
9. **Use of other benefits:** Employees can be offered other rewards, such as medical insurance or care of dependents.

Pay for performance (PFP)

A topic of considerable interest is the whole issue of *performance-related pay:* the idea of linking pay with performance. Piecework and related methods are used most for skilled manual work. There have been many early studies of rates of work when there is payment by results.

Wage incentives can also reduce absenteeism, when a bonus is given for regular attendance. These schemes work better if there is participation over their introduction (Steers & Rhodes, 1984) and simply increasing the rate of pay can have dramatic effects in reducing labour turnover, in one case from 370% to 16% (Scott, Clothier & Spriegel, 1960). Use can be made of non-pay incentives, such as more free time or recognition, but financial incentives have the most effect (Guzzo, Jette & Catzell, 1985).

Problems with these plans arise where particular workers have differential opportunities to produce at a higher level – that is some workers may be unfairly disadvantaged under such a system. Further, wage incentives that reward individual productivity can, and often do, decrease co-operation among workers. Rewarding team productivity is an obvious solution but, of necessity, as the size of the team increases so the clear relationship between any individual's productivity and his/her pay decreases.

Without wage incentive schemes the productivity in any organisation tends to be "normally distributed" in a bell-shaped curve, but the introduction of a system sometimes leads to a restriction of production when workers come to an informal agreement about the norms of production. That is, there is often a restriction of range. This may be because workers fear increased productivity will lead to lay-offs, and/or that rate of payment will be reduced to cut labour costs. Obviously the restriction of range is in part a function of the history and climate of trust in any organisation.

The idea of PFP is that by linking pay with performance people are more inclined to direct and sustain desirable, goal-specified work-related behaviours. The idea is that money has both instrumental and symbolic motivational properties. It establishes behavioural criteria by which rewards are allocated and aligns employee behaviour with organisational values and objectives.

It is recognised that money/pay is one of many rewards at work and that unpaid or voluntary workers have to be managed and motivated without the "stick of money" (Van Vuuren, de Jong & Seydel, 2008).

The effectiveness of performance-related pay on measurable organisational inputs has, as one may expect, attracted considerable interest. Perry, Engbers, and Jun (2009) were interested in why, particularly in the public sector, performance-related pay systems were introduced, then abandoned, and then reintroduced. They noted three things of great interest. First, that there were a number of key variables in performance-related pay. These can be diagrammatically displayed as in Figure 10.2. In short the pay system is influenced by environmental factors and employee characteristics, which have numerous consequences.

Second, they found that the research in this area could be divided into two periods:

1. **1977–1993** – where expectancy and reinforcement theory dominated thinking. These simple causal theories – people will work harder/better/ more productively to get more (desired) rewards – never took sufficient cognisance of other moderator and mediator factors. Various studies and meta-analyses in this period found very little clear evidence that merit pay actually impacts on employee motivation and performance.
2. **1993–present** – here more and better studies were done but the results were very much the same. In short there was evidence of limited efficacy of contingency pay in the public sector. It fails to deliver on its promise.

Third, they drew up a number of lessons from this review. They included:

- PRP may have greater effect at lower organisational levels, where job responsibilities are less ambiguous.

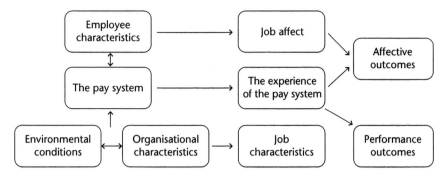

FIGURE 10.2 Key variables in performance-related pay

Source: Perry et al (2009)

- Implementation breakdowns account for failure of PRP systems but are not the only reason.
- Public institutions are more transparent and there is a closer scrutiny of PRP, which means they have to be seen as more fair, valid and non-political. Further, public organisations have more payroll cost containment and therefore there is less money for bonus pay. They also operate in non-market conditions.
- PRP imposed from the outside can seem to contradict the public service ethos.
- It is important to adapt any PRP to one's own organisation. Some politicians see PRP as a mechanism to call bureaucrats to account and conform to both their and the public's expectations.

Studies continue in this area; one looked at the role of public sector civil servants' love of money in China (Liu & Tang, 2011). The researchers found that attitudes to money influence both motivation and satisfaction. Another Chinese study found that PFP had a positive effect on work attitudes if there was a good fit between the employees and organisational values (Chiang & Birtch, 2010). That is, just having PFP is not sufficient. To benefit from PFP both employer and employee need to share the same values. Systems can help align values but are insufficient to do so on their own.

The idea that PFP does not work in the sense that it improves the quality and quantity of output is widespread but there is also evidence that it can be dysfunctional in the sense that it prevents improvements in task performance (Bijleveld et al., 2011). The issue is whether by concentrating so much on extrinsic motivation one actually limits intrinsic motivation.

Self-determination theory suggests that PFP systems are imposed by others (usually bosses) and seen as involving both punishments and rewards. If people identify with these systems and retain a sense of autonomy they may thrive, but if not they may become seriously disengaged (van Beek, Hu, Schaufeli, Taris & Schreurs, 2012).

With the current emphasis on team working (Furnham, 1996) group-level incentive plans have been popular. Profit sharing is a good example. It is assumed that the synergistic benefits of greater cooperation (hopefully leading to productivity) can offset the theoretical benefits of paying for individual performance. Gain-sharing plans involve a system where bonuses are based on the measurable cost reductions (in labour, materials, supplies) that are under the control of the work force. These plans involve *all* members of the work unit – even support staff and managers.

Trade Unions the world over oppose individual incentive plans, arguing that they promote unhealthy competition, increase accidents and fatigue, and disadvantages older or less healthy workers. Some even oppose group incentive schemes because they argue that they ultimately lead to a reduction in the quality of working life. They want people paid for the job they do, not performance on the job: they thus favour equality not equity.

The major problems with performance-related pay systems are, first, the fact that ratings of performance tend to drift to the centre. Feeling unable to deal with conflict or anxiety between people in a team, managers overrate underperformers and underrate better performers, so undermining the fundamental principles of the system. Next, as has been pointed out, merit increases are too small to be effective. Paradoxically in difficult economic times, when higher motivation and effort are required, the size of merit pay awards tends to be slashed.

The aims of such systems are straightforward: good performers should be pleased with, satisfied by, and motivated to continue to work hard because they see the connection between job performance and (merit-pay) reward. Equally, poor performers should be motivated to "try harder" to achieve some reward.

There are different types of PFP systems depending on who is included (to what levels), how performance will be measured (objective counts, subjective ratings or a combination) and which incentives will be used (money, shares, etc.). For some organisations the experiment with PFP has not been a success. Sold as a panacea for multiple ills it has backfired to leave a previously dissatisfied staff more embittered and alienated.

There are various reasons for the failure of PFP systems. First, there is frequently a poorly perceived connection between pay and performance. Many employees have inflated ideas about their performance levels, which translate into unrealistic expectations about rewards. When thwarted, employees complain, and it is they who want the system thrown out. Often the percentage of performance-based pay is too low relative to base pay. That is, if a cautious organisation starts off with too little money in the pot, it may be impossible to discriminate between good and poor performance, so threatening the credibility of the whole system.

The most common problem lies in the fact that, for many jobs, the lack of objective, relevant, countable results requires heavy, often exclusive use of performance ratings. These are very susceptible to systematic bias – leniency, halo, etc., which render them neither reliable nor valid.

Another major cause is resistance from managers and unions. The former, on whom the system depends, may resist these changes because they are forced to be explicit, to confront poor performance and tangibly to reward the behaviourally more successful. Unions always resist equity- rather than equality-based systems because the latter render the notion of collective bargaining redundant.

Further, many PFP plans have failed because the performance measure(s) which are rewarded were not related to the aggregated performance objectives of the organisation as a whole – that is to those aspects of the performance which were most important to the organisation. Also, the organisation must ensure that workers are capable of improving their performance. If higher pay is to drive higher performance, workers must believe in (and be capable of) performance improvements.

PFP plans can work very well indeed, providing various steps are taken. First, a bonus system should be used in which merit (PFP) pay is not tied to a percentage of base salary but is an allocation from the corporate coffers. Next, the band should be made wide whilst keeping the amount involved the same: say 0–20% for lower paid employees and 0–40% for higher levels. Performance appraisal must be taken seriously by making management raters accountable for their appraisals; they need training, including how to rate behaviour (accurately and fairly) at work.

Information systems and job designs must be compatible with the performance measurement system. More importantly, if the organisation takes teamwork seriously, group and section performance must be included in the evaluation. It is possible and preferable to base part of an individual's merit pay on team evaluation. Finally, special awards to recognise major individual accomplishments need to be considered separately from an annual merit allocation.

In short, Miner (1993) has argued that five conditions need to be met to ensure that any sort of incentive plan works:

1. The employee must value the extra money they will make under the plan.
2. The employee must not lose important values (health, job security, and the like) as a result of high performance.
3. The employee must be able to control their own performance so that they have a chance to strive further.
4. The employee must clearly understand how the plan works.
5. It must be possible to measure performance accurately (using indexes of performance, cost effectiveness, or ratings).

Similarly, Lawler (1981) has provided an excellent summary of the consequences of merit-pay systems (Table 10.2).

For many workers, job security is regarded as more important than level of wages/salary, and this is particularly true of unskilled, lower-paid workers, and those with a family history of unskilled work. Having a secure job is not only important for the family; it is also a status symbol. Worry about job insecurity has increased in the 1990s as a result of many jobs being taken over by computers. This is a major problem with the contemporary work scene; the big companies in Japan

Table 10.2 Effectiveness of merit–pay and bonus incentive systems in achieving various desired effects

Type of compensation plan	Performance measure used	Tying pay to performance	Desired effects		
			Minimising negative side effects	Encouraging cooperation	Gaining acceptance
Merit-pay systems					
For individuals	Productivity	Good	Very good	Very poor	Good
	Cost effectiveness	Fair	Very good	Very poor	Good
	Ratings by superiors	Fair	Very good	Very poor	Fair
For groups	Productivity	Fair	Very good	Poor	Good
	Cost effectiveness	Fair	Very good	Poor	Good
	Ratings by superiors	Poor	Very good	Poor	Fair
For organisation as a whole	Productivity	Poor	Very good	Fair	Good
	Cost effectiveness	Poor	Very good	Poor	Good
Bonus systems					
For individuals	Productivity	Very good	Fair	Very poor	Poor
	Cost effectiveness	Good	Good	Very poor	Poor
	Ratings by superiors	Good	Good	Very poor	Poor
For groups	Productivity	Good	Very good	Fair	Fair
	Cost effectiveness	Fair	Very good	Fair	Fair
	Ratings by superiors	Fair	Very good	Fair	Fair
For organisation as a whole	Productivity	Fair	Very good	Fair	Good
	Cost effectiveness	Fair	Very good	Fair	Fair
	Profit	Poor	Very good	Fair	Fair

Source: Adapted from Edward E. Lawler (1981). *Pay and organisation development*, p. 94. Reading, MA: Addison-Wesley.

succeeded for many years in offering job security to their staff, but the subsidiary firms then took the losses. And wage incentives affect whether or not people will work at all; in the past this was a choice between work and a life of leisure for some, today it is choice between work and social security.

However, there are definite limitations to the effects of money on work. Some people are less interested in earning more money; it depends on how much their friends and neighbours earn, how large their family is, whether they are trying to buy a house or a car. On the other hand they may raise their level of financial aspiration, and want a bigger house or car, or they may find new things to buy, or they may regard money as an index of success.

But the central question remains: which pay system has most effect on worker performance and satisfaction? A simple question but one without a simple answer. As noted above there are many alternatives: profit share, small group incentives, individual piece-work. According to Bucklin and Dickinson (2001), at the beginning of the twentieth century relatively simple piece-rates were the norm, but by the end of the century individualised variable performance pay was more common. This change was based on many things: such as changes in the law (employment, tax, social welfare); changes in economic affairs (interest rates, exchange rates); and the ability to measure and monitor performance. They note that the pay for performance system has four important characteristics. This is contrasted with profit sharing, which is based on the performance of the organisation as a whole.

In their lengthy and comprehensive review, Bucklin and Dickinson (2001) considered the literature on a number of very important and difficult questions:

1. *The ratio of incentive to base rate pay.* The question what effect is the power and efficacy of the ratio has on productivity and satisfaction. Should people have a very low base rate and a potentially high incentive pay, as is the case with many salespeople? This could lead to insecurity. Or do relatively small incentive pay opportunities (i.e. 5%) have a sufficiently powerful effect on productivity? For a long time the agreed optimal number was 30% incentive to base rate potential. *The conclusion of many studies was that a much smaller percentage (3–10%) was still very effective.*

2. *The schedule of reinforcement (fixed or variable ratio).* Is it more effective to pay people for every unit of work (hours worked, things made) or on a more variable ratio such as giving an occasional and unpredicted bonus? *The researchers noted that studies showed that monetary incentives improve performance in comparison to hourly wages.*

3. *Whether incentives should be linear, accelerating or decelerating.* The conclusion was that the slope of the payoff curve does not have an effect on productivity.

Table 10.3 Advice for managers

Principles	Implementation guidelines
1. Define and measure performance accurately	• Specify what employees are expected to do, as well as what they should refrain from doing • Align employees' performance with the strategic goals of the organisation • Standardise the methods used to measure employee performance • Measure both behaviours and results. But the greater the control that employees have over the achievements of desired outcomes, the greater the emphasis should be on measuring results
2. Make rewards contingent on performance	• Ensure that pay levels vary significantly based on performance levels • Explicitly communicate that differences in pay levels are due to different levels of performance and not because of other reasons • Take cultural norms into account. For example, consider individualism–collectivism when deciding how much emphasis to place on rewarding individual versus team performance
3. Reward employees in a timely manner	• Distribute fake currencies or reward points that can later be traded for cash, goods, or services • Switch from a performance appraisal system to a performance management system, which encourages timely rewards through ongoing and regular evaluations, feedback, and developmental opportunities • Provide a specific and accurate explanation regarding why an employee received a particular reward
4. Maintain justice in the reward system	• Only promise rewards that are available • When increasing monetary rewards, increase employees' variable pay levels instead of their base pay • Make all employees eligible to earn rewards from any incentive plan • Communicate reasons for any failure to provide promised rewards, changes in the amounts of payouts, or changes in the reward system
5. Use monetary and non-monetary rewards	• Do not limit the provision of non-monetary rewards to non-economic rewards. Rather, use not only praise and recognition, but also non-cash awards consisting of various goods and services • Provide non-monetary rewards that are need-satisfying for the recipient • Distribute non-monetary rewards based on the other four principles of using monetary rewards effectively • Use monetary rewards to encourage voluntary participation in non-monetary reward programmes that are more directly beneficial to employee or organisational performance

Source: Aguinis et al (2013).

Aguinis, Joo and Gottfredson (2013) attempted a helpful, simple but research-based summary of what is important in performance management and guidelines for the implementation of these ideas (Table 10.3).

Executive pay

The issue of executive pay continues to invoke hot debate. There is an academic literature on what people know about pay and what they think is fair pay. It can be summarised by three points. *First*, people are pretty well informed about the pay of different types of professionals as compared to national averages. *Second*, nearly all believe that the differentials are too high: the top earners should receive less and the bottom earners more. *Third*, if people are asked to start all over again and devise pay rates for different jobs, there are some surprises: many believe that currently well-paid jobs, such as TV news reading, should pay well below the national average, while others, such as nursing, should pay as much as judges.

Essentially there are four issues that inform this debate:

1. **The *amount* of (comparative) pay any/all executives should receive.** It is well know that satisfaction with pay is all about *comparatives* and not *absolutes*: that is, not how much you receive but how much you receive relative to your comparison group. The question is, what exactly is that? There are both internal and external comparators. Most top executives prefer the latter and not the former, but it is the exact opposite for observers. There have been strident calls for the implementation of a policy that means the top job is never paid more than ten times that of the bottom job within an organisation. It can be rather embarrassing for the board to try to explain how one job is worth so much more than another. Bosses, however, quite like social comparisons. They note that the world is now one market and if you are not prepared to pay international market rates, there will be a mass exodus of talent to other countries.

2. **How pay is *determined*.** Again there are various issues: one is who is involved and what mechanism they apply. Is it an in-house remuneration committee, or should a review be conducted by some expert outside consultancy company? What sort of algorithm should be used? For instance, should it be based on some sort of performance measure? How is that to be calculated? Anyone interested in performance management knows how difficult it is to measure performance. You can choose some metric: time, money, quality, quantity, customer feedback, but there are three problems here: how to get measures for jobs that don't distort behaviours (see how bus drivers ignore waiting passengers because they are often measured by on-time performance); the

contribution of others (teams) to productivity; and macro economic forces that suddenly occur. Linking pay to the share-price can also have serious and sudden unfortunate consequences as clever CEOs sell properties, re-engineer (sack) middle management, etc., to make the financials look good in the short term, only to have a later crisis.

3. **What *form* should payment take?** Salary, bonus, shares? And delayed salary? What about the perks: the house, the jet, etc.? What should be considered part of the total reward package? Most of the debate is about the end-of-year bonus, which may increase a short-termist approach to things. The paradox is that bonuses often make social comparison much easier because of people's natural boastfulness.

4. **Should pay be secret and *confidential* or made *public*?** While members of the board can usually hide their salary, the CEO's salary is nearly always published. In some countries this data has to be made open so there is no way to make it secret.

Pay secrecy

Surprisingly few companies communicate to employees all the issues about pay: how it is determined and administered, i.e. pay level. But does open communication about pay enhance perceptions of fairness or increase pay satisfaction? Essentially, if a company is open and upfront with respect to its pay policy it has to be able and willing to defend it.

Just after the First World War a big American company put out a "policy memorandum" entitled "Forbidding discussion among employees of salary received". It threatened to "instantly discharge people" who disclosed their "confidential" salary in order to avoid invidious comparison and dissatisfaction. The staff would have none of it. The next day the staff walked around with large signs around their necks showing their exact salaries.

The same issue continues to this day. People are worried that pay discussion simply fuels "hard feelings and discontentment". The question is: does pay secrecy lead to lower motivation and satisfaction or the other way around? There have been studies on this topic that show that secrecy is prevalent in most organisations and that workers actually want it. It may be illegal.

Colella, Paetzold, Zardkoohi and Wesson (2007) looked at the costs and benefits of pay secrecy. They argued that there were various costs:

1. *Employee judgements about fairness, equity and trust may be challenged.* If people don't know exactly what amount individuals are paid and why they surely infer or guess it. Yet uncertainty generates anxiety and

vigilance about fairness. People believe that if information is withheld it is for good reason. This in turn affects three types of justice judgements: *informational* (it being withheld); *procedural* (lack of employee voice and potential bias) and *distributional* (compressing the pay range).

2. *Judgements about pay fairness will, if they have to, be based on a general impression of the fairness in the organisation.* People see all sorts of things (hiring, firing, perks) that are vivid and remembered examples of "fairness". So, even if they have a "fair but secret" pay policy it will be judged unfair if other perhaps unrelated actions do not look fair.

3. *Secrecy breeds distrust.* Openness about pay signals integrity. Secrecy may enhance views about organisational unfairness and corruption. Further, it signals that the organisation does not trust its employees. So secrecy reduces motivation by breaking the pay for performance linkage.

4. *People need to have (and perform best when they are given) goals/targets/ KPI and are rewarded for them.* But if they do not know the relative worth of the rewards (i.e. in pay secrecy) they may well be less committed to those goals.

5. *Pay secrecy could affect the labour market because it could prevent employees moving to better fitting and more rewarding jobs.* Pay-secret organisations may not easily lure or pull good employees from other organisations. Secrecy makes the market inefficient.

On the other hand secrecy can bring real advantages to an organisation:

1. *Secrecy can enhance organisational control and reduce conflict.* Pay differentials can cause jealousy. So, hiding them may prevent problems in corps d'esprit. Making pay open often encourages managers to reduce differences. That is the range distribution is narrower than the performance. So, paradoxically, secrecy increases fairness in the equity sense because people can more easily be rewarded for the full range of their outputs.

2. *Secrecy prevents "political" behaviour, union involvement and conflict.* Openness is both economically inefficient and likely to cause conflict.

3. *Pay secrecy allows organisations more easily to "correct" historical and other pay equity.* So, paradoxically, one can minimise both unfairness and discrimination as well as perceptions of those matters more easily by secrecy.

4. *Secrecy benefits team work particularly in competitive individuals, organisations and cultures.* It encourages interdependence rather than "superstardom".

5.   *Secrecy favours organisational paternalism in that organisations can (and do) argue that employees themselves want secrecy, and a reduction in conflict, jealousy and distress at learning about others.* One can even suggest that workers might make irrational decisions if they know what their colleagues are (really) paid. So, paternalistic secrecy increases control and the "feel good" factor.

6.   *Secrecy is another word for privacy and increasing concern in a technologically sophisticated surveillance society.* Perhaps this is why surveys show people are generally in favour of secrecy because people do not want their salaries discussed by their co-workers. People are willing to trade off their curiosity about the pay of others for not having their own package made open.

7.   *Secrecy may increase loyalty or, put more negatively, labour market immobility.* If people can't compare their salaries they may be less inclined to switch jobs to those that are better paid. So, you get what is called continuance commitment through lack of poaching.

Clearly the cost-benefit ratio depends on different things. Much depends on the history of the organisation. It is pretty difficult to "re-cork" the genie if it has escaped the bottle. It also depends on whether good, up-to-date, accurate industry compensation norms really exist. What does – on average – a senior partner in a law firm, a staff-nurse, a store manager get paid? The public industry norm information can have a powerful effect on organisations that opt for secrecy or privacy.

The next issue is how the organisation does (or claims to) determine criteria for pay allocation. Do they do payment for years of service, for level, for performance on the job or for some combination of the above? The more objective the criteria (number of calls made, number of widgets sold), the more difficult it is to keep things secret. Next, appraisal systems strive to be objective, equitable and fair. The more they are, the less need for secrecy. Where objective criteria are used staff have less concerns for secrecy. So, subjectivity and secrecy are comfortable bedfellows. People don't know under pay secrecy what their pay is based on. And secrecy means they can't predict or believe that they can in any way control their pay.

When companies pay in secret, people have to guess how they rank relative to others at the same level. That, no doubt, is why high performers want secrecy more than low performers; they believe they are equitably being paid more and want to avoid jealousy and conflict. So, you believe you are well paid because of your hard work and all is well with secrecy.

When pay secrecy is abolished some people not only feel angry, they feel humiliated by exposure to relative deprivation. They feel unfairly dealt with and their easiest means of retaliation is inevitably to work less hard.

Pay secrecy is not just an HR issue. It relates to organisations' vision and values as well as individual job motivation. Secrecy can lead to more management control, bigger differentials and less conflict. But can you enforce it? Paradoxically the more enthusiastically an organisation tries to enforce it the more employees might challenge the notion. Individuals and groups choose, or not, to talk.

Three things are clear. Once you have abolished or reduced secrecy the path back is near impossible. Next, if competitors have openness and you have secrecy they might undermine your system. But, most importantly, for openness to work you need to be pretty clear in explaining how pay is related to performance at all levels and to be able to defend your system.

It has been argued that pay communication seeks to establish and increase perceived fairness in various ways (Day, 2012):

- It explains that pay is fair because it is based on relevant, agreed, socially acceptable criteria (i.e. level, performance).
- It is fair relative to market standards.
- It is fair relative to past worker input.
- It is aligned with future pay practices.
- It encourages the focus of attention to relevant peers.

Thus, it is argued that if pay communication is clear and open *and* if the pay is actually equitable, it leads to staff commitment, engagement and satisfaction. Indeed, there are studies to suggest that pay communication often results in lower trust and perception about fairness (Day, 2007). Certainly, early studies of salesmen found open pay policies had little or no effect (positive or negative) on general satisfaction (Futrell & Jenkins, 1998). What seems most important is to explain what determines pay level (i.e. performance, loyalty) and why.

Money at work

There are both intrinsic and extrinsic rewards for people at work. The more intrinsically a person is motivated the less important and powerful the effect of money as a reward. Indeed, increasing the latter can even reduce the former. There are four reasons why people are not simply motivated by money:

- *First*, they adapt to the changes in levels of money very quickly so any effect wears off quickly.
- *Second*, it is not the absolute amount of money that people are paid that is important but rather how much they are paid comparative to those in their work group.
- *Third*, perceptions of fairness are ultimately important, which is why issues around executive pay and pay secrecy are so important.
- *Fourth*, other things such as job security, work–life balance and time off can be more important than money.

There are many subtly different pay schemes, which can have different effects on performance.

11

BEHAVIOURAL ECONOMICS

I buy when other people are selling.

John Paul Getty

Nothing is more disastrous than a rational investment in an irrational world.

John Maynard Keynes

There are two times in a man's life when he should not speculate: when he can afford it, and when he can't.

Mark Twain

Why is the man or woman who invests all your money called a broker?

George Carlin

Introduction

We are all *"people of the heart and people of the head"*. Our everyday decisions are governed by our thought processes but also by our emotions. Despite the fact that we like to think of ourselves as analytical, logical and rational there is considerable evidence to suggest that this is not the case.

We are rationalising rather than rational and psycho-logical rather than analytically logical. It is particularly an issue with money. People can be astonished if for instance they are "natural savers" and they have some sort of (personal or business) relationship with a "spender". Equally, a financial risk taker may see a cautiously investing friend as mad, wasting wonderful opportunities; while the latter sees the former as irresponsible, even wicked in their profligacy.

Indeed, the central message of behavioural economics is that people make "big money mistakes" for well-established reasons. The science has been able to describe and explain the processes by which we take short cuts and make logical errors. In essence, it is suggested that people try to simplify and speed up their everyday decision making by adopting "rules of thumb". They consciously try to reduce complexity and in doing so make predictable and consistent logical errors.

We know why people do not think that all money is the same and treat it differently with regard to how they obtained it in the first place. So, they may be very happy to take wild risks with inherited or gifted money but not with money they earned by hard work. We also know people are much more motivated (and pained) by the prospect/experience of loss as opposed to the opportunity and reality of gain. Many throw good money after bad in an irrational way or suddenly disinvest when the market falls. A lot of people tend to believe that things they own are worth more than they patently are. And very many delay making investment or spending decisions; money issues frighten them.

It has been shown that people often make important money decisions based on unimportant, trivial or irrelevant information. Often there is a lot of evidence of the "ego trap", which is the idea that people are supremely overconfident about their money decisions. We know that very many people make spending decisions without doing much research; that they "take heart" from winning investments and are happy to "explain away" all poor ones. Many think they are always beating the market or simply don't know the rate of return on their investments.

The studies on risk taking are also very illuminating. Some people are amazing risk takers with all aspects of their lives. Risks – be they physical or behavioural – seem to give then a great thrill: a rush of adrenaline that they seem to need to keep them going. Others seem more complicated as they are cautious in some aspects of their life (e.g. physical safety, diet) but almost outrageously risky in others (e.g. their personal relationships).

But do people know how they "stack up" against others in their taste for risk taking? They might believe they are risk takers or risk averse but does their behaviour really show that? Many are ignorant about others' risk taking because the topic is taboo. They are disconnected in the sense that their view of themselves is not what accords with what they do. The person who thinks of themself as "super-cautious" actually turns out to be "quiet risky" while the opposite can also be true.

Money is a great source of anxiety for many people: for the poor how to get more of it; for the rich how to keep it; and for nearly everybody how best to invest it particularly in uncertain times. We all know we have to save for our future and that investing wisely is terribly important for our well-being. However little or much we have "wealth management" is important; and if anything it will get more so. Most of us want good advice from people who understand our "taste", indeed, we have a "need for" financial management whether it be taking no, few, some or great risks. It is fundamentally bound up with our general well-being.

Prospect theory

Behavioural economics has its intellectual foundations in both psychology and economics. It seeks to understand how people select, process and decide upon financial (and other) information. It offers profound and parsimonious information as to why so many seemingly educated and informed people make strangely illogical or irrational decisions with respect to all aspects of their money: borrowing, investing, saving and spending.

It is axiomatic in economics that people make rational decisions about their money. Economists assume we (always) know what we want, which is for our own good, and that we know how to get it. People make cost-benefit analyses in the pursuit of personal satisfaction and getting the most out of life with their individual resources.

Economists have been challenged by certain economic behaviours, which they have not found easy to explain: why do people tip; why do they spend differently with cash than a credit card; why do people have savings accounts which don't offer interest that even keeps pace with inflation; why do we happily and enthusiastically spend more for a product when using a credit card as opposed to cash.

Behavioural economics was "born" in the late 1960s with experiments that showed that people do not understand some basic statistical phenomena (regression to the mean; the importance of sample size). The pioneers in this area – Amos Tversky and Daniel Kahneman – explored the judgemental heuristics or mental short cuts that people use to think about their money and other related issues.

Kahneman and Tversky won the Nobel Prize in economics in 2002 for their work on prospect theory. It is a theory that describes decisions between alternatives that involve risk, i.e. alternatives with uncertain outcomes, where the probabilities are known. The model is descriptive: it tries to model real-life choices, rather than optimal decisions. People decide which outcomes they see as basically identical and they set a reference point and consider lower outcomes as losses and larger ones as gains. The asymmetry of the S-curve (Figure 11.1) is indicative of Warren Buffett's

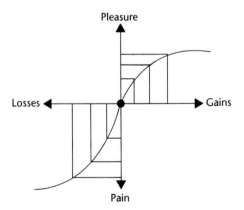

FIGURE 11.1 The pain and pleasure of loss and gain

finding that "losses gain twice the emotional response of gains" and shows that people are risk averse (play it safe) in relation to gains, yet loss averse (gamble to avoid losses).

For individual investors the purchase price of shares is the reference point against which they make all decisions. Thus, they tend to sell too soon after making a small gain or hold on for too long when the loss is terrifying. As we have seen many times the market overreacts to bad news and encourages selling. The fear of loss is over exaggerated.

An important implication of prospect theory is the framing of risky situations. The following example highlights just what an effect framing has on people:

Participants were asked to imagine being a scientist working on an outbreak of an unusual disease, which is expected to kill 600 people. Two alternative programmes to combat the disease have been proposed. The first group of participants were presented with a choice between two programmes:

Programme A: "200 people will be saved"
Programme B: "there is a one-third probability that 600 people will be saved, and a two-thirds probability that no people will be saved"

Seventy-two percent of participants preferred programme A (the remainder, 28%, opting for programme B). The second group of participants were presented with the choice between:

Programme C: "400 people will die"
Programme D: "there is a one-third probability that nobody will die, and a two-thirds probability that 600 people will die"

In this decision frame, 78% preferred programme D, with the remaining 22% opting for programme C. However, programmes A and C, and programmes B and D, are effectively identical. A change in the decision frame between the two groups of participants produced a preference reversal, with the first group preferring programme A/C and the second group preferring B/D.

The framing of risky situations can drastically affect the way a person will react to them and this has been widely used in behavioural economics and applied to a diverse range of situations (investing, lending, borrowing decisions) that appear inconsistent with the old economic viewpoint that humans act rationally. Would you rather get a 5% discount, or avoid a 5% surcharge? The same change in price framed differently significantly affects consumer behaviours and is an area of huge importance to marketing.

It is not the reality of the loss that matters but the perception. Nations have gone to war and "stayed the course" until their doom because of loss aversion. It simply means you refuse to admit you made a mistake. As Aronson puts it, "Once we have committed a lot of time or energy to a cause, it is nearly impossible to convince us that it is unworthy." The real question is: "How bad do your losses have to be before you change course?"

Much research supports the assumption that human decision making across contexts is influenced by perceptual cognitive biases, which are hardwired from birth. These biases are heuristics: short cuts in decision making where we make automatic and "unthinking" decisions, often about purchases on a daily basis.

Most people do not have the capacity or motivation to fully process or evaluate every piece of information that they encounter in their ever-changing worlds. So, to cope with the sheer amount of data and enhance decision making, humans rely on heuristics to deal with the complexity of their daily environments. Such cognitive biases allow us to make rapid judgements about complex information that we are unable to thoroughly evaluate. These stimuli are responded to automatically, without conscious awareness of the underlying cognitive process.

Kahneman (2011) has provided a masterful summary of the cognitive and social psychology underlying behavioural economics. He distinguishes between two types of thinking: fast and slow, or systems 1 and 2. *Fast* thinking is intuitive, relies on heuristics, and is in a sense *automatic*, while *slow* thinking is *effortful*, deliberate and more logical/rational. These two systems interact to minimise effort and optimise performance.

System 2 thinking requires effort, attention and involvement. It involves thinking, memorising and processing. It involves different forms of energy, but as people become more skilled at any task, their demand for energy diminishes. System 2 thinking keeps you busy and can deplete your willpower. People find cognitive effort mildly unpleasant and avoid it as much as possible.

System 1 is lazy while 2 means being more alert, intellectually active, sceptical and rational. Inevitably intelligent people may be better at slow thinking and demanding computation, but that does not mean they are immune to biases and lazy thinking.

Kahneman's book contains 38 short chapters that explain and describe admirably many aspects of fast thinking. These include the power of priming; the idea that people in a state of cognitive ease are more casual and superficial in their thinking; overconfidence and the neglect of base-rate effects; anchoring and priming.

In the final chapter of the book he uses a new metaphor for the two types: the experiencing (System 1) self that does the living and the remembering (System 2) self that keeps the score and makes the choices. The experiencing self is less conscious about time.

Heuristics

Heuristics are biases, mental short-cuts; the products of fast thinking. There are a number of heuristics that are widely discussed in present behavioural economics research. Advertisers and businesses have long known about these because they have understood that the way they frame their message, price option, promotion or proposition has a great impact on whether they will be chosen.

Many of these have been identified and they are briefly reviewed here.

1. Loss aversion

This is the tendency to prefer avoiding losses to acquiring gains. All of us treat losses and gains quite differently. People's decisions are powerfully influenced by how they frame and describe situations. Nearly all people are much more willing to take risks to avoid losses and much more conservative when it comes to opportunities for gain.

People should test their personal threshold for loss. We are all sensitive to an extent: the question is how sensitive are you? So, the good advice is diversify your investments; focus on the big picture, the broader whole, the wider issues; forget the past because you are not there to justify earlier behaviours; reframe losses as gains like lessons learned, taxes saved; spread out your gains and, paradoxically, pay less attention to your investments, otherwise you will overreact.

In one study a bank targeted people who had not used their credit card for some time. Half were told how good/useful was the cards; and half were told it would be withdrawn unless it was used. As predicted from the theory, those who received the loss framed message were twice as likely to act (i.e. use the card) as those that received the positively framed message.

In short the data show that *people give twice the weight to the pain of loss than they do to the pleasure of gain.* We are therefore risk seeking in the realm of gains, but risk averse in the realm of losses: almost the opposite of what most people suspect. There are many good examples of studies where this has been demonstrated. For instance:

a. Homeowners were randomly sent information about the benefits of or losses accruing in not, insulating their home. Those who got the loss message (expressed in daily cash loss) were over 200% more likely to proceed with the insulation.
b. Another case study reported on trying to get people to imagine the benefit of buying new technology. Those asked to imagine what they could not do if they did not buy it were more than twice as likely to purchase it.
c. Supermarkets know that giving out small coupons increases sales, because if they are not redeemed the customer has lost something.
d. The same is true with all sorts of loyalty cards. If these are given to people after they have made a purchase with the acknowledgement or stamp showing they

have already made a purchase (and even better a double stamp as a generous first offer) they are much more likely to use the card, because not doing so represents a loss.

The moral of loss aversion is simple. People are more likely to act if threatened with loss than promised gain in money. The same issue can be framed in opposite ways (losses or gains) but the effects are very different.

2. Endowment

This is the idea that people have the tendency to overvalue things they own. We place a higher value on things that we personally own (a car, a coffee mug, a computer) than their actual, sometimes even printed, market value. These products seem endowed with extra value. People also think a product is more valuable if they get something in return for it, even though it may be of little value. Even little things like stationery, old clothes or books, which are practically worthless, are thought of by owners as potentially high in value.

Curiously, people want more money for a personal product or object that they are trying to sell than the identical object they may want to purchase. This is because the loss of the possession has a greater psychological impact than the benefit derived from gaining it.

People overvalue what they have: they endow it with psychological wealth and are misguided about actual worth. This can lead them to be very disappointed when selling items, but can make manufacturers rich when they explore this heuristic.

3. Anchoring

Anchoring is the impact of an arbitrary reference point upon an estimate of an unknown value. The heuristic bias is caused by people having insufficient adjustment in decisions because final judgements (i.e. agreeing the price) are assimilated towards the starting point of the judge's deliberations.

This area has attracted a great deal of attention (Furnham & Boo, 2011). Anchors can be both internal and external sources of information. Customers seem to have internal expected retail prices (based on all sorts of things), which they use as anchors, basing their response to prices in store upon them. Some customers also base their evaluation of retail price on external sources of numbers such as prices of other products they have come across in store. For instance, if a customer buys a laptop they are often happy to purchase expensive accompaniments. This is because in comparison to the price of the computer they are perceived as being good value.

It is suggested that the anchoring effect occurs as we are not motivated enough to revise our price estimates away from a value that we can anchor upon, and so settle with a similar figure. Further, the authors propose that individuals' original estimates of figures tend to be broad, and so it is cognitively less strenuous to accept whatever an anchor figure is available and focus on more demanding thoughts.

You can anchor by proximity: placing low cost items next to high cost items. Similarly, products of low inherent value can have their value anchored at a higher level if placed next to something expensive.

We also anchor experiences. Against worst case scenarios, less serious issues do not seem as bad. The flight might have been cancelled: it is going but eight hours late.

Curiously, when people have no idea about cost or value they anchor on anything that seems remotely plausible. All free giveaways are thought to be more valuable if the product was seen to have an original cost. Because of the anchoring effect it is usually advised in a negotiation situation to "go in early and go high", to anchor the person around a particular monetary value of your choosing.

4. Salience

Essentially the idea is that the more particular information or data *seem* salient or relevant to a particular problem, the more disproportionate the influence they will have. Thus, even though the information can be demonstrated not to be (at all, or partly) relevant/salient to a particular decision it can carry more weigh if perceived to be so. This information that is said to be salient is that which receives a disproportionate amount of attention in comparison to other information available. Such information also benefits from enhanced recall.

It could be that the salient information is that which is similar to that previously experienced and thus has a large network of nodes in the memory, with a number of linkages. Retrieval of such information is facilitated due to the network associated with it, increasing the ease with which it is retrieved.

5. Fluency

Oppenheimer (2008) described fluency as being "the subjective experience of ease or difficulty with which we are able to process and understand information" (p. 237). This is a simple heuristic, suggesting that we have a preference for information that is processed with ease. Those things (ideas, objects, theories) which are processed faster, more easily and more smoothly appear to have higher value. Simple, straightforward things seem more important than they are.

Alter and Oppenheimer (2006) found that stocks with fluent and easily pronounceable names outperformed non-fluently named stocks. The authors based this finding on fluency, and the fact that fluently named stocks are considered to be more valuable due to the ease with which they are processed.

The real test for any brand is that it "*readily comes to mind*": in fact sooner than all competitive brands. That which is easily read, understood and remembered is always "*top of mind*". That which is easy encourages behaviour: so people spend more on a credit card than in cash and more with notes than coins worth the same amount simply because they are so much easier. This can work in situations as simple as having see-through containers: things "readily available" are more readily consumed.

This is why marketers try so hard to make their product stand out: it should be easily and readily noticeable through packaging colour, shape or logos, which can all have beneficial effects. People also respond to consistency in product design – whether it refers to shape or colour or logo. Pack consistency helps recognisability, which helps sales. It is no surprise that EASY is a brand that has done well.

Fluency can occur in other ways. If a product name rhymes, or is very easy to pronounce and spell, it sells more. That is why car manufacturers struggle to find new car names that can sound attractive and pronounceable in different languages. Equally, the fewer the options people have the better. Having too many options can easily overwhelm people. Less really is more.

Fluency is related to ease: ease of navigation round a store, ease of purchase, and ease of recall.

6. Availability

This is based on the notion that if you can (quickly and easily) think of something, it will be rated as very important. The more often a particular event occurs, the more mentally available this is for retrieval – and this factor is used to estimate likelihood of occurrence.

The trouble is that the frequency with which particular events come to mind is usually *not an accurate* reflection of their actual probability in real life. This short cut also leads to illusory correlations where because people can relatively easily recall events that occurred at much the same time it was believed that they were related to each other.

One famous example is asking people whether dying from a shark attack or having airplane parts fall on your head is more common and they nearly always choose the former.

7. Familiarity

This heuristic works on the basis of current behaviour being similar to a past experience. We assume that previous behaviour and its results can be applied to new situations. What worked in the (very different) past will work in current (and future) situations. In this sense we are "victims" of our past. It also explains why people learn more from failure than from success. The deja vu experience, then, can be very bad for us. It makes us lazy and our decision making poor.

8. Peak-end rule

Kahneman (2011) suggested that the evaluations we keep in mind of previous experiences are based on the peak of either how pleasant or how unpleasant they were, and how the event was perceived at its end. Events are not evaluated rationally, considering how pleasant the experience was on average. Memories are powerfully coloured by powerful positive and negative experiences.

In one study he found that participants evaluated 60 seconds of 14°C ice water followed by 30 seconds of 15°C ice water more positively than simply 60 seconds of 14°C ice water alone. The one degree increase in water temperature was experienced as a pleasant improvement and heightened overall memories of the experience.

This is related to the primacy–recency effect, well known to memory researchers. Here, information that occurs at the beginning and the end is better recalled than the information that occurs "in the middle". The primacy effect is where information that comes first or early is given more weight, while the recency effect is where the information that comes last is given more weight.

9. Recognition

Recognisable objects and information are considered to have more value than those that are novel. If a name or place or shape or colour seems familiar it is judged more positively that if it is not recognised.

10. Simulation heuristic

Kahneman and Tversky (1982) suggest that the ease with which an event is imagined in one's mind is used to make predictions, assess probabilities, evaluate statements and determine the likelihood of that event occurring. This may appear similar to the availability heuristic, but differs in that the simulation heuristic involves *imagining* fictitious experiences, whereas availability refers to the recall of real-life memories.

This heuristic is said to be less automatic than the others, and we do not generally spontaneously generate alternatives to a situation. However, when instructed to imagine an alternative possibility this leads to the automatic generation of additional alternative possibilities.

11. Sunk cost

Economists argue that sunk costs are not taken into account when making rational decisions. It is the situation of throwing good money after bad; of continuing on a loss-making project to "justify" the amount of money already spent on it.

Sunk costs may cause cost overrun. In business, an example of sunk costs may be investment into a factory or research that now has a lower value or no value whatsoever. For example, $20 million has been spent on building a power plant; the value at present is zero because it is incomplete (and no sale or recovery is feasible). The plant can be completed for an additional $10 million, or abandoned and a different facility built for $5 million. It should be obvious that abandonment and construction of the alternative facility is the more rational decision, even though it represents a total loss on the original expenditure – the original sum invested is a sunk cost. If decision makers are (economically) irrational, or have the wrong incentives, the completion of the project may be chosen. For example, politicians or managers may have more incentive to avoid the appearance of a total loss. In practice, there is considerable ambiguity and uncertainty in such cases, and decisions may in retrospect appear irrational that were, at the time, reasonable to the economic actors involved and in the context of their own incentives.

12. Default

Decision making requires effort. Defaulting on a typical response is easy. Some people always default on "no", others on "yes". The former always refuse, the latter always accept. Some people seem always to agree; others always disagree. They don't weigh up the evidence fully before defaulting to a particular position.

The default opt out is well known. It has been shown that if you require people to *opt out* of something, few do so, but if you require them to *sign up* for donorship few do so. They are less likely to opt out than in. Thus, by defaulting on inactivities governments and manufacturers can ensure that they get people to behave in a particular way. In some countries you have to opt out to register as a non-organ donor. That means that everyone has the right to refuse actively. That is they have to opt out. In most countries a very small percentage do, so any or all of their bodily organs are used after death: but they have to be pro-active.

Manufacturers have learnt to tick boxes when offering people products and services. If you have to "un-tick" or cancel the tick, most do as the manufacturer requires.

13. Compromise effects

Faced with a list of options most people avoid extremes. Usually they avoid the cheapest and the most expensive option and compromise. That is why manufacturers have decoy products. It has been argued that "organic" produce in big departmental stores are essentially decoy products making more expensive non-organic products seem cheaper and more attractive.

There is no simple agreed list of these heuristics or what they are called. Some people stress the power of certain heuristics over others. Thus, the power of mental accounting is stressed by some people in the insurance business to try to understand why people think differently about money with different origins while others are fascinated by the observation that although people always say they want more choice (of products/services) when faced by more choice they choose less. It is no surprise that "cheap" shoe shops have a "pile-em-high-an-sell-em-cheap" approach while expensive, highly sophisticated shoe shops may display as few as three to four very expensive shoes.

Practical advice

In a popular book entitled *Why Smart People Make Big Money Mistakes*, Belsky and Gilovich (1999) discuss seven typical issues that demonstrate the problems with "heuristic thinking":

1. Not all money is seen as equal

This is also known as *mental accounting* or fungibility. It means people define and therefore use money differently. People spend £100 obtained from a roulette win, a salary, a tax refund or a lucky find differently. Whether money comes from a bonus, a gift, a rebate or a refund *it is all the same*.

We draw and deposit our own money in different accounts of our own making. If people get a bonus of £200 they are paradoxically more likely to spend it on something "frivolous" than if they got a bonus of £2,000 or even £20,000. The latter is more serious, sacred and "harder to spend". Equally, buying something using a credit card feels diffent to using cash (particularly low denomination notes).

Mental accounting can make people at the same time both spenders and savers: reckless with certain "types of money" but excessively conservative investors with other sorts of money. It means they are more likely to spend tax refunds or gift money recklessly and to use cash quite differently from credit cards.

There are benefits to some mental accounting. It helps that the mortgage gets paid; that retirement money or children's university education money is never touched. But it makes people reckless with windfall money or forgotten cash, rediscovered savings, etc. Equally it is unwise to have savings acquiring low interest while "borrowing" money on a credit charge by not paying off debts at the end of the month. One solution is to imagine that all income – whatever the source – is earned. Work out how long it would take to earn. This, Belsky and Gilovich maintain, can make a big difference.

2. We treat losses and gains quite differently

People's decisions are powerfully influenced by how they frame and describe financial situations. The results are very clear: people are much more willing to take risks to avoid losses and much more conservative when it comes to opportunities for gain.

Prospect theory stresses how important choices are described as gains or losses. The same amount of pain and the same amount of pleasure have very different impacts. This is the psychology of loss aversion. This oversensitivity to loss means that people may respond too quickly to drops in the market. On the other hand the selling of a stock or bond (the pain of making a loss fund) makes some people more willing to take the risk of keeping the investment despite its continual decline. Oversensitivity to loss also means people go for certain gains.

People, Belsky and Gilovich argue, should test their personal threshold for loss. We are all sensitive to loss: the question is how sensitive are you?

Behavioural economists have shown how loss aversion and our inability to ignore sunk costs means people often act unwisely. But they have also explained why people don't act when they should. We sometimes get overwhelmed by choice, and paralysed by having to make a decision – so we defer the actual decision. Decision paralysis happens particularly when we have plenty of – indeed too much – choice. The more time we have to do a task, the more we procrastinate. That is why some people have to be driven by deadlines to react. We also know people like to compromise and have extremeness aversion. Given a choice people choose an intermediate. Thus, people can be persuaded to buy more if a high price item is introduced.

3. We are also prone to inaction

We also opt for the status quo: doing nothing; resisting change; showing unwillingness to rock the boat. The endowment effect is particularly interesting. It means people overvalue what they value. That is why organisations allow for trial periods and money back guarantees. Belsky and Gilovich (1999) claim that there are various telltale signs of this problem: having a hard time choosing between investment options, not having a pension, delaying financial decisions all the time.

The advice from the behavioural economists is simple. Deciding not to decide is itself a decision. All decisions come with opportunity costs. Try to reframe a problem: be a devil's advocate.

4. The money illusion and the bigness bias

This problem classically arises when we confuse nominal changes in money (it goes up or down) with real changes, for instance as a function of inflation or deflation. The question is the current buying power of money as opposed to its actual amount.

Related to this is the idea of base rate: the fact that people buy lottery tickets, which, because of the real odds of winning, have been described as "a tax on the stupid". People simply don't understand the relationship between inflation and buying power. Many ignore or downplay various fees/commissions that people charge, and they don't really understand compound interest. The authors warn against being impressed with short-term success and ignoring the fine print when making money decisions.

5. Anchoring and confirmation bias

This is quite simply the common and strong tendency to latch onto some idea/fact or number and use it, whether relevant or not, as a reference point for future decisions. We are, of course, particularly susceptible to anchoring when we do not have much information about something (the cost of hotels in foreign countries, typical discounts, etc.).

It is confirmation bias that also leads people to make important money decisions based on unimportant or irrelevant information. This is searching out for, treating less critically, and being overly and unjustly impressed by information that confirms your preferences and prejudices. Warning signs include being somewhat over-confident in your ability to bargain and negotiate, making important money decisions without much research, and finding it hard to sell investments for more than you paid for them. Belsky and Gilovich (1999) suggest that people broaden their advisors and try a little humility.

6. Overconfidence is a common "ego trap" that people fall into

Too many people do not know how little they really know about financial issues. They feel that they can do things like sell their own house and pick great investments without specialist advice. Some people persist in the belief that they are beating the market, but do not really know or understand their actual return on investments. They seem to believe that investing in what they know is a guarantee of success. It is really a case of "investor: know thyself". Indeed, there is evidence that people are overconfident in all things, like how safely they drive and how insightful they are.

7. Getting information through the grapevine and relying too much on the financial moves of others

This is the final "big money mistake" documented. This is all about investing with the herd and (mindlessly) conforming to the behaviour of others. This is seen when people invest in "hot stocks and shares": most people buy when stocks are rising and sell when shares are falling. This is about being too reliant on the ideas of colleagues, friends, journalists and financial advisers. The advice is "hurry up and wait"; avoid fashions, "tune out the noise" and actually seek out opportunities to be contrarian. In fact, all the "gurus" of investing say the same thing: that they often buy when shares are going down not up (once, of course, they have looked at them carefully).

Belsky and Gilovich (1999) helpfully end their book with "principles to ponder":

a. **Every dollar/pound/euro spends the same:** It does not matter where money comes from, how it is kept or spent (salary, gifts, wins) it is all the same.
b. **Losses hurt you more than gains please you:** We are all loss and risk averse.
c. **Money that is spent is money that does not matter:** Mistakes from the past should not haunt the present.
d. **It is all about the way you frame/see/look at things:** The way we code potential losses and gains profoundly influences all the choices we make.
e. **All numbers are amounts of money even if you don't count them:** In the old jargon, look after the pennies and the pounds will look after themselves. Don't underestimate small amounts of money.

f. **We pay too much attention to money matters that matter too little:** We tend to weigh some fact and figures too heavily.

g. **Your money-related confidence is often misplaced:** It is so easy and common to over-estimate our money skills and knowledge.

h. **It is very hard to admit one's money mistakes:** This is about pride and hubris but also being very uncomfortable about self-criticism.

i. **The trend may not be your friend:** Trust your instincts before you follow the herd when thinking about investing.

j. **You can know too much:** You can get overwhelmed by financial information – much of which is irrelevant.

The priming power of money

The power of money can be illustrated by its powerful priming ability. This can have powerful, immediate, predictable, but unconscious effects on behaviour. The "mere" exposure to (real) money can trigger a mindset that really influences behaviour. Primes have an effect on beliefs and behaviours because they activate powerful associations. Prime with money, therefore, and you get a set of positive and negative associations that can impact on all sorts of behaviour.

In one celebrated illustration Peter Naish (on a BBC programme in 2013) from the (British) Open University split people into two groups. Both counted pieces of paper with their non-preferred or weaker hand. One counted real money (used banknotes to the value of £250) and the other pieces of paper. Once primed, both groups did three further studies. First, they were asked to eat chocolates to rate them for taste, sweetness, etc. Second, they were asked to test their pain endurance by seeing how long they could keep their hands in freezing cold water. Third, they were confronted by a situation where they could help someone or ignore them.

As predicted the money group ate significantly more chocolate, endured pain significantly longer and were less likely to help others in need. The simple effect of exposing them to money stimulated them to be hungrier, more able to endure pain and more self-oriented (thus projecting this on others).

Bonini et al. (2002) showed that the same amount of money is judged differently after priming. In Canada, DeVoe and House (2012) showed that asking people to think about their income in terms of hourly payments reduced their rating of the pleasure they received from leisure time spent on the Internet. They argued that priming people to think about time in terms of money influences how they experience pleasurable events by creating greater impatience during unpaid time.

In other studies Boucher and Kofos (2012) showed that if you prime people with money they experience greater self-control. They showed in two studies that money priming decreased feelings of fatigue, and made people see difficult tasks as less so and put more effort into them. They noted that "surreptitiously reminding oneself of money (perhaps by installing a money screensaver on one's computer) is vital for helping people achieve their goals and live harmoniously with others" (p. 810).

In a series of interesting and innovative studies, Vohs and colleagues showed the psychological power of money (Vohs, Mead & Goode, 2006, 2008; Zhou, Vohs & Baumeister, 2009). The idea was that if you prime people with money they will take a "market-pricing" orientation to the world. Money primes make people attend to ratios and rates, and ideas of self-sufficiency: an insulated state where people put in effort to attain particular goals and prefer to be separate from others. That is, money is a tool that enables people to achieve their goals without the aid of others.

> The self-sufficient pattern helps explain why people view money as both the greatest good and evil. As countries and cultures developed, money may have allowed people to acquire goods and services that enabled the pursuit of cherished goals, which in turn diminished reliance on friends and family. In this way, money enhanced individualism but diminished communal motivations, an effect that is still apparent in people's responses to money today.
>
> (Vohs et al., 2006, p. 1156)

In later work, Vohs et al. showed that subtle reminders of money elicit big changes in human behaviour. They showed that, compared to people not reminded of/ primed by money, people preferred more solitary tasks and less physical intimacy but worked harder on challenging tasks and even desired to take on more work.

Thus, from an employer's perspective, money priming has contradictory effects, reflecting the ambivalent attitude to money so often shown. The money primed individuals seemed to favour equity over equality, and competitiveness over cooperativeness.

What is interesting is how powerful an effect a little priming has. Just a quick task with "play" money versus "real" money is enough to change behaviour toward fellow workers.

Can money primes have other negative effects? Kouchaki, Smith-Crowe, Brief and Sousa (2013) asked the simple question: "Can mere exposure to money corrupt people?" They hypothesised that money priming leads people to develop a "business decision frame", which includes ideas of self-interest, market pricing, utility calculus, etc. This is the idea of the pursuit of self-interest and the weakening of social bonds resulting from money priming, but also the likelihood of increasing unethical behaviour. In four studies this is exactly what they demonstrated. Money priming objectifies social relations and dampens morality. Cost-benefit analysis makes us selfish.

Kouchaki et al. conclude thus:

Considering the significant role of money in business organisations and everyday life, the idea that subtle reminders of money elicit changes in morality has important implications. Our findings demonstrate that the mere presence of money, an often taken-for-granted and easily overlooked feature of our daily lives, can serve as a prompt for immoral behaviour operating through a business decision frame. These findings suggest that money is a more insidious corrupting factor than previously appreciated, as mere, subtle exposure to money can be a corrupting influence.

Behavioural finance

Behavioural finance, according to Shefrin (2007), is about how psychological processes influence the behaviour of all those involved in the financial world. He argues that there are three themes to this literature:

1. Most financial decision making is based on heuristics/rules of thumb. These "back-of-the-envelope" calculations are generally imperfect and predispose one to numerous (predictable) errors.
2. Finance people's perception of risk and return is powerfully influenced by the way in which decisions are framed.
3. Human biases mean markets are inefficient – that is the price of things does not coincide with fundamental value.

The idea is to help financial practitioners recognise and then reduce their cognitive errors. Further, a small numbers of behavioural concepts explain a large number of financial errors. The whole thesis is explained (again) thus:

- People develop general principles as they find things out for themselves.
- They rely on heuristics and rules of thumb to draw inferences from the information at their disposal.
- People are susceptible to particular errors because the heuristics they use are imperfect.
- People actually commit errors in particular situations.

What is the difference between behavioural economics and behavioural finance? In fact very little, though the latter may be seen as a part of the former. In many ways behavioural finance is simply a way to explain to those in finance the essential message of behavioural economics.

Neuro-economics

The development of a wide range of brain-scanning devices that allow one to map brain activity during various tasks has led to the rise of neuroscience. Various writers and consultants have jumped on the bandwagon and put the prefix neuro- in front of many disciplines, hoping to show their scientific credentials. Hence one has neuro-marketing and also neuro-economics.

Zweig (2009) described neuro-economics as a hybrid field that is beginning to understand what drives the biology of investing behaviour. The argument is familiar:

> Our investing brains often drive us to do things that make no logical sense – but make perfect emotional sense. That does not make us irrational. It makes us human. ... your brain has only a thin veneer of relatively modern analytical circuits that are often no match for the blunt emotional power of the most ancient parts of your mind. (p. 3)

He notes early on seven "basic lessons that have emerged from neuro-economics":

> 1. A monetary loss or gain is not just a financial or psychological outcome, but a biological change that has profound physical effects on the brain and body;
> 2. The neural activity of someone whose investments are making money is indistinguishable from that of someone who is high on cocaine or morphine;
> 3. After two repetitions of a stimulus – like, say, a stock price that goes up one penny twice in a row – the human brain automatically, unconsciously, and uncontrollably expects a third repetition;
> 4. Once people conclude that an investment's returns are "predictable", their brains respond with alarm if that apparent pattern is broken;
> 5. Financial losses are processed in the same areas of the brain that respond to mortal danger;
> 6. Anticipating a gain, and actually receiving it, are expressed in entirely different ways in the brain, helping to explain why "money does not buy happiness";
> 7. **Expecting** both good and bad events is often more intense than **experiencing** them. (pp. 3–5)

The idea is simple: we count on our intuition to make sense of the world around us but only tap into our analytical systems when intuition stalls or fails. Intuition is the first filter of experience. This has been called the reflexive brain system:

the brain leaps to conclusions and operates automatically, unconsciously and uncontrollably.

The argument is to become more self-aware of your two brains/systems. Trust your gut feelings when something seems wrong, but know when your emotional, less rational reflexive thinking kicks in. Ask questions about understanding and certainty before making an economic decision. Try not to prove, but instead disprove assumptions. Beware of emotional words and pictures and get to numbers. Follow sensible investment rules. Wait before deciding – don't let your mood influence your decisions. Be ready to move quickly by understanding long-term plans.

Zweig (2009) has advice for various economic situations:

1. Greed

We are activated by financial reward, which, like sex and drugs, provides a wonderful but dangerous feeling, and hence an addictive experience. So, beware certain deals with potentially massive gains. Remember that lightning seldom strikes twice and that stocks and shares go up and down. "Lock up your 'mad money' and throw away the key" (p. 50) – put a strict cap on how much you will risk on speculative trading. Write a checklist of clear standards every investment must meet before buying and selling. Think twice – don't blink, think; sleep on it; be calm before any major decisions.

2. Prediction

Many economic predictions by experts go wrong because they believe whatever has happened in the past is the only thing that can happen in the future. Further, they post-cast by relying too heavily on the short-term rather than the long-term past. Recommendations include: controlling what you can control (expenses, taxes, expectations) rather than trying to predict the unpredictable; restrict yourself from making too many bets; always ask for (and check) evidence; track your investment portfolio but not obsessively often; check the base rate – that is, is something that seeks to "beat the market" at least now what the market offers; correlation is not causation: most market strategies are based on coincidental patterns – take a break from pattern-seeking predictions; don't obsess by continuous monitoring – remember that investing is a long-term project.

3. Confidence

We are surprisingly overconfident in our ability to predict and understand economic events. There are numerous studies that show overconfidence is misplaced, particularly by "experts" making decisions. Recommendations include: having no shame in saying you don't know when asked questions like, "Which computer/company/country will dominate in the next 10 years?"; know what you don't know and have a pile of "too hard" questions about investment; crop your over hopeful investments to become more realistic; keep an investment diary or log to see how accurate you actually are/were; use trading to see what works and what doesn't; handcuff your "inner conman" by always asking: how much better than average do I think I am? What rate of performance do I think I can achieve? How well have other people performed on average over time? Zweig (2009) also suggests embracing your mistakes and trying to learn from them. Don't buy just what you know and like but also consider other stocks. Equally, do not get stuck in your own company's stock, because diversification is the best defence. Finally, be like a child and ask "why" over and over again.

4. Risk

Highly variable mood factors considerably influence risk tolerance. Our perception of the half-empty/half-full glass depends on how we feel about the glass, which can be relatively easily manipulated. Most people cannot easily distinguish false fears from real dangers. Further, the language of risk and chance powerfully influences what risks we are prepared to take. The recommendations for dealing with risk are similar to others: take time; look back; know yourself; try to prove yourself wrong. Zweig (2009) also recommends guarding from framing issues by reframing. Thus, if someone offers a 90% success rate, think of a 10% failure rate. Try to prove yourself wrong by using the devil's advocate approach.

5. Fear

The emotion of fear or dread acts as a very hot button on the brain. Overreacting to raw, mainly negative feelings of loss leads to very bad decisions. The idea is to try to be calm when making decisions to break out of anxiety. Next, to use cool language to evaluate problems and ask questions like: Other than the price, what else has changed? What other evidence do I need to evaluate in order to tell "whether this is really bad now"? If I liked this investment enough to buy it at a much higher price, shouldn't I like it even more now that the price is lower? Zweig (2009) recommends again that we track our feelings in an emotional register. Also, beware the herd and conforming and consensus.

6. Surprise

Getting one thing when we expected another can cause unexpected shocks, which can easily influence automatic emotional thinking. The best advice is to expect to be surprised. Equally, whenever you are tempted to follow everybody else because "everybody knows", do not: the best investment is the overlooked opportunity. High hopes can cause big trouble because they can cause nasty surprises, which lead to bad decisions. Again track your reactions to surprises. More importantly, look at statistical gimmicks which can manipulate which companies to avoid and sometimes can increase surprise.

7. Regret

The endless cycle of "shouldawouldacoulda" can cause powerful emotions which "eat people up" and stop them learning from both their regrets and their errors. People suffer more from negative regret emotions when they believe they could have chosen other options; they have had near misses; the problem was to do with errors of commission rather than omission. People often get paralysis after loss, not taking action they can and should take to prevent further loss. People are extremely reluctant to admit being a loser and making mistakes. They torment themselves with imagining what might have been. Further, the higher you think the odds of making money, the more regret you will feel if you don't. Zweig (2009) offers various bits of advice for making do and moving on. Just face it, fess up, and stop being in denial. Next, dump your losers and get help getting out of bad investments. Find ways to sell like investing in radically different things. Cut your losses but not too much. Do not let too much cash pile up. Reframe by focusing on how much you made from your starting point rather than how much you lost from the peak.

8. Happiness

> Unfortunately, if you already earn enough cash to live on, the odds that merely having more money will make you happier are pretty close to zero. (p. 228)
>
> Instead of labouring under the delusion that we would be happy if we first had a little more money, we should recognise the reality that we might well end up with more money if we just took a little more time to be happy. (p. 229)

A large number of recommendations of how to become happy are provided.

Zweig (2009) offers ten pieces of advice that are in part informed by neuro-economics:

1. Take a global view of all your investments and your net worth.
2. Hope for the best but expect the worst by diversifying and bracing yourself for disaster.
3. Investigate before you invest. Do your homework.
4. Never say always and never put more than 10% of your portfolio in any investment.
5. Know what you don't know and you won't become overconfident, believing you are an expert.
6. The past is not a prologue: buy low and sell high, not the other way around.

7. Weigh what investors say: get a complete track record of people whose advice you seek.
8. If it sounds too good to be true, it is. People who offer high return on low risk for a short time are a fraud.
9. Costs are killers: lots of people tax you so compare, shop and trade slowly.
10. Never put all your eggs in one basket.

The cognitive miser

Kahneman's (2011) book *Thinking Fast and Slow* has become a best seller. Economists, marketers, psychologists and lay people have become fascinated by the message of, and clear evidence for, behavioural economics. People who resist the message and believe their monetary decision making is coolly rational and logical are poorly informed.

Understanding how and why people think about their money and make money decisions is of considerable interest to many groups. Governments as well as big business are interested in how to shape individuals' and groups' decision making. To say that many groups are eager to exploit the *fast thinking* of individuals may be too cynical. However, it is clearly the case that forearmed is forewarned: the more we know about the "unfortunate" consequences of heuristic thinking the less vulnerable we (hopefully) are to it.

12

PERSUASION, PRICING AND MONEY

Capitalism is what people do if you leave them alone.

Kenneth Minogue

Nothing is illegal if one hundred businessmen decide to do it.

Andrew Young

The creditor hath a better memory than the debtor.

James Howell

It is only the poor who pay cash, and that not from virtue, but because they are refused credit.

Anatole France

Introduction

There are many organisations interested in how people think about, and use, their money. They are predominantly in the financial and commercial sectors. Banks want you to invest and borrow from them. Advertisers are paid to devise commercials that help sell products. Retailers are committed to tempt you to buy certain products. All are in the business of attempting to persuade you to act in a certain way with respect to your money.

This chapter is on the social psychology of persuasion and the marketing psychology of pricing. It is an area of research that has attracted a great deal of attention because of concerns about how "gullible and innocent" people are persuaded to part with their money.

The six principles

Many of us are searching for ways to influence and persuade others in order to reap the most benefits from these individuals.

Cialdini (2001) proposed that there are (only) six key (identifiable) principles of persuasion which can be employed to influence others. His work has been among the most influential in the whole of social psychology.

1. Reciprocity

When we are given something by another person, or treated well, we feel obliged to reciprocate the kind behaviour shown to us. We reciprocate in kind: you send me a Christmas card and I send another back; you buy me a drink and I "return the favour"; you spend money on me and I give it back in some way; you invite me to dinner, I reciprocate.

Charities know the power of reciprocity, often enclosing a small gift (i.e. a pen, personalized address labels) with mail shots. Cialdini (2001) showed how these very cheap gifts could double the number of donations. It is important to note that gifts do not have to be valuable or even tangible: information can act as a gift.

The felt need to reciprocate can make people feel uncomfortably indebted. Hence unemployed people eschew the option to go "drinking with their pals" because they cannot afford a round. Similarly, many organisations have a set (and rather low – £/$5–20) limit on Christmas gifts that people give to each other because a poorly paid worker may not be able to reciprocate a present to equal value and therefore feel uncomfortable and indebted.

It may help to hint at what you would like in return, although this is ground which must be trodden carefully, as some individuals are wary of reciprocation. Those with high reciprocation wariness show traits such as declining assistance and failing to return favours (Cotterell, Eisenberger & Speicher, 1992). With such individuals, taking a different route to persuade would be advantageous. The whole psychology of the "free gift", the coupon and the "taster" is the psychology of reciprocation.

Principle: People (nearly always) repay in kind.
Application: Give what you want to receive.

2. Commitment and consistency

We (particularly in the West) have a drive to be consistent in what we say and do. When we make a commitment to do something, we experience personal and interpersonal pressure to behave as we have suggested we will. Inconsistency is frowned upon and considered to be an undesirable personality trait by (Western) society and so is avoided. It is often called hypocrisy and people are chastised for doing "U turns".

Making a small commitment can therefore result in significant behavioural changes. It is for this reason that politicians are so unwilling to answer questions that would seem to commit them to a certain strategy. It is also why sales people ask very specific questions like, "If the price were right, would you buy today?" They know people feel foolish and dishonest if their words and actions do not match.

In order to persuade people to accept large requests, it is suggested that they are first presented with small requests in the same area. This is called the "foot in the door" technique. People are likely to agree with later larger requests in order to appear consistent in their values and behaviour. Guéguen and Jacob (2001), for example, increased compliance to give a charitable donation when individuals had previously made a small commitment online.

In our society (but not all) people feel they will look weak, confused and dithering if they openly change their mind or do not behave in a way consistent with what they have said or promised. That is why people like to "get things in writing" or use the "foot in the door technique".

Principle: People feel the need to fulfil/act in accordance with written, public and voluntary commitments.

Application: Encourage people to make active, open/public commitments to a behaviour plan you want them to follow.

3. Social proof

We use others' behaviour to determine what is correct and accepted. The more uncertain we are about how to behave, what is valuable and how we should be spending our money the more we look to others to show us "what to do".

We look for social proof: what others do, say and think. This is proposed to be especially true when we are unsure of ourselves. If a decision is ambiguous we are likely to accept others' actions as the correct route. We are more likely to imitate behaviours of those who we consider similar to ourselves.

When you are the first person in a restaurant it is very common for you to be asked to "sit in the window" as social proof that people like to eat there. Faced with different places to eat (in a food court, for example) people often opt for the more crowded choice, even if there is a longer queue, because this (somehow) proves that it is good. Moreover, if they see Indians eating at an Indian restaurant, or Chinese eating in a Chinese restaurant, in a place like London or New York people are reassured that it is a good choice.

Television stations used canned laughter to encourage better ratings. The process goes like this: we see/hear others laughing and we tend to (contagiously) follow suit. The more we see them laugh the more they prove to us they are enjoying the show and the more likely we are to rate it highly.

There are some excellent examples where people have been nudged to behave in a particular way because of social proof. If people are told most people in their area (immediate environment) complete their tax forms on time or own a particular product they are more likely to "follow suit". All parents know the power of peer pressure on their children. This is why hotel chains tell you that previous guests behaved in a particular way (i.e. reused their towels, used room service). The more "people like us" are seen to be doing something positive, the more likely we are to follow.

Principle: People follow the lead of others particularly those with referent power.

Application: Use peer power to influence "horizontally"; prove to people that (valued/liked/admired) others behave in the way you want them to.

4. Authority

People want to follow the lead of real experts. Many in business strive to increase their credibility by assuming impressive titles, wearing expensive clothes and driving expensive cars. It has been shown again and again that merely giving the appearance of authority increases the likelihood that others with comply with (monetary) requests.

We are trained from birth to trust and abide by instructions from authority figures. Once an individual in a position of authority has given an order, we are said to stop thinking about the situation and to start responding as suggested. People show their authority with uniforms and titles, or with particular ways of speaking or acting. In doing so they "command authority", which means you are more likely to follow their advice.

Such a strategy can be employed beneficially by companies with a large budget, who, through paying well-respected celebrities to represent their brand in advertisements, persuade others to purchase products. Charities also often employ the use of celebrities in an attempt to encourage people to make donations to a cause that "must be worthy" if an authority figure is supporting it. People like us can also employ the technique, through hinting to others how much we like a gadget or car belonging to a celebrity, for example; if they have it, it must be good.

Principle: People tend to defer to "experts", "authorities" or "celebrities", who provide and seem to have specialised information. We follow those we respect.

Application: Establish your expertise to others: do not assume that it is self-evident.

5. Scarcity

The language of loss, or closing windows of opportunity, of time and goods running out can be deeply behaviourally motivating. It is the law of supply and demand: the less there is of something (usually) the more valuable it is.

Things are evaluated more favourably when they are less available. Products will be more popular when they are available for "a limited time only", or when they are in short supply and likely to sell out. Organisations have closing down sales showing the scarcity of time. Products have "limited editions". Anything that is rare is seen to be more valuable. Any resource that is "running out" is therefore seen as more desirable.

Further, if you have some information that few other people have, businesses are willing to pay for it. Insights into specific consumer behaviour, for example, can be priced highly. In order to persuade, therefore, the scarcity of an aspect of the product should be highlighted.

When persuading another, the communicator must highlight the features of the recommendation that are unique, telling the person what they will miss out on by failing to follow the recommendation. Humans are motivated more by losses than they are by an equal gain (see previous chapter). Therefore, clued-in advertisements communicate the money that will be lost if an individual does not invest in their product.

Marketing people often advertise scarcity: they have an under-supply, there is a limited stock, there is a closing down sale. "Hurry, limited stocks" has been shown to be an effective marketing campaign. Some customers have been influenced by the idea of future scarcity: because of the weather, the mine running out, the age of the craftsman … there will soon be very serious shortages of a particular product. This is similar to having a limited edition.

Principle: People value (much more) and are eager to acquire what is scarce and rare.

Application: Use "exclusivity/rarity" information about a product or service to persuade.

6. Liking

We like people who are like us, and we tend to follow their advice more. Thus, the more we share with others (language, education, world view, religion) the more we are likely to be persuaded by them. A number of factors lead to "liking". Physical attractiveness plays a role, with research showing that we believe good-looking individuals have more desirable traits, such as kindness and intelligence. We like those who are similar to us; this seems to be the case whether we are alike in terms of opinions, personality or lifestyle. Cooperating and having to work together to achieve mutual goals also results in liking. We also develop liking for those who compliment us, believing and accepting these compliments, as well as developing positive feelings towards those who have praised us.

Therefore, in order to persuade we need people to like us. It may be beneficial to share information about yourself and establish similarities and mutual opinions with people who you later intend to persuade.

Principle: People like others who are similar them, who (also) say they like (compliment) them.

Application: Win friends through showing similarity and praise (Charm to disarm).

Examples

The London-based consultancy Mountainview Learning sought to put some of these principles into practice.

(a) Apple sales techniques

They studied **Apple** and their conclusion from visiting many of their stores in England was the following:

Apple uses heuristics in three ways. First, to increase store traffic; second, to increase in-store sales; and, third, to sustain high or higher margins. Apple's Path to Purchase is simple and effective:

- Reach more people (through communications).
- Get more people to visit the stores or websites (consider) and seek out information.
- Get as many people to play with/use the products as possible (shoppers).
- Increase the conversion ratio (shoppers to buyers).

Heuristics can be evoked at each and every stage in a retailer's "Path to Purchase", amounting to a big difference in sales and margins.

Scarcity is a widely used demand-creating strategy but rarely has it been used as effectively. Apple uses scarcity to get news coverage and to cause line-ups (queues) outside and inside the store, creating even more news value. It is human nature to rate things which are perceived to be scarce higher than things which are not perceived to be scarce.

Apple first started using this as a strategy when it launched the iPod and it was taken to a new level when pre-printed "Out-of-Stock" posters were put in iPhone retailers' stores.

Social proof is a heuristic wherein the value of a course of action is dependent on the number of people doing it. When Apple uses scarcity to increase a product's value, people queue for hours outside stores and these record queues make news headlines. The queues provide social proof that the products must be great and increase their perceived value – driving yet more traffic to the stores.

Social proof is used very effectively in-store. The products are laid out for customers to play with; the store is open plan, so that from any vantage point you can see many people playing with them; experts are on hand to help overcome any problems; and lectures are taking place on the latest developments. Being surrounded by so many Apple disciples exerts a powerful pressure to "follow the crowd".

Reciprocity is where people are more likely to make a purchase having been given a prior free gift. Apple allows people to check their e-mail on computers in store, as well as providing free advice, iPhone charging and tech support. As one sign put it, "Only the Apple store gets you up and running before you leave." This degree of personalisation, and the variety of free services, leaves shoppers indebted and more likely to buy, as well as increasing liking and positive affect.

Imagine. By encouraging us to use products (Apple salespeople are told to encourage customers to use the product not to teach them how to use it). Physically interacting with a product gets us to imagine already owning one.

Apple moved electronics retailing forward by giving the customer enough unmonitored examples of all their products that anyone who enters the store can use them at will. The products are set out such that you are encouraged to pick them up and play with them.

Fluency. Simplicity and ease of buying is at the core of everything Apple does. Whilst other brands were talking about memory or capacity Apple focused on 10,000 songs in your pocket or concepts such as "Plug n Play". Reducing the mental processing involved in both using and buying their products makes them harder to resist.

Contrast this (minimalist/fluent) approach with that of Apple's competitors – electrical retailers and department stores selling exactly the same products as Apple but in a completely different way. And think of how much "clutter" fashion retailers and grocery stores put in the way of the customer making easy (and quick) buying decisions.

Liking. We are more easily influenced by people we like. Apple employs trendy, friendly, attractive young people. We tend to like attractive people, and this increases our tendency to comply. Staff seem to be trained to evoke a natural smile – a sales technique proven to increase bar tips by 140%.

When we see someone smiling, the "smile" mirror neurons in our brains are activated, which puts us in a good mood and lowers our resistance to persuasion. People rate products more highly when they're happy, as they misattribute their good feelings to things around them, and, importantly, they spend more money!

Authority is a tool of persuasion wherein people comply when the source of the request is seen as trustworthy and credible. Apple uses this extremely well to position its products and brand as the epitome of the industry.

Employees are named "specialists", they give "lectures", run "training" programmes and work behind the "Genius Bar". A "Genius" commands more authority than a "Service Assistant", although they both do the same job.

Emotions. Hedonic consumption is no secret in marketing. Apple is, in our view, world-class when it comes to engaging its customers emotions and influencing their mood. Apple adverts use emotions to get noticed and remembered, and to sell the experiential benefits of the product. For example, one advert has a grandfather using his iPhone to see his grandson's face for the first time. And once the customers are in the store, this emotional engagement continues:

- The posters on the walls depict emotional scenes of family bonding.
- The products are laid out for ease of play and there is a sense of childlike excitement.
- The products are described as "magical" with "even more to love".
- The Beatles are strumming away in the background bringing back some emotional memories for some.

These products are arguably not for children, and yet pictures and videos from films like *Toy Story* surround customers, and products are laid out with simple, colourful games ready to be played. Apple cleverly markets these products as a connection to the emotionally laden play of our youth.

(b) Increasing charitable donations

Next Mountainview Learning was asked to help a **charitable organisation** increase the donations that people gave it. After reviewing the very extensive literature it boiled down its recommendations to a number of simple points, which are set out in Table 12.1.

TABLE 12.1 Increasing donations

	Kinship	We are geared to protect our "clan". Emphasise the similarity the donor has to the person in need – even generic values and traits will do.
	Use a single victim	People process groups on an abstract level (i.e. rationally). Single victims are more concrete, and engage emotional thinking – which drives altruism.
	Identify the victim	Identifying the person in need by name makes people more likely to donate – because they become less abstract and more tangible.
	Be emotional	Emotions drive prosocial behaviour: use emotional materials in appeal pictures and narrative. Sad facial expressions are more effective than others.
	Don't be rational	Remove from appeals any material which might engage the reader in rational thinking. Even maths calculations make people less generous.
	Make them happy	People can only think about helping others when they are sure they themselves aren't under threat: where possible, make them feel safe, happy and secure.
	Priming #1	Prime people to behave generously by exposing them to concepts like care-giving, religion, being watched (e.g. mirrors) or exemplary behaviour, like superheroes.
	Priming #2	Don't prime people to concepts of money or individualism, since it makes them antisocial and less generous.
	Tangible results #1	It is very effective to show what the direct effect of donating an exact amount will be (e.g. "1 Pack = 1 Vaccine"); donations should not be shown to pay for abstract costs like overheads.
	Tangible results #2	Donations increase the closer to the fundraising goal the appeal claims to be.

	Social proof	People generally "follow the herd". If everyone else is shown to be donating, or donating a lot, then others will follow suit.
	Authority	Use authority in appeals to persuade donors that donating is the right thing to do.
	Commitment and consistency #1	People behave so as to maintain a coherent concept of self; tell them they are charitable, or remind them of a charitable deed of theirs, and they will be more likely to donate.
	Commitment and consistency #2	First, ask people a question or small request that they can't refuse; then they will be more likely to say "yes" to a follow-up request.
	Reciprocity	People often "return the favour" – prosocial behaviour can be encouraged by first offering a gift.
	Complexity	Keep things as simple as possible – when a choice is (even a little bit) complicated, people tend to just avoid it.
	Opt-out	People tend to stick with the default. Using an opt-out option is a great way to increase donations.
	Deferred donations	People value money more now than they do in the future; so asking them to donate later on, rather than "today", will increase donations.
	Anchoring	Numbers are not judged, or produced, in a vacuum. By showing people figures, you can influence how much they will donate, or how large they perceive a suggested amount to be.
	Decoy	A proposed donation plan will look a lot more attractive if placed next to one which is more expensive, or less appealing in any way.
	Cost saliency	If a proposed donation amount is less reminiscent of a painful financial loss (e.g. removing the pound sign and using fewer zeros), it is more attractive.
	Time isn't money	People value their time less than their money; where possible, it may be more cost-effective to ask people to volunteer than to donate.

Source: Mountainview Learning, London.

Tipping

The term TIP supposedly stands for "To Insure Promptness", which was derived from the eighteenth-century English tradition of giving coins with written words to publicans. It is now estimated that over $10 billion is given as tips in America to waiters/waitresses, porters, hairdressers, taxi drivers, chambermaids and a host of other "professionals".

What is the meaning and function of tipping? Why does it exist? Why tip taxi drivers and hairdressers but not tailors? What are the determinants of tipping? How does tipping affect the service-givers (e.g. waiters), the recipients (i.e. customers) and the relationship between the two parties?

Psychologists suggest that tipping is a form of ego massage calculated to enhance the self-image of the tipper. Also, by giving a tip – above and beyond the agreed set price – the tipper can demonstrate he/she is not fully trapped by market forces and can be capable of voluntary, discretionary action. The tip can sometimes be seen as a result of the customer's insecurity or anxiety. A maid or hairdresser deserves a tip through having access to the customer's private territory or articles that may just pose a threat to the customer's public face. The tip can buy their server's silence because it buys loyalty or indebtedness. Psychologists stress that tipping is intrinsically motivated rather than performed for the sake of the external material or social rewards.

Lynn and Grassman (1990) spelt out, in detail, the three "rational" explanations for tipping:

1. Buying social approval with tips: following the social norms (i.e. 15% tipping) is a desire for social approval or else a fear of disapproval.
2. Buying an equitable relationship with tips: tips buy peace of mind by helping maintain a more equitable relationship with servers.
3. Buying future service with tips: tips ensure better service in the future because the tit for tat works but only with regular customers.

In their study they found support for the first two, but not the third explanation.

Despite the number of people fairly dependent on tips for their income, little research has been done until comparatively recently into this curious and widespread habit. Lynn and Latane (1984) summarised studies done in the 1970s:

1. Most tips are around the 15% American norm.
2. The percentage of the tip to total cost is an inverse power function of the number of people at the table.
3. Physically attractive and/or attractively dressed waitresses receive greater tips than less attractive waitresses.
4. Tips are bigger when paid by credit cards, relative to cash payments.
5. Tips are not related to whether alcohol is consumed.
6. Tips increase with the number of non-task-oriented "visits" by waiter and waitress, but are unrelated to the customer's ratings of service.
7. Often, but not always, males tip more than females.

Some studies have focused on the server's behaviour. Rind and Bordia (1995) noted that server (waiter)–diner interactions were related to tip size.

So the factors/behaviours that encourage a larger tip are:

1. Whether the server touched the diner.
2. Whether the server initially squatted in their interaction with the diner as opposed to stood.
3. The size of the server's initial smile.
4. Whether the server introduced him/herself with their first name.
5. The number of incidental (non-task oriented) visits to the table.

One tool for effective tipping is the "liking" heuristic. Tips can be significantly increased by anywhere up to 140% by:

- Waitresses wearing make-up and a flower in their hair, and drawing smiley faces on receipts.
- Waiters drawing the sun on receipts.
- Writing hand-written messages on the receipts, like "thank you" or a weather forecast.
- Staff using large, open-mouthed smiles.
- Staff giving customers jokes, puzzles and facts; sweets too, if costs permit.
- Staff addressing customers by name, and introducing themselves.
- Staff mimicing customers' body language and verbal behaviour, and touching them appropriately during interactions.

The second useful heuristic for encouraging tipping is reciprocity – people tend to help those who have helped them before. This does not have to be costly, though. Tips are significantly increased by giving customers a puzzle, joke or interesting fact with the receipt; giving customers a hand-written message forecasting the weather or saying "thank you"; waitresses drawing a smiley face on the receipt, though waiters can get the same result by drawing the sun; giving customers a sweet, though giving them two is better, and giving them two at different times is even more effective than that (Guéguen, 2002; Rind & Bordia, 1995; Strohmetz, Rind, Fisher & Lynn, 2002).

In all his many studies on tipping, Lynn is eager to replace homo economicus with homo psychologicus. Most of his recent studies suggest that tipping for all sorts of service in many different countries is primarily driven by three things: the desire to (1) reward good quality service; (2) help the service providers; and (3) personally gain social approval and status. More recently, he has noted two other factors: gaining good quality service in the future as well as conforming to internalised tipping norms (or doing what is right).

Lynn and colleagues have studied car guards in South Africa (Saunders & Lynn, 2010) as well as waiters in America (Lynn, Jabbour & Kim, 2012). These studies have looked at all sorts of factors that might have a small influence on the tipping behaviour of individuals. These include: the sex and race of the server; the sex, race, age, education, income, worship frequency and alcohol consumption of the customer. Inevitably, they did find that the bigger the bill, the bigger the tip.

Nearly all the papers argue that the economists' view is that tipping is irrational and needs to be replaced with the insights of behaviour economics to be understood.

Pricing practices in shops

How do retailers price goods to increase sales? Why are all goods £/\$5.99 and never £/\$6.00? What is the psychological power of BOGOF: *Buy One Get One Free*? Pricing practices used to advertise products and services to consumers, such as "3 for £/\$5", "60% off" or "sale – one week only", are very common. How do they work and how effective are they?

Ahmetoglu and Furnham (2012) undertook a comprehensive review, which is the basis for this section. A version of this report was used by the Office of Fair Trading in Great Britain to warn consumers about pricing practices.

Price consultants advise retailers on how to price their products and brands and the design of price tags, rebates, sale adverts, cell phone plans, bundle offers, etc. These are increasingly based on psychological variables and research findings rather than economic ones (Poundstone, 2009). Competitors can easily respond to price changes, in fact more so than to most other tactics (Sigurdsson, Foxall & Saevarsson, 2010), but pricing practices are more subtle. Marketers have learnt how to tactically manipulate pricing procedures so as to influence buyers' perceptions and purchase decisions. Interestingly, this often does not have to involve any changes to the price and profits but rather to how prices are displayed.

As the price of goods becomes a less important differentiating factor, it is likely that the *"design" of the price* and the manner in which these products are displayed and evaluated will become instrumental. There are *price insensitive* customers as well as those who are much more interested in product features than price.

Pricing strategies have become a great battleground between retailers. Further, various government bodies (such as the Office of Fair Trading in Great Britain) have become interested because of the way some believe shoppers are "duped" or misled by cunning pricing practices.

A significant amount of recent research on consumer decision making has established that consumers are notoriously susceptible to the influence of environmental cues that are often irrelevant to the utility of the offer. For example, consumers have been shown to comply with signs that prompt them to buy higher quantities of a product even when there is no rational incentive to do so. Studies have found that placing a sale sign on an item can lead to increased demand for that item even when the price remains the same (Inman, McAlister & Hoyer, 1990). Recent research even shows that consumers' willingness to pay for a product can be influenced by manipulating the price of an adjacent and functionally unrelated product (Nunes & Boatwright, 2004).

1. Drip pricing (partitioned pricing)

Drip pricing refers to purchases where *consumers only see an element of the price upfront*, and where either *optional or compulsory price increments are revealed as they "drip" though the buying process*. The most common examples are airline taxes or charges to pay for using credit cards. Thus, the total price is only revealed (or can only be calculated) later on in the purchasing process.

When price is separated in this way, it is also called "partitioned pricing". People are "lured" into a buying procedure, more often now online, discovering as they go along that the (total/final) price they understood that was required to be paid was only a small part of the cost demanded by the retailer. Sometimes the total cost (say to include postage and packing) can even double the advertised price.

Sellers can either separate *a surcharge*, in which the charge represents an additional amount inherent to the purchase situation, or a *component of the product* as a consolidated total price for the bundle. While the consumer can choose whether to purchase these options in the latter scenario, in the former situation consumers cannot opt out of them. Both are considered a form of drip pricing.

Several moderator variables have also been examined with regard to the effectiveness of portioning prices. The first is the *size of the surcharge*. Research shows that compared to a single price, partitioning a small (6%) surcharge leads to higher purchase intentions, price satisfaction and perceived value, and lower search intentions. This difference is not observed when the surcharge is high (12%) (Xia & Monroe, 2004). It is noteworthy, however, that while a *large* surcharge (12%) leads to lower perceived value and reduced acceptance of the surcharge, it does not lower consumers' *intentions to buy* the product. Furthermore, partitioning increases value perceptions and willingness to pay when the surcharge is considered reasonable, but decreases when the surcharge is unreasonable (Burman & Biswas, 2007).

Other moderator variables examined in the literature include *number of surcharges, seller trustworthiness, whether the total price is presented or not*, and *individual differences in consumers*. The evidence indicates that one large surcharge leads to higher purchasing perceptions and behaviours than two surcharges of the same total value (Xia & Monroe, 2004).

Furthermore, studies that have taken into account seller trustworthiness have shown that a *larger* number (9 vs. 2) of price components may lower perceived fairness and purchase intentions for less trustworthy sellers, when total price is not presented (Carlson & Weathers, 2008).

Partitioning add-on products may also have a similar anchoring-adjustment effect, particularly in instances where the focal product in the bundle is priced lower than that of a comparison bundle (even if the total price remains constant). Thus, partitioning prices into a base price and (various possible) surcharges can significantly increase consumers' perceived value and purchase intentions for products, and can lower search intentions compared to combined pricing. They are *"lured in"*, not noticing what the total cost really is. This is because consumers may fail to adjust from the initial (lower) price of the base good and underestimate the total price of the partitioned-price product. The result could be for some shoppers "once bitten, twice shy" and the serious loss of reputation for any product, retailer or brand that over zealously applied drip pricing.

2. Reference pricing

A reference price is a price that is communicated to the consumer as being the "normal", most commonly charged, or undiscounted previous price (e.g. was £199, now £169).

There are three basic types of retail reference pricing practices:

> 1. comparing an advertised price to a price the retailer *formerly charged* for the product;
> 2. comparing an advertised price to a price presumably *charged by other retailers* in the same trade area; and
> 3. comparing an advertised price to a *manufacturer's suggested retail price*.

As with drip pricing, the fundamental psychological principle (heuristic) underlying reference pricing is *anchoring*.

There is an abundance of evidence to show that advertised reference prices (ARPs) influence a range of consumer price-related responses, including increasing perceptions of the fair price, the normal price, the lowest available price in the market, the potential savings and the purchase value, and also that they decrease additional search effort.

As Lichtenstein (2005, p. 359) notes:

> ARPs work, a lot of research shows they do, and retailer practice and returns show that they do. This is not new – it is widely known. If I advertise a sale price of, say $29.95 and accompany it with an ARP of, say $39.95, in most contexts, sales will increase relative to a no ARP present situation. Sales will increase as I increase my ARP to $49.95, to $59.95, to $69.95.

A number of studies have since focused on the mechanisms through which reference pricing might work (Furnham & Boo, 2011), as well as the conditions under which it has the most/least impact. Several moderator variables have been put forward; these include *the size of the reference price* (e.g. exaggerated or implausible reference prices), consumer scepticism, price knowledge, and consumers' familiarity with the brand/product.

Surprisingly, evidence shows that implausible or exaggerated (or simply dishonest) reference prices often have similar effects on consumer behaviour as plausible reference prices. Research shows mixed results with regard to price knowledge. Some studies find that shopping experience has no effect on consumers' acceptance of reference prices.

Thus, the presence of a reference price increases consumers' deal valuations and purchase intentions and can lower their search intentions as compared to when a reference price is absent. Reference prices can in some instances influence consumers even when these are very large and when consumers are sceptical of their truthfulness. It is obviously a very common strategy.

3. The use of the word "free"

There are different ways in which the term "free" is used in advertising, for example: "Buy one get one free"; "Free case" with a given broadband package; or "Kids eat free". Thus, the word free is used as a priming mechanism, or to indicate that a free product is being offered as part of a deal. This may be like a gift: something that entails no (direct and obvious) cost, at least in terms of money. Most people have clearly forgotten the well known line that "there is no such thing as a free lunch".

A product offered as "free" may affect consumer behaviour because it eliminates buyers' regret as nothing was spent on the product, causing people to overvalue anything that is free (Shampanier, Mazar & Ariely, 2007). People choose the benefit which avoids trade-offs (including calculating discounts that require cognitive effort). Because free is an absolute price, we know exactly what it means. There is no relative thinking, no calculation required, and therefore no fear of loss.

Few studies have specifically examined the "priming" effect of the word free (as in "kids go free") on consumer behaviour. Raghubir (2004) shows that once a "free" product has been bundled together with another product and offered for one price, consumers are unwilling to pay more for the free product when it is sold alone. Kamins, Folkes and Fedorikhin (2009) found that describing one of the products in a bundle as free decreased the price consumers were willing to pay for each product when these were sold individually. However, other studies have shown positive valuations of the overall bundle when one of the items is described as free, at least relative to when it is offered at a price discount.

This discrepancy creates a degree of uncertainty about the effect of a free designation and the underlying mechanism at work. Thus, free offers can have seemingly inconsistent effects, suggesting the presence of moderator variables. It is interesting that there appear to be no good synonyms for the word free.

4. Bait pricing

Bait pricing involves consumers being enticed with a discount, but subsequently ending up purchasing a more expensive product because there are very few, or indeed no, items available at the discounted price. The mechanism behind bait pricing is likely to be the *commitment and consistency principle* (Cialdini, 2001). Once people have committed to an action (e.g. to buy a product), they are more likely to be consistent with that particular deed (i.e. buy rather than leave the shop or website). They start off thinking they are paying less but end up paying more.

The literature on sales promotions has shown that short-term sales are positively affected by offering promotions (Raghubir, 1998). Darke, Freedman, and Chaiken (1995) showed that consumers use the size of a percentage discount as a heuristic cue to help decide whether a better price is likely to be available elsewhere. This line of research indicates that promotions can serve as baits such that they attract customers in the short term.

Evidence derived from examining the independent effects of discount offers (baits) and consumer behavioural patterns in stock-out situations (predominantly switching within store) makes it possible to infer that bait and switch practices are likely to influence customers' purchase decisions in favour of the retailer employing this pricing strategy.

We do not know what sort of person is particularly prone to "fall" for the bait, or which withdraw during the purchase. Nor do we know the long-term reputation gained by retailers that have lured in many customers by the bait technique. It is possible that customers feel "once bitten, twice shy", so that this method might only make money in the short term.

5. Bundling

Bundling offers come in various forms, including *volume offers* ("3 for 2", "Buy one get one half price" or 3 for £/$20, etc.) and comparative/mixed bundles where comparisons are made across a bundle or "basket" of goods.

Most of these practices will also be based on the anchoring heuristic. In addition to numerical cues, however, bundle offers may be preferable because they signal a saving (even if there isn't one) simply because shoppers consider that bundles usually offer such savings (i.e. this inference may have become a shortcut in itself). People assume things are cheaper in *bulk buys*. For years supermarkets and hypermarkets have tried to persuade us that bulk buying is a very good deal.

Multiple unit price promotions (such as buy 3 for 2) are popular among retailers of packaged goods. Foubert and Gijsbrecht (2007) showed that a bundle discount increases the probability of switching to the bundle, more so than per unit discounts (again with an identical saving). They found that even when the consumer did not purchase enough of the product to qualify for the discount, they would still switch to the promoted items. Thus, the mere communication of a bundle discount is enough to attract consumers to the promoted items, even when they are not obtaining any savings, and potentially incurring a loss.

A number of studies have shown that mixed bundle promotions can have a significant effect on consumer choices. Johnson, Herrmann and Bauer (1999) conducted experiments in which respondents evaluated car offers that varied in bundling. They found that the respondents' positive evaluations of the offers increased as component price information was progressively bundled.

Bundling may also influence consumers simply because it decreases cognitive/thinking effort. Thus, service providers may be able to convince consumers to stay or entice them to switch service providers not by offering the best or cheapest option, but simply by promoting the convenience of having bundled services billed on a single statement.

6. Time-limited offers

Time-limited offers generally refer to offers which only last for the immediate period of negotiation and the customer is advised that the price will not be available at a later date. Time-limited offers are based on a psychological principle called *scarcity* (Cialdini, 2009).

People assign more value to opportunities/items when they are (or are becoming) less available. This is because things that are difficult to obtain are typically more valuable (Lynn, 1989), and the availability of an item can serve as a short-cut cue to its quality.

While there is an abundance of evidence on the effect of scarcity (in general) on consumer behaviour, studies specifically examining time-limited offers are somewhat mixed and suggest the presence of moderator variables. Early research found strong support for the impact of scarcity (though not restricted to time-limited offers) on consumer behaviour.

In a meta-analysis, Lynn (1991) found a strong and reliable (positive) relationship between scarcity and *value* perceptions.

The following inference can be made with a reasonable amount of confidence: under conditions in which time-limited offers *do* trigger feelings of scarcity, consumers are more likely to overestimate the product quality, or the value of the deal, lower their intentions to search, and have higher intentions to buy.

Ahmetoglu and Furnham (2012) have tabulated useful information on pricing practices, their moderators and their effects (Table 12.2).

Thus, from a bottom-up, tactic-by-tactic perspective, there is a substantial amount of evidence that these strategies work. It is, however, also clear that there are a range of variables that may moderate their effect. Specifically, the impact with these strategies may be highest with products that are infrequently purchased or have a relatively high ticket price, or are new, unique or highly customised. Conversely, they are likely to have less impact with established or standardised offers on cheaper or more frequently purchased items.

TABLE 12.2 Common pricing techniques

Pricing practice	Moderator variable	Effect
Drip pricing	Partitioned (vs. consolidated) price	Partitioning into a product and a surcharge (compared to a single price) leads to increased demand, higher purchase intentions, higher perceived value, higher price satisfaction, lower recalled price, lower price estimation, and lower search intentions
	Surcharge size	Compared to a single price, partitioning a small (6%) surcharge leads to higher purchase intentions, price satisfaction and perceived value, and lower search intentions. This difference is not observed when the surcharge is high (12%)
	Reasonableness of surcharge	Partitioning increases value perceptions and willingness to pay when the surcharge is considered reasonable, but decreases them when the surcharge is unreasonable
	Number of surcharges	One large surcharge leads to higher purchasing perceptions and behaviours than two surcharges of the same total value. A larger number (9 vs. 2) of price components lowers perceived fairness and purchase intentions for less trustworthy sellers, when total price is not presented. However, when a total price is presented, a larger number of price components leads to higher perceptions of fairness, as well as a lower recalled total price, resulting in increased purchase intentions (regardless of seller trustworthiness)
	Presenting total price upfront	Presenting the total sale price and then the additional surcharge information results in higher purchase intentions, perceived value, and lower search intentions, compared to a total price alone
	Consumers' need for cognition	Partitioning has no effect on value perceptions or willingness to pay for consumers who have low need for cognition – i.e. those that do not engage in or enjoy effortful cognitive activities
	Partitioning add-on products (not surcharges)	Whilst partitioning surcharges benefits sellers fairly consistently (to the detriment of consumers), the effects of partitioning add-on products (optional or compulsory) seems to be more complex and depend on numerous features of the add-on(s), which may or may not be beneficial for sellers. Thus, there is no general answer to whether partitioning optional or compulsory products will be detrimental to consumers. Rather, this will depend on the particular product(s) added/partitioned, as well as the context
Opt in/out	Default effect	People tend to stick with the default option; they do so because of preference for inaction and/or because they take the default option as the one best recommended

Reference pricing	Presence (vs. absence) of a reference price	Presenting consumers with an external reference price (higher than the sale price) leads to higher purchase intentions, higher inferred savings and lower search intentions, compared to when no external reference price is provided
	Size of reference price	Product valuations increase linearly as the reference price increases
	Plausibility of reference price	Implausible or exaggerated reference prices often have similar effects on consumer behaviour as plausible reference prices. In some cases, these may even increase value perceptions significantly more than plausible reference prices
	Consumer scepticism	Reference prices have their effects even when consumers are sceptical towards the offer. Consumers may believe pricing claims even when they exceed their initial price expectations by 200%
	Price knowledge	Research shows mixed results with regard to price knowledge. Some studies find that shopping experience has no effect on consumers' acceptance of reference prices, while others show that price knowledge of competitors reduces the effect of reference prices. This may be due to different designs (e.g. remoteness of experience) and samples (e.g. amount of knowledge of participants) used in these studies
	Familiarity with product/brand	Effects of reference prices are reduced with familiar brands and with inexpensive (and therefore more frequently encountered) products
Use of the word "free"	Describing a bundle product as "free"	There is a degree of uncertainty about the effects of free designation. Some studies show that a freebie promotion can have negative effects on consumers' valuations of the overall bundle and on the focal product compared to when the same type of promotion lacks a freebie designation. However, other studies have shown positive valuations of the overall bundle when one of the items is described as free, at least relative to when it is offered at a price discount. Thus, freebies can have seemingly inconsistent effects, suggesting the presence of moderator variables
Bait sales	Bait and switch	There is very limited direct evidence, but the results from one large-scale online study show that offering a low-quality product at a low price to attract consumers and then trying to convince them to pay more for a superior product has a strong effect on consumer purchasing behaviour
	Price promotions/baits	Price promotions increase sales in the short term indicating that consumers are attracted by "baits"
	Stock-outs	Faced with an out-of-stock product, over 60% of consumers substitute it with a product from the same store. They are more likely to do this if in a hurry or brand-loyal, but more likely to shop elsewhere if surprised or the shop has high prices

TABLE 12.2 (continued)

Pricing practice	Moderator variable	Effect
Complex pricing	Multiple- (vs. single-) unit promotions	Multiple-unit discounts increase sales by up to 40% more than single-unit promotions of the same value. They also increase purchase intentions (and switching to the bundled products), even when consumers are not buying enough of the product to qualify for the discount
	Number of units	Compared to single-unit promotions, multiple-unit promotions may only increase purchase intentions for large bundles (8 items), but not for small (2 or 4 items) bundles
	Single-unit price information	The presence (vs. absence) of the single unit price in a bundle does not alter the above effect, suggesting the effect is not due to consumers' inability to calculate the relative discount. A large proportion of consumers do not use single unit prices
	Mixed-bundle promotions	Compared to an individual (unbundled) pricing, a mixed-bundle offer increases consumers' evaluations of the offer and purchase intentions and lowers their estimates of the cost of the bundle. This is because consumers generally infer savings from bundled offers and/or because of the convenience that the single bill provides
	Complexity of pricing	Within the utility sector, customers tend to remain with the supplier they have always had rather than switch to a more beneficial supplier. Consumers seem to find it hard to understand the differences in tariffs charged by different companies and are unwilling to spend the time making the necessary comparative calculations. Within the telecommunications industry customers are rarely very accurate in their estimate of call charges
Time-limited offers	Scarcity	Scarcity (not restricted time limits) increases perceptions of value of the offer, as well as purchase behaviour and willingness to buy
	Short-term time pressure	Time pressure or time constraints imposed on consumers can increase perceptions of offer value as well as "drive" their choice to high quality/low risk brands
	Time-limited offer	There have been conflicting findings regarding the impact of time-limited offers on consumer behaviour. At least two studies have found that imposing a time limit on an offer can increase purchase intentions, choice probability, and perceived deal value for the product. However, one study found this effect not to be true. The discrepancies indicate the presence of moderator variables (hypothesised to be scepticism and product category)
	Discount size	Where the effect (of time-limited offers) has been found it has been true only for high-discount offers (20% or 50%), and not for low-discount offers (5%), where the effect actually reverses
	Length of time limit	Shorter time limits increase urgency and, subsequently, purchase intentions; but too short a time limit increases inconvenience perceptions, decreasing deal evaluation and purchase intentions

Source: Ahmetoglu and Furnham (2012).

There are also categories of people who are likely to be more influenced by some of the pricing practices discussed. However, research examining individual differences in susceptibility to these practices is near to non-existent. This is perhaps not surprising as the main aim of this research is to establish pricing strategies that work universally, rather than for a subgroup of individuals. Nevertheless, advances in technology increasingly enable retailers to readily profile and target consumers. Thus, the study of individual differences may provide a fruitful avenue for future research and may prove to be very relevant for retailers and manufacturers.

It is interesting to note that the effects of the three pricing practices mentioned above (i.e. reference pricing, bundling, and drip pricing) can (at least partly) be attributed to the anchoring heuristic. There is a wealth of evidence deriving from a variety of disciplines that shows that this mechanism has a substantial and robust influence on human decision making. The current review of the literature suggests that this mechanism is potent also in terms of influencing consumer behaviour.

Conclusion

There are many people eager to exploit our laziness with respect to thinking about money. All businesses attempt to persuade us to buy their brand at the highest possible amount they are likely to be be able to obtain. Hence the science of persuasion and the disciplines of advertising and marketing.

There are a limited number of strategies to use in the business of persuasion but many organisations use more than one at the same time. Moreover, given that we are often attracted or put off by the price of products and services, how these are priced is very important. Indeed, government agencies dedicated to helping to protect consumers are particularly interested in the legality of some pricing strategies that are essentially aimed at befuddling consumers.

APPENDIX 1

PERSONAL CONFESSIONS

They say psychologist study their own problems. This may have some kernel of truth to it. So, what are mine and how do they inform the content of this book? We all try to be disinterested scientists but obviously interests and beliefs affect what one writes about (and does not write about) and why. In the (British) *Sunday Times* every week there is a celebrity interview in the Money Section of the paper. A (usually) well-known person is interviewed. At the risk of being too disclosive or judged too arrogant, here are my answers to the various questions posed every week. It might, in part explain some aspects of this book.

How much money do you have in your wallet?

£110, and €50. I withdraw around £400 a week in two visits to the "generous wall" as my wife calls the cash machine.

What credit cards do you use?

Never had one, though I do have a Barclays debit card; one of my parental "money-grams" (deeply ingrained messages from parents) is disapproval of credit. Knowledge of fraud makes me even more wary of cards.

Are you a saver or a spender?

Very much a saver, but not I hope a miser. I am a saver, despite the now near pointlessness of this activity. Money represents for me security and autonomy. I am a bargain hunter and rejoice in finding discounted food near its sell-by date.

How much did you earn last year?

My academic salary is around £75,000, but I supplement this in various ways: books; journalism; talks; test publishing. I work hard for it – seven days a week – but enjoy it.

Have you ever been hard up?

Yes, for many years. My wife remembers me stapling my shoes together in Oxford and feigning illness because I could not afford to eat out. I was a student for too long. But I never felt deprived, jealous or unhappy. Many of my friends were roughly in the same boat.

Do you own a property?

Yes three: houses in Islington, and Olney (Buckinghamshire) and a cottage in the country. The latter belonged to my wife when she worked as Strategic Planning Director for Avon. I got on the property ladder as soon as I could and it certainly paid off. I owned a one- and then a two-bedroom flat less than five minutes' walk from the office. I first lived in a University of London hall of residence while at the LSE. Our current house is ideal for our needs: seven minutes by bicycle to work, in a lovely square and recently redecorated.

What was your first job?

I made nursing attendant in the hospital where my mother was matron. I did it for three years during university vacations and never enjoyed it. My mother really wanted me to read medicine but it wasn't for me. I liked the shift work, particularly working weekends. It taught me more about skiving than anything else. But I was always entrepreneurial as a boy, making five times my pocket money returning large empty soft drink bottles and doing waste paper collections on my soap box.

What has been your most lucrative work?

Motivational speaking. I am not in the top of my league by any means but have replaced serious gurus at the last moment. Once I spoke for 11 minutes to 1,600 people in Barcelona and got more than my monthly salary. Text books and successful business books don't make as much money as people think. And I really enjoy the performance aspects of public speaking.

Are you better off than your parents?

Immeasurably, but I have inherited their money habits: middle-class thrift; mend and make do; disapproval of conspicuous consumption. They bought nothing on credits except their house. They tithed at church and gave to charity but hated waste. I have written a book on the *Protestant Work Ethic* to explore their mindset.

Do you invest in shares?

Not much. Anyway, that's my wife's department. She is much more financially literate than I am. I trust her judgement totally.

What's better – property or pension?

Both, but increasingly property. The ageing population has put too much strain on pensions.

What has been your best investment?

Property and I suppose education, though the latter is much more intangible. And I would say that, wouldn't I? I also default on "yes" when people ask me to do things – write books, give talks, help with consultancy assignments. Many of these have led on to further engagements.

What about worst?

After working a lot in Asia in the 1980s and 1990s I became beguiled by the myth of Japanese success. I bought Japanese stocks which went slowly down.

What is the most extravagant thing you've ever bought?

I don't do extravagant really. Once I bought a bottle of wine for £60. And then there are the gold necklaces I buy for my wife. But nothing really serious. It's just not me.

What is your money weakness?

Books, carved boxes, Japanese lacquer work. And good theatre tickets.

What aspect of the tax system would you change?

First, simplification to stop the ever growing army of poachers and gamekeepers trying to differentiate between the avoidance and evasion issue. *Second*, having every tax law with a sell-by date, meaning it has to be reconsidered for issues such as the law of unintended consequences. *Third*, reducing non-dom Scandals by the American system of worldwide tax. *Fourth*, realising how reducing tax rates encourages more growth and more revenue for the government.

What are your financial priorities?

Saving for my son's education and the infirmities of old age. Care home costs.

What is the most important lesson you have learnt about money?

Work out what you need, as opposed to want; cost it and aim to earn that amount of money rather than to earn large amounts that have no effect on well-being, perhaps even the reverse.

APPENDIX 2
MY TEST RESULTS

I was fortunate enough to be able to take a money test, called *The Psychology of Money Profile*, devised by Dr James Gottfurcht, because I supervised his daughter's PhD. It was a self-report questionnaire, designed to give insight into your own money attitudes, beliefs and values. I completed this test and below is part of my feedback from Dr Gottfurcht, which I have permission to publish.

How to understand your scores

In addition to the *seven psychological money skills* defined below, you are receiving an additional score on a scale called **Looking Good**. If your score on **Looking Good** is **H** (High), it suggests you may have tried to look good or better on the Profile than your skills really are. If this is true, your Profile scores may be inflated, and it could mean your real skill levels may be lower than you scored. If your score on **Looking Good** is **L** (Low), it suggests you may be underestimating your skill levels and/or you may have lacked financial guidance when you were growing up. This could mean your true skill levels may be higher than your scores. If you scored **M** (Midrange) on **Looking Good**, it likely means you did not overestimate or underestimate your skill levels, and your Profile scores are more likely to reflect your true scores. **You scored M.**

If you score Low on a *psychological money skill*, it will be denoted by **L**. This suggests your skill in this area is less developed, is probably holding you back from financial success and satisfaction, and is highly likely to be strengthened by coaching, classes, training or therapy. If you score Midrange, it will be denoted by **M**. This suggests your skill in this area is moderately developed, may or may not be holding you back from financial success and satisfaction and likely will be strengthened by coaching, therapy, etc. If you score High Midrange, it will be denoted as **HM**. This suggests that skill is moderately highly developed and is unlikely to be holding you back from financial success and satisfaction. If you score High, it will be denoted by **H**. This suggests that skill is highly developed and can be a valuable resource to accelerate your financial success and satisfaction.

Most people agree with the scores we give them (**L**, **M**, **HM** or **H**) on the seven skills. In other words, they think they are accurate. It is not unusual, however, to score a bit differently than you believe yourself to be on one or two of the *psychological money skills*. This discrepancy can stimulate you to look inward and try to discover why those scores are different than you thought they would be. If you scored differently than you see yourself to be on many of the skills, it is very possible you may not have answered each item accurately. Remember, if none of the answers were an exact fit, you were asked to choose the response that was most true for you.

Here are your scores on the seven psychological money skills

1. **Financial planning** – Integrating financial values, beliefs and feelings into a cohesive set of goals and knowing the concrete action steps that lead from your starting point to your destination. **You scored M**.
2. **Realistic financial expectations** – Aligning financial expectations with long-term financial results. This means perceiving money realistically to be the way it actually is instead of the way you want it to be or the way you fear it may be. **You scored HM**.
3. **Financial confidence** – Believing and feeling deeply optimistic you will reach and enjoy financial success. **You scored H**.
4. **Stepping stones** – Learning new financial behaviours by engaging in gradual steps that progress from smaller financial goals to larger ones. **You scored HM**.
5. **Change tolerance** – Your tolerance for handling and engaging in new behaviour with money. This means overcoming the unsettling or stressful aspects of change so that you may embrace and use them to reach your financial goals. **You scored M**.
6. **Passion** – Having a burning desire and commitment toward attaining and sustaining financial success and an enriched life. **You scored HM**.
7. **Taking charge** – Initiating behaviour to deal with a financial issue or relationship in a proactive way. **You scored HM**.

The three most important psychological money skills for you to develop

1. **Financial planning** is essential because it is difficult to reach your financial and life goals in a timely manner without some sort of a guiding plan. A coherent plan enables you to organise your thoughts and actions in a systematic way to expedite getting from your starting point to your destination. **You scored M**.

2. **Realistic financial expectations** is necessary because even if you have a plan, unless it's realistic, you are likely to be headed in the wrong direction and encounter unnecessary obstacles. If you don't have a plan, you are likely to reach your goal less efficiently or not to reach it all. **You scored HM**.

3. **Financial confidence** is also essential because it provides the energy and stamina to overcome the obstacles on your path. Many research studies show that whatever you truly believe, you are likely to manifest. In fact, recent research has *proven* that when you genuinely believe something, you produce cellular changes in your body that help manifest what you believe. In medicine, we call this the placebo effect. In psychology, we call this the self-fulfilling prophecy. **You scored H**.

Our professional experience is that these *three psychological money skills* are the most important in manifesting and maintaining self-made financial success and satisfaction. Not many people score H on all three skills unless they have had coaching, training or therapy with a professional who specialises in the psychology of money. If you score H on all three skills, it is very likely you already have (or soon will have) a high level of financial success and satisfaction. If you did *not* score H on all three skills, the good news is you can significantly increase your scores and financial success and satisfaction through coaching, telephone classes, workshops or therapy.

The four other important psychological money skills

1. **Stepping stones** – For most people, this is the easiest skill to develop and enhance. It is highly beneficial because it is one of the quickest, most powerful ways to overcome feelings of helplessness and procrastination. Once you accomplish an easier smaller goal, your hope and confidence usually increase and provide you with extra motivation and energy. **You scored HM**.

2. **Change tolerance** – This is important because financial opportunities and risks are constantly evolving and shifting. If you can "investigate before you invest", be aware of potential risks and rewards, and be willing to take calculated risks despite uncertainty, you have an edge on others who are afraid of change. **You scored M**.

3. **Passion** – This is powerful because passion supplies the motivation and fuel to jumpstart and sustain your efforts. It helps you to persevere and overcome adversity until you succeed. It also improves the richness of your life. **You scored HM**.

4. **Taking charge** – This is important because it includes being proactive and assertive rather than reactive. You can anticipate financial challenges accurately and pre-empt them or you can respond quickly and make the most of them. **You scored HM**.

REFERENCES

Abramovitch, R., Freedman, J. & Pliner, P. (1991). Children and money: Getting an allowance, credit versus cash, and knowledge of pricing. *Journal of Economic Psychology*, *12*, 27–46.

Aguinis, H., Joo, H. & Gottfredson, R. (2013). What monetary rewards can and cannot do. *Business Horizons*, *2012*, *16*, 1–9.

Ahmetoglu, G. & Furnham, A. (2012). *Pricing practices: A critical review of their effects on consumer perceptions and behavior*. University College London, unpublished paper.

Alter, A. & Oppenheimer, D. (2006). Predicting short-term stock fluctuations by using processing fluency. *Proceedings of the National Academy of Science*, *103*, 9369–9372.

Anderson, C. & Nevitte, N. (2006). Teach your children well: Values of thrift and saving. *Journal of Economic Psychology*, *27*, 247–261.

Angeles, L. (2011). A closer look at the Easterlin paradox. *Journal of Socio-Economics*, *40*, 67–73.

Argyle, M. (1996). *The social psychology of leisure*. London: Penguin.

Ayllon, T. & Azrin, N. (1968). *The token economy*. New York, NY: Appleton-Century-Crofts.

Ayllon, T. & Roberts, M. (1974). Eliminating discipline problems by strengthening academic performance. *Journal of Applied Behaviour Analysis*, *7*, 71–76.

Baca-García, E., Díaz-Sastre, C., de Leon, J. & Saiz-Ruiz, J. (2000). The relationship between menstrual cycle phases and suicide attempts. *Psychosomatic Medicine*, *62*, 50–60.

Baguma, P. & Furnham, A. (2012). Attributions for, and the perceived effects of, poverty in East Africa. In S. Carr, M. MacLachlan & A. Furnham (Eds.), *Humanitarian work psychology* (pp. 332–350). Basingstoke: Palgrave Macmillan.

Bailey, W. & Gustafson, W. (1986). Gender and gender-role orientation differences in attitudes and behaviours toward money. In K. Kitt (Ed.), *Proceedings of the Fourth Annual Conference of the Association of Financial Counseling and Planning Educators* (pp. 11–20). New York.

——(1991). An examination of the relationship between personality factors and attitudes to money. In R. Frantz, H. Singh & J. Gerber (Eds.), *Handbook of behavioural economics* (pp. 271–285). Greenwich, CT: JAI Press.

Bailey, W. & Lown, J. (1993). A cross-cultural examination of the aetiology of attitudes toward money. *Journal of Consumeer Studies and Home Economics*, *17*, 391–402.

Bailey, W., Johnson, P., Adams, C., Lawson, R., Williams, P. & Lown, J. (1994). An exploratory study of money beliefs and behaviours scale using data from 3 nations. In *Consumer Interests Annual* (pp. 178–185). Columbia, MO: ACCZ.

Baker, P. & Hagedorn, R. (2008). Attitudes to money in a random sample of adults: Factor analysis of the MAS and MBBS scales, and correlations with demographic variables. *Journal of Socio-Economics*, *37*, 1803–1814.

Baker, W. & Jimerson, J. (1992). The sociology of money. *American Behavioural Scientist*, *35*, 678–693.

Ball, R. & Chernova, K. (2008). Absolute income, relative income and happiness. *Social Indicators Research*, *88*, 497–529.

Bandura, A. (1989). Social cognitive theory. In R. Vatsa (Ed.), *Annals of child development* (Vol. 6, pp 1–60). Greenwich, CT: JAI Press.

Bank of Scotland. (2008). http://www.bankofscotland-international.com/news/equivalent-1million-pounds-in-1958.asp

Barclays Wealth. (2011). http://artsandbusiness.org.uk/media%20library/Files/Research/pics-0910/2011-UK-Wealth-Map.pdf

Barnet-Verzat, C. & Wolff, F.-C. (2002). Motives for pocket money allowance and family incentives. *Journal of Economic Psychology*, *23*, 339–366.

——(2008). Pocket money and child effort at school. *Economic Bulletin*, *9*, 1–10.

Barth, F. (2001). Money as a tool for negotiation separateness and connectedness in the therapeutic relationship. *Clinical Social Work Journal*, *29*, 79–93.

Bas, J. (1996). *Parent power: Raising children in a commercial world*. London: Advertising Association.

——(1998). *Parent power 2: A practical guide to children, shopping, and advertisements*. London: Advertising Association.

Becchetti, L. & Rossetti, F. (2009). When money does not buy happiness. *Journal of Socio-Economics*, *38*, 159–167.

Becchetti, L., Trovato, G. & Iondono-Bedoya, D. (2011). Income, relational goods and happiness. *Applied Economics*, *43*, 273–290.

Behrend, H. (1988). The wage–work bargain. *Managerial and Decision Economics*, *18*, 51–57.

Belk, R. W. (1991). The ineluctable mysteries of possessions. In *To have possessions: A handbook on ownership and property*, Special issue of *Journal of Social Behavior and Personality*, *6*, 17–55.

Belk, R. W. & Wallendorf, M. (1990). The sacred meaning of money. *Journal of Economic Psychology*, *11*, 35–67.

Bellack, A. & Hersen, M. (1980). *Introduction to clinical psychology*. Oxford: Oxford University Press.

Beloff, H. (1957). The structure and origin of the anal character. *Genetic Psychology Monograph*, *55*, 141–172.

Belsky, G. & Golivich, T. (1999). *Why smart people make big money mistakes – and how to correct them*. New York, NY: Simon & Schuster.

Benson, A. (2008). *To buy or not to buy*. London: Trumpeter.

Berkowitz, L., Fraser, C., Treasure, F. P. & Cochran, S. (1987). Pay, equity, job qualifications, and comparisons in pay satisfaction. *Journal of Applied Psychology*, *72*, 544–551.

Berti, A. & Bombi, A. (1979). Where does money come from? *Archivio di Psicologia*, *40*, 53–77.

——(1981). The development of the concept of money and its value: A longitudinal analysis. *Child Development*, *82*, 1179–1182.

——(1988). *The child's construction of economics*. Cambridge: Cambridge University Press.

Berti, A. & Grivet, A. (1990). The development of economic reasoning in children from 8 to 13 years old: Price mechanism. *Contribute di Psicologia*, *5*, 37–47.

Berti, A. & Kirchler, E. (2001). Research on representations of the fiscal system. *Giornale Italiiano di Psicologia*, *38*, 595–607.

Berti, A. & Monaci, M. (1998). Third graders' acquisition of knowledge of banking: Restructuring or accretion? *British Journal of Educational Psychology*, *68*, 357–371.

Berti, A., Bombi, A. & de Beni, R. (1986). Acquiring economic notions: Profit. *International Journal of Behavioural Development*, *9*, 15–29.

Berti, A., Bombi, A. & Lis, A. (1982). The child's conception about means of production and their owners. *European Journal of Social Psychology*, *12*, 221–239.

Beutler, I. & Dickson, L. (2008). Consumer economic socialisation. In J. J. Xiao (Ed.), *Handbook of consumer finance research* (pp. 83–102). New York, NY: Springer.

Bijleveld, E., Custers, R. & Aarts, H. (2011). Once money is in sight. *Journal of Experimental Social Psychology, 47*, 865–869.

Biswas-Diener, R. & Diener, E. (2001). Making the best of a bad situation. *Social Indicators Research, 55*, 329–352.

Blaszczynski, A. & Nower, L. (2010). Instrumental tool or drug: Relationships between attitudes to money and problem gambling. *Addiction Research and Theory, 18*, 681–691.

Bodnar, J. (1997). *Dr Tightwad's money-smart kids: Teach your kids sound values for wiser saving, earning, spending and investing*. Washington, DC: Kiplinger.

Boehm, J. K. & Lyubomirsky, S. (2008). Does happiness promote career success? *Journal of Career Assessment, 16*, 101–116.

Bonini, N., Biel, A., Garling, T. & Karlsson, N. (2002). Influencing what their money is perceived to be worth. *Journal of Economic Psychology, 23*, 655–666.

Bonn, M., Earle, D., Lea, S. & Webley, P. (1999). South African children's view of wealth, poverty, inequality and unemployment. *Journal of Economic Psychology, 20*, 593–612.

Bonn, M. & Webley, P. (2000). South African children's understanding of money and banking. *British Journal of Development Psychology, 18*, 269–278.

Bonner, S. & Sprinkle, G. (2002). The effects of monetary incentives on effort and task performance. *Accounting, Organisations and Society, 27*, 303–345.

Borneman, E. (1973). *The psychoanalysis of money*. New York, NY: Unrizen.

Bottomley, P. A., Nairn, A., Kasser, T., Ferguson, Y. L. & Ormrod, J. (2010). Measuring childhood materialism: Refining and validating Schor's Consumer Involvement Scale. *Psychology & Marketing, 27*, 717–740.

Boucher, H. & Kofos, M. (2012). The idea of money counteracts ego depletion effects. *Journal of Experimental Social Psychology, 48*, 804–810.

Bowen, C. (2002). Financial knowledge of teens and their parents. *Financial Counselling and Planning, 13*, 93–101.

Boyce, C. J., Brown, G. & Moore, S. (2010). Money and happiness: Rank of income, not income, affects life satisfaction. *Psychological Science, 21*, 471–475.

Britt, S. & Huston, S. (2012). The role of money arrangements in marriage. *Journal of Family Economic Issues, 33*, 464–476.

Britt, S., Huston, S. & Durband, D. (2010). The determinants of money arguments between spouses. *Journal of Financial Therapy, 1*, 42–60.

Brown, R. (1978). Divided we fall: An analysis of relations between sections of a factory workforce. In H. Tajfel (Ed.), *Differentiation between social groups*. London: Academic Press.

Bruce, V., Gilmore, D., Mason, L. & Mayhew, P. (1983). Factors affecting the perceived value of coins. *Journal of Economic Psychology, 4*, 335–347.

Bruce, V., Howarth, C., Clark-Carter, D., Dodds, A. & Heyes, A. (1983). All change for the pound: Human performance tests with different versions of the proposed UK one pound coin. *Ergonometrics, 26*, 215–221.

Bruner, J. & Goodman, C. (1947). Value and need as organizing factors in perception. *Journal of Abnormal and Social Psychology, 42*, 33–44.

Brusdal, R. (2004). *Growing up commercial*. Olso: NICR.

Brusdal, R. & Berg, L. (2010). Are parents gender neutral when financing their children's consumption? *International Journal of Consumer Studies, 34*, 3–10.

Bucklin, B. & Dickinson, A. (2001). Individual monetary incentives. *Journal of Organizational Behaviour Management, 21*, 45–137.

Burgess, S. M. (2005). The importance and motivational content of money attitudes: South Africans with living standards similar to those in industrialised Western countries. *South African Journal of Psychology, 35*, 106–126.

Burman, B. & Biswas, A. (2007). Partitioned pricing: Can we always divide and prosper? *Journal of Retailing, 84*, 423–436.

Burris, V. (1983). Stages in the development of economic concepts. *Human Relations, 36,* 791–812.

Campbell, A., Converse, P. E. & Rogers, W. L. (1976). *The quality of American life.* New York, NY: Sage.

Caporale, G., Georgellis, Y., Tsitsianis, S. & Yin, Y. (2009). Income and happiness across Europe: Do reference values matter? *Journal of Economic Psychology, 30,* 42–51.

Carlson, J. P. & Weathers, D. (2008). Examining differences in consumer reactions to partitioned prices with a variable number of price components. *Journal of Business Research, 67,* 724–731.

Casserly, J. (2008). *The emotion behind money: Building wealth from the inside out.* Chicago, IL: BYWD.

Cebr Forecasting Eye. (August 2006). http:www.cebr.com

Chan, K. & McNeal, I. (2006). Chinese children's understanding of commercial communications. *Journal of Economic Psychology, 27,* 36–59.

Chen, H. & Volpe, R. (1998). An analysis of personal financial literacy among college students. *Financial Services Review, 1,* 107–128.

Chen, E., Dowling, N. & Yap, K. (2012). An examination of gambling behaviour in relation to financial management behaviour, financial attitudes and money attitudes. *International Journal of Mental Health Addiction, 10,* 231–242.

Chiang, F. & Birtch, T. (2010). Pay for performance and work attitudes. *International Journal of Hospitality Management, 29,* 632–640.

Children's Mutual. (2010). *Save, save, save.* London: CM.

Chown, J. (1994). *A history of money.* London: Routledge.

Christopher, A. N., Marek, P. & Carroll, S. M. (in press). Materialism and attitudes toward money: An exploratory investigation. *Individual Differences Research.*

Churchill, G. A. & Moschis, G. P. (1979). Television and interpersonal influences on adolescent consumer learning. *Journal of Consumer Research, 6,* 23–25.

Cialdini, R. B. (2001). *Influence: Science and practice* (4th ed.). Boston, MA: Allyn & Bacon.

——(2009). We have to break up. *Perspectives on Psychological Science, 4,* 5–6.

Clark, A. E., Frijters, P. & Shields, M. (2008). Relative income, happiness and utility. An explanation for the Easterlin paradox and other puzzles. *Journal of Economic Literature, 46,* 95–144.

Clarke, M. D., Heaton, M. B., Israelsen, C. L. & Eggett, D. L. (2005). The acquisition of family financial roles and responsibilities. *Family and Consumer Sciences Research Journal, 33,* 321–340.

Colella, A., Paetzold, R., Zardkoohi, A. & Wesson, A. (2007). Exposing pay secrecy. *American Management Review, 32,* 55–71.

Coleman, J. W. (1992). Crime and money. *American Behavioural Scientist, 35,* 827–836.

Collier, C. (2006). *Wealth in families.* Cambridge, MA: Harvard University Press.

ComScore. (2009, December). www.comscore.com

Cotterell, N., Eisenberger, R. & Speicher, H. (1992). Inhibiting effects of reciprocation wariness on interpersonal relationships. *Journal of Personality and Social Psychology, 62,* 658–668.

Coulborn, W. (1950). *A discussion of money.* London: Longmans, Green & Co.

Cox, C. & Cooper, C. (1990). *High flyers.* Oxford: Blackwell.

Cram, F. & Ng, S. (1989). Children's endorsements of ownership attributes. *Journal of Economic Psychology, 10,* 63–75.

Cummings, S. & Taebel, D. (1978). The economic socialization of children: A neo-Marxist analysis. *Social Problems, 26,* 198–210.

Dalton, G. (1971). Economic theory and primitive society. *American Anthropologist, 63,* 1–25.

Danes, S. M. (1994). Parental perceptions of children's financial socialization. *Financial Counselling and Planning, 5,* 127–149.

Danes, S. M. & Haberman, H. R. (2007). Teen financial knowledge, self-efficacy, and behavior: A gendered view. *Financial Counseling and Planning Journal, 18*(1), 48–60.

Danziger, K. (1958). Children's earliest conceptions of economic relationships. *Journal of Social Psychology, 47,* 231–240.

Darke, P. R., Freedman, J. L. & Chaiken, S. (1995). Percentage discounts, initial price and bargain hunting: A heuristic-systematic approach to price search behavior. *Journal of Applied Psychology, 80*(5), 580–586.

Davies, P. & Lundholm, C. (2012). Students' understanding of socio-economic phenomena. *Journal of Economic Psychology, 33,* 79–89.

Davis, A. (1964). The relation of cognitive dissonance theory to an aspect of psychotherapeutic practice. *American Psychologist, 19,* 329–332.

Davis, K. & Taylor, R. (1979). *Kids and cash.* La Jolla, CA: Oak Tree.

Dawson, J. (1975). Socio-economic differences in size-judgements of discs and coins by Chinese Primary VI children in Hong Kong. *Perceptual and Motor Skills, 41,* 107–110.

Day, N. (2007). An investigation into pay communication: Is ignorance bliss? *Personal Review, 36,* 739–762.

——(2012). Pay equity as a mediator of the relationship among attitudes and communication about pay level determination and pay secrecy. *Journal of Leadership and Organisational Studies, 19,* 462–476.

De Bens, E. & Vandenbruaene, P. (1992). *TV advertising and children.* Ghent: University of Ghent.

Deci, E. L. (1980). *The psychology of self-determination.* Lexington, MA: D. C. Heath.

Deci, E. L. & Ryan, R. (1985). *Intrinsic motivation and self-determination in human behaviour.* New York, NY: Plenum Press.

De Mause, L. (1988). "Heads and Tails": Money as a poison centre. *Journal of Psychohistory, 16,* 1–11.

Deutsch, F., Roksa, J. & Meeska, C. (2003). How gender counts when couples count their money. *Sex Roles, 48,* 291–304.

DeVoe, S. & House, J. (2012). Time, money and happiness. *Journal of Experimental Social Psychology, 48,* 466–474.

DeVoe, S. & Pfeffer, J. (2007). When time is money. *Organizational Behavior and Human Decision Processes, 104,* 1–13.

——(2011). Time is tight: How higher economic value of time increases feelings of time pressure. *Journal of Applied Psychology, 96,* 665–676.

DeVor, M. (2011). *Money Love.* USA: Meadow DeVor.

Dickinson, J. & Emler, N. (1996). Developing ideas about distribution of wealth. In P. Lunt & A. Furnham (Eds.), *Economic socialization* (pp. 47–68). Cheltenham: Edward Elgar.

Diener, E. (2000). Subjective well-being. *American Psychologist, 55,* 34–43.

Diener, E. & Biswas-Diener, R. (2002). Will money increase subjective well-being? A literature review and guide to needed research. *Social Indicators Research, 57,* 119–169.

Diener, E. & Chan, M. (2011). Happy people live longer: Subjective well-being contributes to health and longevity. *Applied Psychology: Health and Well-Being, 3,* 1–43.

Diener, E. & Oishi, S. (2000). Money and happiness. In E. Diener & E. Suhs (Eds.), *Culture and subjective wellbeing* (pp. 185–218). Cambridge, MA: MIT Press.

Diener, E. & Seligman, M. E. P. (2012). Very happy people. *Psychological Science, 13,* 81–84.

Diener, E. & Tov, W. (2009). Well-being on planet earth. *Psychological Topics, 18,* 213–219.

Diener, E., Diener, M. & Diener, C. (1995). Factors predicting the subjective well-being of nations. *Journal of Personality and Social Psychology, 69,* 851–864.

Diener, E., Ng, W. & Tov, W. (2009). Balance in life and declining marginal utility of diverse resources. *Applied Research in Quality of Life, 3,* 277–291.

Diener, E., Ng, W., Harter, J. & Arora, R. (2010). Wealth and happiness across the world: Material prosperity predicts life evaluation, whereas psychosocial prosperity predicts positive feeling. *Journal of Personality and Social Psychology, 99,* 52–61.

Diener, E., Sandvik, E., Seidlitz, L. & Diener, M. (1993). The relationship between income and subjective well-being: Relative or absolute? *Social Indicators Research, 28,* 195–223.

Diener, E., Suh, M., Lucas, E. & Smith, H. (1999). Subjective well-being: Three decades of progress. *Psychological Bulletin, 125*(2), 276–302.

Diez-Martinez, E., Sanchez, M. & Miramontes, S. (2001). Mexican children's and adolescents' understanding of unemployment. *Children's Social and Economic Education, 4*, 159–169.

Dimen, M. (1994). Money, love and hate: Contradiction and paradox in psychoanalysis. *Psychoanalytic Dialogues, 4*, 69–100.

Di Muro, F. & Noseworthy, T. (2012). Money isn't everything, but it helps if it doesn't look used. *Journal of Consumer Research, 39*, 1330–1341.

Dismorr, B. (1902). Ought children to be paid for domestic services? *Studies in Education, 2*, 62–70.

Di Tella, R. & McCullock, R. (2008). Gross national happiness as an answer to the Easterlin paradox? *Journal of Developmental Economics, 86*, 22–42.

Dittmar, H. (2005). A new look at "compulsive buying": Self-discrepancies and materialistic values as predictors of compulsive buying tendency. *Journal of Social and Clinical Psychology, 24*, 832–959.

Dittmar, H. & Drury, J. (2000). Self-image – Is it in the bag? *International Journal of Advertising, 17*, 131–144.

Dodd, N. (1994). *The sociology of money*. New York, NY: Continuum.

Donovan, N. & Halpern, D. (2003). *Life satisfaction*. London: Cabinet Office.

Douglas, M. (1967). Primitive rationing. In R. Firth (Ed.), *Themes in economic anthropology* (pp. 119–146). London: Tavistock.

Douglas, M. & Isherwood, B. (1979). *The world of goods: Towards an anthropology of consumption*. London: Allen Lane.

Drotner, K. (1991). *To create one-self*. Copenhagen: Gyldendal.

Dulebohn, J. & Martocchio, J. (1998). Employee perceptions of the fairness of work group incentive pay plans. *Journal of Management, 24*, 469–488.

Dunn, E., Gilbert, D. & Wilson, T. (2011). If money doesn't make you happy, then you probably aren't spending it right. *Journal of Consumer Psychology, 21*, 115–125.

Ealy, D. & Lesh, K. (1998). *Our money, ourselves*. New York, NY: AMACOR.

Easterlin, R. A. (1974). Does economic growth improve the human lot? Some empirical evidence. In P. A. David & M. Abrovitz (Eds.), *Nations and households in economic growth* (pp. 89–125). New York, NY: Academic Press.

Easterlin, R. A., McVey, L. A., Switek, M., Swangfa, O. & Zweig, J. S. (2010). The happiness-income paradox revisited. *Proceedings of the National Academy of Sciences, 107*, 22463–22468.

Eckel, C. & Grossman, P. (2002). Sex differences and statistical stereotyping in attitudes toward financial risk. *Evolution and Human Behaviour, 23*, 281–295.

Economidou, M. (2000). *An economic psychology survey on the choice to insure or not insure voluntarily*. Paper presented at the 25th Conference of the IAREC, Austria

Eldar-Avidan, D., Haj-Yahia, M. & Greenbaum, C. (2008). Money matters. *Journal of Family and Economic Issues, 29*, 74–85.

Engelberg, E. & Sjoberg, L. (2006). Money attitudes and emotional intelligence. *Journal of Applied Social Psychology, 36*, 2027–2047.

——(2007). Money obsession, social adjustment and economic risk perception. *Journal of Socio-Economics, 36*, 686–697.

Estes, P. & Barocas, I. (1994) *Kids, Money and Value: Creative ways to teach your kids about money*. Cincinnati: Betterway Books.

Eysenck, H. (1976). The structure of social attitudes. *Psychological Reports, 39*, 463–466.

Fabian, L. & Jolicoeur, D. (1993). Socialisation as an ecological factor of compulsive buying behaviour among young adults. *European Advances in Consumer Research, 1*, 262–268.

Feather, N. (1991). Variables relating to the allocation of pocket money to children: Parental reasons and values. *British Journal of Social Psychology, 30*, 221–234.

Fenichel, O. (1947). The drive to amass wealth. In O. Fenichel & O. Rapoport (Eds.), *The collected papers of O. Fenichel*. New York, NY: Norton.

Ferenczi, S. (1926). *Further contributions to the theory and techniques of psychoanalysis.* New York, NY: Norton.

Ferguson, N. (2009). *The ascent of money: A financial history of the world.* London: Penguin.

Festinger, L. (1957). *A theory of cognitive dissonance.* Stanford, CA: Stanford University Press

Feurstein, C. (1971). Money as value in psychotherapy. *Journal of Contemporary Psychotherapy, 3,* 99–104.

Finn, D. (1992). The meaning of money: A view from economics. *American Behavioural Scientist, 35,* 658–668.

Fischer, R. & Boer, D. (2011). What is more important for national well-being: Money or autonomy? *Journal of Personality and Social Psychology, 101,* 164–184.

Flouri, E. (1999). An integrated model of consumer materialism: Can economic socialisation and maternal values predict materialistic attitudes in adolescents? *Journal of Socio-Economics, 28,* 707–724.

——(2001). The role of family togetherness and right-wing attitudes in adolescent materialism. *Journal of Socio-Economics, 30,* 363–365.

——(2004). Exploring the relationship between mothers' and fathers' parenting practices and children's materialistic values. *Journal of Economic Psychology, 25,* 743–752.

Forman, N. (1987). *Mind over money: Curing your financial headaches with money sanity.* Toronto, Ontario: Doubleday.

Foubert, B. & Gijsbrecht, E. (2007). Shopper response to bundle promotions for packaged goods. *Journal of Marketing Research, 44,* 647–662.

Freud, S. (1908). *Character and anal eroticism.* London: Hogarth.

Frey, B. S. & Stutzer, A. (2002). *Beyond outcomes: Measuring procedural utility* (Working Paper Series 72). Berkeley, CA: Berkeley Olin Program in Law & Economics.

Frijters, P., Haisken-DeNew, J. P. & Shields, M. A. (2004). Money does matter! Evidence from increasing real income and life satisfaction in East Germany following reunification. *The American Economic Review, 94*(3), 730–740.

Furnham, A. (1982). The perception of poverty among adolescents. *Journal of Adolescence, 5,* 135–147.

——(1983). Inflation and the estimated sizes of notes. *Journal of Economic Psychology, 4,* 349–352.

——(1984). Many sides of the coin: The psychology of money usage. *Personality and Individual Differences, 5,* 95–103.

——(1985a). The perceived value of small coins. *Journal of Social Psychology, 125,* 571–575.

——(1985b). Why do people save? *Journal of Applied Social Psychology, 15,* 354–373.

——(1986). Economic locus of control. *Human Relations, 39,* 29–43.

——(1990). *The protestant work ethic.* London: Routledge.

——(1996). Attitudinal correlates and demographic predictors of monetary beliefs and behaviours. *Journal of Organizational Behaviour, 17,* 375–388.

——1998). *The economic socialisaion of young people.* London: SAU

——(1999a). Economic socialisation. *British Journal of Developmental Psychology, 17,* 585–604.

——(1999b). The saving and spending habits of young people. *Journal of Economic Psychology, 20,* 677–697.

——(2001). Parental attitudes to pocket money/allowances for children. *Journal of Economic Psychology, 22,* 397–422.

——(2005). Understanding the meaning of tax. *Journal of Socio-Economics, 34,* 703–713.

——(2008). *The economic socialisation of young people.* London: SAU.

Furnham, A. & Argyle, M. (1998). *The psychology of money.* Routledge: London.

Furnham, A. & Boo, H. C. (2011). A literature review of the anchoring effect. *Journal of Socio-Economics, 40,* 35–42.

Furnham, A. & Cleare, A. (1988). School children's conceptions of economics: Prices, wages, investments and strikes. *Journal of Economic Psychology, 9,* 467–479.

Furnham, A. & Goletto-Tankel, M. (2002). Understanding savings, pensions and life assurance in 16–21-year-olds. *Human Relations, 55,* 603–628.

Furnham, A. & Kirkcaldy, B. (2000). Economic socialisation: German parents' perception and implementation of allowances to educate children. *European Psychologist, 5,* 202–215.

Furnham, A. & Lunt, P. L. (1996). *Economic socialization.* Cheltenham: Edward Elgar.

Furnham, A. & Okamura, R. (1999). Your money or your life: Behavioural and emotional predictors of money pathology. *Human Relations, 52,* 1157–1177.

Furnham, A. & Rawles, R. (2004). Young people's ignorance about the topic of taxation. *Citizenship, Social and Economic Education, 6,* 12–24.

Furnham, A. & Thomas, P. (1984a). Pocket money: A study of economic education. *British Journal of Developmental Psychology, 2,* 205–212.

——(1984b). Adult perceptions of the economic socialization of children. *Journal of Adolescence, 7,* 217–231.

Furnham, A. & Weissman, D. (1985). *Children's perceptions of British coins.* University College London, unpublished paper.

Furnham, A., Wilson, E. & Telford, K. (2012). The meaning of money. *Personality and Individual Differences, 52,* 707–711.

Furnham, M., Fenton O'Creevy, M. & von Stumm, S. (2013). *Sex differences in money pathology in the general population.* University College London, unpublished manuscript.

Furth, H. (1980). *The world of grown-ups.* New York, NY: Elsevier.

Futrell, C. & Jenkins, O. (1998). Pay secrecy versus pay disclosure for salesmen. *Journal of Marketing Research, 15,* 214–219.

Galbraith, J. K. (1984). *The affluent society* (4th ed.). Boston, MA: Houghton Mifflin.

Gallo, E. & Gallo, J. (2002). *Silver spoon kids.* Chicago, IL: Contemporary Books.

Gandelman, N. & Porzecanski, R. (2013). Happiness inequality: How much is reasonable? *Social Indicators Research, 110,* 257–269.

Gardes, F. & Merrigan, P. (2008). Individual needs and social pressure. *Journal of Economic Behaviour and Organisation, 66,* 582–596.

Gardner, D., Van Dyne, L. & Pierce, J. (2004). The effects of pay level on organizational-based self-esteem and performance. *Journal of Occupational and Organizational Psychology, 77,* 307–322.

Gardner, J. & Oswald, A. (2006). Money and mental well-being: A longitudinal study of medium-sized lottery wins. *Journal of Health Psychology, 26,* 49–60.

Gilbert, E. (2005). Common cents: Situating money in time and place. *Economy and Society, 34,* 357–388.

Godfrey, N. (1994). *Money doesn't grow on trees.* New York, NY: Fireside.

——(1996). *A penny saved: Teaching your children the values and life skills they will need to live in the real world.* New York, NY: Simon & Schuster.

Goldberg, H. & Lewis, R. (1978). *Money madness: The psychology of saving, spending, loving and hating money.* London: Springwood.

Goldstein, J. (2011). What does it mean to be a millionaire? *Planet Money,* May 23.

Goodnow, J. J. (1996). From household practices to parents' ideas about work and interpersonal relationships. In S. Harkness & G. Super (Eds.), *Parents' cultural belief systems* (pp. 313–344). London: Guilford Press.

——(1998). Children's household work: Its nature and functions. *Psychological Bulletin, 103,* 5–26.

Goodnow, J. J. & Warton, P. M. (1991). The social bases of social cognition: Interactions about work, lessons about relationships. *Merrill-Palmer Quarterly, 37,* 27–58.

Graham, C. (2011). Does more money make you happier? Why so much debate? *Applied Research Quality Life, 6,* 219–239.

Gresham, A. & Fontenot, G. (1989). The differing attitudes of the sexes toward money: An application of the money attitude scale. *Advances in Marketing, 8,* 380–384.

Gruber, J., Mauss, I. & Tamir, M. (2011). A dark side of happiness? *Psychological Science, 6,* 222–233.

Gruenberg, S. & Gruenberg, B. (1993). *Parents, children and money.* New York, NY: Viking Press.

Grygier, T. (1961). *The Dynamic Personality Inventory*. Windsor: NFER.

Guéguen, N. (2002). The effects of a joke on tipping when it is delivered at the same time as the bill. *Journal of Applied Social Psychology, 32*(9), 1955–1963.

Guéguen, N. & Jacob, C. (2001). Fund-raising on the Web: The effect of an electronic foot-in-the-door on donation. *CyberPsychology & Behavior, 4*(6), 705–709.

Gunter, B. & Furnham, A. (1998). *Children as consumers*. London: Routledge.

Guzzo, R., Jette, R. D. & Katzell, R. A. (1985). The effects of psychologically based interventions programs on worker productivity: A meta analysis. *Personnel Psychology, 38,* 275–291.

Hacker, J. & Pierson, P. (2010). Winner-take-all politics: Public policy, political organization, and the precipitous rise of top incomes in the United States. *Politics and Society, 38*(2), 152–204.

Hagerty, M. R. & Veenhoven, R. (2003). Wealth and happiness. *Social Indicators Research, 64,* 1–27.

Hallachan, T., Faff, R. & McKenzie, M. (2004). An empirical investigation of personal financial risk tolerance. *Financial Services Review, 13,* 57–78.

Hanashiro, R., Masuo, D., Kim, J. H. & Malroutu, Y. L. (2004). Money attitudes and gender comparison between Japanese students and Asian American students. *The Okinawan Journal of American Studies, 1,* 38–45.

Hanley, A. & Wilhelm, M. (1992). Compulsive buying: An exploration into self-esteem and money attitudes. *Journal of Economic Psychology, 13,* 5–18.

Hansen, J., Kutzner, F. & Wanke, M. (2012). Money and thinking. *Journal of Consumer Research, 39,* 1–13.

Harrah, J. & Friedman, M. (1990). Economic socialisation in children in a mid-western American community. *Journal of Economic Psychology, 11,* 495–513.

Harris, M. (1995). Waiters, customers and service: Some tips about tipping. *Journal of Applied Social Psychology, 25,* 725–744.

Hartley, A. (1995). *The psychology of money*. Brookville, Australia: Hart.

Hausner, L. (1990). *Children of paradise*. Irvine, CA: Plaza Press.

Hayhoe, C. & Stevenson, M. (2007). Financial attitudes and inter vivos resources transfers from older parents to adult children. *Journal of Family Economic Issues, 28,* 123–135.

Haynes, J. & Wiener, J. (1996). The analyst in the counting house: Money as a symbol and reality in analysis. *British Journal of Psychotherapy, 13,* 14–25.

Headey, B. W., Muffels, R. & Wooden, M. (2008). Money does not buy happiness. *Social Indicators Research, 87,* 65–82.

Helliwell, J. F. (2003). How's life? Combining individual and national variables to explain subjective well-being. *Economic Modelling, 20,* 331–360.

Herron, W. G. & Sitkowski, S. (1986). Effect of fees on psychotherapy: What is the evidence? *Professional Psychology: Research and Practice, 17,* 347–351.

Herron, W. G. & Welt, S. (1992). *Money matters: The fee in psychotherapy and psychoanalysis.* New York, NY: Guilford Press.

Herskovitz, M. J. (1962). *Human problems in changing Africa*. New York, NY: Knopf.

Hilgert, M., Hogarth, J. & Beverley, S. (2003). Household financial management. *Federal Reserve Bulletin, 6,* 309–322.

Hira, T. & Lobil, C (2006). Understanding the impact of employer provided financial education on workplace satisfaction. *Journal of Consumer Affairs, 39,* 173–194.

Hitchcock, J., Munroe, R. & Munroe, R. (1976). Coins and countries: The value-size hypothesis. *Journal of Social Psychology, 100,* 307–308.

Hogue, M., Fox-Cardamone, L. & Du Bois, C. (2011). Justifying the pay system through status. *Journal of Applied Social Psychology, 41,* 823–899.

Holder, M. & Coleman, B. (2007). The contribution of social relationships to children's happiness. *Journal of Happiness Studies, 9,* 279–302.

Howarth, E. (1980). A test of some old concepts by means of some new scales: Anality or psychoticism, oral optimism or extraversion, oral pessimism or neuroticism. *Psychological Reports, 47*, 1039–1042.

——(1982). Factor analytic examination of Kline's scales for psychoanalytic concepts. *Personality and Individual Differences, 3*, 89–92.

Howell, R., Kurai, M. & Tam, L. (2013). Money buys financial security and psychological need satisfaction. *Social Indicators Research, 110*, 17–29.

Hsieh, C.-M. (2011). Money and happiness. *Ageing and Society, 31*, 1289–1306.

Huppert, F., Baylis, N. & Keverne, B. (Eds.). (2005). *The science of well-being.* Oxford: Oxford University Press.

Inman, J. J., McAlister, L. & Hoyer, W. D. (1990). Promotion signal: Proxy for a price cut? *Journal of Consumer Research, 17*(1), 74–81.

Izraeli, D. (1994). Money matters. *Sociological Quarterly, 35*, 69–84.

Jackson, K. (Ed.). (1995). *The Oxford book of money.* Oxford: Oxford University Press.

Jahoda, G. (1979). The construction of economic reality by some Glaswegian children. *European Journal of Social Psychology, 9*, 115–127.

——(1981). The development of thinking about economic institutions: The bank. *Cashiers de Psychologic Cognitive, 1*, 55–73.

James, O. (2007). *Affluenza.* London: Vermilion.

Jellinek, M. & Berenson, E. (2008). Money talks. *Journal of the American Academy of Child Adolescent Psychiatry, 47*, 249–253.

Johnson, M. D., Herrmann, A. & Bauer, H. H. (1999). The effects of price bundling on consumer evaluations of product offerings. *International Journal of Research in Marketing, 16*(2), 129–142.

Jonas, E., Greitemeyer, T., Frey, D. & Schulz-Hardt, S. (2002). Psychological effects of the euro- experimental research on the perception of salaries and price estimations. *European Journal of Social Psychology, 32*, 147–169.

Judge, T., Piccolo, R., Podsakoff, N., Shaw, J. & Rich, B. (2010). The relationship between pay and job satisfaction. *Vocational Behaviour, 77*, 157–167.

Kahler, R. & Fox, K. (2005). *Conscious finance.* Rapid City, SD: Conscious Finance, LLC.

Kahneman, D. (2011). *Thinking fast and slow.* London: Allen Lane.

Kahneman, D. & Deaton, A. (2010). High income improves evaluation of life but not emotional well-being. *Proceedings of the National Association of Science of the United States of America, 107*, 16489–16493.

Kahneman, D. & Tversky, A. (1982). The psychology of preference. *Scientific American, 246*, 160–173.

Kahneman, D., Krueger, A. B., Schkade, D., Schwarz, N. & Stone, A. (2006). Would you be happier if you were richer? A focusing illusion. *Science, 312* , 1908–1910.

Kamins, M., Folkes, V. & Fedorikhin, A. (2009). Promotional bundles and consumer price judgements. *Journal of Consumer Research, 36*, 666–670.

Kanfer, R. (1990). Motivation theory and industrial and organizational psychology. In M. D. Dunnette & L. M. Hough (Eds.), *Handbook of industrial and organizational psychology* (Vol. 1, pp. 75–170). Palo Alto, CA: Consulting Psychologists Press.

Kardos, P. & Castano, E. (2012). Money does not stink, or does it? *Current Psychology, 31*, 381–385.

Katona, G. (1975). *Psychological economics.* New York, NY: Elsevier.

Kaufman, W. (1956). Some emotional uses of money. *Acta Psytherapeutica, 4*, 20–41.

Kaun, D. (2005). Income and happiness. *Journal of Socio-Economics, 34*, 161–177.

Keller, C. & Siegrist, M. (2006). Money attitude typology and stock investment. *Journal of Behavioural Finance, 7*, 88–96.

Kenney, C. (2008). Father doesn't know best. *Journal of Marriage and Family, 70*, 654–669.

Kerr, M. & Cheadle, T. (1997). Allocation of allowances and associated family practices. *Children's Social and Economic Education, 2*, 1–11.

Kesebir, P. & Diener, E. (2008). In pursuit of happiness: Empirical answers to philosophic questions. *Perspectives on Psychological Science, 3*, 117–125.

Kilbourne, W. E. & LaForge, M. C. (2010). Materialism and its relationship to individual values. *Psychology & Marketing, 27*, 780–798.

King, L. & Napa, C. (1998). What makes a good life? *Journal of Personality and Social Psychology, 75*, 156–165.

Kirchler, E. & Praher, D. (1990). Austrian children's economic socialisation. *Journal of Economic Psychology, 11*, 438–494.

Kirton, M. (1978). Wilson and Patterson's Conservatism Scale. *British Journal of Social and Clinical Psychology, 12*, 428–430.

Kiyosaki, R. (1997). *Rich dad, poor dad.* New York, NY: Time Warner.

Kline, P. (1967). *An investigation into the Freudian concept of the anal character.* Unpublished PhD, University of Manchester.

——(1971). *Ai3Q Test.* Windsor: NFER.

Klontz, B. Britt, S. Mentzer, J. & Klontz, T. (2011) Money beliefs and financial behaviours, *Journal of Finance Therapy, 2*, 1–22.

Knowles, S., Hyde, M. & White, K. (2012). Predictors of young people's charitable intentions to donate money. *Journal of Applied Social Psychology, 42*, 2096–2110.

Kohler, A. (1897). Children's sense of money. *Studies in Education, 1*, 323–331.

Kohn, A. (1999). *Punished by rewards.* Boston, MA: Houghton Mifflin.

Kouchaki, M., Smith-Crowe, K., Brief, A. & Sousa, C. (2013). Seeing green: Mere exposure to money triggers a business decision frame and unethical outcomes. *Organisational Behaviour and Human Decision Making, 121*, 53–66.

Lambert, W., Soloman, R. & Watson, P. (1949). Reinforcement and extinction as factors in size estimation. *Journal of Experimental Psychology, 39*, 637–671.

Langs, R. (1982). *Psychotherapy: A basic text.* New York, NY: Jason Aronson.

Lassarres, D. (1996). Consumer education in French families and schools. In P. Lunt & A. Furnham (Eds.), *Economic socialization* (pp. 130–148). Cheltenham: Edward Elgar.

Lawler, E. (1981). *Pay and organization development.* Reading, MA: Addison-Wesley.

Lea, S. (1981). Inflation, decimalization and the estimated size of coins. *Journal of Economic Psychology, 1*, 79–81.

Lea, S. & Webley, P. (1981). *Theorie psychologique de la Monnane.* Paper presented at the 6th International Symposium on Economic Psychology, Paris.

——(2006). Money as tool, money as drug: The biological psychology of a strong incentive. *Behavioural and Brain Sciences, 29*, 161–209.

Lea, S., Tarpy, R. M. & Webley, P. (1987). *The individual in the economy.* Cambridge: Cambridge University Press.

Leahy, R. (1981). The development of the conception of economic inequality. *Child Development, 52*, 523–532.

Leiser, D. (1983). Children's conceptions of economics. *Journal of Economic Psychology, 4*, 297–317.

Leiser, D. & Ganin, M. (1996). Economic participation and economic socialization. In P. Lunt & A. Furnham (Eds.), *Economic socialization* (pp. 93–109). Cheltenham: Edward Elgar.

Leiser, D. & Halachmi, B. (2006). Children's understanding of market forces. *Journal of Economic Psychology, 27*, 6–19.

Leiser, D. & Izak, G. (1987). The money size illusion as a barometer of confidence? The case of high inflation in Israel. *Journal of Economic Psychology, 8*, 347–356.

Leiser, D., Sevon, G. & Levy, D. (1990). Children's economic socialisation: Summarising the cross-cultural comparison of ten countries. *Journal of Social Psychology, 12*, 221–239.

Leman, P. J., Keller, M. & Takezawa, M. (2008). Children's and adolescents' decisions about sharing money with others. *Social Development, 18*, 711–727.

Lewis, A. (1982). *The psychology of taxation.* Oxford: Martin Robertson.

——(2001). *Money in the contemporary family.* London: Nestlé.

Lewis, A. & Scott, A. (2003). The economic awareness, knowledge and pocket money practices of a sample of UK adolescents. *Children's Social and Economic Education, 4*, 34–42.

Lichtenstein, D. R. (2005). Price perceptions, merchant incentives, and consumer welfare. *Journal of Product and Brand Management, 14*(6), 357–361.

Lim, V. & Sng, Q. (2006). Does parental job insecurity matter? Money anxiety, money motives, and work motivation. *Journal of Applied Psychology, 91*, 1078–1087.

Lim, V. & Teo, T. (1997). Sex, money and financial hardship: An empirical study of attitudes towards money among undergraduates in Singapore. *Journal of Economic Psychology, 18*, 369–386.

Lindgren, H. (1991). *The psychology of money.* Odessa, FL: Krieger.

Linley, A. (2008). *Average to A+.* Warwick: Capp Press.

Liu, B. & Tang, T. (2011). Does love of money moderate the relationship between public service motivation and job satisfaction? *Public Administrative Review, 71*, 718–727.

Luft, J. (1957). Monetary value and the perceptions of persons. *Journal of Social Psychology, 46*, 245–251.

Luna-Arocas, R. & Tang, T. (2004). The love of money, satisfaction and the Protestant Work Ethic. *Journal of Business Ethics, 50*, 329–354.

Lunt, P. (1996). Introduction: Social aspects of young people's understanding of the economy. In P. Lunt & A. Furnham (Eds.), *Economic socialization* (pp. 1–10). Cheltenham: Edward Elgar.

Lyck, L. (1990). Danish children's and their parents' economic understanding, reasoning and attitudes. *Journal of Economic Psychology, 11*, 583–590.

Lynn, M. (1989). Scarcity effects on desirability: Mediated by assumed expensiveness? *Journal of Economic Psychology, 10*(2), 257–274.

——(1991). Scarcity effects on value: A quantitative review of the commodity theory literature. *Psychology and Marketing, 8*(1), 43–57.

Lynn, M. & Grassman, A. (1990). Restaurant tipping: An examination of three "rational" explanations. *Journal of Economic Psychology, 11*, 169–181.

Lynn, M. & Latane, B. (1984). The psychology of restaurant tipping. *Journal of Applied Social Psychology, 14*, 551–563.

Lynn, M., Jabbour, P. & Kim, W. G. (2012). Who uses tips as a reward for servive and when? *Journal of Economic Psychology, 33*, 90–103.

Lyons, A. C., Scherpf, E. & Roberts, H. (2006). Financial education and communication between parents and children. *The Journal of Consumer Education, 23*, 64–76.

Madares, C. (1994). *The secret meaning of money.* San Francisco, CA: Jossey-Bass.

Malka, A. & Chatman, J. (2003). Intrinsic and extrinsic work orientations as moderators of the effect of annual income on subjective well-being. *Personality and Social Psychology Bulletin, 29*, 737–746.

Marshall, H. (1964). The relation of giving children an allowance to children's money knowledge and responsibility, and to other practices of parents. *Journal of Genetic Psychology, 104*, 35–51.

Marshall, H. & Magruder, L. (1960). Relations between parent money education practices and children's knowledge and use of money. *Child Development, 31*, 253–284.

Masus, D., Malroutu, Y., Hanashiro, R. & Kim, J. (2004). College students' money beliefs and behaviours. *Journal of Family and Economic Issues, 25*, 469–283.

Matthews, A. (1991). *If I think about money so much, why can't I figure it out.* New York, NY: Summit Books.

Mauldin, T., Mirmura, Y. & Uni, M. (2001). Parental expenditure on children's education. *Journal of Family and Economic Issues, 22*, 224–241.

Maurer, W. (2006). The anthropology of money. *Annual Review of Anthropology, 35*, 15–36.

Mayer, S. & Norton, P. (1981). Involving clinicians in fee collections: Implications for improving clinical practice and increasing fee income in a community mental health centre. *Community Mental Health Journals, 17*, 214–225.

McBride, M. (2010). Money, happiness and aspirations. *Journal of Economic Behaviour and Organisation*, *74*, 262–276.

McClure, R. (1984). The relationship between money attitudes and overall pathology. *Psychology*, *21*, 4–6.

McCurdy, H. (1956). Coin perception studies in the concept of schemata. *Psychological Review*, *63*, 160–168.

McLellan, D. (ed.) (1997) *Karl Marx: Selected Writings*. Oxford: Oxford University Press.

McLuhan, M. (1964). *Understanding media*. Cambridge, MA: MIT Press.

Medina, J., Saegert, J. & Gresham, A. (1996). Comparison of Mexican-American and Anglo-American attitudes towards money. *Journal of Consumer Affairs*, *30*, 124–145.

Medvedovski, D. (2006). *Fathers, families and economic issues*. St Paul, MN: Department of Business and Economics, Bethal University.

Meeks, C. (1998). Factors influencing adolescents' income and expenditures. *Journal of Family and Economic Issues*, *19*, 131–150.

Meier-Pesti, K. & Penz, E. (2008). Sex or gender? Expanding the sex-based view by introducing masculinity and femininity as predictors of financial risk-taking. *Journal of Economic Psychology*, *29*, 180–196.

Menninger, K. A. & Holzman, P. S. (1973). *Theory of psychoanalytic technique* (2nd ed.). New York, NY: Basic Books.

Micromegas, N. (1993). *Money*. Paris: Micromegas.

Middleton, J. & Langdon, K. (2008). *Sort out your money*. Oxford: Recession.

Mikulincer, M. & Shaver, P. R. (2008). "Can't buy me love": An attachment perspective on social support and money as psychological buffers. *Psychological Enquiry*, *19*, 167–173.

Miller, J. & Yung, S. (1990). The role of allowances in adolescent socialization. *Youth and Society*, *22*, 137–159.

Milner, R. & Furnham, A. (2013). *A study of beliefs about pocket money*. University College London, unpublished paper.

Miner, J. (1993). *Industrial–organizational psychology*. New York, NY: McGraw-Hill.

Mogilner, C. (2010). The pursuit of happiness: Time, money, and social connection. *Psychological Science*, *21*, 1348–1354.

Moore, R. (1965). The meaning of money: A psychiatric-psychological evaluation. *Pastoral Psychology*, *16*, 41–48.

Morgan, E. (1969). *A history of money*. Harmondsworth: Penguin.

Mortimer, J. & Shanahan, M. (1994). Adolescent experience and family relationships. *Work and Occupation*, *21*, 369–384.

Mortimer, J., Dennehy, K., Lee, C. & Finch, M. (1994). The prevalence, distribution and consequences of allowance arrangements. *Family Relations*, *43*, 23–29.

Moschis, G. P. (1985). The role of family communication in consumer socialisation of children and adolescents. *Journal of Consumer Research*, *11*, 898–913.

Myers, D. G. (1992). *The pursuit of happiness*. New York, NY: Morrow.

Myers, D. G. & Diener, E. (1996). The pursuit of happiness. *Scientific American*, May, 54–56.

Newcomb, M. D. & Rabow, J. (1999). Gender, socialisation, and money. *Journal of Applied Social Psychology*, *29*(4), 852–869.

Newson, J. & Newson, E. (1976). *Seven-year-olds in the home environment*. London: Allen & Unwin.

Ng, S. (1983). Children's ideas about the bank and shop profit. *Journal of Economic Psychology*, *4*, 209–221.

——(1985). Children's ideas about the bank: A New Zealand replication. *European Journal of Social Psychology*, *15*, 121–123.

Niemi, R., Mueller, J. & Smith, T. (1989). *Trends in public opinion: A compendium of survey data*. New York, NY: Greenwood Press.

Norvilitis, J. M., Merwin, M. M., Osberg, T. M., Roehling, P. V., Young, P. & Kamas, M. M. (2006). Personality factors, money attitudes, financial knowledge, and credit card debt in college students. *Journal of Applied Social Psychology*, *36*, 1395–1413.

Nunes, J. C. & Boatwright, P. (2004). Incidental prices and their effect on willingness to pay. *Journal of Marketing, 41*, 457–466.

Office for Fair Trading (2010). *Pricing Practices.* London: ONS.

Oishi, S., Kesebir, S. & Diener, E. (2011). Income inequality and happiness. *Psychological Science, 22*, 1095–1100.

O'Neill, J. (1999). *The Golden Ghetto: The psychology of affluence.* New York, NY: The Affluenza Project.

O'Neill, R. (1984). Anality and Type A coronary-prone behaviour patterns. *Journal of Personality Assessment, 48*, 627–628.

O'Neill, R., Greenberg, R. & Fisher, S. (1992). Humour and anality. *Humour: International Journal of Human Research, 5*, 283–291.

Oppenheimer, D. (2008). The secret life of fluency. *Trends in Cognitive Science, 12*, 237–241.

Ott, J. (2001). Did the market depress happiness in the US? *Journal of Happiness Studies, 2*, 433–443.

Otto, A., Schots, P., Westerman, J. & Webley, P. (2006). Children's use of saving strategies. *Journal of Economic Psychology, 27*, 57–72.

Ozgen, O. & Bayoglu, A. (2005). Turkish college students' attitudes towards money. *International Journal of Consumer Studies, 29*, 493–501.

Pahl, J. (1995). His money, her money: Recent research on financial organisation in marriage. *Journal of Economic Psychology, 16*, 361–376.

Papp, L., Cummings, E. & Goeke-Morey, M. (2009). For richer, for poorer. *Family Relations, 58*, 91–103.

Perry, J., Engbers, T. & Jun, S. (2009). Back to the future? Performance-related pay, empirical research, and the perils of persistence. *Theory to Practice, 69*, 39–51.

Pfeffer, J. & DeVoe, S. E. (2009). Economic evaluation: The effect of money and economics on attitudes about volunteering. *Journal of Economic Psychology, 30*, 500–508.

Piachaud, D. (1974). Attitudes to pensions. *Journal of Social Policy, 3*, 137–146.

Pine, K. J. & Fletcher, B. (2011). Women's spending behaviour is menstrual-cycle sensitive. *Personality and Individual Differences, 50*, 74–78.

Pinto, M., Parente, D. & Mansfield, P. (2005). Information learned from socialization agents. *Family and Consumer Sciences Research Journal, 33*, 357–367.

Pliner, P., Freedman, J., Abramovitch, R. & Darke, P. (1996). Children as consumers: In the laboratory and beyond. In P. Lunt & A. Furnham (Eds.), *Economic socialization* (pp. 35–46). Cheltenham: E. Elgar.

Pollio, H. & Gray, T. (1973). Change-making strategies in children and adults. *Journal of Psychology, 84*, 173–179.

Pope, K. S., Geller, J. D. & Wilkinson, L. (1975). Fee assessment and outpatient psychotherapy. *Journal of Consulting and Clinical Psychology, 43*, 835–841.

Poundstone, W. (2009). *Priceless: The myth of fair value (and how to take advantage of it).* New York, NY: Hill & Wang.

Pouwels, B., Siegers, J. & Vlasblom, S. (2008). Income, working hours and happiness. *Economic Letters, 99*, 72–74.

Powdthavee, N. (2010). How much does money really matter? *Empirical Economics, 39*, 77–92.

Prevey, E. (1945). A quantitative study of family practices in training children in the use of money. *Journal of Educational Psychology, 36*, 411–428.

Price, D. (2000). *Money magic.* Novato, CA: New World Library.

Prince, M. (1993). Self-concept, money beliefs, and values. *Journal of Economic Psychology, 14*, 161–173.

Promislo, M. D., Deckop, J. R., Giacalone, R. A. & Jurkiewicz, C. L. (2010). Valuing money more than people: The effects of materialism on work–family conflict. *Journal of Occupational and Organisational Psychology, 83*, 935–953.

Raghubir, P. (1998). Coupon value: A signal for price? *Journal of Marketing Research, 35*, 316–324.

———(2004). Free gift with purchase: Promoting or discounting the brand? *Journal of Consumer Psychology*, *14*, 181–185.

Rendon, M. & Kranz, R. (1992). *Straight talk about money*. New York, NY: Facts on file.

Richins, M. & Dawson, S. (1992). Materialism as a consumer value: Measure, development and validation. *Journal of Consumer Research*, *19*, 303–316.

Rijken, M. & Groenewegen, P. P. (2008). Money does not bring well-being, but it does help! The relationship between financial resources and life satisfaction of the chronically ill mediated by social deprivation and loneliness. *Journal of Community & Applied Social Psychology*, *18*, 39–53.

Rim, Y. (1982). *Personality and attitudes connected with money*. Paper given at Economic Psychology Conference, Edinburgh.

Rinaldi, E. & Bonanomi, A. (2011). Adolescents and money. *Italian Journal of Sociology of Education*, *3*, 86–120.

Rinaldi, E. & Giromini, E. (2002). The importance of money to Italian children. *Young Consumers*, *3*, 53–55.

Rinaldi, E. & Todesco, L. (2012). Financial literacy and money attitudes. *Italian Journal of Sociology of Education*, *2*, 143–165.

Rind, B. & Bordia, P. (1995). Effect of servers' "thank you" and personalization on restaurant tipping. *Journal of Applied Social Psychology*, *25*, 745–751.

Robertiello, R. (1994). Psychoanalysts and money. *Journal of Contemporary Psychotherapy*, *24*, 35–38.

Roberts, J. & Sepulveda, C. (1999). Money attitudes and compulsion buying. *Journal of International Consumer Marketing*, *11*, 53–79.

Robertson, A. & Cochrane, R. (1973). The Wilson–Patterson Conservatism scale. A reappraisal. *British Journal of Social and Clinical Psychology*, *12*, 428–430.

Rodgers, Y., Hawthorne, S. & Wheeler, R. (2006). *Teaching economics through children's literature in the primary grades* (Economic Working Papers Series). New Brunswick, NJ: Rutgers University.

Roland-Levy, C. (1990). Economic socialization: Basis for international comparisons. *Journal of Economic Psychology*, *11*, 469–482.

Rose, G. M. & Orr, L. M. (2007). Measuring and exploring symbolic money meanings. *Psychology and Marketing*, *24*(9), 743–761.

Rothstein, A. (1986). The seduction of money. *Psychoanalytic Quarterly*, *55*, 296–300.

Rubinstein, S. (1980). Your money or your life. *Psychology Today*, *12*, 47–58.

Ruspini, E. (2012). Girls, boys, money. *International Review of Sociology*, *22*, 514–529.

Sabri, M. F., Hayhoe, C. R. & Goh, A. (2006). Attitudes, values and belief toward money: Gender and working sector comparison. *Pertanika Journal of Social Sciences & Humanities*, *14*(2), 121–130.

Salemi, M. (2005). Teaching economic literacy. *International Review of Economics Education*, *4*, 46–57.

Sato, T. (2011). Minding money. *Integrative Psychology and Behaviour*, *45*, 116–131.

Saunders, S. & Lynn, M. (2010). Why tip? An empirical test of motivations for tipping car guards. *Journal of Economic Psychology*, *31*, 106–113.

Schneider, B., Hanges, P., Smith, D. & Salvaggio, A. (2003). Which comes first: Employee attitudes or organizational, financial and market performance? *Journal of Applied Psychology*, *88*, 836–851.

Schofield, W. (1971). Psychotherapy: The unknown versus the untold. *Journal of Consulting and Clinical Psychology*, *36*, 9–11.

Schor, B. (2004). *Born to buy*. New York, NY: Scribner.

Schor, J. (1991). *The overworked American*. New York, NY: Basic Books.

Scott, W. D., Clothier, R. C. & Spriegel, W. R. (1960). *Personnel Management*. New York, NY: McGraw-Hill.

Scragg, R., Laugesen, M. & Robinson, E. (2002). Cigarette smoking, pocket money and socioeconomic status. *Journal of the New Zealand Medical Association*, *115*, 1158.

Self, J. (2007). *The teenager's guide to money.* London: Quercus.

Seligman, M. (2008). Positive health. *Applied Psychology, 57,* 3–18.

Shampanier, K., Mazar, N. & Ariely, D. (2007). Zero as a special price: The true value of free products. *Marketing Science, 26,* 742–757.

Shapiro, M. (2007). Money: A therapeutic tool for couples therapy. *Family Process, 46,* 279–291.

Shefrin, H. (2007). *Beyond greed and fear.* Oxford: Oxford University Press.

Shim, S., Xio, J., Barber, B. & Lyons, A. (2009). Pathways to life success: A conceptual model of financial well-being for young adults. *Journal of Applied Developmental Psychology, 30,* 708–723.

Shipton, B. & Spain, A. (1981). Implication of payment of fees for psychotherapy. *Psychotherapy: Theory, Research and Practice, 18,* 68–73.

Siegler, R. & Thompson, D. (1998). "Hey, would you like a nice cold cup of lemonade on this hot day?": Children's understanding of economic causation. *Developmental Psychology, 34,* 146–160.

Sigurdsson, V., Foxall, G. & Saevarsson, H. (2010). In-store experimental approach to pricing and consumer behavior. *Journal of Organizational Behavior Management, 3,* 234–246.

Skandia. (2012). *Millionnaires monitor.* Old Mutual Compass.

Smelser, N. (1963). *The sociology of economic life.* Englewood Cliffs, NJ: Prentice Hall.

Smith, G. & Sweeney, E. (1984). *Children and television advertising.* London: Children's Research Unit.

Smith, H., Fuller, R. & Forrest, D. (1975). Coin value and perceived size. *Perceptual and Motor Skills, 41,* 227–232.

Smith, S. & Razell, P. (1975). *The pools winners.* London: Caliban Books.

Sohn, S.-H., Joo, S.-H., Grable, J., Lee, S. & Kim, M. (2012). Adolescents' financial literacy. *Journal of Adolescence, 35,* 969–980.

Solheim, C., Zuiker, V. & Levchenko, P. (2011). Financial socialization family pathways. *Family Science Review, 16,* 97–112.

Sonuga-Barke, E. & Webley, P. (1993). *Children's saving: A study in the development of economic behaviour.* Hove: Earlbaum.

Spectrem Group. (2011). *Affluent market insights 2011.*

——(2011). http://www.millionairecorner.com/article/sources-wealth

Stacey, B. & Singer, M. (1985). The perception of poverty and wealth among teenagers. *Journal of Adolescence, 8,* 231–241.

Steed, L. & Symes, M. (2009). The role of perceived wealth competence, wealth values, and internal wealth locus of control in predicting wealth creation behaviour. *Journal of Applied Social Psychology, 39,* 2525–2540.

Steers, R. M. & Rhodes, S. R. (1984). Knowledge and speculation about absenteeism. In P. S. Goodman, R. S. Atkin & Associates (Eds.), *Absenteeism* (pp. 229–275). San Francisco, CA: Jossey-Bass.

Strauss, A. (1952). The development and transformation of monetary meaning in the child. *American Psychological Review, 53,* 275–286.

Strohmetz, D., Rind, B., Fisher, R. & Lynn, M. (2002). Sweetening the till: The use of candy to increase restaurant tipping. *Journal of Applied Social Psychology, 32,* 300–309.

Sutton, R. (1962). Behaviour in the attainment of economic concepts. *Journal of Psychology, 53,* 37–46.

Tajfel, H. (1977). Value and the perceptual judgement of magnitude. *Psychological Review, 64,* 192–204.

Takahashi, K. & Hatano, G. (1989). *Conceptions of the bank: A developmental study* (JCSS Technical Report No. 11). Tokyo: Japanese Cognitive Science Society.

Tang, L.-P., Chen, Y.-J. & Sutarso, T. (2008). Bad apples in bad (business) barrels. *Management Decisions, 46,* 243–263.

Tang, T. (1992). The meaning of money revisited. *Journal of Organizational Behaviour, 13*, 197–202.

——(1993). The meaning of money: Extension and exploration of the Money Ethic Scale in a sample of university students in Taiwan. *Journal of Organizational Behaviour, 14*, 93–99.

——(1995). The development of a short money ethic scale: Attitudes toward money and pay satisfaction revisited. *Personality and Individual Differences. 19*, 809–816.

Tang, T. & Gilbert, P. (1995). Attitudes towards money as related to intrinsic and extrinsic job satisfaction, stress and work-related attitudes. *Personality and Individual Differences, 19*, 327–332.

Tang, T. & Kim, J. (1999). The meaning of money among mental health workers: The endorsement of money ethic as related to organisational citizenship behaviour, job satisfaction and commitment. *Public Personnel Management, 28*, 15–26.

Tang, T. & Liu, H. (2011). Love of money and un ethical behaviour intention. *Journal of Business Ethics, 107*, 295–312.

Tang, T., Furnham, A. & Davis, G. (1997). *A cross-cultural comparison of the money ethic, the protestant work ethic and job satisfaction.* University College London, unpublished paper.

Tang, T., Tang, T. & Homaifar, B. (2006). Income, the love of money, pay comparison, and pay satisfaction. *Journal of Managerial Psychology, 21*, 476–491.

Tatarko, A. & Schmidt, P. (2012). *Social capital and attitudes to money.* Higher School of Economics Research Paper WP/BRP/07/SOC/2012.

Tatzel, M. (2002). "Money worlds" and well-being: An integration of money dispositions, materialism and price-related behavior. *Journal of Economic Psychology, 23*, 103–126.

——(2003). The art of buying: Coming to terms with money and materialism. *Journal of Happiness Studies, 4*, 405–435.

Teplitsky, I. J. (2004). *Psychology of money.* Oakland, CA: Julius Books.

Thompson, D. & Siegler, R. (2000). Buy low, sell high: The development of an informal theory of economics. *Child Development, 71*, 660–677.

Thozhur, S. M., Riley, M. & Szivas, E. (2006). Money attitudes and pay satisfaction of the low paid. *Journal of Managerial Psychology, 21*, 163–172.

Thurnwald, A. (1932). *Money.* London: Methuen.

Twist, L. (2003). *The soul of money.* London: W. W. Norton.

Van Beek, I., Hu, Q., Schaufeli, W., Taris, T. & Schreurs, B. (2012). For fun, love or money. *Applied Psychology, 61*, 30–35.

Van Vuuren, M., de Jong, M. & Seydel, E. (2008). Commitment with or without a stick of paid work: Comparison of paid and unpaid workers in a nonprofit organisation. *European Journal of Work and Organisational Psychology, 17*, 315–326.

Veblen, T. (1899). *The theory of the leisure class.* New York, NY: Viking.

Verplanken, B. & Herabadi, A. (2001). Individual differences in impulse buying tendency: Feeling and no thinking. *European Journal of Personality, 15*, S71–S83.

Vogler, C., Lyonette, C. & Wiggins, R. D. (2008). Money, power and spending decisions in intimate relationships. *The Sociological Review, 56*, 117–143.

Vohs, K. D., Mead, N. L. & Goode, M. R. (2006). The psychological consequences of money. *Science, 314*, 1154–1156.

——(2008). Merely activating the concept of money changes personal and interpersonal behavior. *Current Directions in Psychological Science, 17*, 208–212.

Von Stumm, S., Fenton-O'Creevy, M. & Furnham, A. (2013). Financial capability, money attitudes and socioeconomic status. *Personality and Individual Differences, 54*, 344–349.

Walker, R. & Garman, E. (1992). The meanings of money: Perspectives from human ecology. *American Behavioural Scientist, 35*, 781–785.

Wang, A. (2009). Interplay of investors financial knowledge and risk-taking. *Journal of Behavioural Finance, 10*, 204–213.

Ward, S., Wackman, D. & Wartella, E. (1977). *How children learn to buy.* London: Sage.

Ware, J. (2001). *The psychology of money.* Chichester: Wiley.

Warner, S. (1989). Sigmund Freud and money. *Journal of the American Academy of Psychoanalysis and Dynamic Psychiatry*, *17*, 609–622.

Webley, P. (1983). *Growing up in the modern economy*. Paper presented at the 6th International Conference on Political Psychology.

Webley, P. & Nyhus, E. (2006). Parents' influence on children's future orientation and saving. *Journal of Economic Psychology*, *27*, 140–164.

Webley, P., Levine, M. & Lewis, A. (1991). A study in economic psychology: Children's saving in a play economy. *Human Relations*, *44*, 127–146.

Webley, P., Burgoyne, C., Lea, S. & Young, B. (2001). *The economic psychology of everyday life*. London: Psychologist Press.

Wernimont, P. & Fitzpatrick, S. (1972). The meaning of money. *Journal of Applied Psychology*, *56*, 248–261.

Wilder, B. (1999). *Money is love: Reconnecting to the sacred origins of money*. Santa Fe, CA: Wild Ox Press.

Wilhelm, M., Varese, K. & Friedrich, A. (1993). Financial satisfaction and assessment of financial progress. *Financial Counselling and Planning*, *4*, 181–199.

Williams, M. L., McDaniel, M. A. & Ford, L. R. (2006). Understanding multiple dimensions of compensation satisfaction. *Journal of Business and Psychology*, *21*, 429–459.

Wilska, T.-A. (2005). Gender differences in the consumption of children and young people in Finland. In T.-A. Wilska & L. Haanpaa (Eds.), *Lifestyle and social change* (pp 159–176). Turku: Turku University.

Wilson, E. O. (1975). *Sociobiology: The new synthesis*. Cambridge, MA: Harvard University Press.

Wilson, G. & Patterson, J. (1968). A new measure of conservatism. *British Journal of Social and Clinical Psychology*, *7*, 164–168.

Wiseman, T. (1974). *The money motive*. London: Hodder & Stoughton.

Witryol, S. & Wentworth, N. (1983). A paired comparisons scale of children's preference for monetary and material rewards used in investigations of incentive effects. *Journal of Genetic Psychology*, *142*, 17–23.

Wolfenstein, E. V. (1993). Mr Moneybags meets the Rat Man: Marx and Freud on the meaning of money. *Political Psychology*, *14*, 279–308.

Wood, M. (2005). Discretionary unplanned buying in consumer society. *Journal of Consumer Behaviour*, *4*, 268–281.

Wosinski, M. & Pietras, M. (1990). Economic socialization of Polish children in different macro-economic conditions. *Journal of Economic Psychology*, *11*, 515–529.

Wyatt, E. & Hinden, S. (1991). *The money book*. New York, NY: Somerville House.

Xia, L. & Monroe, K. B. (2004). Price partitioning on the internet. *Journal of Interactive Marketing*, *18*, 63–73.

Yamanchi, K. & Templer, D. (1982). The development of a money attitude scale. *Journal of Personality Assessment*, *46*, 522–528.

Yang, Q., Wu, X., Zhou, X., Mead, N., Vohs, K. & Baumeister, R. (2012). Diverging effects of clean versus dirty money on attitudes, values and interpersonal behaviours. *Journal of Personality and Social Psychology*, *104*, 473–489.

Yodanis, C. & Lauer, S. (2007). Managing money in marriage. *Journal of Marriage and Family*, *69*, 1307–1325.

Yoken, C. & Berman, J. S. (1984). Does paying a fee alter the effectiveness of treatment? *Journal of Consulting and Clinical Psychology*, *52*, 254–260.

Yong, J. & Li, N. (2012). Cash in hand, want better looking mate. *Personality and Individual differences*, *53*, 55–58.

Zelizer, V. (1989). The social meaning of money: "Special monies." *American Journal of Sociology*, *95*, 342–377.

Zhang, X., Tian, P. & Grigoriou, N. (2011). Gain face, but lose happiness? It depends on how much money you have. *Asian Journal of Social Psychology*, *14*, 112–125.

Zhou, X. & Gao, D.-G. (2008). Social support and money as pain management mechanisms. *Psychological Inquiry, 19,* 127–144.

Zhou, X., Vohs, K. & Baumeister, R. (2009). The symbolic power of money. *Psychological Science, 20,* 700–706.

Zuo, J. (1997). The effect of men's breadwinner status on their changing gender beliefs. *Sex Roles, 37,* 799–816.

Zuzanek, J. (2013). Does being well-off make us happier? *Journal of Happiness Studies, 14,* 795–815.

Zweig, J. (2009). *Your money and your brain.* New York, NY: Simon & Schuster.

INDEX

[Note: page numbers in **bold** refer to tables; page numbers in *italics* refer to figures.]

Aarts, H. 77
Abramovitch, R. 119, 147–9
abundance zone 207
accelerating incentives 229
achievement 95
acquisition centrality 108
Adams, Scott 33
addiction 38
advice for parents 153–8
affirmation 206, 208
affluenza 62–4, 163–4
Affluenza 62–3
age and subjective wellbeing 70
agency theory 216
aggregation 4
Aguinis, H. 229
Ahmetoglu, G. 270, 275
Al-Fayed, Mohamed 26–7
alchemy 2, 82
alcoholism 189
Alexander, Scott 21
alienation 92
all money is equal 248
allowances 143–51; studies on 147–51
Alter, A. 244–5
altruism 50, 142–6
Amazon 17
American Express 16
anchoring 30, 243–4, 250, 271–2
Anderson, C. 143
Angeles, L. 67

anhedonia 192
anxiety 46, 57, 86, 88–9, 92, 95, 178, 196
Apple 264–6
approaches to topic of money 33–54;
    economic anthropology and primitive
    money 42–4; economics of money
    39–42; introduction 33–9; money in
    literature 51–2; other approaches 52–4;
    religion and money 47–51; sociology of
    money 44–7
Arora, R. 70
Ascent of Money 5
assertiveness training 202
attachment 74, 76
attitudes towards money 1–14, 81–114,
    99–100; history of money 5–12;
    introduction 1–5; *see also* behaviours
    towards money
attribution therapy 206
authority 262, 265
autonomy 73, 195–6
availability 244
avoidance of tax 3, 6, 23, 130

bait pricing 274
Baker, P. 92
Baker, W. 44
balanced mutual funds 159
Ball, R. 66
Bank of England 12
bank money 41

banking 123–5, 175
bankruptcy 24, 64, 101, 142
banks 11–12
Barclays Wealth 19
bargain hunters 194, 200
Barnet-Verzat, C. 142–3
bartering 6, 40
Barth, F. 204
basic economic utility model 66–7
Batt, Al 33
Bauer, H. H. 275
Baumeister, R. 78
Beccheti, L. 68, 77
behavioural economics 237–58;
    behavioural finance 253–4; cognitive
    miser 258; heuristics 242–8; introduction
    237–8; neuro-economics 254–8;
    practical advice 248–51; priming power
    of money 251–3; prospect theory
    239–41
behavioural finance 253–4
behaviours towards money 81–114;
    financial risk taking 110–113;
    introduction 81–2; materialism 106–110;
    measuring economic beliefs 103–5;
    money ethics 82–5; money locus of
    control 85; structure of money attitudes
    85–103; thinking about money 113–14;
    unconscious/conscious finance 105–6
behaviourist approaches to money 54
beliefs about money 81–114
Belk, R. W. 49–50
Belsky, G. 248–51
beneficial therapeutic outcome 204–6; see
    also positions on therapy payment
Benson, A. 189–91
Berg, L. 140
Berggruen, Nicholas 22
Berkowitz, L. 218
Berman, J. S. 205
Berti, A. 119–21, 124–5
Beutler, I. 175
"bi-metallism" 9
Biel, A. 252
big money mistakes 248–51
big spenders 105
Biggins, John 16
bigness bias 249
Bijleveld, E. 77
Billings, Josh 1
binge eating 189
biological psychology of money 37–9; drug
    theory 37–8; tool theory 37–8
Bird's Eye Walls 144

Biswas-Diener, R. 65, 69
black or white thinking 201
boasting 184
Bodnar, J. 155–7
Boehm, J. K. 70
Boer, D. 73
BOGOF see buy one get one free
Bombi, A. 119–20, 125
Bonini, N. 252
Bonner, S. 215
boom to bust 3
Bordia, P. 269
Borneman, E. 186, 188
borrowing 154, 170, 248
Bottomley, P. A. 107, 109
Boucher, H. 252
bouncing cheques 12
Boyce, C. J. 67
brand awareness 107
bribery 161
bride payments 43–4
Brief, A. 253
Brin, Sergey 25–6
Bristol Pound 18
Britt, S. 168
Brixton Pound 18
Brown, G. 67
Brown, R. 218–19
Bruce, V. 29
Bruner, J. 27–8
Brusdal, R. 140
Bucklin, B. 229
budgeting 83, 85, 95, 154, 160, 175
buffer against pain 74–6
Buffett, Warren 24–5, 239–40
bundling 274–5
Burgess, S. M. 101
Burgoyne, C. 116
business decision frame 253
buy one get one free 270, 273–4
buying happiness 55–7
buying locally 18–19
buying love 195
buying and selling 119–21
B£ see Brixton Pound

Campbell, A. 56
Carlin, George 237
Carroll, S. M. 101, 107
cash 9–10, 41; coins 9–10; paper 10;
    plastic/virtual money 10
Casserly, J. 208
Castano, E. 30, 113
catastrophisation 191

causal effects of money 70
CBT *see* cognitive behaviour therapy
Cerreto, Salvatore 21
Chaiken, S. 274
Chan, K. 135
Chan, M. 70
change-making strategies 118–19
changing forms of money 31
"Charge-It" programme 16
charitable donations 50–51, 155, 266–7
Chatman, J. 66
Chaucer, Geoffrey 51
Chechov, Anton 183
Chen, E. 101
Chen, H. 159
Chen, Y.-J. 84
Chernova, K. 66
childhood-related money problems 160–62
children and development of economic
    ideas 116–18
chocolate balls 122
Chown, J. 9
Christopher, A. N. 101, 107
chronic congestion 64
Cialdini, R. B. 260
Clark Graham, Robert 21
Clarke-Carter, D. 29
clean money 78; *see also* dirty money
Cleare, A. 120
clipping 9
co-dependency 105
co-partnerships 223
coaching 175
Cochran, S. 218
cognitive behaviour therapy 191–2, 201
cognitive dissonance therapy 204–5
cognitive maturation 127
cognitive misers 258
cognitive triggers 190
coins 9–10, 27–30, 38; experimental studies
    of 27–30; perception of 38
Colella, A. 232
Coleman, J. W. 53
Collier, C. 172–3
commercial communications 133–5
commitment 260–61
commodity money 41
compensation 219–21
compromise effects 247–8
compulsive buying 101, 107, 189–91
compulsive savers 193
confidence 256
confirmation bias 250
confiscation of money 148

conflict reduction 232–3
conformity 199–200
conscious finance 105–6
conservatism 38, 92, 94, 103–4
consistency 260–61
Consumer Involvement Scale 107
consumer orientation 107
consumer's dilemma 108
Converse, P. E. 56
convertible paper 10
Corey, Irwin 165
costs and benefits of pay secrecy 232–3
Coulbourn, W. 40
counter-transference 202
counterfeiting 9
couples and money 166–8
cowries 6–7, 43
Cram, F. 125
credit 41
credit cards 16–17
crimes of passion 53
criminology of money 52–3
cultural sociology of money 44–5
Cummings, S. 116
currency 41
Custers, R. 77

Danes, S. M. 171, 175
dark side of happiness 61–2; time/place for
    happiness 62; ways to pursue happiness
    62; wrong degree of happiness 61;
    wrong types of happiness 62
Darke, P. 148–9, 274
Davies, P. 120
Davis, A. 204
Davis, G. 84
Davis, K. 154
Dawson, S. 108
de Beni, R. 120
De Bens, E. 134–5
de-stressing 201
debasing currency 9
decelerating incentives 229
Deci, E. L. 213–14
Deckop, J. R. 106, 110
default 247
deferring to experts 262
defining money 1–5; overlooked topic
    3–5
degrees of happiness 61
demagnetisation 191
demand–change questions 122–3
depression 57, 59, 61, 192
desacralisation 50

determining fair pay 222
detrimental therapeutic outcome 205; *see also* positions on therapy payment
Deutsch, F. 167–8
development of economic ideas in children 116–18
development of economic thinking 118–37; banking 123–5; commercial communications 133–5; life assurance 136–7; market forces 121–3; money 118–19; other issues 137; pensions 135–6; possession and ownership 125; poverty and wealth 131; prices and profit 119–21; saving 131–3; taxation 125–30
development of symbolism 34
DeVoe, S. E. 77, 252
DeVor, M. 207
Di Muro, F. 30, 113
Dickens, Charles 51
Dickinson, A. 229
Dickinson, J. 117
Dickson, L. 175
Diener, E. 56–8, 65, 69–70, 73–5
Diez-Martinez, E. 137
digesting 188
diligence 47
Dimen, M. 203–4
dirty money 30, 47, 78, 113, 187
disconnect 110
discovering money 2
disempowerment 181
dissatisfaction 107
distrust 88–9, 92–3, 232
Dittmar, H. 107, 178
Dodd, N. 45
Dodds, A. 29
domestic money usage 47
dopamine 76
Dormanen, Craig 33
double coincidence of wants 6
Douglas, M. 43
Dow Jones Industrial Average 25
Dowling, N. 101
dreams 205–7
drip pricing 271–2
Drotner, K. 178
drug theory 37–9
Drury, J. 178
Dulebohn, J. 220
dummies for money 97, 112
durability: of money 41
Durband, D. 168
Durkheim, Émile 44
Dworkin, Andrea 165

Ealy, D. 178–81
early learned experience 185
Easterlin paradox 64–9; economic utility model 66–7; is happiness a good thing 69; reanalysis of data 68–9
Easterlin, R. A. 64–6
EASY brand 245
Economic Belief Scale 104–5, **104**
economic beliefs 103–5
economic socialisation 116–17, 139–64, 169–70, 175; advice for parents 153–8; allowances and family rules 143–6; childhood-related money problems 160–62; introduction 139–40; parental involvement and motivation 140–43; poor little rich kids 162–4; quizzing your children 151–3; studies on pocket money/allowances 147–51; teaching economic theory 158–60
economic theory 158–60
economic thinking, development of 118–37
economic world, understanding 115–38
economics anthropology 42–4
economics of money 39–42
Economidou, M. 136
economising 36
"economy of gratitude" 167
educating about money 139–40
effort and task performance 215–16
ego massage 268
"ego traps" 250
electronic money 27, 41
electrum 7–8
elevation 59
embezzlement 183
Emler, N. 117
emotional intelligence 101
emotional spending 180
emotional triggers 190
emotional under-pinning of money pathology 192–201; freedom 195–201; love 195; power 194–5; security 193–4
emotions 265
empire builders 194
empowerment 181
endowment effect 243, 249
Engbers, T. 224
Engelberg, E. 101
environmental degradation 67
envy 89
equitable payment 217
equity theory 216–19
eroticism 186

ethics of money 82–5, 186
etiquette 184
evaluation 95
Evangelista, Linda 81
evolution 111
executive pay 229–31
expectancy theory 216
expelling faeces 188
experimental studies of coins 27–30
exploiting laziness 279
exterior finance 105
external locus of control 85
extreme consumerism 133–4
extrinsic motivation 212–15

face-consciousness 73
factors influencing relation between wealth
    and happiness 70–75; amount of money
    74–5
factors in risk tolerance 110–111
failure of PFP systems 226
fair day's wage 216–19
fairness of pay 232
fake consciousness 206
falling into the "ego trap" 250
familiarity 244–5
family accounting 172
family disorders 160–61, 197–8
family and money 165–82; see also sex
    differences
famous people with odd money habits
    22–7; investors 24–6; misers 22–3;
    spendthrifts 23–4; tycoons 26–7
fanatical collectors 194
fast thinking 242, 258; see also heuristics
fate 89
fear 49, 105, 256–7
Feather, N. 148
Fedorikhin, A. 273
fees in psychotherapy 202–6; positions on
    204–6
fending off fights 157
Fenichel, O. 186
Fenton-O'Creevy, M. 101, 184
Ferenczi, S. 186
Ferguson, N. 5
Ferguson, Y. L. 107, 109
fetishism of commodities 4–5
Feuerstein, C. 205–6
fiat money 41
financial literacy 149, 158–60, 173–4
financial moves of others 250–51
financial parenting 173
financial risk taking 110–113

financial security 112
fining 148
Finn, D. 39–40
Fischer, R. 73
Fisher, S. 186
Fitzpatrick, S. 85
Fletcher, B. 178
Flouri, E. 106, 109, 141
fluency 244–5, 265
Folkes, V. 273
folklore about money 2, 187, 206–7
following suit 261–2, 264
Fontenot, G. 88, 177
football cards 121–2
Forbes list 75
Forman, N. 199–201
Forrester Research 18
Foubert, B. 274–5
Fox, K. 105–6
France, Anatole 259
frankness 112
Fraser, C. 218
Freedman, J. 119, 147–9, 274
freedom 195–6
freedom fighters 196
Freud, S. 3, 53, 186, 192, 195, 202–3, 205–6
Frey, D. 30, 74–5, 113
Friedman, M. 126
Friedrich, A. 94
Frijters, P. 69
frugality 92–3
functional use of money 42
fungibility 30, 44, 113, 248
Furnham, A. 28–30, 84–5, 89–93, 101–4,
    120, 127, 131–2, 135–7, 143–4, 148–9,
    177–8, 184, 270, 275
Furth, H. 120

Galbraith, J. K. 5
Gallo, E. 156
Gallo, J. 156
gambling 34, 97, 101, 112, 189, 192, 200
Gandelman, N. 69
Ganin, M. 118
Gao, D.-G. 74, 76
Gardner, D. 220
Gardner, J. 69
Garling, T. 252
Gates, Bill 25
Geller, J. D. 205
gender **88**, 165–82; see also sex differences
Getty, John Paul 237
"ghost money" 9
Giacalone, R. A. 106, 110

gifts 38, 42, 47–9, 143, 155
Gijsbrecht, E. 274–5
Gilbert, E. 6
Gilbert, P. 84
Gilmore, D. 29
Gilovich, T. 248–51
goal-setting theory 216
godfathers 194
Godfrey, N. 154–5
Goh, A. 177
Goldberg, H. 192–5, 201
Goldstein, H. 19
Goletto-Tankel, M. 135–7
good money 41–2
good parenting 139–64; *see also* economic
  socialisation
"good Samaritans" 51
good tax vs. bad tax 129
Goode, M. R. 252
Goodman, C. 27–8
Google Earth 26
"Google Guys" 25–6
Gottfredson, R. 229
Gottfurcht, James 285
government use of tax monies 128
Graef, Akilin 21
Graham, C. 68
Grassman, A. 268
Gray, T. 118–19
Great Depression 5
greed 2, 184, 193, 202, 255
Green, Russell 81
Greenberg, R. 186
Greitemeyer, T. 30, 113
Gresham, A. 88–9, 98, 177
Grigoriou, N. 73
Grivet, A. 121
Groenewegen, P. P. 73
group piece work 222
growing money 2
Gruber, J. 61–2, 69
Guégen, N. 261
guilt 105, 113, 171, 180, 192–3, 202–3
Gunther IV 21

Haberman, H. R. 171
habituation 66–7
Hacker, J. 74
Hagedorn, R. 92
Haisken-DeNew, J. P. 69
Halachmi, B. 121
Halifax Pocket Money Survey 145
Hanashiro, R. 178
Hanges, P. 221

Hanley, A. 92
Hansen, J. 78
happiness and money 55–80, 257–8;
  affluenza 62–4; buying to increase
  happiness 76–8; dark side of happiness
  61–2; Easterlin paradox 64–9; impacts on
  75; introduction 55–7; life evaluations
  70; money and pain 75–6; other
  variables 70–75; success 70; variations in
  happiness 78–9; wellbeing 57–61
Harrah, J. 126
Harter, J. 70
Hatano, G. 124
hatred 185
Hausner, L. 162
Hayhoe, C. 101, 177
Haynes, J. 202
Headey, B. W. 69
hedonism 77
heirlooms 49
Helliwell, J. F. 74
Hendersen, Harold 15
Herrmann, A. 275
Herron, W. G. 202, 204
heuristics 239, 241–51, 264–6; anchoring
  243–4; availability 245; compromise
  effects 247–8; default 247; endowment
  243; familiarity 245–6; fluency 244–5;
  loss aversion 242–3; peak-end rule 246;
  problems with 248–51; recognition 246;
  simulation heuristic 246; sunk cost
  246–7
Heyes, A. 29
high street banking 12
higher order needs 73
Hill, Benny 22
Hinden, S. 154
Hira, T. 171
hire purchase 11
history of money 5–12; banks 11–12; cash
  9–10; precious metal 7–9
Hitchcock, J. 28
HNS *see* National Health Service
Holzman, P. S. 204
Homo economicus 40, 269–70
homogeneity of money 41
horizontal influence 262
House, J. 252
how money is used 35
Howarth, C. 29
Howarth, E. 187
Howell, James 259
Hughes, Howard 23
Huston, S. 168

iconography of national currency 6
ignoring money 3–5
illusion of money 38, 249
imagination 265
imagining fictitious experiences 246
immorality of stock market 112
impulse disorders 189
impulsive spending 178–80
"in specie" valuation of coinage 9
inaction 249
incentive plans see performance-related pay
incentive power of money 37
inconvertible paper 10
increasing charitable donations 266–7,
  266–7
individualism and subjective wellbeing 73
inertia of money 2
inflation 30, 112–13, 249
influence of menstrual cycle 178
information through grapevine 250–51
ingesting 188
Ingram, Kay 165
inheritance tax 130
inherited beliefs 208
inherited wealth 162, 172–3
Inland Revenue 23
insecurity 101
Interbank lending system 12
interest in financial matters 112
interest in use of money 259
intergenerational transfer of money altruism
  142–6
intergroup rivalry 185
interior finance 105
internal locus of control 85
interpersonal triggers 190
interval/ratio measurement of money 34
intimacy avoidance 180
intrinsic motivation 212–15
intrinsic reward 211–12
intuition 255
investors 24–6; "Google Guys" 25–6;
  Warren Buffett 24–5
Iondono-Bedoya, D. 77
iPod 264
irrationality of financial activities 3–4,
  183–6
Izak, G. 30, 112–13

Jackson, K. 51
Jackson, Michael 23–4
Jacob, C. 261
Jahoda, G. 120, 123
James, Oliver 62–4

Jimerson, J. 44
job satisfaction 219–21
Johnson, M. D. 275
Jonas, E. 30, 113
Joo, H. 229
Journal of Happiness Studies 59
Journal of Positive Psychology 59
Judge, T. 220
Jun, S. 224
Jurkiewicz, C. L. 106, 110

Kahler, R. 105–6
Kahneman, Daniel 239, 241, 246, 258
Kamins, M. 273
Kardos, P. 30, 113
Karlsson, N. 252
Kasser, T. 107, 109
Katona, G. 36
Kaufman, W. 188
Kaun, D. 73
"keeping up with the Joneses" 189
Keller, C. 96, 112
Kesebir, P. 57–8, 74
Keynes, John Maynard 237
Kids and Cash 154
Kim, J. 84, 178
King, L. 56–7
Kirchler, E. 126
Kirkaldy, B. 149
Kiyosaki, R. 173–4
kleptomania 82, 106, 195
Kline, P. 187
Kofos, M. 252
Kohn, A. 214–15
Kouchaki, M. 253
Krantz, R. 154
Kutzner, F. 78

lack of impact on therapeutic outcome
  205–6; see also positions on therapy
  payment
Langdon, K. 207
Langs, R. 204
Lassarres, D. 149
Latane, B. 268–9
Lawler, E. 227
Lea, S. 4, 29–30, 33–4, 36–9, 116
Leahy, R. 131
learning about money 138
Lebowitz, Fran 139
legal tender 41, 45
Leiser, D. 30, 112–13, 118, 121, 125–6
Lesh, K. 178–81
Levchenko, P. 141, 175, 177

levels of money at work 234–5
levels of taxation payable 128
Levy, D. 125
Lewis, A. 145–6, 169
Lewis, R. 192–5, 201
Li, N. 77–8
Lichtenstein, D. R. 272
life assurance 136–7
life evaluation 70
lifestyle 139–43
liking 125, 263, 265, 269
Lilly, Doris 165
Lim, V. 95, 177
limitations of money 41
Lindgren, H. 3
linear incentives 229
liquid money 9, 11
Lis, A. 125
literary references to money 51–2
Lloyd Wright, Frank 55
Lobil, C. 171
local currencies 10, 18–19
locus of control of money 85
loss aversion 242–3, 248–9
loss of control 192
losses vs. gains 248–9
lottery money 30, 69, 82, 113, 212,
    249
love 195–6
loyalty 233
loyalty cards 18
Luna-Arocas, R. 85
Lundholm, P. 120
Lunt, P. 116
luxury fever 63
Lyck, L. 126
Lynn, M. 93, 268–70, 275
Lyonette, C. 166–7
Lyubomirsky, S. 70

McClure, R. 89
Machiavellianism 84, 88
McNeal, I. 135
McVey, L. A. 66
Madares, C. 171–2
madness and money 183–210; *see also*
    mental health
magic of money 118–19
Magruder, L. 147
making money 2
Malka, A. 66
malleable desire for material goods 73–5
Malroutu, Y. L. 178
Mandela, Nelson 137

manipulators 194
Mansfield, P. 174
Marcos, Imelda 81
Marek, P. 101, 107
marital break-up 79, 166
market forces 121–3
Marshall, H. 147
Martocchio, J. 220
Marx, Karl 4, 44, 53, 206
MAS *see* Money Attitude Scale
Mason, L. 29
MasterCard 16
Masuo, D. 178
materialism 47, 106–110, 208–9
Materialism Values Scale 106–7
mating preferences 77–8
Matthews, A. 160–61, 175, 197–9
Maurer, W. 42
Mauss, I. 61–2, 69
Mayer, S. 205
Mayhew, P. 29
Mead, N. 78, 252
measured day work 222
measuring economic beliefs 103–5
measuring worth 6
media of exchange 6, **7**, 43
Medina, J. 89, 98
meditation 207
Meeska, C. 167–8
Menninger, K. A. 204
mental accounting 248
mental health 183–210; compulsive buying
    189–91; emotional under-pinning of
    money pathology 192–201; introduction
    183–6; paying for psychotherapy 202–6;
    psychoanalysis of money 186–8; self-help
    books 206–9; treating pathology 201–2
Merchant of Venice 11
merit ratings 223
MES *see* Money Ethic Scale
messages about money 175–7
Microsoft 26
"Midas" scale 86, 206
Middleton, J. 207
Mikulincer, M. 75–6
Milken, Michael 15
Miller, J. 148
Milligan, Spike 55
millionaires 19–22; eccentric behaviour
    21–2
mindful shopping 191
Miner, J. 227
Minogue, Kenneth 259
Miramontes, S. 137

misers 22–3, 187, 200; Benny Hill 22; Howard Hughes 23; Lester Piggott 22–3
modelling 141–2, 156, 159–60, 175
modern family economic activities 169–72
Mogilner, C. 77
Monaci, M. 124
monetary groupings 41
monetary incentives 215–16
monetisation 46–7
Money Attitude Scale 87–8, 92, 101, **102**
money avoidance 97–8
"money biography" 207–8
"Money in the Contemporary Family" 169
money disorders 175–7, 188
Money Ethic Scale 82–4, **83**
"money game" 2
"money grams" 161, 175–7, **176**
Money is Love 207
Money Magic 207
money problems, childhood-related 160–62
money scripts 97–8, 105
"money shadow" 208
money smartness 143, 152, 154, 159–60
money status 38, 95, 97–8
MoneySense 145
monthly productivity bonus 222–3
mood swings 178
Moore, R. 206
Moore, S. 67
motivation of parents 140–43
Mountainview Learning 197–9, 264–7
Muffels, R. 69
multiplying money 2
Munroe, R. 28
Myers, D. G. 56, 70

Nairn, A. 107, 109
Naish, Peter 251–2
Naito, Fern 183
Napa, C. 56–7
National Health Service 204
National Opinion Research Centre 56, 70
natural human faculties 44
near money 10
negative reinforcement 187
negligence 3–4
Nestlé 169
net worth 159, 168
neuro-economics 254–8; confidence 256; fear 256–7; greed 255; happiness 257–8; prediction 255–6; regret 257; risk 256; surprise 257
neuroscience 254

neurosis 199–202
Nevitte, N. 142–3
new money 18
Newcomb, M. D. 170
Newson, E. 148
Newson, J. 148
Ng, S. 123–5
Ng, W. 65, 70
Nicholson, Viv 24
Nobel Prize 239
nominal measurement of money 34
non-generosity 95
non-spenders 105
Norton, P. 205
Noseworthy, T. 30, 113
"not enough theory" 179
novelty 76
Nyhus, E. 119, 140, 142

obsession 92, 94–5, 112
obsessive–compulsive disorder 23, 186
odd money habits of famous people 22–7
Office of Fair Trading 270
Oishi, S. 73–5
Okamura, R. 178
O'Neill, J. 162–4
O'Neill, R. 186–7
oniomania 189
online banking 17–18
open books 97, 112
Oppenheimer, D. 244–5
optimality 47
ordinal measurement of money 34
Ormrod, J. 107, 109
Orr, L. M. 95
Oswald, A. 69
other issues for children to understand 137
Otto, A. 133
overconfidence 250, 256
overdrafts 41
overestimation effect 28
overpayment inequity 217
overseas taxation 128
overshopping 189–91
ownership 125

pack thinking 199–200
Paetzold, R. 232
Page, Larry 25–6
pain and money 74–6, 105–6
paper money 10
parental involvement 140–43
parental socialisation 174–5
Parente, D. 174

Parker, Suzy 1
parsimony 186, 239
partitioned pricing 271–2
pathology of money 177–81, 192–202;
    emotional under-pinning 192–201;
    treating 201–2
Patterson, J. 103
Pay by Text 18
Pay Per Click 25
pay for performance *see* performance-
    related pay
pay satisfaction 94, 219–21
paying for psychotherapy *see* fees in
    psychotherapy
PE subjects *see* Protestant ethics
peak-end rule 246
peer power 262
Pendrill, Graham 21
pensions 135–6
percentages of tax payable 130
perception of coins 38
perennial child syndrome 163
performance-related pay 223–9, *224*;
    failure of systems 226
Perry, J. 224
personality variables 85–6
persuasion and pricing 259–80; conclusion
    279; introduction 259; pricing practices
    in shops 270–79; six principles 260–67;
    tipping 267–70
persuasion principles in practice 264–7;
    Apple sales technique 264–6; increasing
    charitable donations 266–7
Pfeffer, J. 77
PFP *see* performance-related pay
philosophy of money 53
physical health and subjective wellbeing 73
physical triggers 190
Piachaud, D. 135–6
Piaget, Jean 116–17
Piccolo, R. 220
piece work 222
Pierce, J. 220
Pierson, P. 74
Pietras, M. 126, 131
Piggott, Lester 22–3
Pine, K. J. 178
Pinto, M. 174
Pizza Hut 17
plastic money 10, 27, 31, 41
playground economy 140
Pliner, P. 119, 147–9
pocket money 143–51; studies on 147–51
Podsakoff, N. 220

"political" behaviour 233
Pollio, H. 118–19
Polyani, Karl 42
poor calibration 111
poor fathers 173–4
"poor little rich kids" 162–4
Pope, K. S. 205
pornography 37
portability of money 41
Porzecanski, R. 69
positions on therapy payment 204–6;
    beneficial therapeutic outcomes 204;
    detrimental therapeutic outcomes 205;
    no impact on therapeutic outcome
    205–6
positive psychology 58–61
Positive Psychology Centre 58
positive thinking 206
possession 49, 125
possession-defined success 108
post-materialism 108, 142
Pouwels, B. 73
poverty 5, 47, 131
power 2, 95, 194–6
power–prestige 88–9, 92–3, 101
PPC *see* Pay Per Click
Praher, D. 126
precious metal 7–9
prediction 3, 255–6
Presidential Savings Bank 17
Prevey, E. 147
Price, D. 207–8
prices/profit 119–21
pricing *see* persuasion and pricing
pricing practices in shops 270–79, **276–8**;
    bait pricing 274; bundling 274–5; drip
    pricing 271–2; reference pricing 272–3;
    time-limited offers 275–9; use of the
    word "free" 273
priming power of money 251–3, 273
primitive money 6, 42–4
Prince, M. 89
principles of persuasion 260–67; authority
    262; commitment/consistency 260–61;
    examples 264–7; liking 263; reciprocity
    260; scarcity 262–3; social proof 261–2
problems with heuristic thinking 248–51;
    anchoring and confirmation bias 250;
    illusions of money 249; inaction 249;
    information through grapevine 250–51;
    losses vs. gains 248–9; not all money is
    equal 248; overconfidence 250
Prochnow, Herbert 183
profanity 49–51

profit-sharing 223
profligacy 177
projective identification 203
Promislo, M. D. 106, 110
proneness to inaction 249
prospect theory 239–41
Protestant work ethic 57, 84, 94, 283
proximity 244
psychoanalysis of money 186–8
psychological money skills 285–8
psychological "theories" of money 33–9;
    biological psychology of money 37–9;
    factors 34–5
Psychology of Money 4
Psychology of Money Profile 285–8
Psychology Today 86
psychophysical perception of money 28–30
psychosomatic illness 86, 192
punishment 214
Puritanism 192
purpose of taxation 128
pursuit of happiness 62, 108

quality 88–9
questioning whether happiness is good
    thing 69
quizzing children 151–3

Rabeder, Karl 21
Rabow, J. 170
radiating wealth 207
Raghubir, P. 273
rank–income hypothesis 67
ratio of incentive to base pay rate 229
rationalisation 13, 237–8
rationality 33–6
Rawles, R. 127
RBS Group 145
ready money 9–10
real worth of money 42
reanalysis of better data 68–9
reciprocity 43, 78, 260, 264, 269
recognisability: of money 41
recognition 246
recording dreams 207
redistributive transactions 43
reference pricing 272–3
reflections on money 52–4; behaviourist
    approaches to money 54; criminology of
    money 52–3; philosophy of money 53;
    social ecology of money 53–4
regret 257
relastionships within money 38
relative deprivation 216–19

relative value of products 6
reliance on others' financial moves 250–51
religion and money 47–51, 186, 208–9;
    sacred and profane 49–51
Rendon, M. 154
repayment in kind 260
repossession 101
representative money 41
resolving family issues with money 165–6
restrictions on money 38
retention 92, 94–5
retention time 88–9
reunification of Germany 69
reward systems 221–3
Rich, B. 220
rich equals happy 78–9
rich fathers 173–4
Richins, M. 108
Rijken, M. 73
Rim, Y. 85
Rinaldi, E. 159
Rind, B. 269
risk 256
risk seekers 97, 112
risk tolerance 110
rituals of money 43–4, 49
Robertiello, R. 202
Roberts, J. 101
Rogers, W. L. 56
Roksa, J. 167–8
Roland-Levy, C. 127
Rose, G. M. 95
Rosenberg, Harold 33
Rossetti, F. 68
Rothstein, A. 186
Rubinstein, S. 86–7
rules of the family 143–6
Ryan, R. 213

Sabri, M. F. 177
sacred vs. profane 49–51, 203–4
sacrificial effect of money 43–4, 204
sadomasochism 53, 186, 206
Saegert, J. 89, 98
safe players 96, 112
sales techniques 264–6
salience 244
Salvaggio, A. 221
Sanchez, M. 137
saving 112, 131–3, 147–8, 154, 175
scarcity 207, 262–4, 275
schedule of reinforcement 229
schizophrenia 3
Schmidt, P. 101

Schneider, B. 221
Schofield, W. 205
Schor, B. 107
Schor, J. 56
Schots, P. 133
Schulz-Hardt, S. 30, 113
Scott, A. 145–6
Second Life 21
secrecy over pay 231–4
Secret of making money 4
security 95, 193–4, 196
seignorage 9
Self, J. 157–8
self-aggrandisement 107
self-denial 193–4
self-determination theory 225
self-efficacy theory 216
self-enhancement 106
self-esteem 57, 84–5, 92, 109, 162–3, 189, 200, 202, 220
self-help books 206–9
self-hypnosis 207
self-medication 105
self-transcendence 101
self-worth 49, 76
selfish capitalism 63
Seligman, M. E. P. 75
selling love 195
sensible shopping 207
Sepulveda, C. 101
Sevon, G. 125
sex differences 165–82; conclusions 181; introduction 165–6; money in couples 166–8; money and families 169–72; in money grams 175–7; money pathology in men and women 177–81; parental socialisation 174–5; rich and poor fathers 173–4; wealth in families 172–3
Shand, Karen 21
Shapiro, M. 167
Shaver, P. R. 75–6
shaving coins 10
Shaw, J. 220
Shefrin, H. 253
Shields, M. A. 69
Shinawatra, Thaksin 22
Shipton, B. 205
shopping fever 64
shops' pricing practices 270–79
Siegers, J. 73
Siegler, R. 118, 121
Siegrist, M. 96, 112
simulation heuristic 246
Singer, M. 131

Sitkowski, S. 204
situational triggers 190
Sjoberg, L. 101
Skandia 20–21
slang words 81–2
Smith, Adam 6, 44
Smith, D. 221
Smith, G. 133
Smith-Crowe, K. 253
social capital 101
social comparisons and subjective wellbeing 66–7, 73, 216–17, 230–31
social ecology of money 53–4
"Social Meaning of Money" 46
social proof 261–2, 264
socialisation pathways 141
socioeconomic understanding 123
sociology of money 44–7
Solheim, 175, 177
Solheim, C. 141
Sonuga-Barke, E. 131–2, 147
Sort Out Your Money 207
Sousa, C. 253
Spain, A. 205
Spectrem Group 19–20
Spencer, Herbert 44
spendthrifts 23–4, 187, 200; Michael Jackson 23–4; Viv Nicholson 24
spilt-over theory 141
Sprinkle, G. 215
squandering 188
stability of money 41
Stacey, B. 131
stage-wise theories about development of economic ideas 115–16
stamp duty 130
start age for taxation 129
status symbols 4–5, 43–4
stealing love 195
Steed, L. 85
Steinem, Gloria 183
Stevenson, M. 101
stocks and bonds 111–12, 173
story of online shopping 17–18
Stout, Rex 15
Stroud Pound 18–19
structure of money attitudes 85–103
structured sociology of money 44–5
studies of notes 27–30
studies on pocket money/allowances 147–51
Stutzer, A. 74–5
subjective wellbeing 57–8, 70–75; factors associated with 70–75

substitute money 41
success measured by money 70, 108
Sunday Times 281
sunk cost 246–7
superstition 184
supply of money 41
surprise 257
surveillance society 233
Sutarso, T. 84
Swangfa, O. 66
swapping 140
SWB *see* subjective wellbeing
Sweeney, E. 133
Switek, M. 66
symbolic compensation 212
symbolism 3, 33–5, 41, 43, 113–14
Symes, M. 85
systematic bias 226
systematic relaxation 201

taboo topic 3, 28–9, 164, 166, 175, 181, 184, 238
Taebel, D. 116
Tajfel, H. 28
Takahashi, K. 124
Tamir, M. 61–2, 69
Tang, L.-P. 84
Tang, T. 82–5
Tarpy, R. M. 33–4, 36
task performance 215–16
Tatarko, A. 101
Tatzel, M. 107–9
tax relief 50
taxation 125–30; avoidance 130; definition 128; good or bad? 129; government use of 128; income tax vs. others 128–9; inheritance tax 130; levels 128; other countries' 128; percentages 130; stamp duty 130; start age 129; VAT 130
Taylor, R. 154
teaching economic responsibility 139–40; *see also* economic socialisation
teaching economic theory 158–60
team working 225
technological changes 31
Telford, K. 101
Templer, D. 87–8, 94
Teo, T. 95, 177
Teplinsky, I. J. 206–7
thinking about money 113–14
Thinking Fast and Slow 258
Thomas, P. 148
Thompson, D. 118, 121
threshold to achievement of happiness 74–5

thrift 142
Thurnwald, A. 43
Tian, P. 73
time-limited offers 275–6
time/place to be happy 62
tipping 267–70
Todesco, L. 159
toilet training 186–7
token coins 9–10, 41
token economies 54
Tolstoy, Lev 181
tool theory 37–9
"tough love" 143–4, 152–3, 160
Tov, W. 65, 69
Toy Story 266
Treasure, F. P. 218
treating pathology 201–2
treatment of losses and gains 248–9
"tri-metallism" 9
Trovato, G. 77
Tversky, Amos 239, 246
Twain, Mark 237
Twist, L. 208–9
tycoons 26–7, 200; Mohamed Al-Fayed 26–7
types of bonus 223
types of happiness 62
types of tax 128–9
typologies of money madness 197–8

unconscious finance 105–6
underpayment inequity 217
understanding economic world 115–38; development of economic concepts in children 116–18; development of economic thinking 118–37; introduction 115–16; learning about money 138
unemployment 67, 79, 86, 137
unwise spending for happiness 76–8
use of money 35
use of other benefits 223
use of word "free" 273
usury 11
utility theory 40

value seekers 107
value–size hypothesis 28
Van Dyne, L. 220
Vanderbruaene, P. 134–5
Varese, K. 94
VAT 130
Vaughan, Bill 55
Veblen, T. 4–5
vigilance re money 97–8

virtual money 10
visualisation 207
Vlasbom, S. 73
Vogler, C. 166–7
Vohs, K. 78, 252
Volpe, R. 159
voluntary commitments 261
volunteering 155
Von Stumm, S. 101, 184
vulnerability 184

wage–work bargain 221–2
Wallendorf, M. 49–50
Wanke, M. 78
wealth 131, 172–3; in families 172–3
Wealth in Families 172–3
wealth management 132, 238
Weber, Max 44
Webley, P. 4, 33–4, 36–9, 116, 119,
    131–3, 140, 142, 147
Weissman, D. 29
wellbeing 57–61
Welt 202
Welt, S. 202
Wernimont, P. 85
Wesson, A. 232
Westerman, J. 133
Wiener, J. 202
Wiggins, R. D. 166–7
Wilder, B. 207
Wilhelm, M. 92, 94
Wilkinson, L. 205
Wilson, E. 101
Wilson, Earl 1
Wilson, G. 103
Wilson, Gahan 55
Wiseman, T. 82
withholding of excrement 187–8
withholding income 148
Wolfenstein, E. V. 53
Wolff, F.-C. 142
Wooden, M. 69
work and subjective wellbeing 73

workaholism 105
workplace motivation 211–36;
    compensation 219–21; equity and
    relative deprivation 216–19; executive
    pay 229–31; incentives/effort/task
    performance 215–16; intrinsic/extrinsic
    motivation 212–15; introduction
    211–12; money at work 234–5; pay for
    performance 223–9; pay secrecy 231–4;
    reward systems 221–3
world of money today 15–32; credit card
    story 16–17; experimental studies of
    coins/notes 27–30; introduction 15;
    local currencies 18–19; millionaires
    19–22; odd money habits 22–7; online
    banking/shopping story 17–18;
    technological changes 31
worry *see* anxiety
worship of money 49, 97–8
Wosinski, M. 126, 131
wrong type of happiness 62
Wu, X. 78
Wyatt, E. 154

Yahoo! 26
Yamanchi, K. 87–8, 94
Yang, Q. 78
Yap, K. 101
Yoken, C. 205
Yong, J. 77–8
Young, Andrew 259
Young, B. 116
Yung, S. 148

Zardkoohi, A. 232
Zelizer, V. 45–6
Zhang, X. 73
Zhou, X. 74, 76, 778
Zuiker, V. 141, 175, 177
Zuo, J. 177
Zuzanek, J. 68
Zweig, J. S. 66, 254–8